THE AGRARIAN QUESTION IN SOUTH AFRICA

This volume is dedicated to the memory and example of

Harold Wolpe (1926–96)

The Agrarian Question in South Africa

edited by

Henry Bernstein

FRANK CASS
LONDON • PORTLAND, OR

First published in 1996 in Great Britain by
FRANK CASS & CO. LTD.
Newbury House, 900 Eastern Avenue, London IG2 7HH England

and in the United States of America by
FRANK CASS
c/o ISBS, 5804 N.E. Hassalo Street, Portland, Oregon 97213-3644

British Library Cataloguing in Publication Data

A catalogue record for this book is available from the British Library.

ISBN 0–7146–4737 3 (hardback)
0–7146–4292 4 (paperback)

Library of Congress Cataoging in Publication Data

The agrarian question in South Africa / edited by Henry Bernstein.
    p.   cm.
    "This group of studies first appeared in a special issue on 'The
agrarian question in South Africa' of the journal of peasant
studies, vol.23, nos.2 & 3, 1996" -- T.p. verso.
    "Earlier versions of most of the studies in this volume were
presented as papers at a workshop on South Africa at the Congress on
Agrarian Questions: the Politics of Farming anno 1995" -- P. [1].
    Includes bibliographical references (p.).
    ISBN 0-7146-4737-3. -- ISBN 0-7146-4292-4 (pbk.)
    1. Land reform--South Africa--Congresses. 2. Apartheid--South
Africa--Congresses. 3. Agriculture and state--South Africa-
-Congresses.4. Agricultural laborers--South Africa--Congresses.
5. South Africa--Economic conditions--1991- --Congresses.
I. Bernstein, Henry
HD1333.S6A37   1996   96-8787
333.3'168--dc20   CIP

This group of studies first appeared in a Special Issue on
'The Agrarian Question in South Africa' of The Journal of Peasant Studies,
Vol.23, Nos.2 & 3, January/April 1996, published by Frank Cass & Co. Ltd.

Printed in Great Britain by
Redwood Books Ltd, Trowbridge, Wilts.

Contents

South Africa's Agrarian Question: Extreme and
Exceptional?   **Henry Bernstein**   1

The Theory and Practice of the Agrarian Question
in South African Socialism, 1928–60   **Allison Drew**   53

The Politics of Land Reform in South Africa
after Apartheid: Perspectives, Problems,   **Richard Levin and**
Prospects   **Daniel Weiner**   93

The Political Economy of the Maize *Filière*   **Henry Bernstein** 120

Labour Organisation in Western Cape   **Joachim Ewert and**
Agriculture: An Ethnic Corporatism?   **Johann Hamman**   146

Livestock Production and Common Property
Struggles in South Africa's Agrarian Reform   **Ben Cousins**   166

Land Reform in the Eastern Free State: Policy
Dilemmas and Political Conflicts   **Colin Murray**   209

The Agrarian Question and Industrial Dispersal
in South Africa: Agro-Industrial Linkages
Through Asian Lenses   **Gillian Hart**   245

Peasants Speak: The Land Question in   **Richard Levin and**
Mpumalanga   **Daniel Weiner**   278

Abstracts   302

South Africa's Agrarian Question: Extreme and Exceptional?[1]

HENRY BERNSTEIN

INTRODUCTION

Earlier versions of most of the studies in this volume were presented as papers at a workshop on South Africa at the Congress on Agrarian Questions: The Politics of Farming anno 1995, held at Wageningen Agricultural University, the Netherlands, 22–24 May 1995.[2] All of the contributors, except Allison Drew, participated in the workshop. The occasion provided a unique forum for discussion between the authors. We had not all met together before, although some individuals amongst us have enjoyed close working relationships for some time.[3]

Beyond the circumstance noted, this collection is distinguished by two features that deserve emphasis. First, its contributors share a commitment to the use of a critical political economy in exploring South Africa's agrarian question, notwithstanding (inevitable) shades of difference in under-standings of political economy, its objectives and means. Second, all the studies are based on recent research, conducted since the 'transition' from apartheid began with the the unbanning of opposition organisations (and release from prison of Nelson Mandela) in February 1990.[4]

Political and social change in the (almost) six years since then, has been volatile and charged with the intense contradictions inherited from over three centuries of colonisation and white supremacy; current and future developments are marked by great uncertainty, as a number of the papers illustrate vividly. Despite such flux, and its tensions – or, better, helping to illuminate them – a particular strength of the collection is its presentation and analysis of recent research findings.

At the same time, in a number of instances the topical work presented builds on previous research by the authors that enriches its content in various ways. One example is Allison Drew's contribution, drawing on her long-standing project of uncovering the ideas of earlier generations of South

Henry Bernstein, Department of Anthropology and Sociology, School of Oriental and African Studies (SOAS), University of London, Thornhaugh Street, Russell Square, London WC1H 0XG, UK.

African socialists [Drew, 1991, 1995–96]. Another example, and very important for reflection on South African realities (see notes 37, 40, 41), is the substantial research experience of several authors in neighbouring African countries – Ben Cousins and Daniel Weiner in Zimbabwe [Cousins, 1989; 1992; Cousins, Weiner and Amin, 1992; Weiner, 1989], Richard Levin in Swaziland [Levin, 1996], and Colin Murray in Lesotho [C. Murray, 1981]. Colin Murray's contribution here also builds on his extraordinary historical reconstruction of the social dynamics of land ownership and use in the eastern Free State over a hundred year period [C. Murray, 1992]. As a final, and somewhat different illustration, Gillian Hart's recent return to research in South Africa utilises the comparative 'lenses' of her work in South East and East Asia to illuminating effect.

This introductory essay aims to do three things. First, it sketches the historial context of South Africa's agrarian question, to provide a framework of basic information, and some key reference points for the contributions that follow, to international readers with limited knowledge of South Africa.[5] The next section introduces the studies within the context sketched, and a final section discusses some of their implications for the extreme – and exceptional? – characteristics of South Africa's agrarian question.

HISTORICAL CONTEXT

The sketch of historical context is, unavoidably, most schematic. At the same time, it narrows the lens, so to speak, the nearer it approaches the present through three key phases of modern South African history: the 'mineral revolution' following the discovery of diamonds in the 1860s and of gold in the 1880s; the processes that led to the formation of the Union of South Africa in 1910, and that followed it (industrialisation and a consolidating segregation); and the period of apartheid under the National Party (NP) state from 1948 to 1994.[6]

Colonial Settlement and Expansion, 1652–1860s

Prior to the start of mining of the world's largest deposits of diamonds at Kimberley (in the Northern Cape) in 1867, and of gold on the Witwaterstand (in the Transvaal) in 1886, the territory of present-day South Africa had been subject to over two centuries of European colonial expansion. This developed from the small beginning of a refreshment station established by the Dutch East India Company at the Cape of Good Hope in 1652, to supply ships plying the trade route between Europe and Asia. The principal processes of change during this long intervening period (mid-seventeenth to late nineteenth centuries) were as follows.

– the growth of Dutch settlement in the Western Cape, including the development of a commercial agriculture (wheat, wine, cattle) and mercantile economy with substantial landowners and burghers at the apex of its class structure and unfree labour at its base (drawn from the survivors of the indigenous Khoisan people and slaves imported from the Dutch East Indies);

– the rapid establishment of formal institutions and informal structures of white supremacy, entrenched in the evolving 'Africanised' (Afrikaner) culture of Dutch colonial settlement;

– the expansion of the frontier of Afrikaner settlement, spearheaded by groups of *trekkers* (pastoralists and hunters) and mediated by their encounters with African social formations (for example, the Xhosa of the Fish River region who fought a long series of wars with the Dutch, and later the British, from the mid-eighteenth century);

– the widespread disruption of the *Mfecane*, a series of wars and migrations from the late eighteenth century to the 1830s that consolidated five powerful indigenous kingdoms in the central and eastern areas of present day South Africa: those of the Zulu, Ndebele, Swazi, Basotho, and Bapedi;

– the entry and expansion of British colonialism, including rule of the Cape from 1806 and settlement in the Eastern Cape and eastern seaboard (Natal); the impetus of British imperialism in the region brought it into increasing collision with the social formations of the interior, both African and Afrikaner (the two principal republics consolidated by *trekkers* in the highveld of the Orange Free State and Transvaal in the mid-nineteenth century).

By the 1860s, on the eve of the 'mineral revolution',

> ...British colonialism had overseen the emergence of significant capitalist farming by white settlers in the Western and Eastern Cape and Natal. There also existed pockets of commercial capitalism around the ports of Cape Town, Port Elizabeth and Durban. A network of migrant merchants was slowly insinuating commodity relations into all the societies of the region ... The Afrikaans-speaking Boer colonialists (of the interior, HB) ... lived mainly off the rents in labour and in kind from the various squatters on their extensive landholdings. They justified this pre-capitalist form of colonial exploitation in terms of rigid racist ideologies which forbade any 'equality in church or state' between white master and black servant [*Davies et al.*, 1988: 6].

The Mineral Revolution and the Union to 1948

Despite the instances and forms of commoditisation that had developed (very unevenly and often haltingly) in the colonial situations outlined, it was the mineral revolution, above all in gold mining, that definitively shaped the trajectory of capitalist development. The geological conditions of gold mining (low grade ores in deep and widely dispersed deposits) made it profitable only with a high rate of exploitation of labour and large investments of capital. Exploitation rested on the construction of a rapidly expanding and increasingly regulated system of migrant (male) African labour, with some foundations in earlier colonial practices and the social geography of settler expansion and African dispossession. In 1889 the gold mines employed some 17,000 African workers and 11,000 whites; by 1909 these numbers had grown to 200,000 and 23,000 respectively. This labour system returned African migrants, at the end of their contracts, to rural homes where agriculture supported (or 'subsidised') their low wages and the reproduction of their labour power.[7]

The massive regional system of migrant mine labour (extending beyond South Africa to the neighbouring colonies of Basutoland [now Lesotho], Nyasaland [now Malawi], Mozambique, etc.), its emergent contradictions and how they were managed by mining capital and the state, constitute one of the most important and enduring keys to the political economy of South Africa. The same is true of one particular contradiction manifested from the early days of mining: the fission of the working class on racial lives. White miners, confronting capital and its preference for cheaper (and more oppressed) 'coloured' labour, pursued a militant course that climaxed in the Rand Revolt of 1922 with its slogan of 'Workers of the World Unite for a White South Africa'. The brutal suppression of the general strike on the Rand was followed by the mutual accommodation of capital and white labour under the aegis of an explicitly white supremacist state that generated policies of an 'industrial colour bar' and 'job reservation' for whites. On the side of capital, the scale of investment required for profitable mining, especially with the advent of deep mining in 1897, produced a rapid centralisation and concentration of capital. By about 1910, virtually all gold production was controlled by six mining houses, one of the two principal origins of the huge conglomerates whose dominance is a striking feature of South Africa's economy today.

The raw dynamic of the mineral revolution elevated the significance of South Africa in the global horizons of British imperialism, leading to a renewed offensive against those social forces still obstructing its ambitions. The colonial conquest of remaining independent African formations was completed, and the Anglo-Boer war of 1899–1902 overturned the Afrikaner republics whose territory incorporated and surrounded the gold fields and their frantically growing centre at Johannesburg. The now four British colonies post-war became the four provinces of the Union of South Africa established in 1910 (Transvaal, Orange Free State, the Cape and Natal).

During the transitional period from 1902 to 1910 the British and Afrikaners forged a particular type of 'historic compromise', in effect between imperial mining capital and still predominantly agrarian settler formations. While it contained unresolved tensions (manifested subsequently), it 'resulted in the imposition of a colonial peace which ended more than a century of war' and also transferred 'the economic muscle and bureaucratic sophistication of an advanced capitalist country' to the formation of the new state [*Beinart*, 1994: 3]. This historic compromise, of course, was achieved at the expense of Africans, many of whom had participated in the British war effort [*Warwick*, 1983] and reclaimed lands seized by Afrikaner settlers [*Krikler*, 1993].

The new state (and the historic compromise it incorporated) was central to systematising the 'racial order' [*Greenberg*, 1980] deposited by its various Afrikaner and British colonial antecedents, adapting it to the demands of capitalist development in mining, agriculture and industry, and managing the tensions generated by the underlying contradictions of extreme national oppression thus combined with class formation and exploitation.

These processes were initially translated into the policies and legislation of 'segregation' by the South African Party (SAP) governments of Louis Botha (1910–19) and J.C. Smuts (1919–24), in which the Chamber of Mines was the dominant influence. Of all the measures enacted by the SAP, the Land Act of 1913 was the most fundamental in material terms and also symbolically the most potent up to the present day.[8] The Act introduced (even if it did not complete) the definitive division, and its legal sanctification, of the land of South Africa between areas of white and black settlement and permanent residence, in the proportions of 92 per cent and eight per cent respectively. In formalising the racial division of land and thereby the spatial basis of social 'segregation', and in further limiting the areas 'reserved' for African occupation and use, the Land Act served to consolidate the migrant labour system noted above. At the time this was of most concern to mining capital, but the Act also aimed to limit the numbers of Africans settled on white farms. This contributed to the dual process of undermining agricultural commodity production developed by Africans (often on white owned land) during the previous half century [*Bundy*, 1979; *Keegan*, 1986], and stimulating the transitions (protracted and uneven as they were) from sharecropping and other rent arrangements to labour tenancy, and from labour tenancy to (unfree) wage labour, in a gradually capitalising white agriculture [*Morris*, 1976; 1981; *Marcus*, 1989].

While restricting African land and organising the flows of African migrant labour, mining capital and the SAP governments otherwise pursued a course of economic liberalism at a time when the living standards of white as well as black workers declined, leading to the Rand Revolt of 1922 noted above. This was a turning point that paved the way for the election of the Pact governments of 1924–33 that allied the Afrikaner National Party (NP) and the mostly anglophone Labour Party in common opposition to the SAP and the Chamber of Mines. To Afrikaner nationalism the latter represented the domination of '*foreign*' interests, and to organised white workers a threat to their jobs and incomes by manipulation of the recruitment and employment of black workers.

The Pact was more interventionist than the SAP governments in terms of public investment, protectionism and the beginnings of a racially exclusive (whites only) state welfarism. In the early 1920s industry in South Africa was limited to the production of some mining supplies and wage goods. Manufacturing enterprises were mostly small in scale with an artisanal character. The Pact encouraged domestic industry with protective tariffs and established the first major capital goods enterprise ISCOR (Iron and Steel Corporation) as a parastatal company in 1928. It also extended support to white farmers, and extended earlier measures protecting white employment through job reservation in the mines, railways, and government services, and introducing minimum wage levels for some categories of white workers (the 'civilised labour' policy).

With the advent of the global depression, South Africa's GDP declined by six per cent a year between 1928 and 1932, but the economy then revived due to the importance of gold production. When Britain abandoned the gold standard in September 1931, the price of gold rose rapidly, marginal mines due for closure were saved, and the taxation of mining profits (providing one third of government revenues in the 1930s) favoured a continuing expansion of industry: the South African economy grew at five per cent annually during the office of the 'Fusion' government of 1933–39 (fusing Hertzog's NP and the SAP in the new United Party, UP). The gold boom stimulated new investment in mining (taxation of which had led to significant disinvestment under the Pact government) and allowed the protection of agriculture and manufacturing against the opposition of mining capital.

Economic and social change in the 1930s, including industrialisation and urbanisation, put the political structures and processes of the racial order under increasing strain in ways that are key to subsequent events. First was growing African proletanisation beyond the migrant labour system that supplied the mines and labour tenancy on the farms, to employment in manufacturing industry and urban services, accompanied by increasing and more permanent urban migration. Industrial employers started to circumvent the industrial colour bar to meet their labour requirements, and even negotiated informal agreements with embryonic black trade unions in some branches of manufacturing. The 1920s had seen the rapid rise, spread and fall of the ICU (Industrial and Commercial Workers' Union of Africa) which mobilised the oppositional energies of many rural black people as well as urban workers [*Bradford*, 1988]. Despite the demise of the ICU as an organisation that catalysed and helped connect class and popular struggles in many parts of the country, economic and social change in the 1930s provided conditions for the emergence of industrial unionism [*Hirson*, 1989: Ch.4]. At the same time, opposition by mining capital blocked any official recognition, however limited, of black trade unions.

Second, the cumulative impact of the 1913 Land Act served to intensify pressure on subsistence and reproduction in the African 'reserves'.⁹ 'Beginning in the 1930s, a series of government commissions warned of acute landlessness, overcrowding, severe soil erosion, the creation of "desert conditions" and the "spectre of mass starvation" in the reserves' [*Davies et al.*, 1988: 16]. Legislation in 1936 (The Natives' Land and Trust Act) extended land 'reserved' for Africans from eight to 13 per cent, but this additional land had still not been fully allocated by the end of apartheid almost sixty years later. Moreover, the Act – like that of 1913 – was also designed to control labour on white farms and rationalise the conditions of its exploitation; its implementation was delayed by bitter resistance by labour tenants.

Third, the capitalisation of agriculture and its differentiation of white farmers, compounded by the years of depression and the terrible drought of the early 1930s, accelerated Afrikaner urban migration. These migrants were at the core of 'poor whiteism', a highly charged preoccupation of Afrikaner politics (in both government and opposition parties), and which stimulated the first extensive survey of poverty in South Africa. The Carnegie Commission of 1932 reported that there were 300,000 'very poor' whites (of a total of under two million), 90 per cent of whom were Afrikaners [*Welsh*, 1971: 176]. The 'civilised labour policy' focused more on measures to absorb these urban migrants into semi-skilled jobs in secondary industry than to accommodate the demands of the ('English') white labour aristocracy.

By the late 1930s, industrialisation faced shortages of skilled labour, and Afrikaner nationalism blocked government assisted immigration schemes to overcome skills shortages. The development of Afrikaner nationalism as a more cohesive political force addressing the economic and social changes noted, was the fourth significant process in the 1930s and the harbinger of what was to follow. The social character of Afrikaner nationalism and its evolving programme in the 1930s are detailed and analysed in the outstanding study by O'Meara [1983: Parts I and II]. It is sufficient to note here the leading role of the Afrikaner petty-bourgeoisie and its intelligentsia, and their links with small Afrikaner capital in finance, trade and manufacturing, as well as the more substantial agrarian capital of the Cape in particular. The political formation of Afrikaner nationalism centred on the 'purified' National Party of DF Malan, which had split from the Fusion government in 1934, and the activities of the secret and highly active *Broederbond* with its host of 'front' organisations in cultural activity, in 'Christian-national' trade unionism, and in the 'economic movement' of *Volkscapitalisme.*

The Second World War was a period of profound change in South Africa, as elsewhere. Opposing entry to the war, the Prime Minister Hertzog and 36 other MPs resigned from the UP to join forces with Malan in a 'reunited' National Party; Hertzog was replaced by Smuts in his second period of office from 1939 to 1948. In this period, the growth of manufacturing industry was accelerated by the imperatives of wartime production, state support and increasing investment by foreign capital, with a consequent rapid expansion of African urbanisation and industrial employment. Between 1936 and 1951 the African urban population doubled (from 1.1 to 2.3 million) to exceed white urban population for the first time, while the proportion of those classified as peasants in the economically active African population declined from 51 per cent to 17 per cent to eight per cent in the censuses of 1936, 1946 and 1951.

The number of black workers in manufacturing industry increased by 115,000 during the war years, behind whom gathered a growing urban reserve army of labour in the segregated 'locations' or townships. Many black urban migrants came from the white farms where labour shortages (already experienced in the 1930s) intensified accordingly, and the mine labour force also declined by 20,000 workers. The improved bargaining position of black workers, together with continuing deterioration of the conditions of subsistence in the reserves, generated a new militancy manifested in the 1946 strike of some 70,000 African miners.

The Apartheid Regime, 1948–73

Accelerated economic and social change between 1940 and 1948 generated a new wave of struggles, both urban and rural, that challenged the 'segregationist' racial order, and in turn intensified the tensions between the social forces of white supremacy, paving the way for the general election victory of the NP. The elements of the social bloc of Afrikaner nationalism noted above now gained the adherence of key sections of white workers, won over by 'Christian-national' unionism after a bitter internecine struggle in white labour organisations, and by agrarian capital in the highveld.

In immediate terms, the agrarian interest was the most strategic to the success of the NP in 1948. Most of the 36 MPs who left the UP with Hertzog in 1939 represented rural constituencies; 22 of these seats were regained by the UP in the general election of 1943 when wartime conditions guaranteed markets and prices to white farmers. Post-war conditions were less certain. Further expansion and profitability were threatened by acute shortages of farm labour, and the government was under pressure from mining and industrial capital to use its powers under the Marketing Act to depress food prices, of special concern to the grain farmers of the highveld.[10] Agricultural interests in the Cape (in wine, fruit, and wool) had supported Malan in 1934, and been a key element in the Afrikaner 'economic movement' that followed. They were now joined by the maize farmers of the highveld, until then allied with mining capital in a 'union of gold and maize' that provided the social base of the SAP and subsequently the UP.[11] In 1948 all 15 rural constituencies in the Transvaal returned National Party MPs. Moreover, the weighting of rural constituencies enabled the NP's election victory with a minority of the total votes cast.

The NP was to remain in government from 1948 to 1994, first to construct, and then to try to 'reform', the apartheid state. It is convenient to distinguish three phases of apartheid: a formative phase from 1948 to 1960, the phase of its heyday during the 1960s and early 1970s, and a phase of accumulating crisis thereafter which led to its eventual demise in 1994.

In the historic moment of 1948: 'apartheid represented primarily an attempt to restructure relations of exploitation to cope with agriculture's labour crisis, and to establish a system of stabilised [black – HB] urban labour which would threaten neither farm labour supplies nor compete with the petty bourgeoisie or white labour' [Davies et al., 1976: 27]. Central to these connected aims was 'efflux' and 'influx' control of the movements of Africans, to regulate the distribution of their labour power between agriculture, mining and urban sectors (as well as to complete their disenfranchisement). Efflux control was effected by the establishment of district labour bureaux in white farming areas, influx control by extended and ramified Pass Laws and a proliferation of rules governing the conditions of African residence, above all in the cities (see, inter alia, Greenberg, [1980; 1987]; Hindson [1987]; Posel [1991]). A particular point of connection between the two was the widespread use of black prisoners (many of them convicted under the pass laws) to augment farm labour supplies [Wilson, 1971].

The industrial colour bar was retained and extended, but the government allowed it to float upwards to meet the growing demand for (semi-skilled) industrial labour, while promoting white wage earners to supervisory, technical and clerical positions, including in an expanding civil service and public sector. The peculiar type of (white) state welfare capitalism of apartheid was built up through a comprehensive process of state (re)formation in which the NP and *Broederbond* staffed all apparatuses with their 'own people'. Industrial growth was promoted through strategic parastatal companies in transport, iron and steel, chemicals and energy, and armaments, and state contracting and other means were deployed to promote the rapid accumulation of Afrikaner finance capital in particular (the other major source than the mining houses of South Africa's giant conglomerates today), but also Afrikaner capital in other branches of the economy.

These measures were inscribed in, and accompanied by, the legislative and bureaucratic consolidation and refinement of the racial order as an elaborate system of social and political oppression, encompassing 'Coloured' and Asian' as well as African people. The 1950s saw the successive enactment of the fundamental statutes of apartheid, including the Population Registration and Group Areas Acts of 1950 (which defined the four 'population groups' and their mutually exclusive areas of urban residence); the (self-explanatory) Suppression of Communism Act of 1950 (also used to smash non-racial and black trade unions), the Natives' Settlement of Disputes Act of 1952 (barring black workers from registered trade unions), the Criminal Law Amendment Act of 1953 (used to suppress the Defiance Campaign – see below), and the Riotous Assemblies Act of 1956 (also aimed at black worker actions); the Bantu Authorities Act of 1951 and Promotion of Bantu Self-Government Act of 1959 (which laid the foundations of the bantustans – see below), and a host of other legislative provisions covering all spheres of social existence.

This process of establishing the structures of apartheid was punctuated by a decade of widespread, diverse and continuous resistance, with roots in the social change of the 1940s. Most important was the transformation of the ANC from a small, mostly petty-bourgeois formation of 'responsible' opposition to an organisation of mass action. A Youth League was established in 1943 which soon demonstrated its militancy, and whose Programme of Action of 1949 was adopted by the ANC. The ANC initiated the mass Defiance Campaign of 1952 and saw its membership increase from 7,000 to over 100,000 within months. The Congress Alliance, linking the ANC with the South African Coloured People's Organisation (renamed Coloured People's Organisation in 1959), South African Indian Congress, the (white) Congress of Democrats, the Federation of South African Women, and the South African Congress of Trade Unions (established 1955), organised the 'Congress of the People' in 1955, at which 3,000 delegates adopted the Freedom Charter, which remained the programmatic statement of the national liberation struggle for the next four decades.

Despite the repressive means available to the state, the 1950s had a political vitality and momentum that often originated outside, and also fed into, formal (and national) organisations. There was a number of cases of rural insurrection against 'homeland' authorities and the impositions of 'betterment' planning in the bantustans (Drew, this volume), as well as widespread industrial action and struggles against pass laws, housing and transport conditions in the townships and Bantu education, and resistance to removals under the Group Areas Act.[12]

On 21 March 1960, South African police fired on a demonstration in the township of Sharpeville, killing 69 people. This led to the watershed between the first and second phases of apartheid. A state of emergency was declared, the ANC and PAC banned, and a reign of state terror unleashed on opposition forces. In May 1961, South Africa left the British Commonwealth and became a republic, while a rapid outflow of foreign capital (above all in 1960 and 1961) created a crisis of accumulation and growth in the economy.

The crisis was transitory and indeed was followed by the 'golden period' of apartheid from 1963 to 1972. State terror was effective in crushing the mass resistance that flourished in the 1950s, to establish a political 'stability' that attracted the return of foreign capital in the global economic boom of the 1960s. Repression kept the wages of black workers at depressed levels, thereby contributing to the record rates of profit on investment in the South African economy which grew in real terms at between six to eight per cent a year.

This decade also saw the definitive formation of the contemporary bantustan system. While African dispossession and restriction to 'native reserves' is a central thread running through the country's colonial history, furthered in the twentieth century by the effects of such measures as the 1913 and 1936 Land Acts, it reached a new stage with the perverse social and spatial engineering of 'grand' apartheid. On foundations laid down by the Promotion of Bantu Self-Government Act of 1959, and in response to the political upheavals of the 1950s, all Africans were to become citizens of first eight, then ten 'nations' or ethnic 'homelands' shown in Map 1.

The map is too small in scale to illustrate adequately the many territorial fragments of which some bantustans were composed, notably KwaZulu (44), Ciskei (18) and Lebowa (14). Such fragmentation marked the spatial configurations of white settlement and African dispossession in Natal (KwaZulu) and the Eastern Cape (Ciskei), while Lebowa manifested the effects of both white settlement in the northern and eastern Transvaal and the juxtaposition with other 'homelands' (Gazankulu, KwaNdebele, KaNgwane; see Levin and Weiner, 'Peasants Speak', this volume). It was the intention of the NP state that in time all these bantustans would become

MAP 1

APARTHEID SOUTH AFRICA, SHOWING THE TEN BANTUSTANS

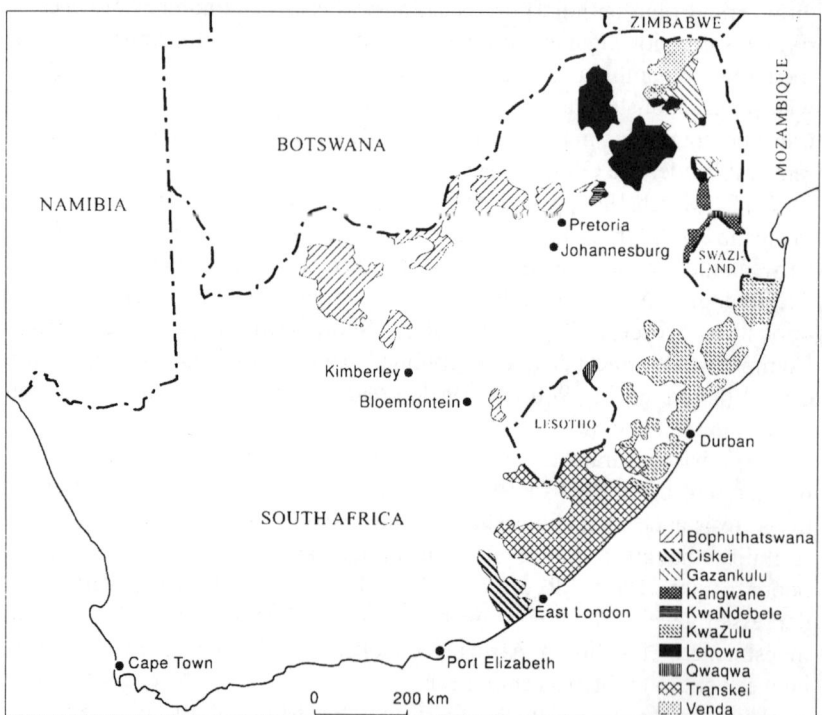

'independent' countries, but only four were to acquire this status: the Transkei in 1976, Bophuthatswana in 1977, Venda in 1979, and the Ciskei in 1981. Farcical as their 'sovereignty' was, recognised only by the South Africa state, the character of the bantustans in the changing socio-economic conditions of apartheid is of central importance, not least to the concerns of this volume, which justifies jumping ahead of the historical narrative somewhat.

First, and in a not unfamiliar paradox of capitalist development, at a time of rapid economic growth the bantustans were undergoing a shift from 'cheap breeding grounds for black labour' (see note 7) to a dumping ground for a growing relative surplus population as agriculture and industry became more capital intensive. There was an acceleration of forced removals from 'white' South Africa, which affected some 3.5 million Africans between 1960 and 1983 [*Platzky* and *Walker,* 1985]. They were expelled from white farming areas (some 1.1 million), rural 'black spots' (areas of African freehold owned land, purchased before 1913), and urban 'locations' or black townships through 'endorsements out' under the pass and other laws and the resiting of locations inside bantustans borders. The scale of these forced removals, together with demographic growth, exacerbated already serious pressures of population density in the bantustans. At the time of the 1970 census, 46.6 per cent of Africans resided in the bantustans (rising to 54 per cent in 1980), 24.4 per cent in the 'white' countryside, and 29 per cent in the urban areas of the Republic (up from 23 per cent in 1946).

Second, the South African state aimed at, and to a considerable extent achieved, the creation of a collaborationist petty bourgeoisie in the bantustans as a counterweight to popular opposition. This petty bourgeoisie had its base in 'homeland' administrations, including their 'tribal authorities' (and under the eye of the Afrikaners who occupied the senior positions in the security and bureaucratic apparatuses of the bantustans). The funding of bantustan regimes by the South African state reached massive dimensions in the final phase of apartheid, going into their proliferating ministries and government departments, development corporations and schemes, parastatal companies, universities, and so on – and with all that, the numbers on their payrolls. The structures of repression in the bantustans were thus combined with opportunities for 'accumulation from above' (Levin and Weiner, 'Politics', this volume), expanded as the South African state provided incentives successively to encourage African business in the bantustans, to site new factories just outside bantustan boundaries ('border industries') to take advantage of 'cross-border' commuter labour (Hart, this volume), and to promote joint ventures within bantustans by South African capital and bantustan governments. Most of these efforts were economically unsuccessful other than in mining and casino and 'entertainment' resorts, especially in Bophuthatswana with its rich uranium deposits and gambling and vice centre at Sun City.[13]

Apartheid's Gathering Crisis, 1973–90

At the beginning of the 1970s, white South Africa enjoyed the fruits of strong economic growth, of social and political 'peace' and regional security. All this changed during the 1970s, and even more dramatically in the 1980s. Growth in the 1960s represented the peak of a trajectory of accumulation, in which manufacturing had become the leading sector of the economy, stimulated by the global boom and inflow of foreign capital, and accompanied by the rapid expansion of commerce and finance. As the world economy began to slide into recession, South Africa entered the crisis of what Gelb [1991] termed its 'racial Fordist' regime of accumulation.

As at other key moments in its history (like the 1930s, noted above) the fortunes of gold proved strategic, now alleviating (and obscuring) the emergent structural crisis of the economy. New mining areas in the Orange Free State and on the far West Rand had been opened up by Anglo-American, the country's largest conglomerate. Following the freeing of international gold prices in 1968 and their rapid rise with the movement of oil prices and a weakening US dollar in the 1970s, gold mining profits in South Africa rose dramatically as did their contribution to national income (by more than ten times in current prices between 1970 and 1980). This helped pay for large imports of machinery and for the inflated costs of oil imports,[14] and for a while cushioned the impact of the faltering performance of manufacturing industry from the second half of the 1970s.

As the structural cracks in the economy started to appear, they were increasingly exposed and magnified when the 'stability' of the racial order, on which the previous boom was promised, was shattered by a new wave of class and popular struggles[15] (also encouraged by shifts in the regional balance of forces, with the independence of Angola and Mozambique in 1975). Probably of greatest importance was the emergence and growth of militant black trade unionism, with a wave of mass strikes starting in Durban in late 1972 and early 1973 and then spreading across the country. The momentum of this largely spontaneous action was sustained over time by the development of a strong union movement, consolidated in the eventual formation of COSATU (Congress of South African Trade Unions) in 1985, with a membership of nearly half a million workers.

The social engineering of 'grand' apartheid in the 1960s had expanded greatly the numbers of black youth entering secondary education but exposed them to notoriously under-funded and overcrowded schools supervised by the hated Department of Bantu Education. Secondary school together with university students were the principal social base of the Black Consciousness Movement, which emerged in the late 1960s. Opposition to Bantu education fed into the pivotal Soweto events of 1976. A peaceful mass demonstration against the extension of Afrikaans in the school curriculum was violently attacked by the police. This provoked virtual insurrection in Soweto and stimulated, and connected with, a new wave of community organisations and actions in the black townships that contested the impositions, high costs and oppression of daily existence under apartheid.

The shocks to the racial order from the revived and growing resistance of black workers and their unions, of the Soweto uprising and its aftermath, and of the range of popular struggles and the organisations they generated, were compounded by the changed balance of forces in the region. The independence of Angola and Mozambique from Portuguese colonialism in 1975 allowed the military wing of the ANC – Umkhonto we Sizwe or MK (established in 1961) – to operate from bases in those countries and to intensify its strategy of 'armed propaganda' through sabotage and raids in South Africa.

The response of the apartheid regime to the growing crisis of the racial order was the Total Strategy instituted by the regime of PW Botha (Prime Minister 1978–84, then State President, 1984–89). The Total Strategy sought to integrate a number of policies and instruments of repression and 'reform', both domestically and within the Southern Africa region. One key set of measures entailed a reorganisation, and militarisation, of the form of the apartheid state. The executive powers of the state (symbolised in the new office of State President) were strengthened and concentrated above all in the State Security Council (SSC), in effect an 'inner cabinet' of senior ministers and military officers. The SSC put in place an elaborate National Security Management System (NSMS), a set of parallel structures from central to local levels of the state to monitor resistance and organise repression throughout the country. Military expenditure also rose rapidly as South Africa forces engaged in a series of wars, international raids, assassinations, and support for anti-government forces in Angola and Mozambique.

A second key aspect of the Total Strategy was attempts to co-opt new collaborators and allies and to strengthen existing ones. This included increased financial support for bantustan regimes, and close political coordination with them in forming their own political parties as a counter-weight to popular opposition, as well as using bantustan security apparatuses to terrorise oppositional forces. In 1983 the regime also established the Development Bank of Southern Africa, as a kind of mini-World Bank to finance 'homeland' economic 'development'. Concerning the 'Coloured' and 'Indian' populations (outside the bantustan system), the government proposed to establish a tri-cameral parliament, adding to the white chamber a 'Coloured' chamber (House of Representatives) and Indian Chamber (House of Delegates), each with their ('Own Affairs') government departments. The proposal was approved by a (whites only) referendum in 1983, and stimulated the formation in the same year of the United Democratic Front (UDF), an alliance of over 600 organisations with two million supporters, to oppose the tri-cameral parliament. The UDF organised a successful boycott of the elections to the new chambers in 1984.[16]

This founding campaign of the UDF was followed by another wave of urban insurrection in many parts of South Africa between 1984 and 1986. Often sparked by local grievances about rent increases and other mounting pressures on living standards as the economy slumped, mass actions such as boycotts and stay-aways increasingly expressed direct political opposition to the state. The slogan 'Make apartheid unworkable and the country ungovernable' was launched in 1985 by the ANC, which underwent a political resurgence in the 1980s. In the aftermath of the Soweto uprising, many student activists who escaped to exile joined the ANC and MK. The UDF was, in effect, an ANC aligned organisation, and COSATU adopted the Freedom Charter of the ANC in 1987.

In July 1985 the regime declared an indefinite State of Emergency. The ferocity of state repression, organised through the hierarchy of Joint Management Committees of the NSMS, took a heavy toll of the energies and cadres of the urban insurrection. In the first eight months of the Emergency, 8000 people were detained and 22,000 charged; between June 1986 and May 1987 a further 26,000 people were detained. Mass arrests and detentions were accompanied by a growing incidence of targeted assassinations of activists in both South Africa and neighbouring countries by regime hit squads.

By 1987 systematic state terror had succeeded in halting the momentum of mass opposition, and also revealed the escalating costs of reproducing the racial order. A key index of this was the fragmentation of the original social bloc of the NP. In 1982 the Conservative Party (CP) was formed by a split from the NP and gained control of the rural constituencies of the Transvaal and parts of the Orange Free State, also attracting sections of Afrikaner wage earners and the petty bourgeoisie disaffected by 'reform' measures.

Also increasingly disaffected was big business.[17] It was accommodating itself, gradually if uneasily, to black trade unionism, whose actions generated the first significant gains in real wages for black workers since the Second World War (in manufacturing) or even the turn of the twentieth century (in mining). Large capital was also nudging the apartheid regime towards economic liberalisation, including the beginnings of privatisation of major state companies. With the insurrection of 1984, big business became convinced of the inability of the regime to (re)create the 'stability' necessary to the pursuit of profits, and concerned about the effects of international economic sanctions against South Africa. Its shifting stance was symbolised in the (public) opening of lines of communication between South African capital and the ANC in September 1985, when a high profile business delegation went to Zambia for talks with the ANC leadership.

In the late 1980s the apparent impossibility of overthrowing apartheid by mass insurrection and the escalating costs of maintaining the racial order, were now considered in an international conjuncture profoundly marked by the accelerating collapse of Soviet state socialism. The political stalemate in South Africa generated intensified exchanges between key elements in the regime, big business, and the leadership of the opposition movement, concerning a negotiated end to apartheid.[18]

When PW Botha suffered a stroke in January 1989, he was succeeded as national leader of the NP and then as President of South Africa by FW de Klerk, the conservative boss of the Transvaal party machine. In the general election of 1989, the NP's share of the vote dropped to below 50 per cent and it lost 27 seats, with the CP the major opposition party in the white parliament. In February 1990 de Klerk announced the unbanning of the ANC, SACP and other organisations and the impending release from prison of Nelson Mandela, thereby establishing key conditions of the negotiated end to apartheid that followed.

Negotiating the End of Apartheid, 1990–94

Rather than detailing the complex course of events between 1990 and 1994 (see, *inter alia*, Friedman and Atkinson [1994]; M.J. Murray [1994]), it is more useful for present purposes to note key aspects of the terminal crisis of apartheid, that both provide the context for the 'transition' of 1990-1994 and define the challenges confronting the new Government of National Unity (GNU).

First, the 1980s revealed the depth and extent of the crisis of the economy [*Gelb (ed.)*, 1991; *MERG*, 1993]. The price of gold dropped in 1983, followed by massive devaluation of the rand, chronic inflation, capital flight and increasing difficulty in international borrowing. The government response was to institute sharp increases in interest rates and cut public spending, at the same time as it was introducing creeping liberalisation. There was negative growth in output and in key sectors of employment, including manufacturing and mining which shed 150,000 jobs between 1986 and 1993 (from 534,000 to 380,000).

Second, widespread and increasing unemployment and poverty 'could no longer be externalised to the homelands' [*Beinart*, 1994: 239]. Even before many influx controls were removed in 1986, black urban migration was turning from a steady flow into a flood. Pickles and Weiner [1991: 18] state that 'the black population of white farms declined by one million between 1980 and 1985 alone. A total of 1.6 million blacks left rural white South Africa during this short period ... the highest rate of black outmigration ever recorded.' The growing pressures on highveld farming (Bernstein, 'Maize', this volume), as well as on survival in the bantustans, were compounded by years of severe drought in the early 1980s, and again in 1991–92 (the worst drought for 60 years) which generated another wave of evictions of farm labour families [*C. Murray*, 1995].[19] By 1990, an estimated seven million people were living in shack settlements on the peripheries of South Africa's cities and towns.

Third, and of more direct and serious political consequence, was the crisis of everyday social existence in the burgeoning shack settlements and in many longer established townships, and its effects. The urban insurrection of the mid-1980s incorporated an offensive against the incumbents and supporters of township local government, seen as stooges of the apartheid regime, especially by youthful militants – the 'comrades'.[20] In turn, local councillors, business people and criminals organised vigilante formations, often supported – and armed – by the police. In one notorious incident in 1985, a conflict between vigilantes and comrades resulted in the destruction of much of the Crossroads shack settlement outside Cape Town, leaving 60,000 people homeless. Another major rift, and source of extensive violence, was that between township residents (and 'comrades') and the inhabitants of hostels housing migrant workers. Some authors [*Morris and Hindson*, 1992: *Mamdani*, forthcoming] attribute this to a political failure of the democratic movement: hostility to migrant workers, and the lack of attempts to build alliances with them, enforced their social isolation and susceptibility to recruitment as vigilantes. The urban insurrection succeeded in making the townships largely ungovernable by the apartheid state, but alternative structures of 'people's power' – despite the vitality of the UDF-linked civic associations or 'civics' in many places – were not strong enough to curb the mounting violence, also stimulated by widespread gangsterism that organises patronage and protection in relation to residential plots, housing, services, transport and jobs, often under the confusing cover of political claims and rivalries.

This connects with a fourth theme central to events since the mid-1980s: the role of the Inkatha Freedom Party (IFP) led by Mangosuthu Gatsha Buthelezi. Inkatha's principal power base was the bantustan regime of KwaZulu. Its emergent and bitter rivalry with the ANC, founded in Buthelezi's political ambition and the complexities of Zulu history [*Maré and Hamilton*, 1987; *Mzala*, 1988], exploded into an extremely violent (Zulu) civil war in the townships and shack settlements around Pietermaritzburg in the Natal Midlands from 1987 [*Kentridge*, 1990]. From 1990, Inkatha extended its activities to the Rand, turning hostels housing Zulu migrant workers into bases for raids against the neighbouring townships. While other bantustan regimes opposed to the ANC (notably those of Bophuthatswana and the Ciskei) collapsed in the face of popular resistance before the elections of April 1994, that of KwaZulu under Buthelezi – with its Inkatha extension in the Rand – occupied centre stage among the forces that constrained the position of the ANC in the difficult negotiations of CODESA (Conference for a Democratic South Africa).

The CODESA talks took place between December 1991 and May 1992 when they broke up, and were resumed in March 1993, preparing the way for South Africa's first general election by universal franchise in April 1994 with the agreement of an Interim Constitution (1994–99) and provisions for a Government of National Unity. The high drama of the four years of 'transition' culminating in the general election, involved sometimes strategic shifts and compromises by all the leading parties involved (the ANC/SACP/COSATU alliance, the NP and IFP, together with the PAC and the fractious, and fragmenting, Afrikaner extreme right), in a context of strikes and other mass actions and widespread violence (including that instituted by the 'third force' of groups within the state security apparatus), compounded by continuing economic deterioration. All these factors, together with others, contributed to a dangerous combination of attrition and exhaustion of the activist base of the democratic movement with popular expectations that a new government would quickly solve the economic – and social – crisis, and deliver jobs and adequate incomes, decent housing, education and health services, social peace and personal security.

The New Conjuncture

An estimated 86.7 per cent of eligible voters participated in the general election of 1994. Percentages of votes cast for the main parties (with numbers of National Assembly seats gained) were: ANC 62.65 (252), NP 20.39 (82), and IFP 10.54 (43).[21] The Government of National Unity is thus led by the ANC which has the State President (Mandela), one of two Deputy Presidents (Thabo Mbeki) and 18 of 27 Ministerial posts; the NP has the other Deputy President (FW de Klerk) and six Ministries (including Agriculture); the IFP has three Ministries (including Buthelezi at Home Affairs). In the simultaneous election for the assemblies of the nine new provinces established under the Interim Constitution (see Map 2), the ANC gained a clear majority in six and also control of the Northern Cape with half of the seats, while the Western Cape went to the NP and KwaZulu-Natal to the IFP.[22]

The key challenges to the GNU, or more precisely its ANC majority, were indicated earlier. They include the inherited economic and social crisis, linked above all to structural unemployment estimated at more than 40 per cent of the labour force; the high expectations of the dispossessed majority who voted for the ANC; and the enormous problems of restructuring the state. The last refers to creating a coherent, effective and democratic system of government at national, provincial and local levels from the bureaucratic and fiscal nightmare of the apartheid state with its 13 demarcated structures of legislation and administration: the three branches of the tri-cameral parliament (dealing with both 'Own Affairs' and 'General Affairs') and, of course, the ten bantustans.

At its inception, the 'new' South Africa is a capitalist society, and will remain so for the foreseeable future. In short, capitalism has not collapsed with the demise of apartheid, as the socialist wing of the national democratic movement long believed it would – at least until the latter part of the 1980s.[23] Three strategic, and connected, sets of issues confront South African socialists in the new conjuncture: what kind of capitalist society is South Africa? What are the implications of 'democratic transition as unfinished business' (Levin and Weiner, 'Politics', this volume)? What are the possibilities of developing and advancing a national democratic programme to achieve what Saul [1991] termed 'structural reform'?

The sketch of historical context presented here at least suggests some elements in answering the first question. The second question is grounded in the evident observation that the demise of apartheid has left intact the relations of property, production and economic power established under the racial order. This leads directly to the third question, which concerns issues of substantive (as distinct from formal) democracy in any capitalist society: how the nature, degree, and effectiveness of class and popular democratic forces affect struggles over the character of the state and of markets, over their mutual links, what they deliver and to whom [*Rueschmeyer et al*, 1992; *Wuyts et al.*, 1992].

MAP 2

NEW PROVINCES OF SOUTH AFRICA

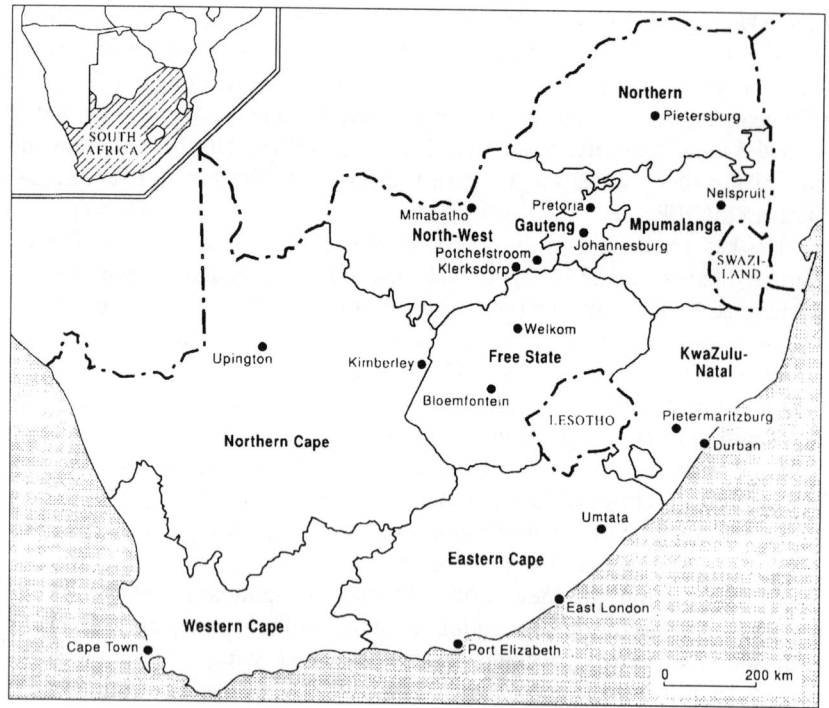

Serious theoretical work on such issues, in the wake of the definitive collapse of the Soviet system, is in its early stages in relation to South Africa, as more generally.[24] The fruits of such endeavour will emerge only from the test of the political practise that it seeks to illuminate and inform. The balance of forces that generated the eventual demise of apartheid, as sketched above, also points to some acute tensions of political theory and practice in the new conjuncture in South Africa, which the ANC leadership, above all in government, has confronted so far with extreme caution. This reflects, *inter alia*, the heterogeneous class character of the ANC as a national liberation movement; the alliances it entered and compromises it accepted during the negotiation process from 1990 to 1994; the problematic relationship between leadership and its constituencies, between the ANC in government and in civil society; the intensely contradictory nature of civil society itself in South Africa, permeated by 'contradictions amongst the people' and their effects within the overarching contradiction of capital and labour.

Important insights into, and analyses of, such issues in relation to the agrarian question are presented in the papers in this collection, which are reviewed next.

THE COLLECTION

The first contribution that follows, by Allison Drew, offers a valuable perspective on a period when the agrarian question was vigorously debated by South African socialists, even if there was much that was problematic in connecting more general theory with a concrete analysis of the concrete South African situation and in assessing the nature of rural struggles. From the 1920s to the 1950s, debate centred on issues of the migrant labour system and conditions in the African reserves, that Drew sketches first. Socialist theory in South Africa followed the classic agrarian question that originally addressed historical experiences and political preoccupations in Europe, and then extended its scope to issues of national democratic revolution in colonial conditions (subject to shifts in Comintern positions and those of Trotsky and his adherents). Issues included the progressive nature of capitalist farming and arguments for and against land redistribution, and the relations of peasantry and working class, of countryside and town, and of the agrarian and national questions.

Drew argues that the theoretical contestation of the CPSA and early Trotskyists in the 1920s and 1930s, was doctrinal in character, shaped by the currents and fissures of international socialism, and – apart from a specific moment in the late 1920s – largely detached from political practice that addressed the concerns of migrant workers and the pressured social base of their reproduction in the reserves. In the changing conditions of the 1940s and 1950s outlined above (industrialisation, urbanisation, strikes and popular struggles), activist intellectuals in both Communist and Trotskyist organisations (notably Govan Mbeki and I.B. Tabatha respectively) started to converge in more concrete analyses of migrant labour and the links between rural and urban struggles. Their analyses contain themes of continuing and more general relevance, including restrictions on the freedoms of the proletarian condition (freedom of movement and exchange of labour power) and struggles to attain and/or maintain those freedoms [Brass, 1986; 1990; Brass and Bernstein, 1992], and forms of constitution of the state, and of political oppression, specific to *rural* (*vs* urban) Africa [Mamdani, forthcoming].

Why the agrarian question virtually disappeared from the agenda of national liberation in South Africa after the 1960s (with the partial exception of the slogans of the PAC) is suggested in the next section of this essay. The effects of this strategic lacuna are an important reference point of the paper by Levin and Weiner on 'The Politics of Land Reform' in the current conjuncture. They suggest that constraints on land reform include the historic difficulties of political organisation in the countryside and the limitations imposed by the negotiated transition from apartheid between 1990 and 1994. An instructive point of connection between the two which they elucidate is the alliance between the ANC and so-called 'progressive' chiefs. The depredations of chiefly rule in the bantustans, its widespread authoritarianism and corruption, stimulated opposition that made its own contribution to the political upheaval of the 1980s; the energies and capacities demonstrated in such local struggles were then dissipated by the ways in which an increasingly 'statist' ANC [Neocosmos, 1995] positioned itself from 1990.

As a consequence, post-apartheid land reform policies are limited, both politically and economically, by an ethical discourse and rationale of restitution, on one hand, and a narrowly technicist view of redistribution, on the other hand – neither of which promises to deliver much land to many black rural people. Levin and Weiner advocate an alternative process of democratic land reform, driven and controlled by communities in the (former) bantustans. They suggest a number of practical measures and organisational forms to this end, informed by their participatory research in villages in the central lowveld of Mpumalanga (described in their second contribution to this volume). In putting forward their proposals they acknowledge, without elaborating, the complex and problematic nature of 'community' and of the 'rural' in the (former) bantustans, and of the heterogeneous (inter- and intra-class) social elements of any democratic process of land reform, issues also illuminated by the papers of Cousins and

Murray (and taken up in the last section of this essay).

The two contributions addressing the historical and contemporary politics of the agrarian question are followed by those of Bernstein and Ewert and Hamman, that investigate contrasting branches – and regions – of capitalist agriculture, respectively the maize economy of the highveld, and the wine and fruit sectors of the Western Cape. Bernstein's focus is on the commodity chain of maize and its regulation. The study first introduces the method of *filières vivières* (food commodity chains) that traces the journeys and transformations of a given food commodity (as both exchange value and use value) from farm field to consumer's plate, and suggests its utility to political economy. The framework constructed is then applied in an analysis of the structures, dynamics and recent history of the maize economy.

The study suggests the inadequacies of restricting 'reform' of a commodity branch that was highly regulated (in the conventional sense of statutory control of markets and prices) to measures of 'deregulation' and market liberalisation. The *filière* approach enables identification and assessment of regulation in its broader (political economy) sense, which in the South African maize industry is increasingly concentrated in, and shaped by, agribusiness capital, both corporate and 'co-operative'. While the system of controls (and subsidies) under apartheid influenced the specific forms, and patterns of accumulation, of agribusiness capital – especially as constituted by the giant grain co-operatives – the types of regulation agribusiness capital exercises will survive the abolition of statutory controls. This has two important implications, among others, for the agrarian question: first, the possible effects on prices of maize meal as an African staple food and wage good, and, second, the capacity of the giant co-operatives to reproduce the historic Afrikaner hegemony over the land and rural economy of the highveld.

Ewert and Hamman's essay is on labour recruitment and farm labour regimes in the wine and fruit producing areas of the Western Cape, the original region of Dutch colonisation and settlement where capitalist farming is longest established. Founded on slave and bonded labour, labour regimes in these prosperous agricultural areas were still typically characterised by (farmer) paternalism and violence, and (farmworker) dependency and poverty, into the 1970s. Ewert and Hamman investigate how this started to change from the late 1970s towards more 'modernised' forms of labour exploitation which they term 'neo-paternalism, formal collective bargaining, and corporatist equity-sharing and decision making'. The reason for this transition is the response of Western Cape farmers to increased export opportunities (accelerated with the end of trade sanctions from 1990) in the face of growing assertiveness by farmworkers.

On one hand, it would be possible to narrate this story within a discourse of the 'normal' dynamic of accumulation in advanced capitalist agriculture (as Bernstein shows in relation to recent changes in the maize industry). On the other hand, these connected processes of commercial expansion, accumulation and changing labour organisation are inscribed in the structures of South Africa's racial order, specifically its distinctive forms in the Western Cape. Ewert and Hamman show how the emergent 'modern' labour regime builds on the historic division of labour (and social tensions) between 'Coloured' farmworkers and African migrants from the Eastern Cape, to generate a new version of the 'ethnic corporatism' at the core of the racial order.

The contributions by Cousins and Murray redirect attention to land and livelihood issues in the (former) bantustans. At the same time, they demonstrate the necessity of addressing the historical specificities and spatial and social complexities of the land question in particular bantustan areas: in Cousins' case studies a fragment of KwaZulu in the Natal Midlands and a fragment of Ciskei on the border with the former ('white') Cape Province, in Murray's study fragments of Bophuthatswana and Qwa Qwa in the eastern Free State.

Cousins first maps a comprehensive conceptual framework, and agenda of issues, concerning livestock production and common property resources in the bantustans. This draws extensively on recent work in other parts of Africa, and on a review of the limited literature on livestock production by black South Africans.[25] The kind of theoretical and empirical overview thus provided is unique in the South African context, and of great value in identifying and connecting neglected aspects of land tenure, land reform and common property resources, their emergent (and uncertain) political and institutional framework, and the local struggles they are likely to generate: between white farmers and black rural communities, and between and within (socially differentiated) communities.

The second part of Cousins' study illustrates and develops such issues in short case studies of two very different rural areas, exemplifying the specificities and complexities indicated above. The case study of Cornfields – Tembalihle concerns 'black spot' land located on the frontiers of (former) KwaZulu and Natal, which groups of original African freehold owners were able to repossess in the 1990s. Historic conflict between white and black landowners is also intertwined with the relations of both groups with their tenants (including labour tenants evicted from white farms), in disputes over land access and use and representation of 'communities'. The other case study is set in the mid-Fish River Basin of the Eastern Cape, which is marked by the effects, and memories, of one of the longest (and most bitterly) contested regions of white settlement. One manifestation of local tensions (as in the first case study) is the conflict generated by stock grazing and other forms of foraging by black rural people on white farms. Here, pressures on land and livelihood resources – and disputes over land claims, tenure and use – are compounded by return, or 'reverse', migration in the face of high urban unemployment.

Some of the themes of Cousins' case studies are also evident in Murray's paper on the eastern Free State. Drawing on his unique scholarly knowledge of the social history of land in Thaba Nchu (former Bophuthatswana) and Botshabelo (former Qwa Qwa), Murray presents a number of cases in those areas that demonstrate the local complexities and tensions of three central aspects of government land reform policy: restitution, redistribution, and forms of tenure. Land restitution is analysed in relation to diverse experiences of dispossession under the racial order, that can generate conflicting claims to the same land by quite different social groups. Redistribution ('the most important single element of land reform policy'), and issues of mechanisms of allocation, of access to and uses of land, are analysed through disputes over redistribution of state-owned land in Botshabelo. Questions of tenure are examined in the context of different tenurial forms in Thaba Nchu.

The richness of Murray's account is combined with an exemplary clarity in detailing first, the complex histories of particular tracts of land and of the groups that occupy and/or claim them; second, the 'proliferation of overlapping and often conflicting authorities' in the political transition from 1990 to 1994; and third, the social character of different land users and claimants 'in a climate of widespread land hunger'. The sociological dramatis personae include white farmers; the heirs of original (Barolong) freeholders with restitution claims, who are not farmers but 'all well-educated members of the middle class'; a small number of active, accumulating black farmers on rented land; groups dispossessed by both apartheid policies and the ethnic chauvinism of despotic bantustan regimes; the great numbers of those concentrated in the townships and shack settlements of Thaba Nchu and Botshabelo (including evicted farmworkers), whose pursuit of any means of survival threatens the viability of nearby farming enterprises. Such expressions (and axes) of social differentiation disclose the danger of a 'chasm between the rhetoric of benefiting "the poor" and the reality of their practical exclusion', in (limited) measures of land reform designed by the state and 'captured' by elements of the local (black) bourgeoisie and petty bourgeoisie.

The history of dispossession and its effects is also one of the central threads of Hart's paper which offers an original and stimulating perspective on issues of industrial-agrarian linkages, illuminated by the author's expert knowledge of the political economy of Southeast and East Asia. Hart begins by considering the 'miracle of the multiplier' – in which small-scale farming generates locally linked non-farm employment – deployed in the World Bank's vision of land reform in South Africa. She provides a compelling critique of both the neo-classical logic of this model, and its inspiration and claims to validity (and generalisation) by certain Asian experiences of growth.

Hart's analysis of some key social conditions and mechanisms of these Asian exemplars (especially China and Taiwan) then informs her case study of industrial decentralisation, investment and employment in northwestern KwaZulu-Natal. This combines several strategic lines of argument. First, manufacturing investment in 'interstitial places' in South Africa, in this case by Taiwanese capital in Newcastle-Madadeni and Ladysmith-Ezakheni, is not simply the product of the incentives made available through apartheid industrial decentralisation policies, but reflects more global tendencies in contemporary capitalism. Second, that while this investment has generated a 'classically Taiwanese form of networked production', it remains much more fragile than in East Asia for two reasons: the African townships that supply labour lack both 'familistic forms of labour discipline' and opportunities to combine wage employment with income from cultivation. Third, there are possibilities of overcoming the latter by redistribution of the substantial 'buffer zones' (separating white towns and black settlements) and adjacent lands, which are well suited to small, intensively worked agricultural holdings.

Finally, while most of the other contributions acknowledge, and in some cases illustrate, the importance of gender relations to the issues they discuss, Hart centres gender in her analysis of labour markets and labour regimes, domestic production and reproduction, and their interconnections and contestations.

It is gratifying to complete this collection with a piece on 'Peasants Speak'.[26] While not presented in the form of 'direct voice', it contains a set of four Village Policy Documents generated by participatory research in the eastern Transvaal (now Mpumalanga) during the period of political transition. The documents are an expression, so far unique, of the knowledge, aspirations and proposals of black rural people in the (former) bantustans concerning land and farming. Levin and Weiner explain the process, within their research project, that produced the documents from a series of workshops in the villages. The notes of the workshop discussions were written up in English, and translated into Zulu and Siswati for checking by the villagers concerned. The documents display a comprehensive and sophisticated approach to issues such as where to get land, how to allocate land, how land should be used, and who should benefit from land reform, grounded in detailed ecological and social knowledge of the area: forced removals, the farming practices of white agriculture, the practices of the chieftancy, the claims of different uses, and users, of land and how to negotiate them.

The value of these ideas can not be overstated, without in any way idealising or romanticising them. The proposals are neither uniform nor formulaic (unlike those of most 'experts'); they can not be read as applicable to all former bantustan areas; there are ambiguities and possible tensions; their implementation, inevitably, would entail confronting the contradictions within rural communities shaped by the ubiquitous (if not uniform) social differences of class, of gender, generation and other 'contradictions amongst the people' illustrated in the studies by Cousins and Murray. On the wider plane, these documents serve to inform the case for 'structural reform' in the countryside (argued by Levin and Weiner's first contribution in this volume) as opposed to what is otherwise on offer: 'a limited 'deracialisation' of land and farming designed by experts, delivered by the state, and driven by the logic of the market' [*Bernstein*, 1994: 180].

EXTREME AND EXCEPTIONAL?

The extreme features of South Africa's trajectory of capitalist development since the mineral revolution over a century ago, were sketched in the previous sections. Among their effects is one of the most extreme distributions of income in the world, and the poverty associated with it. Analysis of the 1991 household census suggests that the bottom 40 per cent of the population (which is overwhelmingly African) received just four per cent of total personal income [*Whiteford*, 1994]. A government report using figures from the late 1980s estimated that 52.7 per cent of Africans – at least 16.3 million people – were living below the Minimum Subsistence Level, including a quarter of the population of metropolitan areas and well over 60 per cent in the bantustans [*RSA*, 1992c]. On a number of health and other social indicators, South Africa compares unfavourably with many countries with much lower average per capita incomes, including elsewhere in Africa [*LAPC*, 1994].

South Africa also has one of the most extreme distributions of land. 60,000 or so white farms occupy 86 per cent of rural land, some 85.8m ha of which 10.6m ha are under arable cultivation. The 14 million people of the (former) bantustans occupy a land area equivalent to one-sixth of that fenced by white farms. There is a dearth of reliable socio-economic and demographic data on the bantustans, itself a result of apartheid, but potentially arable land has been estimated at 0.2 ha per person [*Levin and Weiner*, 1991].

Of course, there is great variation in ecological conditions and population density in the (former) bantustans, which are mostly located in

the eastern half of the country (see Map 1) that receives relatively greater
rainfall and generally contains the better soils.[27] However, large areas are
marked by severe land degradation and problems of water supply; their
inability to furnish an adequate level of subsistence has long been a matter
of investigation and comment (including in government reports), and
evidently intensified over time due to forced removals and demographic
growth. State 'betterment' schemes to promote yeoman farmers and to
enforce land planning and conservation measures (another source of forced
removals within bantustans), foundered on the socio-economic realities of
land shortage and population pressure and on political resistance and
evasion [*Yawitch*, 1981].

It is hardly surprising then that the (former) bantustans are so dependent
on purchased (and 'imported') food staples. Preliminary indications from
CPLAR survey data in Mpumalanga are that an average 50 per cent of
household income is spent on food, and less than two per cent of income
derived from crop and livestock production; while a common, and blanket,
'guesstimate' is that ten per cent at most of the bantustan population derives
any significant part of its livelihood from farming [e.g. *Hindson*, 1991:
237]. Of course, these kinds of figures also mask great variation, including
the effects of social differentiation. The majority of those who farm are
women cultivating 'sub-subsistence' plots, to which they typically have no
claim or access in their own right, nor access to credit, extension services
and other means of support. Their primary objective is contributing to
household food needs.

Otherwise, there is a limited but significant (and probably growing)
number of petty commodity and other petty capitalist producers. Some are
contract farmers in schemes promoted by public agencies like the DBSA
and (former) bantustan agricultural development corporations and/or by
private capital, notably sugar outgrowers in KwaZulu and KaNgwane
[*Vaughan*, 1992]. Some are clustered around official smallholder irrigation
schemes, as in Tshiombo, Venda,[28] while others have developed commodity
production independently, like the farmers described in Murray's paper, and
those growing irrigated maize (for profitable sale as green cobs) and tropical
fruits in one of CPLAR's study villages in the eastern lowveld [*Woodhouse*,
1994:201]. Whether in contract, other scheme or independent farming, petty
commodity and petty capitalist production is associated with male control,
with savings from wages and salaries, and accumulation from non-
agricultural activity (above all in services and trade) and/or positions in
bantustan government structures (bureaucrats, chiefs, headman, their clients
and allies). Finally, there are some larger African capitalist farmers in the
(former) bantustans and since 1990 even in the (former) 'white
countryside'.[29] They are few but undoubtedly increasing, and may have a

political significance far beyond their numbers.

The last point, and other implications of this brief description of African agriculture commodity production, are considered further below. For the moment, it is necessary first to reiterate that the incomes of most black rural people are derived predominantly from wages, remittances and government pensions,[30] and second to recall the problematic and elusive nature of the 'rural', noted earlier. Forced removals commonly resulted in 'displaced urbanisation' [C. Murray, 1987], exemplified by the dense settlements of the eastern Free State and northwestern KwaZulu-Natal that feature in Murray's and Hart's contributions to this volume.

To illustrate the point further: the 1980 Population Census in South Africa gave a figure of 15 per cent of bantustan population as 'urban', namely those living in 'proclaimed' (that is, formally constituted, or gazetted) townships. By adding figures of 15 per cent for 'peri-urban populations (those dependent on commuting to proclaimed towns for employment)' and 26 per cent for 'semi-urban concentrations (settlements of 5,000 or more people)', de Villiers Graaf [1985] arrived at a figure of 56 per cent of bantustan population as 'functionally' (or dysfunctionally) urbanised (see also Hindson [1991]; Bernstein [1994]).[31] By 1994 65 per cent of all South Africans were 'functionally urbanised', while the residual of non-urban African population does not translate readily into usual conceptions of the 'rural', if by that is meant 'access to rural resources or farm employment' [Beinart, 1994: 264].

These observations of the distinctive and extreme conditions of life in the (former) bantustans – in terms of dependence on non-agricultural income, of severely constrained availability of, and access to, the means of farming – underlie much of the consideration of South Africa's 'exceptional' agrarian question and what makes it exceptional.

The Agrarian Question and the Transition to Capitalism

To begin, the classic agrarian question as concerned with transitions to capitalism. This investigates and analyses, first, the historical processes through which capitalist social relations are established in agriculture, with resulting transformations of production and productivity; and, second, the mechanisms through which increased agricultural production and productivity contribute to the formation and development of industry. The agrarian question, in this sense, is resolved when the transition to both capitalist agriculture *and* industry is completed [Byres, 1991].

Different paths of agrarian transition – their contours, timing, duration, relative success or failure – are the outcomes of specific configurations of class forces and class struggle. Agrarian transformations are shaped by contending forces of landed property and agricultural labour; patterns of industrialisation are affected by relations between landed property and agrarian capital on one side and (emergent) industrial capital on the other, as well as by the interventions of states in those relations and in the conditions of accumulation more widely [*ibid.*] In such transitions, agricultural production can be transformed by the metamorphosis of a class of (pre-capitalist) landed property into agrarian capital. Alternatively – and more radically – the class of pre-capitalist landed property may be overthrown and its land distributed to a former tenant peasantry. This establishes the conditions of petty commodity production and its subsequent class differentiation, which generates the formation of capitalist agriculture 'from below'.[32]

This outline, however schematic, helps to identify distinctive features of the development of capitalism in South Africa. First, agrarian transformation did not precede, and establish the conditions of, the development of manufacturing industry. Rather, both the transformation of agriculture (in most branches and regions) and industrialisation followed in the wake of the mining revolution.[33] Second, the capitalist transformation of agriculture (which followed a 'Prussian path' that both reflected and crystallised South Africa's racial order, note 32) is complete. Together with accelerated industrialisation in the post-war period, this means that the agrarian question, in the sense outlined, has been resolved, as reflected in the degree of concentration, scale, productive forces and practices in capitalist farming.

Of course, this 'resolution' via South Africa's variant of the Prussian path had a number of distinctive effects, including those stemming from the central place of the agrarian interest in the social bloc of the apartheid state, with its commitment to solving the agricultural 'labour problem'. How the latter was achieved may well have protracted the transition to wage labour in capitalist farming and the pace of mechanisation. Labour tenancy was still important in some areas (especially the southeastern Transvaal and parts of Natal) at the end of the apartheid era; grain farming became fully mechanised only during the 1970s, with the comprehensive adoption of combine harvesters.[34]

The privileged ('Prussian'-like) place of the agrarian interest in the apartheid state was also expressed in the extensive subsidises and pervasive instruments of regulation that supported white farming, and which generated recurrent tensions with mining, manufacturing and other urban capital. Again with reference to the classic agrarian question, the supply and cost of food occupies a special place. To expand the supply and lower the cost of food, in order to depress wages and enhance its rate of profit (hence accumulation), industrial and urban capital may support land reforms, and/or attack policies that favour agrarian interests, and/or seek sources of cheaper food staples through imports.

Large-scale capital in South Africa never displayed any interest in land reform, and has placed relatively little emphasis on liberalising agricultural imports in the more recent period (with the exception of feed grains). Its fire has been directed mostly at the subsidies, guaranteed markets, administered prices and farm income supports, that underwrote the post-war golden period of capitalist farming. Such measures were deemed to inflate staple food prices (hence wages), to strain the government budget, and to induce macroeconomic 'distortion', as a result of direct political 'interference' with market mechanisms. They were thus ready targets of the gathering ideoological and political campaign for market liberalisation during the combined economic and political crisis of the 1980s, and which intensified during the political transition. Big business and its media (above all the *Financial Mail*) applauded two government reports published at the end of 1992, a year of widespread mass action, acute political tension and galloping food price inflation: a report on price formation in the 'food chain' [*RSA*, 1992a] attacked the practices and powers of the marketing boards (dominated by producer organisations), and a second report on the Marketing Act [*RSA*, 1992b] argued for comprehensive deregulation of agricultural markets (Bernstein, 'Maize', this volume).

The more general point about the conjuncture of the 1980s, as an historical footnote to the earlier 'resolution' of the agrarian question in South Africa, is that the remaining 'Prussian' features of white agriculture were eroded as large-scale capital, with the state in its wake, planned for the end of apartheid. Agrarian politics fractured as highveld farmers shifted allegiance from the NP to the CP, partly in response to early indications of the withdrawal of state support to white agriculture. This also eased the way for the incremental, if still gradual and uneven, advance towards greater 'market orientation' (as official discourse put it). The 'accumulation crisis' of farming in the 1980s analysed by de Klerk [1991] added the effects of diminishing state support to those of extravagant investment by farmers in the 1970s and their resultant debt burden. Increased capitalisation and technical change led to both a secular decline in aggregate agricultural wage employment and to experiments with more 'modern' forms of labour organisation, at least in certain branches of farming (Ewert and Hamman, this volume).

To summarise, agrarian transition through a variant of the Prussian path in South Africa is complete. The legacies of this path of transition were increasingly unpicked in the 1980s – in terms of the declining political strength of the agrarian interest, some changes in farm labour regimes and greater 'market orientation' in the more dynamic branches of agriculture – as the political foundations of apartheid were undermined by mass

opposition, and South Africa's most powerful economic force (conglomerate capital) repositioned itself for an impending 'deracialised' capitalist
order.

The effects of the resolution of the agrarian question in this sense
underlie certain positions in debates about agricultural policy in the new
dispensation in South Africa. For example, from the side of capital neo-
liberalism has only to press for continuing deregulation and market
liberalisation (reinforced by the disciples of international competition in
relation to agricultural imports and exports), with the customary asserted
benefits of greater competitiveness and efficiency to all in a now
'deracialised' capitalist society.

Also following in the tracks of the inherited trajectory of capitalist
agriculture, but in more interventionist fashion, the report of the ANC-
aligned Macroeconomic Research Group (MERG) advocates 'carrots and
sticks to elicit the co-operation of capitalist farmers':

> Indeed, there are immense possibilities for putting economic pressure
> on farmers, by *expanding*, eliminating, and redirecting the array of
> state expenditures and tariffs affecting their *incentives*. The purpose of
> such pressures should be to encourage all farmers to begin to invest in
> a wage labour intensive, technologically dynamic and internationally
> competitive farm production structure [*MERG*, 1993: 194; emphasis
> added].

This position is premised on an underlying (and non-problematised)
assumption of the progressive nature of large-scale capitalist agriculture. It
also argues that the numbers of farm workers in South Africa tend to be
underestimated, 'especially casual and seasonal employees commuting or
temporarily migrating from the homelands and from neighbouring countries
in Southern Africa', and that 'well over half of the rural poor depend on
agricultural wage employment for their survival' [*ibid.*: 187].[35] Accordingly,
the MERG report opposes any land reform involving significant
redistribution, and recommends a limited allocation of (mostly state-
owned?) land 'to benefit adult female members of landless households in the
rural homelands' [*ibid.*: 191], on apparently welfarist (and opportunistic?)
grounds.

For this reading of the classic agrarian question and its resolution in
South Africa, the way forward now is policies to encourage capitalist
farmers to generate additional employment with better rates of pay and
conditions than prevail currently. To gain a perspective on this position, I
turn next to reconsider the agrarian question from the viewpoint of the
political, as well as economic, agenda of national democratic struggle.

The Agrarian Question and National Democracy

First, a brief elaboration of the logic of the path of agrarian transition designated by Lenin as the 'American' path (note 32). This has a resonance far beyond the specificities (and indeed exceptional features) of the historical experience from which Lenin named it: there was no feudal (or 'feudal' like) agrarian class structure in North America (although there was plantation slavery and the dispossession of indigenous peoples). The wider relevance of the American path is the logic of the development of capitalist agriculture from below through the class differentiation of petty commodity producers (peasants, 'family farmers', etc.). Establishing the conditions of this path by the destruction of 'feudal' (like) landed property explains the centrality of land reform to national democratic struggle, not least in colonial conditions. Land reform combines an economic rationale (removing obstacles to the development of the productive forces in agriculture) and a political rationale (overturning the power of landed property to facilitate both industrial accumulation and the formation of [bourgeois] democracy).

Because of its national democratic character, the emblematic slogan of this path – 'land to the tiller' – may be championed by anti-colonial nationalists, agrarian populists, bourgeois modernisers, and socialists, in particular conjunctures of social and political struggle. Not surprisingly, it was reflected in the demand of the ANC Freedom Charter in 1955 that land should be given to those who work it. The implication that the agrarian question is synonymous with the 'peasant question' in national democratic revolution was more plausible at that time in South Africa than it is now, for reasons that have already been outlined. In the 1950s there were far more black people living and working on the farms of 'white' South Africa, with a fresher historic memory of organising their own farming through sharecropping and labour tenancy [*Nkadimeng and Relly*, 1983; *Keegan*, 1988]. Today capitalist agriculture in South Africa exhibits similar tendencies to elsewhere: a diminishing core of permanent, more skilled workers, and a much larger (and possibly growing) casual labour force of seasonal and day labourers in South Africa, many of them women and children drawn from rural townships or 'commuting' from bantustans and subject to appalling conditions of work and pay [*Marcus*, 1989].

Another key difference marked by the watershed of apartheid's 'golden period' of the 1960s concerns the course of political struggle in the countryside. The 1940s to early 1960s was the last period of widespread and overt rural political agitation [Drew, this volume; also *Lodge*, 1983: Ch.11; *Bundy*, 1984; *Delius*, 1990]. Govan Mbeki was the last major figure in the leadership of the ANC in his own and subsequent generations to participate in and analyse the struggles of rural people (Drew, this volume).[36]

Thereafter, and despite continuing, typically covert, resistance in the countryside, repression and the functioning of bantustan apparatuses made rural political organisation beyond the most local level extremely difficult (Levin and Weiner, 'Politics', this volume). When the revival and upsurge of political resistance to apartheid occurred from the early 1970s, it was mostly urban in character, organisation and political vision.

These observations connect with the above account of the 'resolution' of the classic agrarian question in South Africa, but they also qualify it. As the essays by Bernstein and Ewert and Hamman in this volume show, the most 'modernising' forms of capitalist agribusiness and regulation can draw on, adapt, and serve to reproduce, the historic features of the racial order. And there remains the inheritance of the economic crisis of the last phase of apartheid, manifested in massive structural unemployment, widespread poverty, and crises of everyday reproduction, above all in the former bantustans.

This points to an extension of the agrarian question to focus on the 'colonial' formation of South Africa's class structure, that combined capitalist development with extreme national oppression and that remains central to democratic transition as 'unfinished business' in South Africa.[37] In short, this extension requires the recovery of the *politics* of the agrarian question. To assess the project of this recovery (initiated by Levin and Neocosmos [1989], and continued in the papers by Levin and Weiner in this volume), it is necessary to confront two contentious areas of theory and practice, so far only briefly noted: the strategic lacuna on the agrarian question in the programme of the South African national liberation movement and of its current leadership (inside and outside government), and the apparent absence, or weakness, of a mass democratic politics of agrarian reform.

If the liberation movement failed to advance beyond the Freedom Charter's demand of land to the tiller, this was not unique to its thinking about agrarian issues. As an ANC economist remarked: 'From 1955 till the unbanning of the ANC in 1990, the economic policy of the ANC remained the same' [*McMenamin*, 1992: 245]. Her explanation is that 'economic policy formulation was not the priority for a movement which was waging a liberation struggle. What economic thinking existed was contained in general documents and manifests' [*ibid.*] This is accurate as far as it goes, but deserves elaboration.

First, the socialist wing of the movement long believed that capitalism would collapse with the demise of apartheid, and be replaced by some or other form of socialist state and economy (see note 23). Its nature was not detailed or debated (at least publicly) for tactical reasons, as the ANC sought political support from western governments and public opinion.

Second, many cadres were educated, and underwent political and military training, in the countries of the Soviet bloc, and probably assumed that the capitalist farms and plantations of South Africa would be nationalised and collectivised after apartheid. (The ANC in exile had its own large farm in Zambia, managed by cadres who were agriculture graduates of eastern European universities.) Third, even with the resurgence of support for the ANC in South Africa in the 1980s, there remained a large gulf between its leadership in exile (and indeed in prison in South Africa) and the militants of the industrial and township wings of the mass resistance movement, who were developing new forms of democratic political practice and organisation, as well as economic demands.

The implications of the above emerged and were highlighted in the conjuncture of transition. First, the collapse of Soviet state socialism was a moment of profound demoralisation and improvised revision of its positions by the SACP. Second, many movement cadres were based in Tanzania, Zambia, Mozambique and Angola, and observed for themselves the crises of the various socialisms of those countries, both 'African' and 'scientific', through the weight of internal contradictions as well as of external pressure. Third, the circumstances of the transition, and the course of negotiations, enlarged the political space and influence of the 'statist' tendencies in the ANC and the aspirant petty-bourgeois and bourgeois elements of its (inevitably) heterogeneous class alliance.[38]

These factors are reflected in the negotiating stance of the Congress Alliance during the political transition, and in the extreme caution, indeed conservatism, of the economic and social policies of the Government of National Unity. The policy objectives of the Alliance's Reconstruction and Development Programme published on the eve of the election [ANC, 1994], were diluted in the subsequent government White Paper on the RDP, and the implementation of the RDP sidelined to a minister without portfolio [RSA, 1994; Adelzadeh and Padayachee, 1994]; (also Levin and Weiner, 'Politics', this volume). The conservatism of GNU policies is not peculiar to agriculture and land reform; the GNU has also ignored the macro-economic, fiscal and sectoral (including agricultural) policy recommendations of the MERG report.[39] At the same time a number of specific factors can be suggested to explain the conservatism of agricultural and land policy, given the political – and in many cases economic – weakness of white farmers at the end of apartheid.

First, agriculture is bigger and more powerful than the position and interests of farmers only would suggest. In contemporary capitalism the 'agricultural sector' includes, and is largely integrated and regulated by, corporate agribusiness capital upstream and downstream of farming (Bernstein, 'Maize', this volume). Additionally, in South Africa corporate capital is active in production in timber, viticulture, fruit, and the typically 'industrial' branches of sugar, feedlots and poultry. And while agriculture contributed 5.3 per cent of GDP in 1988, with its 'substantial linkages and multipliers' the total impact of agriculture in the economy was estimated at 12.4 per cent of GDP and 24.4 per cent of total employment [*van Zyl and van Rooyen*, 1991]. Second, the ANC may be inhibited from confronting the weaker sectors of white farming because of the negative 'signals' that any action against private property rights would transmit to 'business confidence' and foreign investors. Other possible reasons could include the fear of (much threatened) 'reprisals' from the most intransigent areas of rural Afrikanerdom, and the costs of implementing large-scale agrarian reform through state purchase of land for redistribution.

There are other reasons too, including the view of mechanical or essentialist Marxism that large-scale farming (whether capitalist or socialist) exhibits intrinsically superior 'efficiency'. This can also link with the more pragmatic concern of trade unions and food consumers with food price inflation, and their fear that food prices would increase as a consequence of land reform. There are counter-arguments to both these positions in the South African context [*Levin and Weiner*, 1991; *Raikes*, 1993; *Bernstein*, 1994; 1996], but more important for present purposes is that they often conceal other assumptions and prejudices. One is assimilated from colonial ideology: that black people in Southern Africa are incapable of being committed and effective farmers because they are 'by nature' cattle keepers, foragers rather than tillers. This connects with another, untested, assumption: that black rural people have no desire to be serious farmers (even if they want land for sentimental reasons) but aspire to regular wage employment. At the same time, ANC leaders in government (and those they feel they have to reassure) may harbour an unexpressed fear that any strong position and initiative on land redistribution might catalyse a dynamic of rural mobilisation. This would then complete a vicious circle of mass action in the countryside that threatens the ANC's 'politics of reconciliation', the confidence of capital, and the GNU's pledge to deliver order and stability, *and* that seeks to transfer a vital productive asset from those with the means and culture to use it efficiently (white capitalist farmers) to those unwilling and/or unable to do so (the black rural poor and dispossessed).

This last observation connects the first set of issues noted above (the lacuna on the agrarian question in the programme of national liberation, and of ANC leadership today) with the second: the apparent absence or weakness of a popular politics of agrarian reform. This is evidently of central importance to the project of recovering the politics of the agrarian question, and to debate of agricultural policy and land reform. Those opposed to land reform (on any of the grounds discussed in this section) are likely to invoke the argument that black rural people don't want land and/or do not want to be farmers: if they did, there would be widespread agitation around demand for land, and redistribution would have to be accommodated more seriously (rather than cosmetically) in the agendas of the ANC and GNU.

Such views (whether held with conviction or opportunistically) are both uninformed and misconceived, as the papers in this volume by Levin and Weiner, and those by Cousins and Murray, show. The widespread desire for land is evident, although subject to its own (necessary) complexities in terms of who wants land, for what purposes, where, and what they are prepared to invest (politically and economically) to acquire (and work) land. The answers to such questions will exhibit marked variation in terms of local histories and forms of social differentiation.

Misconception occurs at the point of connection between desire for land and its articulation as a basis for political mobilisation [*Bernstein*, 1992]. If, as suggested above, there are fears that any strong signal about land reform may catalyse ('uncontrollable') rural mobilisation, they embody a different assessment of political potential in the countryside than the contention that rural 'civil society' lacks any capacity to formulate and struggle for popular democratic demands. This is also widely held, and expressed more explicitly than is usual by McIntosh *et al.* [1993] who reason as follows. First, black rural people are dependent overwhelmingly on wages, remittances and other external sources of income; deprived of productive assets and means of rural economic activity, they are unable to satisfy a necessary condition of 'mutual aid organisation'. Nor are they placed to struggle for improved infrastructure and services, as urban constituencies are. Second, and linked with those factors, rural society in South Africa is characterised by severely disabling ties of personal dependence and lack of power (and vision?) of oppressed groups – farmworkers with farmers in the 'white' countryside, villages with tribal authorities and the bureaucracy in the (former) bantustans.

This position is stereotypical, static, innocent of politics – and unrecognisable from the accounts of the dynamics of rural areas presented in this volume. Also, and paradoxically, it omits another reason for the difficulties of effective rural political organisation, implied by Levin and Weiner in their 'Politics' study, namely the ways in which the ubiquitous (if not uniform) class differentiation of black rural society and pervasive 'contradictions amongst the people' combine to generate profound ambiguities of social experience, ideology and action.

One manifestation arises from the history of removals when different dispossessed groups present conflicting claims to the same (original or subsequent) land (see Murray, this volume; Maluleke *et al.*, [1994], on a case in the eastern Transvaal). This is an obvious example but one with deep roots that merit consideration. First, the variant experiences of dispossession, together with the politico-legal constitution and functioning of the bantustans, give a particular weight to the discourses of 'community' in South Africa. Rural community is a kind of corporate status, whether imposed (under the system of tribal authorities) and/or claimed. The claim is that of a common identity and inheritance in relation to specific land. (Of course, the social composition and character of such communities is now very different from that of their historic or 'imagined' origins.) Second, discourses of 'community' (as ideology and basis of collective action) connect with ambiguities about the chieftancy, discussed by Levin and Weiner in their 'Politics' study. Claims to restitution of ancestral land are typically articulated through chiefs as bearers of the community inheritance ('the land of the people of Chief X ...'), even when the right of chiefs to allocate land within the community is contested, as in Mpumalanga (Levin and Weiner), the eastern Free State (Murray), and the Eastern Cape (Cousins). Third, and more generally, Mamdani (forthcoming) argues that such ambiguities express the distinctive political order in rural Africa established by colonial states and reproduced by their post-colonial successors.[40]

Another intense set of issues derives from no doubt the most entrenched and intractable of 'contradictions amongst the people', namely those of gender relations. Just as the class differentiation of black South Africans is shaped by capitalist development in conditions of extreme national oppression, so is it also deeply imprinted with forms and effects of patriarchy that, evidently, are not explicable by appeals to 'custom' and 'tradition' (much as these appeals are invoked in the ideological construction of patriarchy). Nor are the disadvantages of women concerning rights to land, and access to other means of farming, simply the expression of historical continuity. The productive and reproductive resources and activities of black rural women are constrained by the changing dynamics of (male) labour migration, and how chiefly and patriarchal authority seeks to intervene in them. The effects of these processes, then, are expressed in the (interrelated) social relations of sexuality and parenting, marriage and kinship, family and household, property, work and income, 'community' and local politics.[41]

A final example concerns generations, also closely linked to issues of community, of gender and patriarchy, and conveyed in that South African keyword: the 'youth' (meaning, in most instances, *male* youth). The sociology of black youth was put squarely on the political agenda by the events of Soweto and after, especially in the context of the metropolitan townships. Rural youth, on the other hand, has been little investigated.

Levin and Weiner ('Politics') refer to its militancy in the bantustans in the 1980s and how it challenged patriarchal control, and also note that youth politics centred on Bantu education and other aspects of the apartheid state rather than on questions of land. Whether young people have a desire to farm, and the implications of this for the politics of land reform, also remain largely unexplored to date.

In short, there is much that is not known about the social formation and dynamics of black rural life in South Africa, as well as much that suggests its complex and contradictory features. This is hardly a startling observation other than to policy-makers, 'experts' and consultants certain that they know what black rural people want and do not want, are capable of – and more to the point – incapable of. Just as this certainty works to close off discussion, the purpose of this volume is to open up investigation and debate concerning, *inter alia*, community, gender, generational and other potent divisions and tensions, to grasp better how they combine with, mediate – and often obscure – rural class formation, and to assess what advances or inhibits popular democratic politics in the countryside.

It can be suggested, without recourse to stereotypical notions of the fatalism and passivity of rural 'civil' society, that its politics are often introverted, both socially and spatially; that the pressures of everyday reproduction (for most) and pursuit of petty accumulation (for some) mean that political energies are absorbed (and exhausted) in struggles over resources between and within tribal authorities, 'communities' and households. The conditions of an outward directed politics, that can connect and organise local struggles on a wider terrain, are discussed by Levin and Weiner ('Politics') who are also sceptical that the ANC has a vision or commitment that would direct its political resources to this purpose.

Moreover, in the absence of a broader political organisation committed to democratic agrarian reform, the limited land available for redistribution, and the institutional mechanisms of its allocation, are likely to be captured by established agricultural commodity producers: 'those who clamour the loudest for land reform are often those who already have access to the means of production' [*Levin and Neocosmos*, 1989: 244] – who are most likely to be middle-aged men, as noted earlier, if not necessarily 'gentleman farmers' (Hart, this volume).[42] They are also best placed to position themselves at the centre of political and institutional processes linking (former) bantustan 'communities' with government structures and land reform and 'smallholder agriculture' initiatives. The more astute elements of 'organised agriculture' (white farmer unions and co-operatives, combined in the SAAU) began to court larger black farmers, with their own regional associations and National African Farmers' Union (NAFU), immediately after February 1990 (and possibly before).

African agricultural commodity producers emerged within the constrained conditions of the racial order and its divisions of land and income; there is suggestive if fragmentary evidence that their numbers and strength increased in the latter part of the 1980s and during the transition of 1990–94, when their associations were established (NAFU started as an off-shoot of NAFCOC, the National African Federated Chambers of Commerce). These African farmers too constitute a contradictory force in the social equation of the agrarian question: on one hand, exemplars of the 'deracialisation' of land and farming, sharing the general interests of agrarian property and capital, but on the other hand constrained by the racial order and possible allies of struggles for more far-reaching land reform (Levin and Weiner, 'Politics').[43]

The contradictory character and potential importance of a developing black agrarian interest must be assessed in the limited context of a national democratic agrarian programme. This remains rooted in commodity relations while aiming to release a dynamic of 'accumulation from below' with both economic and political objectives [*Mamdani*, 1987; *Neocosmos*, 1993]. Accumulation from below contests both the monopolistic position of white farming and corporate capital (the results of the privileges and rents of apartheid, both direct and indirect), and the historic structures of chiefly and bureaucratic power key to access to land, and to other assets and rents, in the (former) bantustans. Thus its democratic content, in economic terms it can generate employment and competition and stimulate the development of more diverse forms of commodity production, both in farming and in agricultural trade, transport and processing [*Bernstein*, 1996].

CONCLUSION

The conclusion of this discussion, exploratory and tentative as it is, is that South Africa's agrarian question is extreme – and also exceptional for a number of connected reasons. First, after a long history of dispossession and capitalist development, land reform has entered the agenda of policy, in however attenuated a fashion, at a time when the classic agrarian question is no longer of concern to capital on a world scale.[44]

Second, Mamdani's thesis (note 37): that features of an 'apartheid' generic to Africa have deeper historical roots than the formal racial order, hence survive its demise, and connect questions of democracy in South Africa with those in the rest of Africa. This original and compelling argument goes further than any other in properly (re)inserting South Africa in its continental framework. Within that framework, however, South Africa retains exceptional as well as extreme characteristics – in the historical span of its colonisation, the extent of African dispossession, the transition to capitalist agriculture and industry, and its effects, that have been discussed in this essay.

Third, a project of democratic land reform in South Africa addresses social constituencies whose links with land and farming have been significantly ruptured, if less completely – and in many instances more recently – than is often appreciated. 'Land to the (former) tiller' is not an absurd notion in South Africa, nor is it intrinsically anachronistic or populist. It is exceptional in the historical record of the agrarian question, however, and links to the difficulties of democratic political struggle in the countryside. These difficulties are the result not only of longstanding repression, but also of the contradictions of rural society in which class formation is so marked and mediated by the combined effects of migrant labour systems, the centrality and ambiguities of 'community', and pervasive 'contradictions amongst the people', above all those of gender relations and particular forms of patriarchy.

The resolution of their agrarian questions was completed for white farmers by apartheid, and for big capital is being completed by the new wave of deregulation and market liberalisation. The agrarian question of the dispossessed is not thereby resolved nor completed. The intensity of land hunger, deprivation, insecurity and frustration in the (former) bantustans will continue to fuel at least local struggles, especially in those 'border' areas where the rich resources of white farmers (and vacant lands of 'buffer zones') are often literally within sight of impoverished villages and settlements. With its extreme and exceptional character, the agrarian question is a potent constituent of the contradictions inherited by post-apartheid South Africa and a source of social forces that can contribute to shaping its future development.

NOTES

1 Here I am adapting the title of the seminal article by Mahmood Mamdani [1987].
2. The session was convened by the author, who was also on the Organising Committee of the Congress. The Congress Proceedings have been bound in four volumes [WAU, 1995].
3. Five of the nine contributors also participated in the final workshop of the research project on Community Perspectives on Land and Agrarian Reform (CPLAR) held in Johannesburg in March 1994; on CPLAR see Levin and Weiner's 'Peasants Speak' in this volume, also Levin and Weiner [1994; 1996].
4. These combined features distinguish this volume from other recent collections on land and agrarian issues in South Africa: Matlhape and Munz (eds.), [1991]; Pickles and Weiner (eds.), [1991]; de Klerk (ed.), [1991]; Csaki et al. (eds.) [1992]; Murray and Williams (eds.) [1994].
5. Given the intense international interest in South Africa (revived after the Soweto revolt of 1976), there was an even larger than usual gap between external solidarity with mass resistance and knowledge of the country's complex history and its legacies. This can have a negative political effect when uninformed triumphalism (the end of apartheid) immediately

gives way to equally uninformed 'pessimism'.

6. While the following sketch claims no originality, neither can it claim innocence, of course. The flourishing historical scholarship of the last 25 years concerning many of the themes merely noted (or asserted) here, has generated intense polemics between liberal, Marxist and 'social history' approaches. The landmark of liberal scholarship is the *Oxford History of South Africa*, edited by Wilson and Thompson and published in two volumes in 1969 and 1971. A short but seminal article by Trapido [1971] anticipated and stimulated new currents of both Marxist history, theoretically informed by readings of Althusser and Poulantzas, and a counterposed social history inspired by the work of E.P. Thompson.

   In the sketch presented here I have drawn on the conceptual framework, as well as the information, of the valuable reference work by Davies, O'Meara, and Dlamini, 1988. Monographs by two of these authors [*Davies, 1979; O'Meara, 1983*] are the most notable (published) examples of the 'structuralist' Marxist history of South Africa, and, in this author's opinion, have stood up well against the criticism by the social historians. Most of the points of contestation between 'structuralists' and 'social' historians more generally are evident in debates about agrarian history, reviewed and argued in Beinart [1987], Morris [1987], M.J. Murray [1989] and Bradford [1990].

7. In the 1970s the logic of the migrant labour system in South Africa was theorised in terms of the articulation of modes of production, notably in the seminal article by Wolpe (1972). This logic had long been transparent to both labour and capital in South Africa. An early communist, DI Jones, wrote in 1921:

   > This, then, is the function of the native territories, to serve as cheap breeding grounds for black labour – the repositories of the reserve army of native labour – sucking it in or letting it out according to the demands of industry. By means of those territories capital is relieved of the obligation of paying wages to cover the cost to the labourer of reproducing his kind (quoted by Legassick and Wolpe [1976: 87]).

   While a spokesman of the mining industry stated to a government Commission on Mine Wages in 1944:

   > It is clearly to the advantage of the mines that native labourers should be encouraged to return to their homes after the completion of the ordinary period of service. The maintenance of the system under which the mines are able to obtain unskilled labour at a rate less than ordinarily paid in industry depends on this, for otherwise the ordinary means of subsistence would disappear and the labourer would tend to become a permanent resident upon the Witwatersrand with increased requirements (quoted by Davies *et al.*, [1988: 9]).

8. A powerful eyewitness account of evictions following the Land Act is given in the classic work by the African intellectual Solomon Plaatje [1987; first published 1916], who directed his rage at the viciously racist settler farmers of the Orange Free State in particular. Beinart [1994: 55] suggests that 'in order to get his point across, Plaatje romanticised life on the farms before the Act ... (and) also exaggerated the immediate effects of the Act'. Plaatje was the first Secretary General of the African National Congress (ANC), founded in 1912 to oppose the forthcoming Land Act – see the fine scholarly biography by Willan [1984].

9. Which does not mean that the African 'reserves' were immune to social differentiation generated by commoditisation – see the observations by Drew in this volume; also the critique of the 'linear proletarianisation thesis' by Levin and Neocosmos (1989).

10. The Marketing Act of 1937, allowing for statutory marketing channels and administered prices, echoed measures adopted in many capitalist countries during the depression, and was introduced against the opposition of leading economists expressed in a series of articles in the *South African Journal of Economics*. Under apartheid, the Act became one of the central pillars of regulation supporting white farmers, above all maize farmers (Bernstein, 'Maize', this volume).

11. The 'union of gold and maize' was coined by Trapido [1971], as an explicit analogy of 'iron and rye' in Gerschenkron's classic study of Prussia [1943], which actually refers to the '*compromise* between iron and rye'.

12. The most informative single work is that by Lodge [1983], which is largely about the 1950s, and is illuminating on dynamics specific to different localities and political campaigns. Two other important political developments were the clandestine formation of the South African Communist Party (SACP) in 1953, after the original Communist Party (CPSA) abolished itself following the Suppression of Communism Act, and the breakaway of an 'Africanist' faction of the ANC in 1958 to form the rival Pan-Africanist Congress (PAC).

13. Gambling and sexual relations between whites and blacks were illegal in the 'white' Republic of South Africa.

14. The strains of oil supply were cushioned by imports from Iran until the overthrow of the Shah's regime in 1979, and by expanded production of oil from coal by the parastatal SASOL (South African Coal, Oil and Gas Corporation). An attack on the main SASOL plant in 1980 was one of the most successful instances of 'armed propaganda' by Umkhonto we Sizwe.

15. On the trade union movement in the 1970s and 1980s, informative sources are Maree (ed.) [1987], Friedman [1987], Baskin [1991], and Kraak [1993]; M.J. Murray [1987], and Marx [1992] cover the politics of the United Democratic Front (UDF) as well as industrial action, and Murray also details the urban insurrection of the mid-1980s; Lodge, Nasson et al. [1991] concentrate on the UDF, with a general analysis and a number of regional and local studies. On the shifting politics of the NP and the state, Schrire [1992] is useful, while O'Meara (in press) covers the whole period of apartheid in the much awaited sequel to his earlier work on *Volkscapitalisme* [1983].

16. UDF calculations of the poll as percentages of the eligible populations of voters (with government figures in brackets) were: House of Representatives, 17.5 (30), and House of Delegates, 15.5 (20).

17. The composition, nature and political role of capital, and how they changed during the various phases of capitalist development in twentieth-century South Africa, are (or were) at the centre of intellectual and political debates in which liberals and Maxists contested the connections between capitalism and apartheid, class and race, state and economy (see also note 23). The most detailed and sophisticated statement of the liberal thesis of the incompatibility of capitalist rationality and apartheid irrationality is by Merle Lipton [1986], conveniently summarised in Lipton [1987], and discussed in an illuminating review essay by Freund, [1987]). Lipton focused above all on the problems of racially segmented labour markets for capitalist development (and to a much lesser extent on the constraints imposed by income distribution under apartheid on the growth of the domestic market). She traced the labour problems experienced (virtually *ab initio*) by manufacturers, and later by mining companies and farmers, and the various moments at which capital in each of these three main sectors of production started to push for (economic) reform. A striking feature of Lipton's account (which has a number of incidental subtleties) is the economic determinism of its central argument – the very attribute with which South African Marxism was typically (and erroneously) charged by liberal critics!

The twin sources of South Africa's contemporary conglomerates, noted in the text – the ('English') mining houses and Afrikaner finance capital – discovered their commonality of interest during the boom of the 1960s. This was symbolised in the transfer of the General Mining and Finance Company (later known as Gencor) by Anglo American to the mining subsidiary of SANLAM, the largest Afrikaner insurance and finance conglomerate. Davies *et al.* [1988], Gelb (ed.) [1991] and MERG [1993] contain much useful information and analysis concerning South African conglomerate capital; O'Meara (in press) will be indispensable for its political strategies and shifts during the period 1948–94.

18. A fascinating journalistic account of many of these secret meetings is given by Allister Sparks [1994].

19. In the early 1990s, evictions of farm labour families also expressed the fears of white farmers about agricultural workers' rights – and land claims – under a new government.

20. Seekings [1993] is a useful review of youth politics in the 1980s.

21. Preparations for the historic general election cast light on the dubious quality of official (apartheid) population statistics. The 1992 census estimated just under 21 million eligible voters of whom 68.5 per cent were African. In 1994 the Independent Electoral Commission

revised these figures to 22.7 million and 73 per cent respectively [*Reynolds*, 1994: 187].

22. The population of the Western Cape is 55 per cent 'Coloured', 25 per cent white, 19 per cent African and one per cent Indian. The NP gained 53.3 per cent of votes cast and the ANC 33 per cent. NP success came from winning 70 per cent of the 'Coloured' vote, 'using quite crude tactics of racial division' [*Harber and Ludman*, 1995: 293].

In KwaZulu-Natal, the IFP gained fractionally over 50 per cent of the vote, having agreed at the very last moment to enter, rather than boycott, national and provincial elections. Apart from the logistical problems this caused, the most serious allegations of election fraud were levelled at areas administered by the IFP run KwaZulu bantustan government. The ANC poll of just over 32 per cent included a clear majority in the urban areas of greater Durban and Pietermaritzburg. As Harber and Ludman [1955: 283] comment:

> the ANC chose not to contest allegations of fraud in KwaZulu, and the IFP in turn did not challenge national or other regional results. In effect, the ANC ceded control over the province for the sale of national reconciliation ... secret negotiations allowed the ballots to be counted without reference to fraud, which is believed to be what gave the IFP its slim majority. The result provided the IFP with its regional base, but caused a degree of disenchantment among many ANC radicals who felt they had been sacrificed for the sake of national reconciliation.

Since the elections KwaZulu-Natal has continued to have the worst incidence of political violence in South Africa.

23. The best known statement of the 'no middle road' position was by Joe Slovo [1976], the leader of the SACP. Harold Wolpe, whose seminal article of 1972 was seized on by critics as the definitive statement of the 'functionality' of apartheid to capitalist accumulation, later developed an argument about their 'historically contingent' relationship [*Wolpe*, 1988]. Between 1990 and 1994, it fell principally to the immensely respected Slovo to argue for a new orientation of the SACP following the collapse of the USSR, and to justify strategic shifts in the negotiating stance of the Congress Alliance. Harris [1993] tried to turn the earlier 'no middle road' position against Slovo in a polemic that failed to address the problem of the balance of forces during the political transition, and also seemed to equate a more radical stance with greater statism.

24. I have found of most use work by Gibbon [1993], Mamdani [forthcoming], and Neocosmos [1995], which I draw on in the third section of this essay.

25. Cousins shows the importance of livestock to black rural livelihoods, however constrained its conditions of production, which presents another vivid contrast with the *filière* of the commercial red meat industry: one of the most regulated and concentrated in slaughtering, processing, storage and distribution [*Karaan et al.*, 1993] – and run for many years through a mafia-like politics. Cousins is currently investigating the possibilities of commercial livestock production by black farmers, within a research project on Restructuring Agriculture in South Africa directed by Nick Amin of the University of Natal.

26. 'Peasants Speak' was a strong feature of the early years of the *Journal of Peasant Studies* [*Bernstein, Brass and Byres*, 1994], which the editors are keen to revive. Articles published more recently under this rubric include Mendes [1992] and van Onselen [1993].

27. The 500 m rainfall line running north–south bisects South Africa virtually in the middle; only ten per cent of the country receives an average 750mm or more of rainfall a year.

28. Current research by Edward Lahiff of SOAS.

29. Incidental examples encountered by Edward Lahiff and the author in parts of Northern and Mpumalanga provinces include: an entrepreneur with businesses in Soweto who is developing a new farm of 150ha in the Mutale Valley, Venda, with irrigated tomato production as well as feedlots, employing 200 workers to date, doing its own packing and trucking of produce to Johannesburg; a former senior civil servant of the Gazankulu government also growing irrigated tomatoes, okra, chillies, etc. near Giyani, who in effect runs his own cooperative and is active in African farmer organisations regionally and nationally; a businessman who bought a former white farm of 40 ha near Nelspruit on which he is developing irrigated vegetable production, with 30 permanent workers to date, trucking produce to local markets within a radius of 150 km, also a leader of the regional African

farmers' organisation.
30. The operation of the pension system and its importance to survival in the former bantustans, where one pension may help support ten or twelve people, are investigated in the work of Lund [e.g. 1992].
31. de Villiers Graaf's analysis was a necessary corrective to the assumption that most people in the bantustans are 'rural', but all such statistical measures are arbitrary of course, hence likely to mislead. Compare his definition of settlements with more than 5,000 people as 'semi-urban' with the (1989) population figures for the four villages of the CPLAR study – Marite: 29,872, Cork: 8,792, Malekutu: 6,634, and Manzini (a cluster incorporating Makushu and Phola): 45,232.
32. These two broad alternatives, that became known as the 'Prussian' and 'American' paths, were sketched by Lenin in the Preface to the second edition [1907] of his *Development of Capitalism in Russia* (1973/1899). The various strategic meanings of the 'classic' agrarian question are distinguished in Byres [1991], a remarkable comparative analysis of paths of agrarian transition that extends the range of Lenin's original exemplars. Byres [1995] further discusses the comparative method in research on the agrarian question, and his forthcoming book (in press) is a full historical and theoretical exploration of the experiences of Germany and the United States. The definitive statement to date of the 'Prussian' path in agrarian transition in South Africa remains the work of Morris [1976; 1981].
33. This was one of the key points of the doctoral thesis [1969] of the *verligte* ('enlightened') Afrikaner Simon Brand. Brand was a key organic intellectual of apartheid 'reform': a pioneer of development economics in South Africa, member of the Agriculture Committee of the *Broederbond*, economic adviser to P.W. Botha (and in this capacity, frequently and approvingly cited by Lipton [1986]), founding president of the Development Bank of Southern Africa, and following his death recipient of a warm tribute by Thabo Mbeki [1992], now Mandela's Deputy President and possible successor.
34. Migrant seasonal labour is still used extensively in maize farming, for example, for gleaning, especially workers from former Bophuthatswana in the western highveld [*Husy*, 1994] and from the Eastern Cape in the north-eastern highveld. The eastern highveld around Bethal is the best maize growing region in South Africa and was notorious for its farm labour practices [*First*, 1959; *Bradford*, 1993]. Labour demand and supply in the Bethal area found a perverse equibrium in the late 1980s and early 1990s as some farmers countered the escalating cost inflation of machinery and fuel by reverting to hand harvesting of maize, recruiting large numbers of desperate workers from the Transkei. One farmer told me that on arrival these workers required a week of solid 'feeding' before they could provide efficient field labour, and that they wanted to be paid in sacks of maize to take back to their homes.
35. More accurate data on farm workers – their numbers, distribution by branch of agriculture, conditions of work and pay and so on – should be available from research undertaken by the current Presidential Commission on Labour Markets and an associated ILO research project.
36. Govan Mbeki [1964] provided an account of rural resistance in the African reserves and a prescient analysis of bantustan formation. His book was edited for publication by Ruth First after Mbeki's arrest (like Mandela, he spent most of the next three decades in prison). First's biographical sketch of Mbeki noted that he 'presents material never reported anywhere before on the fate of the ordinary peasant at the hands of the tax collector, the authoritarian chief, and the tribal court' [*First*, 1964: 14].
37. In the most sophisticated general theoretical essay on the agrarian question in South Africa, Levin and Neocosmos [1989: 243] argue that 'the agrarian question is an issue pertaining to capitalism, and not primarily to a period of transition, or 'articulation' between capitalism and pre-capitalist modes of production'. In my view, the force of their analysis loses nothing by replacing 'primarily' with 'exclusively' in this statement; the specific form of (agrarian) transition to capitalism shapes the subsequent form of the agrarian question within any given capitalist social formation.

An important underlying issue at this point and elsewhere in this essay should be indicated, even though its proper consideration deserves a full study in its own right: namely, appropriate comparative frameworks for South Africa. The seminal article by Trapido [1971; note 6 above] on 'South Africa in a comparative study of industrialisation' used as reference points for comparison imperial Germany in its development of capitalist agriculture through coercive labour regimes, the anti-bellum US South in the centrality of a single export commodity to capital accumulation (respectively gold and cotton), and tsarist Russia in the use of state-controlled labour migration to supply workers to mines and factories. The comparative framework of labour-repressive regimes in transitions to capitalism is helpful, as is the inclusion of South Africa in wider studies of unfree labour in capitalism (notably Miles [1987]), and indeed the application of the 'Prussian' path used here (note 32). These comparisons are partial, however, to the extent that South Africa is seen as one example of a species of capitalist transitions, to which institutional racism is then added on, as it were. On the other hand, some works have taken the latter as the organising principle of comparison. These include the study of white supremacy by Frederickson [1981], which is particularly fertile on ideology, culture and politics (as well as labour regimes and economic power) in South Africa and the USA from the beginning of colonisation, and Greenberg [1980] who compares accumulation and the role of the state in the capitalist 'racial orders' of South Africa, the US South, Ireland/Ulster, and Palestine/Israel.

It remains striking, however, that such comparative studies have not located South Africa in its African context. The most notable advance in this respect is a forthcoming book by Mahmood Mamdani. The first part, on 'the structure of power', argues that the practices of 'indirect rule' and 'customary law' used to fashion the colonial state (and absorbed by its successors) denied any bourgeois principles of political society, hence 'civil society', to rural Africa and generated instead 'decentralised despotism' and 'non-racial apartheid'. While South Africa was a limiting case because of its constitutional racism, the demise of the latter will reveal the underlying structural division of 'non-racial apartheid' as that between the social and political spheres of countryside and town. The second part of the book concerns the 'anatomy of resistance'. First, an account of peasant movements in Equatorial Africa explores the dialectic of national ('tribalist') forms: as a channel for popular democratic energies as well as a source of despotism selected and reinforced by colonial (and post-colonial) states. Second, there is an analysis of urban migrant labour in South Africa, whose rural origins are a source of strength in working class struggles but which is isolated and alienated by the urban movement and its ideologies. Third, Mamdani considers how urban/rural divisions – generic to capitalism but with specific and politically highly problematic forms in Africa – can be confronted in the course of struggles for democracy.

The breadth and depth of Mamdani's framework enables more systematic (rather than piecemeal) appreciation of insights gained from limited and specific comparisons between South Africa and other African countries; see further notes 40 and 41, also O'Laughlin [1996] on agricultural policies in Mozambique in relation to the dynamics of rural social differentiation, an illuminating analysis of great relevance to the agrarian question in South Africa.

38. See in particular Neocosmos [1995], who points to parallels with the suppression of popular democratic forces in the moment of independence elsewhere in Africa, as analysed by Mamdani [1990] and Gibbon [1994].

39. The authors of the MERG report took care to limit their projections and proposals to what seemed feasible in the light of the critical condition of the economy and the political balance of forces. This has not inhibited criticism from the 'new realism' of (erstwhile) social democratic economists in South Africa, notably Nattrass [1994a; 1994b] and the responses of Fine [1994] and Sender [1994].

40. An interesting example is how the Sotho kingship became a rallying point of opposition to the proposed incorporation of Lesotho (then Basutoland) in the Union of South Africa, while the Schedule to the Act of Union of 1910 entrenched 'the complex of hereditary chieftainship – land – Sotho Law' [Kimble, 1985a: 63] – that is, pillars of what Mamdani calls 'decentralised despotism' that have been contested ever since.

41. Themes explored in fine work on Lesotho that includes C. Murray [1981], Kimble [1985b], and Ferguson [1990].

42. The examples of accumulating black farmers in Murray's study in this volume, and even of those investing in farming from a base in business or the bureaucracy (note 29), are not accurately conveyed by the term 'gentleman farmer', even if other cases would be.

Woodhouse [1994: 201] provides another example of the energy and skill, as well as capital, committed to 'accumulation from below' – a farmer who 'had invested R5000 and considerable ingenuity in constructing a filtration chamber under the (Saringwa) streambed, which enabled him to pump water, free of sand, to irrigate a holding of about 10ha'.

43. The latter should not be exaggerated, in my view. The opposition of the SAAU to a proposed land tax, noted by Levin and Weiner ('Politics') was shared by NAFU. All three entrepreneur farmers cited in note 29 oppose any widespread distribution of small(er) plots of land; it is interesting that in Thaba Nchu 'there was hostility to the allocation of land by headmen *or* by elected farmers' committees', which included private landowners (Murray, this volume).

44. This is a bold assertion which I hope to explore in a future essay. Suffice it to say here that I have more sympathy with the observation of Hobsbawm [1994: 289; 289–93 *passim*] that the 'most dramatic and far-reaching social change of the second half of this century … is the death of the peasantry', than some of his discussants [e.g. *Therborn*, 1995: 88]. The passing of the classic agrarian question, *from the viewpoint of global capital*, is reflected in the virtual disappearance of (bourgeois) land reform from the agenda of 'agricultural development policy' since the 1950s and 1960s, with the symptomatic exception of the World Bank's desire to replace 'indigenous' forms of tenure in Africa with private property rights in land.

REFERENCES

Adelzadeh, A. and V. Padayachee, 1994 'The RDP White Paper: Reconstruction of a Development Vision?', *Transformation* 25.

ANC, 1994 *The Reconstruction and Development Programme*, Johannesburg: Umanyano Publications.

Baskin, J., 1991 *Striking Back: A History of COSATU*, Johannesburg: Ravan.

Beinart, W., 1987 'Agrarian Historography and Agrarian Reconstruction', in Lonsdale (ed.) [1987].

Beinart, W., 1994 *Twentieth-Century South Africa*, Oxford: Oxford University Press.

Bernstein, H., 1992 'Agrarian Reform in South Africa: Who? What? How?', paper to tenth Ruth First Memorial Colloquium, University of the Western Cape.

Bernstein, H., 1994 '"And Who Now Plans Its Future?" Land in South Africa after apartheid', in C.M. Hann (ed.), *When History Accelerates. Essays on Rapid Social Change, Complexity and Creativity*, London: Athlone.

Bernstein, H., 1996 'Land and Food in South Africa's Agrarian Question', in Levin and Weiner (eds.) [1996].

Bernstein, H., Brass, T. and T.J. Byres, 1994, *The Journal of Peasant Studies. A Twenty Volume Index 1973–1993*, London: Frank Cass.

Bradford, H., 1988, *A Taste of Freedom. The ICU in Rural South Africa, 1924–1930*, Johannesburg: Ravan.

Bradford, H., 1990, 'Highways, By-ways and Cul-de-sacs: The Transition to Agrarian Capitalism in Revisionist South African History', *Radical History Review*, Vol.46, No.7.

Bradford, H., 1993, 'Getting Away with Murder: "Mealie Kings", the State and Foreigners in the Eastern Transvaal, c1918–1950', in P. Bonner, P. Delius and D. Posel (eds.), *Apartheid's Genesis, 1935–962*, Johannesburg: Witwatersrand University Press.

Brand, S.S., 1969, 'The Contributions of Agriculture to the Economic Development of South Africa', Ph.D. thesis, University of Pretoria.

Brass, T., 1986, 'Unfree Labour and Capitalist Restructuring in the Agrarian Sector: Peru and India', *Journal of Peasant Studies*, Vol.14. No.1.

Brass, T., 1990, 'Class Struggle and the Deproletarianisation of Agricultural Labour in Haryana (India)', *Journal of Peasant Studies*, Vo.18, No.1.

Brass T., and H. Bernstein, 1992, 'Introduction: Proletarianisation and Deproletarianisation on the Colonial Plantation', in V.E. Daniel, H. Bernstein and T. Brass (eds.), *Plantations, Proletarians and Peasants in Colonial Asia*, special issue *of Journal of Peasant Studies*, Vol.19, Nos.3 & 4.

Bundy, C., 1979, *The Rise and Fall of the South African Peasantry*, London: Heinemann.

Bundy, C., 1984 'Land and Liberation: The South African National Liberation Movements and the Agrarian Question, 1920s–1960s', *Review of African Political Economy* 29.

Byres, T.J., 1991 'The Agrarian Question and Differing Forms of Agrarian Transition: An Essay with Reference to Asia', in J. Breman and S. Mundle (eds.), *Rural Transformation in Asia*, Delhi: Oxford University Press.

Byres, T.J., 1995 'Political Economy, the Agrarian Question and the Comparative Method', *Journal of Peasant Studies*, Vol.22, No.4.

Byres, T.J. (in press), *Capitalism from Above and Capitalism from Below. An Essay in Comparative Political Economy*, London: Macmillan.

Cousins, B. (ed.), 1989, *People, Land and Livestock*, Harare: University of Zimbabwe.

Cousins, B., D. Weiner and N. Amin, 1992, 'Social Differentiation in Communal Lands of Zimbabwe', *Review of African Political Economy* 53.

Csaki, C., Dams, Th.J., Metzger, D. and J. van Zyl (eds.), 1992, *Agricultural Restructuring in Southern Africa*, Windhoek: Association of Agricultural Economists in Nambia with International Association of Agricultural Economists.

Davies, R.H., 1979, *Capital, State and White Labour in South Africa 1900–1960*, Atlantic Highlands, NJ: Humanities Press.

Davies, R., Kaplan, D., Morris, M. and D. O'Meara, 1976, 'Class Struggle and the Periodisation of the State in South Africa', *Review of African Political Economy* 7.

Davies, R, O'Meara, D. and S. Dlamini, 1988, *The Struggle for South Africa*, 2 vols. (Revised Edition), London: Zed Books.

de Klerk, M., 1991, 'The Accumulation Crisis in Agriculture', in Gelb (ed.) [1991].

de Klerk, M., (ed.), 1991, *A Harvest of Discontent: The Land Question in South Africa*, Cape Town: IDASA.

Delius, P., 1990, 'Migrants, Comrades and Rural Revolt: Sekhukhuneland 1950–1987', *Transformation* 13.

de Villiers Graaf, J., 1985, 'The Present State of Urbanisation in the South African Homelands and Some Future Scenarios', paper to Conference of the Development Society of Southern Africa, Cape Town.

Drew, A., 1991, 'Events were Breaking above Their Heads: Socialism in South Africa, 1921–1950', *Social Dynamics*, Vol.17, No.1.

Drew, A, (ed.), 1995–96, *South Africa's Radical Tradition: A Documentary History, Volume 1: 1907–1950, Volume 2, 1943–1964*, Cape Town: University of Cape Town Press, Mayibuye Books and Buchu Books.

Ferguson, J., 1990, *The Anti-Politics Machine. 'Development' Depoliticization and Bureaucratic State Power in Lesotho*, Cambridge: Cambridge University Press.

Fine, B, 1994, 'Politics and Economics in ANC Economic Policy: An Alternative Assessment', *Transformation* 25.

First, R., 1959, *Exposure: the Farm Labour Scandal*, Johannesburg: New Age.

First, R, 1964, Preface to Mbeki [1964].

Freund, B, 1987, 'Defending South African Capitalism' (review article on Lipton [1986]), *Transformation* 4.

Friedman, S., 1987, *Building Tomorrow Today: African Workers in Trade Unions, 1970–1984*, Johannesburg: Ravan.

Friedman, S. and D. Atkinson (eds.), 1994, *South African Review 7. The Small Miracle. South Africa's Negotiated Settlement*, Johannesburg: Ravan.

Frederickson, G.M., 1981, *White Supremacy. A Comparative Study in American and South African History*, New York: Oxford University Press.

Gelb, S., 1991, 'South Africa's Economic Crisis: An Overview', in Gelb (ed.) [1991].

Gelb, S., (ed.), 1991, *South Africa's Economic Crisis*, Cape Town: David Philip.

Gerschenkron, A., 1943, *Bread and Democracy in Germany*, Berkeley, CA: University of California Press.

Gibbon, P., 1993, '"Civil Society" and Political Change, with Special Reference to Developmentalist States', unpublished paper, Uppsala: Scandinavian Institute of African Studies.

Gibbon, P., 1994, 'Some Reflections on State, Civil Society and the Division of Labour in late Colonial Tanganyika', paper to Conference on Dimensions of Economic and Political

Reform in Contemporary Africa, Kampala.

Greenberg, S.B., 1980, *Race and State in Capitalist Development: South Africa in Comparative Perspective*, New Haven, CT: Yale University Press.

Greenberg, S.B., 1987, *Legitimating the Illegitimate: State, Markets and Resistance in South Africa*, Berkeley, CA: University of California Press.

Harber, A. and B. Ludman (eds.), 1995, *Weekly Mail and Guardian A–Z of South African Politics*, Johannesburg: Penguin.

Harris, L., 1993, 'South Africa's Economic and Social Transformation: From "No Middle Road" to "No Alternative"', *Review of African Political Economy* 57.

Hindson, D., 1987, *Pass Controls and the African Urban Proletariat*, Johannesburg: Ravan.

Hindson, D., 1991, 'The Restructuring of Labour Markets in South Africa; 1970s and 1980s', in Gelb (ed.).

Hirson, B., 1989 *Yours for the Union. Class and Community Struggles in South Africa, 1930–1947*, Johannesburg: Witwatersrand University Press.

Howe, G. and P. le Roux (eds.), 1992, *Transforming the Economy. Policy Options for South Africa*, Durban: University of Natal.

Hobsbawm, E, 1994, *Age of Extremes: The Short Twentieth Century, 1914–1991*, London: Michael Joseph.

Husy, D., 1994, 'Migrant Farm Workers in the Maize Sector: Addressing Structural Powerlessness', in Levin and Weiner (eds.) [1994].

Karaan, M., Lubbe, W., Nkosi, A. and J. van Zyl, 1993, *Agricultural Marketing: Red Meat*, Johannesburg, LAPC.

Keegan, T., 1986, *Rural Transformations in Industrializing South Africa: The Southern Highveld to 1914*, Johannesburg: Ravan.

Keegan, T., 1988, *Facing the Storm: Portraits of Black Lives in Rural South Africa*, Cape Town: David Phillip.

Kentridge, M., 1990, *An Unofficial War. Inside the Conflict in Pietermaritzburg*, Cape Town: David Phillip.

Kimble, J., 1985a,'"Clinging to the Chiefs": Some Contradictions of Colonial Rule in Basutoland, c1890–1930', in H. Bernstein and B.K. Campbell (eds.), *Contradictions of Accumulation in Africa*, Beverly Hills, CA: Sage.

Kimble, J, 1985b 'Migrant Labour and Colonial Rule in Southern African: The Case of Colonial Basutoland, 1890–1930', Ph.D. thesis, University of Essex.

Kraak, G., 1993, *Breaking the Chains: Labour in South Africa in the 1970s and 1980s*, London: Pluto.

Krikler, J., 1993, *Revolution from Above, Rebellion from Below: The Agrarian Transvaal at the Turn of the Century*, Oxford: Clarendon.

LAPC (Land and Agriculture Policy Centre), 1994, *Food Security and Staple Foods: Policy Issues for South Africa*, Johannesburg: LAPC.

Legassick, M., and H. Wolpe, 1976, 'The Bantustans and Capital Accumulation in South Africa', *Review of African Political Economy* 7.

Lenin, V.I., 1973 (1899), *The Development of Capitalism in Russia*, Moscow: Progress Publishers.

Levin, R., 1996, *When the Sleeping Grass Awakens: Land, Power and Hegemony in Swaziland*, Johannesburg: Witwatersrand University Press.

Levin, R. and M. Neocosmos, 1989, 'The Agrarian Question and Class Contradictions in South Africa: Some Theoretical Considerations', *Journal of Peasant Studies*, Vol.16, No.2.

Levin, R. and D. Weiner, 1991, 'The Agrarian Question and the Emergence of Conflicting Agricultural Strategies in South Africa', in Matlhape and Munz (eds.) [1991].

Levin, R, and D. Weiner (eds), 1994, *Community Perspectives on Land and Agrarian Reform in South Africa*, Johannesburg: University of the Witwatersrand, Department of Sociology.

Levin, R. and D. Weiner (eds.), 1996, *We Have No More Tears to Cry for Land: Community Perspectives on Land and Agrarian Reform in South Africa*, Trenton: Africa World Press.

Lipton, M., 1986, *Capitalism and Apartheid: South Africa 1910–1986*, London: Wildwood House.

Lipton, M., 1987, 'Capitalism and Apartheid', in Lonsdale (ed.) [1987].

Lodge, T., 1983, *Black Politics in South Africa Since 1945*, Johannesburg: Ravan.

Lodge, T., Nasson, B. *et al.*, 1991, *All, Here, and Now: Black Politics in South Africa in the 1980s*, Cape Town: David Phillip.

Lonsdale, J. (ed.), 1987, *South Africa in Question*, Cambridge: Cambridge University Press.

Lund, F.J., 1992, *The Way Welfare Works: Structures, Spending, Staffing and Social Work in the South African Welfare Bureaucracies*, Pretoria: HSRC.

Macroeconomic Research Group (MERG), 1993, *Making Democracy Work. A Framework for Macroeconomic Policy in South Africa*, Bellville: University of the Western Cape.

McIntosh, A., Quinlan, T. and A. Vaughan, 1993, 'Towards an Independent Civil Society: Limits and Possibilities in Rural Areas', Durban: University of Durban-Westville, ISER (draft).

McMenamin, V., 1992, 'Shifts in ANC Economic Policy', in Howe and le Roux (eds.) [1992].

Maluleke, T, Small, J. and H. Winkler, 1994, 'Land Claims in the Bushbuckridge/Graskop Area', in Levin and Weiner (eds.) [1994].

Mamdani, M., 1987, 'Extreme but not Exceptional: Towards an Analysis of the Agrarian Question in Uganda', *Journal of Peasant Studies*, Vol.14, No.2.

Mamdani, M., 1990, 'State and Civil Society in Contemporary Africa: Reconceptualising the Birth of State Nationalism and the Defeat of Popular Movements', *Africa Development*, 15, 3/4.

Mamdani, M., forthcoming 'Decentralized Despotism, Fragmented Resistance: The Making of Non-Racial Apartheid in Africa' (provisional title).

Marcus, T., 1989, *Modernising Super-Exploitation: Restructuring South African Agriculture*, London: Zed Books.

Maré, G. and G. Hamilton, 1987, *An Appetite for Power: Buthelezi's Inkatha and the Politics of 'Loyal Resistance'*, Johannesburg: Ravan.

Maree, J, (ed.), 1987, *The Independent Trade Unions 1974–1984: Ten Years of the South African Labour Bulletin*, Johannesburg: Ravan.

Marx, A, 1992, *Lessons of Struggle: South African Internal Opposition, 1960–1990*, Cape Town: Oxford University Press.

Matlhape, B. and A. Munz (eds.), 1991, *Towards a New Democratic Agrarian Order*, Amsterdam: SAERT.

Mbeki, G., 1964, *South Africa: The Peasants' Revolt*, Harmondsworth: Penguin.

Mbeki, T., 1992, 'Tribute to Simon Brand', in Howe and le Roux (eds.) [1992].

Mendes, C., 1992, 'Chico Mendes – The Defence of Life', *Journal of Peasant Studies*, Vol.20, No.1.

Miles, R., 1987, *Capitalism and Unfree Labour: Anomaly or Necessity?*, London: Tavistock.

Morris, M., 1976, 'The Development of Capitalism in South African Agriculture: Class Struggle in the Countryside; *Economy and Society*, Vol.5, No.3.

Morris, M., 1981, 'The State and the Development of Capitalist Social Relations in the South African Countryside: A Process of Class Struggle', D.Ph. thesis, University of Sussex:.

Morris, M., 1987, 'Social History and the Transition to Capitalism in the South African Countryside', *Africa Perspective* (NS), Vol.1, Nos.5/6.

Morris, M. and D. Hindson, 1992, 'South Africa: Political Violence, Reform and Reconstruction', *Review of African Political Economy* 53.

Murray, C., 1981, *Families Divided. The Impact of Migrant Labour in Lesotho*, Cambridge: Cambridge University Press.

Murray, C., 1987, 'Displaced Urbanisation', in Lonsdale (ed.) [1987].

Murray, C., 1992, *Black Mountain: Land, Class and Power in the Eastern Orange Free State 1880s–1980s*, Edinburgh: Edinburgh University Press.

Murray, C., 1995, 'Structural Unemployment, Small Towns and Agrarian Change in South Africa', *African Affairs* Vol 94.

Murray, C. and G. Williams, (eds.), 1994, *Land and Freedom in South Africa*, special issue of *Review of African Political Economy* 61.

Murray, M.J., 1987, *South Africa: Time of Agony, Time of Destiny: The Upsurge of Popular Protest*, London: Verso.

Murray, M.J., 1989, 'The Origins of Agrarian Capitalism in South Africa: A Critique of the Social History Perspective', *Journal of Southern African Studies*, Vol.15, No.4.

Murray, M.J., 1994, *The Revolution Deferred: The Painful Birth of Post-Apartheid South Africa,* London: Verso.

Mzala, 1988, *Gatsha Buthelezi: Chief with a Double Agenda,* London: Zed Books.

Nattrass, N., 1994a, 'Politics and Economics in ANC Economic Policy', *African Affairs,* Vol 93

Nattrass, N., 1994b, 'Economic Restructuring in South Africa: The Debate Continues', *Journal of Southern African Studies,* Vol.20, No.4.

Neocosmos, M., 1993, *The Agrarian Question in Southern Africa and 'Accumulation from Below',* Uppsala: Scandinavian Institute of African Studies.

Neocosmos, M., 1995, 'From People's Politics to State Politics: Aspects of National Liberation in South Africa, 1984–1994', draft paper.

Nkadimeng, M. and G. Relly, 1983, 'Kas Maine: The Story of a Black South African Agriculturalist', in B. Bozzoli (ed.), *Town and Countryside in the Transvaal,* Johannesburg: Ravan.

O'Laughlin, B., 1996, 'Through a Divided Glass: Dualism, Class and the Agrarian Question in Mozambique', *Journal of Peasant Studies,* Vol.23, No.4.

O'Meara, D., 1983, *Volkscapitalisme: Class, Capital and Ideology in the Development of Afrikaner Nationalism, 1934–1948,* Cambridge: Cambridge University Press.

O'Meara, D., (in press), *Forty Lost Years: The Apartheid State and the Politics of the National Party, 1948–1994,* New Haven: Yale University Press.

Pickles, J. and D. Weiner, 1991, 'Rural and Regional Restructuring of Apartheid: Ideology, Development Policy and the Competition for Space', *Antipode,* Vol.23, No.1.

Pickles, J. and D. Weiner (eds.), 1991, *Rural and Regional Restructuring in South Africa,* special issue of *Antipode,* Vol.23, No.1.

Plaatje, S.T., 1987, (1916), *Native Life in South Africa,* London: Longman.

Platzky, L. and C. Walker, 1985, *The Surplus People: Forced Removals in South Africa,* Johannesburg: Ravan.

Posel, D., 1991, *The Making of Apartheid 1948–1961: Compromise and Conflict,* Oxford: Clarendon.

Raikes, P., 1993, 'Food Aid, Security and Experience', paper to Conference on Food Security in South Africa, Johannesburg.

Reynolds, A., 1994, 'The Results', in A. Reynolds (ed.), *Election '94 South Africa: The Campaigns, Results and Future Prospects,* Cape Town: David Philip.

RSA (Republic of South Africa), 1992a, *An Investigation into the Price Mechanism in the Food Chain,* Pretoria: Board of Tariffs and Trade.

RSA, 1992b, *Report of the Committee of Inquiry into the Marketing Act,* Pretoria: Department of Agriculture.

RSA, 1992c, *Report of the Committee for the Development of a Food and Nutrition Strategy for Southern Africa,* Pretoria: Department of Agriculture.

RSA, 1994, *White Paper on Reconstruction and Development: A Strategy for Fundamental Transformation,* Pretoria: RSA.

Rueschmeyer, D., Huber Stephens, E. and J.D. Stephens, 1992, *Capitalist Development and Democracy,* Cambridge: Polity.

Saul, J.B., 1991, 'South Africa: Between "Barbarism" and "Structural Reform"', *New Left Review* 188.

Seekings, J., 1993, *Heroes or Villains? Youth Politics in the 1980s,* Johannesburg: Ravan.

Sender, J., 1994, 'Economic Restructuring in South Africa, Reactionary Rhetoric Prevails', *Journal of Southern African Studies,* Vol.20, No.4.

Schrire, R., 1992, *Adapt or Die: The End of White Politics in South Africa,* New York: Ford Foundation.

Slovo, J., 1976, 'South Africa – No Middle Road', in B. Davidson, Slovo, J. and A.R. Wilkinson, *Southern Africa: the New Politics of Revolution,* Harmondsworth: Penguin.

Sparks, A., 1994, *Tomorrow is Another Country. The Inside Story of South Africa's Negotiated Revolution,* Sandton: Struik.

Therborn, G., 1995, 'The Autobiography of the Twentieth Century', *New Left Review* 214.

Trapido, S, 1971, 'South Africa in a Comparative Study of Industrialization', *Journal of Development Studies,* Vol.7, No.3.

van Onselen, C., 1993, 'The Reconstruction of a Rural Life from Oral Testimony: Critical Notes on the Methodology Employed in the Study of a Black South African Sharecropper', *Journal of Peasant Studies*, Vol.20, No.3.

van Zyl, J. and J. Van Rooyen, 1991, 'Agricultural Production in South Africa', in de Klerk (ed.) [1991].

Vaughan, A., 1992, 'Options for Rural Restructuring', in R. Schrire (ed.), *Wealth or Poverty? Critical Choices for South Africa*, Cape Town: Oxford University Press.

Warwick, P., 1983, *Black People and the South African War, 1899–1902*, Cambridge: Cambridge University Press.

WAU (Wageningen Agricultural University), 1995, *Agrarian Questions: The Politics of Farming anno 1995, Proceedings*, Vols.1–4, Wageningen; WAU.

Weiner, D., 1989, 'Agricultural Restructuring in Zimbabwe and South Africa', *Development and Change*, Vol.20, No.3.

Welsh, D., 1971, 'The Growth of Towns', in Wilson and Thompson (eds.) [1971].

Whiteford, A., 1994, 'The Poor get Even Poorer', *Weekly Mail*, March 11–17.

Willan, B., 1984, *Sol Plaatje: A Biography*, Johannesburg: Ravan.

Wilson, F., 1971, 'Farming 1866–1966', in Wilson and Thompson (eds.) [1971].

Wilson, M. and L. Thompson (eds.), 1969, *A History of South Africa to 1870*, Oxford: Clarendon.

Wilson, M. and L. Thompson, (eds.), 1971, *South Africa, 1870–1966*, Oxford: Clarendon.

Wolpe, H., 1972, 'Capitalism and Cheap Labour Power: from Segregation to Apartheid', *Economy and Society*, Vol.1, No.4.

Wolpe, H., 1988, *Race, Class and the Apartheid State*, London: James Currey.

Woodhouse, P., 1994, 'Soils and Irrigation Systems in the Hazyview Area of the Eastern Transvaal', in Levin and Weiner (eds.).

Wuyts, M., Mackintosh, M. and T. Hewitt (eds.), 1992, *Development Policy and Public Action*, Oxford: Oxford University Press.

Yawitch, J., 1981, *Betterment: The Myth of Homeland Agriculture*, Johannesburg: South African Institute of Race Relations.

The Theory and Practice of the Agrarian Question in South African Socialism, 1928–60

ALLISON DREW

INTRODUCTION

With few notable exceptions, the political organisations forming South Africa's liberation movement have historically underestimated the theoretical and practical significance of political aspirations and social movements in the countryside [*Jordaan,* 1959; *Bundy,* 1987: 257; *Weiner and Levin* 1991: 109–10; *Claassens,* 1991: 156–7]. Throughout much of this century, the principal efforts to address the political dimensions of the agrarian question came from socialists who, influenced by Communist and Trotskyist thought and experience, were concerned with the peasantry's political potential, particularly its potential to align with a proletarian-led revolution. South African socialists struggled for decades with the problem of the relationship between rural proletarianisation and peasant consciousness, a problem which bedeviled European socialists as well [*Banaji,* 1990], and they anticipated more recent scholarly debates on rural development and consciousness.[1] None the less, their own theoretical and practical attention to the agrarian question has been sporadic rather than sustained. From the 1920s through the 1950s South African socialists held polarised views of the peasantry and its political potential, a theoretical polarity which manifested itself in an oscillating practice between town and country.

This theoretical polarity reflected, in part, the international socialist milieu in which the South African movement emerged and from which it drew inspiration. Socialist thought in South Africa developed within a broader, European-centred movement which, from the mid-nineteenth century, had privileged the urban proletariat as the leading force in social change, a view reinforced by the 1917 Russian Revolution, which most socialists used as a lens through which they evaluated other societies and

Allison Drew, Department of Politics, University of York, Heslington, York YO1 5DD. The research for this article was facilitated by a Research Grant from the American Political Science Association and a Post-doctoral Research Fellowship at the University of Natal, Pietermaritzburg. An earlier version of this study was presented as a paper at the Wits History Workshop, University of the Witwatersrand, Johannesburg, July 1994. The author wishes to thank Henry Bernstein, David Howell, Ronald Kieve, Gavin Williams, Crawford Young and Ralph Young for their comments.

other attempts at socialist mobilisation.

Reflecting internal power struggles within the Soviet Union, which spilled into the international socialist movement, by the 1930s South African socialism had split into two tendencies. The dominant tendency, represented by the Communist Party of South Africa (CPSA) retained its allegiance to the Communist International (Comintern). The minority supported the struggle of Leon Trotsky and the Left Opposition, a movement against Stalin's leadership of the Soviet Union which broke from the Comintern's Third International to form the Fourth International in 1938. Theoretically, the Comintern adhered to Stalin's [1940] aspiration to build socialism in one country and the corollary notion of moving towards socialism in stages. Trotsky [1982], by contrast, had formulated the theory of permanent revolution to explain the circumstances in which proletarian revolutions could take place in less developed countries without passing through a stage of bourgeois democracy.

Cutting across the Communist–Trotskyist cleavage, however, South African socialists were divided between a majority giving primacy to the urban working class movement and a minority which saw the agrarian question as the backbone of any social revolution [*Drew*, 1991: 199–224; 456–505; *Delius*, 1993: 293–294, 302–3; *Basner*, 1993: 106–8]. The theoretical dominance of the urban bias has been accentuated by two other specifically South African factors: first, the long-term practical difficulty of political organising amongst rural farmworkers and labour-tenants, due to the dispersed and extremely repressive conditions on white farms; second, and more recently, the rapid development and national visibility of an organised, militant, urban black working class. The dramatic upsurge of the black trade union movement in the 1970s shifted discussion away from considerations of an agrarian revolution to prognostications of a black proletarian revolution.

Thus, for much of socialism's history in South Africa, the discourse and the concepts that its proponents used to analyse the agrarian question were formulated with respect to agrarian conditions and socialist experience in Europe. In the 1940s and 1950s, however, as a number of activists began organising in rural areas, socialists began developing concepts and analyses based on South Africa's specific conditions. Not coincidentally, this was also a period when, despite the intense sectarianism dividing the Left, the observations of rural activists often coincided and their analyses began to converge. Relatively little has been written about these theoretical and practical endeavors and their significance for understanding the relationship between theory and practice in South Africa. The blanket of repression which covered South Africa following the notorious Sharpeville massacre of 1960 not only put an end to open political activity in the next decade, it effectively concealed many of these historical experiences.

The experiences of South African socialists raise questions about the extent to which their methodological approaches illuminated or obscured social conditions in South Africa, and to which models or concepts, as abstractions derived from particular empirical conditions and prioritising certain concerns over others, can be applied in an illuminating manner to other conditions.[2] These experiences also indicate the centrality of practical political work in validating or modifying such models or concepts in the light of specific historical conditions and experiences.

THE PEASANTRY AND MIGRANT LABOUR

Two principal alternative perspectives have shaped discussions of the peasantry and its political potential this century: one stressing the primacy of political economy and rural class formation [*Lenin,* 1974], the other, the primacy of the peasantry's moral economy [*Wolf,* 1966; 1987; *Scott,* 1985; *Brass,* 1991: 174–5].[3] Lenin [1974: 176] saw the peasantry as a bedrock of capitalism, even as the weight of peasant tradition slowed down capitalism's transformative effects. The social disintegration and class formation produced by capitalism was critical in understanding the peasantry's political potential, he maintained. The development of commodity relations hastened the break-up of the traditional peasantry into an intermediate stratum or middle peasantry, squeezed between a rural proletariat and capitalist farming class. This social disintegration set the basis for class struggle in the countryside.

While Lenin stressed the peasantry's vulnerability and disintegration into opposing classes, Eric Wolf has emphasised the resilience of peasant social structures to external change. It is capitalism's threat to peasant society which pushes peasants out of their traditional conservatism to participate in revolutionary movements [1987: 368–9]. Migrant labour provides the clue to this paradox of cultural conservatism and revolutionary potential. The middle peasantry engaged in migrant labour has ties to both town and country, making it a transmitter of urban ideas. Thus, according to Wolf, it is the migrant industrial workforce which retains rural ties which is most potentially revolutionary, rather than the industrial proletariat *per se.* Moreover, he maintains, those peasants with tactical leverage over resources like land or with freedom to maneuver have the greatest potential to sustain long-term revolt. This includes the middle peasantry, which uses family labour to cultivate its securely-held land, as well as peasants whose relative independence from landlord control allows them 'tactical mobility' [1987: 371–2].

CAPITALIST DEVELOPMENT IN THE SOUTH AFRICAN RESERVES

The distinctive development and disintegration of the South African peasantry poses a challenge to these dual perspectives, both of which also ignored the salience of gender in peasant societies.[4] South Africa's distinctive racial path of capitalist development, as Hendricks [1995: 47–50; 1993: 4–7; 1990: 16, 162; c.1986: 2] has argued, was based on blocking the development of an African peasantry and impeding the development of a stable black urban working class by deflecting proletarianisation to designated rural areas, called reserves and later bantustans. This reserve-based population was drawn into the labour force through the migrant labour system. Moreover, through a gendered process of proletarianisation, men were drawn into the migrant labour system far earlier and in far greater numbers than women. As a result, the prominent role which women had traditionally played in subsistence agriculture became even more accentuated while they worked in increasingly adverse conditions. This gendered proletarianisation was buttressed by state policies which increased the power of chiefs and legislated the subordination of women as legal minors [*Walker*, 1990: 173, 177ff.].

If nineteenth-century South Africa was dominated by struggles amongst European colonisers and Africans over land, by the end of the century, with British imperialism's development of gold mining, capital's need for labour became paramount. Control of land was assimilated to the need to incorporate rural labour into the migrant labour system [*Jordaan*, 1959: 12–17; *Wilson*, 1972: 234–56].

In 1894 the Glen Grey Act in the Cape implemented the 'one man, one lot' principle in areas reserved for Africans. This was premised on the liberal ideal of individual land tenure and formulated with the hope of providing rural subsistence for as many Africans as possible and weakening the chieftainship's control of land allocation. But in practice, the 'one man, one lot' principle was economically unviable and led to stagnation in the reserves. Although initially supported by some of the more prosperous peasants, the limitations on the size of land holdings in the restricted area of the reserves impeded the development of an African farming class and at the same time led to loss of landholdings and landlessness for many.[5]

These contradictions manifested themselves first in the Cape, where the reserve system had begun, and which, after 1908 was the main area of mine labour recruitment in South Africa. Far from promoting a homogenous peasantry, the 'one man, one lot' principle accelerated class differentiation and proletarianisation as land became fragmented into economically unviable holdings. Following the Union of South Africa in 1910, the 1911 Native Labour Regulation Act implemented an extensive system of pass controls to regulate the recruitment and movement of African male labour, and the 1913 Native Land Act attempted to standardise state policy towards the reserves [*MacMillan,* 1919, 1949: 120–32; *Roux,* 1949: 171–2; *Jordaan,* 1959: 12–13, 22; *Beinart and Bundy,* 1980: 276–80, 294].[6]

In the late nineteenth century, female-based subsistence agriculture was far more important than male migrant labour for social reproduction. Although a minority of cultivators in the late nineteenth century had turned to commercial production and developed into a prosperous peasantry, by the early twentieth century poverty was driving increasing numbers of young, unmarried African men from the reserves into migrant labour on farms and mines [*Bundy,* 1988; *Lewis,* 1984]. By 1920, agricultural production in the reserves met less than 50 per cent of subsistence needs, and the majority of rural households depended on migrant labour income [*Walker,* 1990: 173, 177]. By 1925 the process of proletarianisation was in some places virtually complete. At Herschel, MacMillan [1949: 123] baldly notes,

> ... local production came nowhere near maintaining the people ... .
> Their chief export by far was labour; the final estimate being that 75
> per cent of the adult male population was absent at work outside the
> district at least six months of the year.

Despite regional variations, the tendency was to greater involvement in migrant labour and longer periods away from home. In the late 1930s, about 70 per cent of Ciskeian men aged 15 to 44 were migrant labourers, as opposed to 50 per cent in Basutoland and the Transkei, and 28 per cent in Bechuanaland. Growing numbers of older and married men engaged in migrant labour, and agricultural production shifted even more to women, 'the widows of the reserves', who worked in increasingly arduous conditions as access to land was squeezed and soil depleted [*Ntantala,* 1992. 167; *Walker,* 1990: 176; *Beinart and Bundy,* 1980: 293–4].[7]

Black tenants and sharecroppers suffered deteriorating conditions on white farms, which were typically undercapitalised. As competitive pressure intensified, farmers increased the exploitation of tenant labour. The 1904 Master and Servants Ordinance deprived black tenants of legal protection by defining them as servants instead of wage labourers. The 1913 Land Act prohibited land occupancy and sales to blacks outside reserved areas and outlawed sharecropping and squatting, making labour service the only legal means by which tenants could pay rent, and precipitating mass evictions of blacks from farms to the reserves [*Plaatje,* 1987: 49–66; *Jordaan,* 1959: 18–19; *Keegan,* 1986b: 182–4, 192–3]. Labour-intensive farming methods typically remained more profitable than capital-intensive ones well into the twentieth century. Only after the Second World War, when state policy sought to modernise white farming and capitalist investment in agriculture shot up dramatically, did mechanisation and wage and prison labour displace labour-intensive tenant production [*Jordaan*, 1959: 25–6; *Keegan*, 1986b: 30, 190–206; *Mabin*, 1991: 34, 40; *Claasens*, 1991: 150].

By the 1930s and 1940s, rural poverty had reached epidemic proportions. Africans flooded into towns, despite the legislative controls on their movements, a process encouraged by the temporary relaxation of pass laws during the Second World War to facilitate industrial production for the war effort [*Wilson*, 1972: 161; *Jordaan*, 1959: 19]. The state enacted a series of measures, including the Natives Land and Trust Act of 1936, the Control and Improvement of Livestock in Native Areas Proclamation No.31 of 1939 – popularly known as the Betterment Proclamation – and the Rehabilitation Scheme of 1944, which aimed to stabilise the economic deterioration of the reserves to ensure their viability for a permanent class of migrant labour. The Betterment Proclamation was designed to check the deterioration of the reserves and prevent further erosion. This was to be done by fencing land and reducing stock through cattle culling. Similarly, the Rehabilitation Scheme implemented after the Second World War aimed to arrest soil erosion through a massive reorganisation of African land-use. The Scheme attempted to resettle sections of the population into a variety of newly constructed villages where, in some cases, government programmes of afforestation and soil conservation would be implemented to create reserve-based proletarian settlements for migrant labourers and their families [*Hendricks*, 1990: 96–119; *Roux*, 1949: 189; *Hirson*, 1977: 2–3, 11; *Beinart and Bundy*, 1980: 297–8; *Basner*, 1993: 100–105].

The effect of such measures on the confined areas of the reserves was to further increase economic stratification and rural poverty, as a minority of wealthier reserve dwellers benefited from these interventionist policies. By the 1930s, the key variables in explaining stratification and differentiation were access to administrative posts and education. In the Transkei, Beinart and Bundy contend [1980: 294–5], the principal line of class differentiation was between an administrative stratum – composed of local government officials, teachers and clerks – and the rest of the population, whose income came from various combinations of migrant wages and agricultural production. This administrative stratum invested in land and cattle, ownership of which became increasingly concentrated during the inter-war period. By 1941 only about 3.3 per cent of the Transkei population owned more than 25 cattle, and about 70 per cent owned between one and five [*Hendricks*, 1990: 100–01]. Thus, although differential levels of migrant wages amongst the rest of the population meant that some families had greater funds to spend on rural cultivation or livestock, nonetheless, most were poor, and about one-quarter of the population had no land or stock at all.

For example, the Witzieshoek reserve in the Transvaal was proclaimed a Betterment area in 1939, and cattle culling began in 1942. The result, according to one report was that ' ... rich stockowners got off very lightly and the poorer ones lost from 25 to 100 per cent of their animals' ['Dealer's Evidence' 1950]. By 1950, it was estimated that of a total population of 14,000 households, about 4,000 had no land or cattle and had to find work outside the reserve and about 75 per cent had no stock ['Chief Mopeli' 1950]. While in some of the reserves a thin stratum could be categorised as wealthy peasants, the majority of reserve dwellers, even those who might be classified as middle peasants, eked out an insecure existence, with about one-third being completely proletarianised.[8]

MOMENTS OF THEORETICAL DEBATE I: THE CPSA AND THE NATIVE REPUBLIC THESIS IN THE 1920s

South African socialism emerged in the early twentieth century from the traditions of skilled British workers and Eastern Europeans fleeing Tsarist repression [*Johns*, 1976; *Mantzaris*, 1987]. This white, urban-based social composition reinforced the classical socialist emphasis on the vanguard role of the urban proletariat but gave it a particular twist. Imbued with the racial ideology which rationalised colonial conquest and British imperial penetration, early South African socialists superimposed a racial paradigm on this model and assumed white workers to be the political vanguard [*Ntsebeza*, 1988]. Africans, they believed, were better off in the rural areas where they were not a threat to white workers. But by the 1910s, the continuing influx of black people to the cities and mines made this position untenable. Now recognising that blacks were a permanent part of the industrial workforce, socialists began calling for working-class unity across the colour line. In July 1921 a number of tiny socialist groups merged to form the Communist Party of South Africa (CPSA) on the basis of their common acceptance of the 21 points of the Comintern [*Bunting*, 1981: 58–62]. The CPSA's 1924 draft programme called for a working class revolution which would expropriate and redistribute large landholdings amongst the landless rural population [*Bunting*, 1981: 80–4].

In the late 1920s, under Comintern pressure, the CPSA began to seriously reconsider the agrarian question. Between 1927 and 1929 the Comintern's agitation for the adoption of the Native Republic thesis in South Africa pushed the CPSA haltingly towards a new assessment of the relationship between national democratic and socialist struggles and between the urban working class and rural majority [*Bunting*, 1981: 90–106; *Roux*, 1993: 118–30]. The version of the thesis proposed by the Comintern in 1928 read: ' ... An independent native South African republic as a stage towards a workers' and peasants' republic, with full equal rights for all races, black, coloured and white' [*Bunting*, 1981: 93–4].

The theoretical roots of the Native Republic thesis lie in Marxist discussions on the national question early this century, and the exchanges between Rosa Luxemburg and V.I. Lenin, both of whom theorised from varied Eastern European experiences, established the framework for subsequent Marxist discussions.[9] In a crucial respect, the Native Republic thesis differed from earlier Marxist discussions and preceding Comintern policy. While previous formulations had spoken of the *right* of oppressed nations to self-determination, the Native Republic thesis proposed majority rule as a specific form of national self-determination which would be a stage towards socialism. The thesis proposed national-self determination through a struggle against British imperialism, defined not by its capitalist essence but by its colonial aspect, which included both national and racial domination. From its emphasis on the seemingly colonial character of South African society, flowed the characterisation of the black peasantry as the moving force of the South African revolution in the absence of a black bourgeoisie and the view that ' ... the national question in South Africa, which is based upon the agrarian question lies at the foundation of the revolution in South Africa'. By giving primacy to the satisfaction of black land hunger, argued the Comintern, South African Communists would induce rural blacks to align themselves under proletarian leadership, as Russian peasants had done during the 1917 Russian Revolution [*Bunting*, 1981: 94].

South African Communists polarised around the thesis, reflecting their varied perceptions of working-class development in towns and social class formation in the countryside. Some broke from the Party over what they saw as the slogan's alienation of white labour, which they still considered to be a potentially revolutionary social force. Others, like Jimmy La Guma and Douglas and Mary Wolton, applauded the slogan's emphasis on the needs of the black majority. Still others, notably S.P. Bunting, E.R. Roux and T.W. Thibedi, thought the thesis overemphasised the peasantry to the neglect of the proletariat, black and white, although Bunting and Roux later modified their views, and Bunting campaigned for election in Tembuland under the Native Republic slogan [*Roux*, 1993: 118–40].

The polarisation over the relative political significance of workers and peasants can be seen in the contrasting arguments of Bunting and another Communist, Albert Nzula. In explaining his scepticism about the thesis at the Sixth Comintern Congress, held in Moscow during July and August 1928, Bunting [1928a; 1928b] focused on the differentiated class structure of the African population and the underlying tendency towards proletarianisation, even claiming that there had not yet been any significant black rural movement in South Africa. But Bunting's assessment of rural movements was seriously off the mark in the late 1920s. The decade began with a wave of rural anti-tax protests, and over the next several years, the Industrial and Commercial Workers' Union (ICU), formed as a trade union of black dockworkers in 1919, stretched across the countryside. In 1922 it began making efforts to organise farmworkers, and by 1926–27, which Roux [1930: 54] calls ' ... the grand period of the I.C.U.', it was organising black sharecroppers and labour-tenants seeking to retain possession of their meagre means of production. The ICU's fragmentation in the late 1920s and its decline through the 1930s can be understood both in terms of the nature of its leadership and the severe repression faced by both members and organisers; at the structural level, its degeneration reflected its inability to stop the process of rural proletarianisation [*Nzula et al.,* 1979: 210–11; *Roux,* 1929; 1930; *Bradford,* 1988: 1–20, 266]. Nor were rural protests confined to struggles to resist proletarianisation. In the Western Cape, African National Congress (ANC) organisation of rural farmworkers became a groundswell, only halted in the early 1930s by the brutality of farmers and the state [*Hofmeyr,* 1983; 1985].

In contrast to Bunting's initial dismissal of rural movements, Nzula argued that British expropriation of peasant land gave peasant revolts their anti-imperialist thrust, manifested in their demand for 'more land, less taxes' [*Nzula et al.,* 1979:104]. In South Africa, imperialist exploitation occurred chiefly through the reserve system, which made agricultural subsistence impossible for the black majority. The concentration of landholdings and the landless-ness of the majority were barriers to peasant-based economic development. Following the Comintern, Nzula called for a two-stage revolution to eradicate pre-capitalist relations and allow for free peasant development as the basis for the gradual transition of national democracy into socialism [*Nzula et al.,* 1979: 163, 199–201].

Just as Bunting's initial position did not accurately reflect the development of rural movements in the late 1920s, Nzula's analysis, too, abstracted away critical social forces, seen in his dismissal of the South African working class as even a potential social vanguard and in his presumption that the democratic revolution would be bourgeois-led. In the late 1920s, 44 per cent of all workers employed in private manufacturing were Africans, who performed unskilled manual labour, while 38 per cent were white, typically performing skilled or supervisory work. By contrast, there was no African bourgeoisie able to accumulate capital by exploiting the labour-power of others, and less than one per cent of Africans could be described as formally-educated and trained professionals [*Van der Horst,* 1949: 112–18, 123].

The *de facto* proletarianisation of reserve dwellers who, despite being domiciled on the land, depended on wage labour, lent credibility to Bunting's scepticism about the possibility of a peasant-based revolution. In the mid-1930s, close to 83 per cent of all Africans lived in rural areas, mostly in reserves or other scheduled areas where they had access to small plots of land, or on white farms, and approximately 62 per cent of African males and 87 per cent of African females worked in agriculture and forestry. The majority were not self-sufficient peasants, however. Most men based in the reserves were contract or migrant workers on farms or mines; about 17 per cent worked in mining, and nine per cent, in manufacturing. Typically, in the 1930s, a third of the total male population was absent from the reserves. In some areas, like the Ciskei, this approached 100 per cent of the adult male population. Outside the reserves, most rural blacks worked on white-owned farms as wage workers, squatters or tenant farmers, and the demands of farmworkers organised by the Western Cape ANC and Independent ANC in the late 1920s and early 1930s indicated a proletariat concerned with working conditions rather than a land-hungry peasantry [*Van der Horst*, 1949: 112–18; *Natal University College*, 1949: 312–13; *Hofmeyr*, 1985: 321–8].

Although the Native Republic thesis pushed South African Communists to examine the agrarian question and laid the basis for organisational work which gave the Party a foothold in the countryside [*Roux*, 1993: 131–47; *Simons and Simons*, 1983: 411–13], the Comintern's analysis was inadequately grounded in South Africa's material conditions. While the implicit demand for return of the land struck a chord with recently colonised blacks, the Comintern too readily characterised most Africans as a homogeneous peasantry.

The version of the thesis finally adopted by the CPSA at its seventh annual conference in 1929 proposed: 'An Independent South African Native Republic as a stage towards the Workers' and Peasants' Republic, guaranteeing protection and complete equality to all national minorities' [*Bunting*, 1981: 104].

The CPSA's 1929 programme gave greater content to the thesis by including demands which represented a variety of rural interests. It called for repeal of the Natives Land Act; expropriation of large landholdings for redistribution amongst landless squatters and black and white land-hungry peasants and workers; security of tenure for squatters; regulation of farm labour under the Wage Act; implementation of a nation-wide irrigation scheme and development of cooperative farms [*Bunting*, 1981: 106]. None the less, these demands were incorporated into a framework based on a colonial analogy which privileged black peasant-based development and polarised the national and class struggles through its two-stage conception of social change.

MOMENTS OF THEORETICAL DEBATE II: TROTSKYISTS AND THE
AGRARIAN QUESTION IN THE 1930s

In mid-1928, with fascism dominant in Italy and the Left in retreat
elsewhere in Europe, the Comintern took a sharp left turn and adopted its
New Line – Class against Class. It now argued that the contradictions of the
capitalist system were rapidly leading to its collapse, that the immiseration
of the working class provided the conditions for revolutionary proletarian
class consciousness, and stipulated that Communists break from social
democratic organisations. Accordingly, when the CPSA adopted the New
Line in 1930, the Native Republic thesis went into eclipse for several years
as Communists repudiated popular work in national organisations in an
effort to streamline and bolshevise the Party [*Roux, 1993*: 148–79; *1964*:
269].

Notwithstanding this abrupt shift, the Native Republic thesis had a
profound impact on the socialist movement, catalysing the development of
Trotskyism in South Africa. Numerous individuals either left or were
expelled from the CPSA because of their objection to the top–down manner
in which the Comintern imposed the thesis. Others still adamantly rejected
what they saw as its subordination of the working class struggle to
bourgeois democratic aims [*Roux, 1993*: 156–8; *Roux, 1964*: 256; *Simons
and Simons, 1983*: 424]. The thesis led to a polarisation in the way in which
socialists conceptualised the relationship between town and country which
can be traced through several decades.

Initially, Trotskyists simply inverted the Native Republic thesis,
substituting the notion of a proletariat united across color lines for the
assumption of a homogenous peasantry. Thus, the Cape Town-based Lenin
Club, formed in 1933 by a number of former Communists, argued that the
thesis

> ... is in complete contradiction to Marxism-Leninism, for it places at
> the head of the Revolution the backward Native peasantry, which is by
> far the dominating element in the Native population, instead of giving
> the sole leadership in the transition period to the Working Class, black
> and white alike. The Communists' cry for a 'Native Republic' would
> doom the Revolution beforehand to failure, for never in past history
> have the peasants alone been able to carry a revolution to a successful
> issue [*Lenin Club, 1934a*: 4; also *Southall, 1978*: 33–4].

Despite their common rejection of the thesis, Trotskyists rapidly polarised
over the agrarian question, and in 1934 the Lenin Club split into two
factions. The next year the majority faction formed the Workers' Party of
South Africa (WPSA), and the minority, the Communist League of South

Africa (CLSA). In striking respects, their arguments replicated the Communist debates of the previous decade.

The WPSA took as its point of departure social relations on the land. This was, it argued, the material basis for the oppression of blacks, for the racial division of the working class and for South Africa's economic stagnation. The racial distribution of land meant landlessness and land hunger for the majority of blacks, forcing them to labour on mines and white-owned farms. This huge pool of ultra-cheap black labour was then used to threaten the job security of white workers and push their wages down. Finally, the extremely low income of the black majority restricted the domestic market and impeded industrial development. The WPSA characterised the rural black population, even the agricultural proletariat, as a landless peasantry, and contended that black land hunger would be the mobilising force and the pivot of a permanent revolution, which must be led by a working class united across color lines [Lenin Club, 1934b: 6].

Although its own argument was strikingly close to the Native Republic thesis, the WPSA believed that the thesis pandered to a black nationalism which would impede working-class unity. Instead, it put forward 'Land to the Natives' and 'Every man has the right to as much land as he can work' as slogans to mobilise the black majority. In this way, it wrote,

> The unconditional active support of the peasantry will thus be assured to the proletarian revolution. *By popularising among the workers the needs of the peasantry, and vice versa, the Bolsheviks succeeded in their revolution.* So also can our revolution succeed. By uniting and defending in combined effort the common aims and interests of the workers and peasants, black and white, the revolutionary movement can bring about the overthrow of Capitalism and the establishment of a Soviet South Africa [Lenin Club, 1934b: 6; emphasis in original].

By contrast, the CLSA argued that the immediate priority lay in trade union work as a means to bridge the colour bar and to weaken British imperialism. To the extent that any rural grouping had anti-imperialist potential at that stage, argued the CLSA, it was the Afrikaner *bywoners* (tenant-farmers), not the 'backward' black peasantry. But in its hope for a progressive role for Afrikaner nationalism, the CLSA underestimated the potential for the Afrikaner struggle against British imperialism to pursue a purely reactionary path due to racialist attitudes [Drew, 1991: 194–9]. Despite the CLSA's critique of the WPSA's stress on the agrarian struggle as the pivotal point of the revolution, in effect it came to a similar position when it concluded that the rural anti-imperialist struggle against British imperialism is the *first* stage of the struggle. Once, having got rid of the biggest bandit, we can turn our attention to the lesser bandit – the local capitalist class. We can then rally the workers of South Africa for the *final* struggle, the overthrow of capitalism and the setting up of workers' rule [*CLSA* 1935: 9; my emphasis].

Aside from the particular reference to the *Afrikaner* peasantry and bourgeoisie, this passage is remarkably close to the Native Republic thesis in its conception of an initial *national*, rather than class-based alliance against imperialism!

The division in the Lenin Club provoked a series of exchanges between South African Trotskyists and the International Secretariat (IS) of the Left Opposition, with particular reference to the majority faction's draft thesis on the Native Question. The IS criticised what it saw as the WPSA's overly quantitative approach, which led the WPSA to overemphasise the agrarian struggle on the basis of the demographic predominance of the rural black population, and its mechanical application of the Russian model to South Africa. Thus, wrote Ruth Fischer (Dubois) on behalf of the IS, the call for 'Land to the Natives', while correct in itself, was inadequate in that it was not linked to any other political slogan except an abstract 'South African October', echoing Russia's October 1917 revolution. In effect, she maintained, the WPSA conception of the agrarian revolution lacked political content because it neglected the national question. The agrarian revolution, Fischer wrote,

> ... poses and resolves, at the same time, what is called the national question of this country. This is why the two questions are inseparable. The thesis, instead of indicating the connection, neglects it, separating the two sides of the *same* question quasi-independently of one another. This is why this thesis remains weak, not providing any tactical guidelines and offering only an inadequate and abstract propaganda [*International Communist League,* 1935: 15; translated from the French].

The seemingly nationalist Native Republic thesis, Fischer contended, might not be antithetical to the socialist struggle, given the absence of a black bourgeoisie in the 1930s, and it had the potential to mobilise a mass movement against British imperialism. Indeed, she noted, the WPSA did not propose any effective counter-slogan to the Native Republic thesis [*Drew,* 1991: 199–209].

Trotsky replied to the majority faction's draft thesis in April 1935 [*Trotsky,* 1974]. His analysis was framed in terms of his theory of permanent revolution, which sought to explain the possibility of a proletarian revolution in a less developed society, like early twentieth-century Russia, in the absence of revolution in the advanced industrialised countries [*Trotsky*, 1982; *Burawoy*, 1989: 781–3]. According to this theory, the weak bourgeoisie characteristic of 'backward' countries, those with relatively recent and limited capitalist development built on feudal institutions, is unable to fulfil popular democratic aspirations. Moreover, the peasantry's intermediate class position in the capitalist era precludes it from playing an independent, let alone leading, political role, and it will align either with the bourgeoisie or the proletariat. Hence, the task of completing the bourgeois democratic revolution falls to the proletariat. Yet, due to the small size of the proletariat in backward countries, an urban-based proletarian revolution cannot extend beyond the bourgeois democratic stage unless class struggle extends to the countryside, enabling urban workers to gain support from the poorer strata of the peasantry. Similarly, peasant uprisings are a response to the immediate question of land ownership and, on their own, could not destroy the state power which supports landowners. In this sense, Trotsky concluded, just as the success of the proletarian revolution depends on the peasantry, the fate of the agrarian revolution is determined in cities [1982: 108].

In this theory, capitalism's combined and uneven nature sets the parameters for domestic class struggles and national revolutions.[10] This conception of revolution contains a threefold notion of permanence: first, social transformation develops continuously, albeit unevenly and in a combined manner, rather than through stages; secondly, the interconnection of the various struggles against social oppression which are reproduced through capitalist social relations, means that the resolution of one struggle flows into and shapes the outcome of others; finally, social revolution in one nation is immanently part of an international struggle against world capitalism. Thus, national struggle spills over into the international arena. Conversely, the failure of a national revolution to gain international support means that it remains isolated and limited.

In the mid-1930s, with fascism on the upsurge across Europe, the Comintern shifted away from the New Line of its Third Period and began advocating the formation of people's fronts which united anti-fascist opposition across class lines. The People's Front strategy was formally unveiled at the Seventh Comintern Congress in August 1935. Trotsky's letter reflected his criticism of that strategy in South Africa. He argued that although any social upheaval in South Africa would begin from an agrarian revolution, such an upheaval was predicated on the prior overthrow of British imperialism. This could occur, he maintained, through either military defeat or revolution in Britain and its possessions, both possibilities catalysing the disintegration of the Empire. In Trotsky's estimation, a social revolution would in all likelihood begin first in Britain, facilitated by a movement against British imperialism in the colonies and dominions. In South Africa, he argued, any proletarian-led revolution which had the support of the peasantry would necessarily transform both class and national relations. In turn, a proletarian dictatorship would allow socialist construction.

In such a context, he wrote, it was vital that a working-class party uphold the right of national self-determination, supporting the ANC against white supremacy and the progressive over the reactionary tendencies in the national movement. However, its solution to the national question must be based on the method of class struggle rather than on the classless anti-imperialist front proposed by the Comintern. Therefore, revolutionaries needed to develop a series of tactical slogans which reflected the living conditions and struggles of workers and peasants and which would link the national and agrarian questions. The greatest practical difficulty lay in the fact that black workers lacked a tradition of organisation, while white workers were arrogant and privileged [*Trotsky*, 1974].

Certainly, Trotsky's optimism about the prospects of the collapse of the British Empire was misplaced, although to a certain degree he anticipated its post-war dismantling. But in linking the agrarian and national questions to British imperialist policies, and in pointing to the practical difficulties posed by a racially-divided working class, Trotsky was essentially advising the South African Trotskyists to move away from abstractions and to engage with practical conditions.

Over the next decade, both Trotskyist groupings used Trotsky's letter to re-evaluate the relationship of the agrarian and national struggles to the class struggle. The WPSA changed its original slogan 'Land to the Native' to the Bolshevik slogan of 'Land and Liberty', to indicate the inter-relationship of the agrarian and political struggles [*Trotsky*, 1974: 253].[11] In 1939, fearing the coming of fascism in South Africa, the WPSA ceased publication of its organ, *The Spark*, and went underground. In the early 1940s, its members were amongst the founders of the Non-European Unity Movement (NEUM), and thereafter the WPSA operated on a clandestine level within the NEUM and its affiliated organisations. Its influence in the NEUM is seen in the formulation of the Ten Point Programme of minimum democratic demands in 1943, in which the franchise (Point One) is seen as the key to the agrarian question (Point Seven) [see further below]. Likewise, the Fourth International Organisation of South Africa (FIOSA), successor to the CLSA, now admitted the significance of the agrarian question for social mobilisation. The FIOSA's M.N. Averbach (A. Mon) argued that implementation of the right to own land entailed the expropriation of large land-holdings and thus was part of the socialist struggle:

... the struggle for 'democracy" embraces the struggle ... not merely
for the right to the land, but for the actual division of the land ... .since
the land cannot be won except through a struggle against imperialism
and the South African capitalists, and since the land can be divided
only after it has been expropriated from the big landowners, farmers
and land-companies, the struggle for land, as part of the struggle for
the realisation of the tasks of bourgeois democracy in South Africa
can be won only through the socialist revolution ... [*Mon* 1945: 7].

Thus, influenced by Trotsky's letter, both the WPSA and the FIOSA
attempted to apply the notion of a permanent revolution to South Africa:
that democratic demands, including the right to land, represented a
transitional programme and that the road to democracy would pass through
socialism.

CONFRONTING THE CHALLENGE OF PRACTICE I: MIGRANT LABOUR AND 'TRIBAL PROLETARIANS' IN THE 1940s

Despite the emergence of a Trotskyist tendency in the early 1930s, that was
a still a decade of relative fluidity on the South African Left in terms of
political allegiances and organisational affiliation.[12] But by the 1940s,
collaborative work between Communists and Trotskyists was becoming
increasingly difficult. Several conjunctural factors, including Trotsky's
assassination in 1940 and the differences between Communists and
Trotskyists over the war effort, from 1941, and over participation in the
Native Representative Council (NRC), contributed to an increasingly rigid
sectarian divide which permeates the South African Left to this day, despite
the collapse of the Soviet Union. It is striking, therefore, that those
Communists and Trotskyists who did engage in rural mobilisation in the
1940s and 1950s focused specifically on migrant labour and the rural
reserves. In this attention to migrant labour, South African socialists began
to grapple in earnest with South Africa's empirical realities and came
closest to breaking from polarised conceptions of either a homogeneous
peasantry or a rural proletariat.

This concern with migrant labour in the reserves reflected both the
experience of practical organising difficulties and a growing recognition of
South African specificities. On the one hand, the extreme difficulties of
organising black farmworkers or labour tenants on white farms, seen in the
brutal smashing of the Western Cape ANC and ICU in the late 1920s and
early 1930s, precluded socialist work on white-owned farms, leaving the
reserves as the only option for rural organising [*Hofmeyr,* 1985: 281–311;
Interview with Alexander, 1987].[13] On the other, the difficulties which

socialists confronted in their repeated attempts to reach migrant workers on the mines pushed them to consider reaching them in the reserves [*Moodie*, 1986: 16–17].

Socialist efforts to organise black mineworkers began in 1930, when Bunting and Thibedi formed the African Mineworkers Union (AMWU) [*Simons and Simons*, 1983: 587]. Later, the tiny Johannesburg WPSA made several attempts to reach black mineworkers, seeing them ' … as the battering ram that will smash down British Imperialism in South Africa' [*International Communist League*, 1936: 27–8].[14] But it was Max Gordon, briefly in the WPSA and the leading trade unionist on the Rand between 1935 and 1940, who successfully fanned the discontent over the deteriorating war-time conditions so that the defunct AMWU could be revived [*Stein*, 1978; *Hirson*, 1986: 235–6; *Basner*, 1993: 223, n.5]. Following Gordon's internment in 1940 for opposition to the government's war efforts, the CPSA once again turned its attention to the mines and in August 1941 relaunched the AMWU. Kept in check by the CPSA's anti-strike policy during the war, in 1946 workers engaged in a series of spontaneous strikes which culminated in a strike initiated by the AMWU. Although brutally squashed by the state, the strike demonstrated the explosive character and potential economic strength of an organised migrant labour force on the mines [*Simons and Simons*, 1983: 512, 569–79, 587; *Basner*, 1993: 140–41; *Moodie*, 1986: 34–5].

Much as Wolf [1987: 371–2] would argue later, socialists saw migrant labour as a vector of transmission facilitating the diffusion of political ideas from town to country. According to I.B. Tabata, a member of the WPSA and a rural organizer for the NEUM-affiliated All African Convention (AAC), the WPSA realised early on that as long as the reserves remained unorganised, migrant labour could easily be used by capitalists to break the strikes of black workers in towns:

> Already black workers were fighting for their rights as workers; but it occurred to us that they were isolated because they were the minority at that time … Whenever the workers from the reserves asserted themselves they could be sacked and then they'd just ship in [more] blacks from the reserves and that factor alone made it absolutely imperative to organise the peasantry as well (Interview with Tabata and Gool, 1987).

While there is scant evidence that the CPSA in the 1940s and 1950s tried to theorise concepts of the peasantry or migrant labour [*Delius*, 1993: 303], Trotskyists were consumed with the agrarian question.[15] The WPSA assumed that rural Africans were overwhelmingly peasants or aspirant peasants. But the FIOSA's Averbach argued that aside from a minute layer of farmers scattered about some reserves, landless Africans were peasants in aspiration only, and those on white farms were agricultural proletarians. Averbach coined the term 'tribal proletariat' to characterise South Africa's migrant labour force and rural proletariat, indicating what he took to be their janus-faced character: proletarian in day-to-day outlook; peasant in aspirations [*Mon*, 1945].

Clearly influenced by Trotsky's letter of 1935, Averbach pointed out that South Africa lacked the advanced working class stratum which the Bolsheviks had relied on to educate the masses and link town and country, as only the white workers, who fought for labour protectionist policies, had a tradition of self-conscious political activity. None the less, he argued, migrant labour could fulfil the vanguard role which Lenin and Trotsky saw as vital to the formation of a town–country alliance. The alliance fostered by migrant labour was not the classical alliance of proletariat and peasantry but one of urban and rural workers commonly oppressed by their lack of democratic rights. Accordingly, Averbach concluded, the basis of this alliance must be the struggle against the colour bar and all forms of racialism [*Mon*, 1945: 6–11].

In his attention to the ongoing proletarianisation of the countryside, Averbach grasped an aspect of change which the WPSA underestimated. The concept 'tribal proletariat' assumes, as Jordaan has pointed out (Interview, 1987), that migrant labour would necessarily retain rural ambitions and tribal perspectives and that the major social cleavage to be overcome was between town and country rather than between classes or strata. It does not encapsulate the twin processes of differentiation and disintegration of the peasantry which Lenin thought to be critical in understanding social transformation in the countryside. Moreover, the focus on migrant workers had gender implications: despite the increasing numbers of African women settling in towns, in the 1940s the overwhelming majority of migrant workers were male [*Walker*, 1990: 187–92].

However, the concept anticipates Wolf's thesis that it is culturally conservative middle peasants engaged in migrant labour to maintain their position on the land who paradoxically play a progressive social role by transmitting ideas from town to countryside. It also presages more recent findings about the operations of the AMWU in the 1940s; namely, that faced with the strength of 'home-boy' networks on the mines, the AMWU was often unable to promote a working-class consciousness that cut across tribal affiliations, and that it was the *tshipa* or absconders who had broken their links with their rural homes who formed the main base of the AMWU. Yet, even though the *tshipa* were the principal organisers during the series of black mineworkers' strikes in 1946, the success of the strikes depended on making the link between food shortages on the mines and drought in the rural areas [*Moodie,* 1986: 2–3, 26–7].

CONFRONTING THE CHALLENGE OF PRACTICE II: ORGANISING THE RESERVES IN THE 1940s AND 1950s

The 1940s and 1950s saw a series of rural protests and uprisings across South Africa's reserves, amongst others Zoutpansberg in the Northern Transvaal in the 1940s; Witzieshoek in 1950; Zeerust in the Western Transvaal and Sekhukhuneland in Eastern Transvaal in the mid-1950s; and Pondoland in the Transkei at the end of the decade [*Hirson,* 1977; *Lodge,* 1983: 261–94; *Basner,* 1993: 99–108; *Hooper,* 1989; *Mbeki,* 1964]. This rural discontent reflected the long-term economic deterioration produced by state policies which locked Africans in the reserves while stifling the development of an African peasantry. More specifically, the protests were catalysed by the increased state intervention of the post-Second World War period which imposed conservationist policies without local consultation, political restructuring and controls on movement.

It was through their organisational work in the reserves from the late 1930s through the 1950s, that socialists were able to develop and to modify their ideas about the role of migrant labour in the countryside. Despite differences in social background and organisational allegiance, rural activists displayed striking similarities both in their attention to the reserves and their analyses of rural mobilisation and protest. Essentially, they found that it was in the reserves rather than in towns that social protests transformed into sustained mass-based uprisings potentially capable of challenging state power. The observations of rural activists pose a challenge to the Leninist and Trotskyist argument that it is urban proletarian struggles which activate and provide leadership for rural uprisings, and it raises the question of whether socialist revolution was the viable possibility in the early 1960s that socialists believed it to be.

By the late 1930s the CPSA was moving away from the Native Republic thesis, and in 1950, when the CPSA disbanded following the Suppression of Communism Act, it maintained that the Africanist call for the right of self-determination meant the right of political secession, tantamount to apartheid [*Delius,* 1993: 302; *Bunting,* 1981: 209]. Hence, the Party's continued prioritisation of urban politics over rural struggles. None the less, the CPSA was certainly aware of the need to address the rural areas. In April 1944 the CPSA organised ' ... the first Communist Party Conference to be held in the country districts', addressed by Moses Kotane, the CPSA General Secretary and Advocate Harry Snitcher, who optimistically proclaimed the Party's intention to penetrate rural areas. Delegates from Paarl, Stellenbosch, Kraaifontein, Worcester and other areas discussed the need to publicise the conditions of farmworkers and the possibility of running black candidates for Municipal and Divisional Councils in rural areas ['Communists Hold First Rural Conference' 1944].

Despite such initiatives, from the late 1930s through the 1950s it was the exceptional Communist like Alpheus Maliba in Zoutpansberg, Northern Transvaal, Flag Boshielo in Sekhukhuneland, Eastern Transvaal and Govan Mbeki in the Transkei, who worked in rural areas. Those Communists who engaged in rural work tended to be migrant workers who gained trade union experience through employment in urban industry, and who, as Delius points out, were much more sensitive to the possibilities of rural organisation than the largely urban-based Party leaders [*Delius*, 1993: 306–08, 310; *Hirson*, 1977: 4, 6–7; *Basner*, 1993: 105–08; cf. *Bunting*, 1981: 138].

Alpheus Maliba was one such migrant worker-activist who had been involved with Thibedi's short-lived Communist League of Africa in 1932, then joined the CPSA in 1936, and from 1939 through 1950 served on the Party's Johannesburg District Committee. Maliba wrote several political pamphlets based on his experiences of organising in the Northern Transvaal. His 1939 pamphlet, *The Conditions of the Venda People* [*Bunting*, 1981: 138–47; *Delius*, 1993: 303–04], described an area where subsistence production was supplemented by barter of occasional surplus, and where by the late 1930s, poverty had driven most men into migrant labour, mainly on the mines, as the white farms already had large numbers of labour tenants. The solution to rural poverty, Maliba argued, was not to cull cattle, as the state proposed. Rather, it was to increase the land available to rural people by redistributing large estates and Crown lands; to replace the corrupted form of tribal tenure with individual tenure as an incentive to improve the land; to establish agricultural schools and to abolish the 'useless' NRC.[16]

In 1939 Maliba founded the Zoutpansberg Cultural Association, later renamed the Zoutpansberg *Balemi* (Ploughmen's) Association (ZBA). It was there that the state first began implementing its Betterment Proclamation, ostensibly aimed at stopping erosion in the reserves by culling cattle and limiting stock. Under Maliba's leadership, the ZBA gained some recognition. In May 1944 the CPSA claimed that ' ... [f]or the first time May Day was celebrated by Africans in the countryside when 7,000 Africans marched through the centre of Louis Trichardt' to a meeting called by the ZBA and addressed by Maliba ['May Day 1944'; *Mageza*, 1944]. Yet, despite the ZBA's success at resisting this state intervention, as the 1940s unfolded it began declining due to state repression [*Basner*, 1993: 106–8, 219, n.1; *Delius*, 1993: 303–5].

Other Communists engaged in rural organising, like Flag Boshielo, drew on Maliba's experience. The Party that regrouped in 1953 as the underground South African Communist Party (SACP) was more squarely committed to an alliance with the ANC, rather than explicit working-class politics [*Everatt*, 1991]. Thus, when Boshielo and other Communist migrant worker-activists formed *Sebatakgomo* in Sekhukhuneland in 1954, they affiliated it to the ANC. *Sebatakgomo* was conceived as an organisation linking farm workers and reserve dwellers. Boshielo and other activists responded to increasing repression in the reserves by organising in urban-based hostels and amongst migrant workers, and *Sebatakgomo*'s membership grew in the late 1950s as the struggle against Bantu Authorities escalated into the Sekhukhuneland Revolt in 1958, although its focus became more localised as its leading activists were banned [*Delius*, 1993: 308–9, 311–13].

While Communists worked closely with the ANC, Trotskyists either worked in or gave their critical sympathy to the NEUM. Within NEUM ranks, practical work in rural areas was largely the work of the AAC and its affiliate, the Cape African Teachers Association (CATA). In contrast to the migrant labour base of rural activists aligned with the Congress movement, those in the AAC tended to be teachers, a reflection of the NEUM's use of 'teachers as a vanguard' who could penetrate South Africa's towns and *dorps* (villages) with progressive ideas [*Kies*, 1943; *Drew*, 1991: 424–30, 470–74].

The different social backgrounds of rural activists in both political tendencies reflected and reinforced differences in the social base and outlook of the two wings of the liberation movement. Through the SACP, the ANC was able to draw in a wider working-class base, but its practice lacked a long-term strategy. The NEUM's teacher base explains the organisation's continuous efforts to engage with theory and its criticism of the Congress movement's lack of strategy but over time this became a brake on practical work, although more so in the Western Cape than in the Transkei, where pressure for militant action was keen [*Alexander*, 1986]. Both migrant workers and teachers were important points of access into the reserves in the 1940s and 1950s, and their activities in combatting the state should have been complementary rather than antagonistic.

The AAC's practical work concentrated on the Transkei and began in earnest with the struggle against Rehabilitation. In a pamphlet called *The Rehabilitation Scheme: 'A New Fraud'*, Tabata [1945], who was born near the farming community of Queenstown and organised for the AAC in the Transkei, argued that the reserve policy was premised on the restriction of land as the basis of ensuring a cheap migrant workforce. Land hunger, he concluded, was the root of the problem in the reserves. Like Maliba, he argued that the means to rehabilitate the reserves was not to cull cattle, as this would only intensify hunger and malnutrition, but to increase land availability. This conception of a land hungry peasantry was voiced in the AAC organ, *Ikhwezi Lomso*:

> The demand for an equitable distribution of land among the peasant population is and will continue to be for a long time the most powerful driving force of our struggle for it touches the heart-strings of the majority of the oppressed, the African peasant (quoted in *Jordaan*, [1959: 35]).

The first implementation of the Rehabilitation Scheme was in Libode, West Pondoland in 1947, an area, Ganyile [n.d.] notes, reputed for the docility of its inhabitants. Yet the degree of local resistance to Rehabilitation indicated that preparations against its implementation had begun well in advance. Government-sponsored meetings to explain the policy were boycotted, collaborating chiefs threatened, government officials attacked, and livestock hidden. The testimony of chiefs and headmen revealed ' ... great fears because we people who accepted the rehabilitation scheme move about among the people risking our lives' (quoted in Hendricks [1990: 112]). People ' ... voluntarily formed Location Committees against their headmen and *Bungas* [advisory general councils] to assert their right to decide how they should own their land'. AAC influence grew, with the affiliation of the clandestine, mountain-based Kongo movement and the Transkei Organised Bodies [*NEUM*, 1948; *AAC*, 1948: 5–6, 14–16; *Beinart and Bundy*, 1980: 301–02].

Throughout the Transkei, teacher activists used the CATA network to link up small rural *dorps* and larger towns. W.M. Tsotsi, later AAC General Secretary, addressed the Transkei Organised Bodies on the Rehabilitation Scheme and N. Honono addressed local Vigilance Committees on the Bantu Authorities Act. CATA activists successfully promoted boycotts of activities sponsored by Bantu Authorities, laying the basis for a local branch of the Society of Young Africa, another NEUM-affiliate [*Hyslop*, 1986: 92–3; *Hyslop*, 1987: 11–12; *Tsotsi*, 1953: 13]. However, CATA's influence declined in the late 1950s as it was hit by intense state repression and weakened by internal dissension in the NEUM. In 1955 the entire CATA executive were dismissed from their teaching jobs in retaliation for their struggle against Bantu Education; its members were harassed into the 1960s, and its organ, *The Teachers' Vision*, which had appeared regularly since the early 1940s, was forced out of publication [*NUM*, 1989: 16; *Hyslop*, 1987: 16; 22ff.].

It is in the analyses of Tabata and Communist Govan Mbeki that the South African Left came closest to developing an indigenous theory of rural mobilisation that reflected local empirical conditions. Given the intense sectarianism between Trotskyist and Communists, mirrored in the relationship of the NEUM and the Congress movement, the similarity of Tabata's and Mbeki's analyses of rural protests is striking. Essentially, both conceived the relationship of urban and rural protests as one of intense, short-lived urban protests which periodically intersected with slower, longer-lived rural protests, with migrant labour as the critical link. Tabata recalls:

> We noticed that there was some kind of a seesaw [relationship]. The workers in the towns would fight and fight and fight and the graph would go up, up, up. And the peasantry was simply down there but now when we had begun to organise the peasantry they also would be fighting against the Rehabilitation Scheme and then they would go up. Now the peasants were very slow in going up while the workers just went like that [snap] and they reached a zenith and after that they would come down. The peasants were simply going slowly up and they crossed at a point. But now the workers don't go right down to the bottom, they hold at some point by the peasantry that's going up (Interview with Tabata and Gool, 1987).

The Transkeian-born Mbeki served as secretary of the Transkei Voters' Association in the early 1940s and as general secretary of the Transkei Organised Bodies from 1943–48 (see, *inter alia*, 'Successful Transkei Conference' 1944). Mbeki's argument that the rural areas had a greater capacity to sustain uprisings over a longer period of time than urban areas overlapped in many respects with Tabata's, and was echoed by the tiny, ephemeral Socialist League of Africa [1961: 11] a few years later. In Mbeki's words,

> ... a struggle based on the reserves had a much greater capacity to absorb the shocks of government repression and was therefore capable of being sustained for a much longer time than a struggle based on the urban locations. The urban-based campaign, which starts on a high note after very intensive and costly propaganda work, consumes itself by the intense energy it generates to carry the masses to the climax – usually a general strike ... The struggles of the peasants start from smaller beginnings, build up to a crescendo over a much longer time, are capable of pinning down large government forces, and are maintained at comparatively much lower cost [1964: 130–31].

The virtually continuous upheaval in South Africa's reserves, to which Tabata and Mbeki referred, reflected the widespread reaction to their economic deterioration and mounting state intervention. In 1955 the United Transkeian Territories General Council, whose nickname *Utata Woj' Inj'*

Emsini [Father has had dog's meat blackened with smoke] indicated its lack of popular credibility, passed the Bantu Authorities Act, precursor to the state's future policy of so-called independence for tribal homelands, and its acceptance by authorities in other reserves soon followed. The Act outlined a four-tier authority structure resting on Tribal Authorities of chiefs and headmen, whose legitimacy declined as they became direct symbols of the corrupt and oppressive state. Popular participation in local elections was curtailed and unauthorised public meetings of more than ten people prohibited, making open political organising difficult and risky [*Mbeki*, 1964: 34, 40–42; *Beinart and Bundy*, 1980: 305–06; *Delius*, 1993: 303–05].

This repression did not succeed in smothering popular protests, and an evolutionary pattern of protests can be discerned, as both Tabata and Mbeki indicated. Initially, people resisted the various measures designed to strip them of remaining land and cattle and turn them into exclusive and perpetual migrant workers. Later, these protests merged into broader, political struggles against Tribal Authorities which, in addition to enforcing rehabilitation, controlled the movement of Africans to and from the reserves through the notorious pass laws.

The prolonged process of reserve-based protests indicates that in the 1950s the reserve-based population did indeed have more capacity to sustain uprisings than urban areas, even though state intervention was more brutal in the reserves than in the townships [*Lodge,* 1983: 261]. In part, as Mbeki argued, the reason was tactical and accords with Wolf's thesis that peasants with tactical leverage over resources or freedom to maneuver have the greatest potential for sustained mobilisation. In contrast to blacks labouring on white farms, who had little or no mobility or independence, some reserve dwellers had access both to means of subsistence, even if limited, and to income from wage labour. Their relative independence from direct supervision allowed them to flee from their villages and hide in caves and mountains, as they did in the Witzieshoek and Pondoland uprisings (see, *inter alia*, '8,000 Natives Disappear' 1950), adapting their traditional institutions to new political ends.[17] The 1960 Pondoland uprising in the Transkei, suppressed finally by armed state intervention and the imposition of a State of Emergency, demonstrates how a protest against Rehabilitation became a politicised and broad-based rejection of Bantu Authorities. Resistance came together in a highly structured organisation which led a nine-month revolt, functioned as an alternative authority, and intimidated with threat of force those chiefs who did not support the struggle [*Turok,* n.d.; *Lodge,* 1983: 279–83; *Bunting,* 1981: 271–4, 432–4].

This high degree of solidarity, which helps to explain the rural capacity to sustain protests, is notable given the economic stratification of reserve dwellers. In Pondoland, Lodge [1983: 279–83] attributes this solidarity to a number of specific factors: the extreme powers of the Paramount Chief whose financial corruption pitted him and his functionaries against the rest of the population; the presence of an unusually large proportion of unemployed migrant workers; and a tradition of external political involvement. Throughout the reserves, women were particularly hard hit by the Bantu Authorities Acts, which codified land distribution in a manner which curtailed women's traditional land rights. The high degree of female participation in these protests flowed from the erosion of their customary rights to land and the increasing restrictions on their movement into towns through the extension of passes to women [*Mayer*, 1978: 15–17; *Lodge*, 1983: 139, 265, 274]; (see Hooper [1989] on women's protests in Zeerust).[18]

The political consciousness of reserve-dwellers and migrant labour was, indeed, far from uniform. Tabata argued that while the structural position of migrant labour enabled it to link urban and rural struggles, it also fostered a dual consciousness, a notion similar to Averbach's janus-faced tribal proletariat:

> The migrant labour played a part in this and therefore we began now to turn our attention to the migrant labour and organise them. And we organised them as peasants. Now they found when they came to town there were trade unions and they joined the strikes of the black workers. But they had to go back again to [the reserves] and fight Rehabilitation there ... which was entirely for the peasantry. So from the point of view of organisation they go from one kind of organisation to another (Interview with Tabata and Gool, 1987).

But what Tabata, like Averbach, saw as the dual consciousness of a seemingly homogeneous category was actually a reflection of a stratified population with diverse aspirations. In the 1950s, only a thin stratum of households owned more than 25 cattle while the vast majority owned a handful or less. About one-third of the reserve population was reported as landless. Not surprisingly, it was the most proletarianised migrants who formed the AMWU's main base of support on the mines. Similarly, during the Pondoland uprising, it was the unemployed migrant sugar workers who played a central coordinating and organising role through their migrant labour associations, and whose protests against unemployment and pass laws indicated the desire to control the sale of their labour power. Other reserve dwellers, by contrast, fought to retain their meager holdings of land and cattle, while a thin stratum continued to accumulate larger holdings [*Hendricks*, 1990: 100–101; *Moodie*, 1986: 2–3, 26–7; *Beinart and Bundy*, 1980: 308–9].

These findings indicate that the stratified reserve population, a peasantry that had been disintegrating for decades, sought control over subsistence and livelihood in a variety of ways. Their perceptions about how to achieve this evolved historically as state policies turned them more and more into rigidly controlled migrant wage labour. Those reserve dwellers with land and cattle had a vested interest in their retention. Writing in 1957 under the pseudonym R. Mettler, Baruch Hirson observed:

> At this stage the struggle in the Reserves is against the rehabilitation scheme, and there is no doubt that the Reservist is correct in opposing the vicious culling of cattle. This opposition stems from the clear logic that says that overstocking is the result of the lack of land, and the lack of land is the most pressing problem. But to put the entire stress on the rehabilitation scheme is to bypass several important questions. The reservist without land (and he numbers from 30% to 40%) has not always supported the struggle against the rehabilitation scheme and has in fact often been on the opposite side, as he has mistakenly believed that he might even gain from the new plan [Mettler, 1957: 19].

Drawing upon Mettler, Beinart and Bundy [1980: 303, 311] hypothesise that in contrast to proletarianised and landless migrants, it was the 'middle migrants' or 'peasant migrants' – those able to use their wages to retain some land and cattle as opposed to landless migrants – who had the most to lose from Rehabilitation and who formed the social base of these protests. But the common denominator was not a rejection of wage labour status *per se* but a desire to prevent their perpetual status as a particular type of wage labour: rightless and effectively homeless migrant labour. For many, retention of some minor means of production would make them less vulnerable to the state's efforts to freeze them into total dependency on its industrial plans. The protests against pass laws were struggles for freedom of movement and the free sale of labour-power; the protests against Bantu Authorities, a struggle for democracy and self-determination which drew in all strata and classes.

Yet Tabata and Mbeki did not focus on the actual or potential differences amongst the reserve population but stressed its virtually unanimous solidarity. Thus, Mbeki wrote: 'It was in these reserve areas, too, that the struggle assumed the truly mass character which it lacked elsewhere. Every peasant had to show himself in favour of or hostile to Bantu Authorities' [1964: 128]. Although the varied responses to Rehabilitation undoubtedly reflected different class aspirations and interests, virtually the entire population had a common interest in fighting Bantu Authorities. Tabata's and Mbeki's immediate concern was drawing the rural population into the national democratic struggle, and their practical work aimed at this common denominator.

A final explanation for the capacity of the reserves in the 1950s to sustain uprisings lay in the combined nature of rural oppression. It is notable that Tabata and Mbeki stressed the strength and endurance of reserve protests, while most scholarly analyses emphasise their localised and limited nature. But it was in the reserves that economic and political oppression merged. There, the state owned the land, given 'in trust' to Africans, and state administrators accumulated wealth through corruption and enforced policies restricting African autonomy. Virtually all protests in the reserves during these years indicated the social class antagonisms emanating from the relationship between collaboration and capital accumulation. In the Pondoland revolt of 1960–61, for instance, people attacked chiefs both because they collaborated with the regime in enforcing these unpopular measures and because their collaboration was a means to accumulate wealth [*Chaskalson,* 1987: 51–2; *Beinart and Bundy,* 1980: 309–10]. Precisely because of the convergence of economic exploitation and political oppression, the South African countryside at that period was the base of the national democratic struggle.

In towns, by contrast, economic and political issues could be divided. Within the ANC, internal tensions between its nationalist leadership, still hoping to influence and accommodate whites, and its trade union membership continually resurfaced in controversies over tactics which diluted the success of several generally single-issue campaigns. ANC leaders, influenced by Gandhi's passive resistance, called for mass demonstrations and petitions; trade unionists pushed for minimum wage campaigns and stay-at-homes. Similarly, NEUM leadership resisted growing pressure from its youth and left-wing factions for a more aggressive urban strategy; even though the NEUM scorned single-issue struggles in theory, its own campaigns divorced economic and political issues, eschewing the former as piecemeal and reformist [*Lodge,* 1983: 193–197; *Drew,* 1991: 482–8].

In the 1950s, the predominant form of urban black working-class struggle was not the strike at the point of production but the stay-at-home, during which workers remained in the townships rather than going to work. The black trade union movement, which had been slowly developing since the 1910s, experienced a brutal setback in 1946 with the smashing of the black mineworkers' strike, closing a period of trade union organising and worker militancy dating from the 1930s. The 1950s trade union movement began rebuilding in the harsh conditions of apartheid, in which blacks were uprooted and relocated into Group Areas, and strikes were illegal. The overcrowded and overwhelmingly working-class townships provided fertile conditions for organising and building solidarity. Yet the development of the stay-at-home tactic was a response to social conditions which strengthened racial and national forms of consciousness, and although this was a working-class tactic, the solidarity it fostered was based on community rather than explicitly on class. As the Socialist League of Africa [1961: 7–8] argued, the stay-at-home had particular limitations both for the development of working-class consciousness and for long-term resistance, as state repression was relatively easy to enforce in the densely concentrated townships, which had been designed to be easily sealed off with a minimum number of forces.

Does this mean that the South African case contradicts the Leninist and Trotskyist thesis that urban proletarian struggles show greater strength, continuity and intensity than rural uprisings, which they held to be essentially limited? Their argument suggests that when social classes have reached particular levels of development, all other things being equal, urban areas will be the moving force for social transformation. Given the relatively recent formation of South Africa's urban black working class, and the differential conditions in town and country, it is not surprising that reserve-based uprisings of the 1950s showed more capacity for sustained rebellion. Such capacity has its own implications: the more prolonged an insurrection or uprising, the greater the opportunity for the radicalisation of political consciousness. The struggles in the reserves appear to have been undergoing such a development, as the anti-proletarianisation struggles of the 1940s and 1950s matured by the 1960s into the mass-based struggles for democracy to which Tabata and Mbeki referred. The relative fragility of urban working-class protests in that period, compared to reserve-based struggles, suggests a structural barrier against socialist transformation.

MOMENTS OF THEORETICAL DEBATE III: THE NEUM AND THE AGRARIAN QUESTION IN THE 1950s

Within the NEUM, the decision of Tabata and other AAC activists to organise in the reserves on a classically democratic programme provoked a controversy which catalysed its split in December 1958. To a large degree, but with significant exceptions, the NEUM split between its two main organisations, the AAC, strongest in Johannesburg and the Eastern Cape, and the predominantly Western-Cape based and urban Anti-Coloured Affairs Department movement (Anti-CAD), formed in 1943 to fight the government's attempt to establish separate political institutions for Coloureds.

This split echoed the South African Trotskyist debates of the 1930s and 1940s, which revolved around a polarised conception of the peasantry. Both sides concurred in the essential unity of the land and national questions; hence, their common support of the Workers' Party slogan 'Land and Liberty' to link the two struggles. The dispute boiled down to conflicting interpretations of Point 7 of the NEUM's Ten Point Programme and the implications for rural mobilisation along democratic and socialist lines.[19] Point 7 read: 'Revision of the land question in accordance with the above', the 'above', referring to the programme's preceding democratic demands. The explanatory remarks attached to Point 7 read:

> The relations of serfdom at present existing on the land must go, together with the *land acts*, together with the restrictions upon acquiring land. A new division of the land in conformity with the existing rural population, living on the land and working the land, is the first task of a democratic State and Parliament.

Strikingly, neither interpretation adequately considered the differentiated nature and political role of migrant labour. The majority in the AAC saw rural Africans as peasants or aspirant peasants and interpreted the abolition of restrictions on acquiring land as the right to buy and sell land [*SOYA, c.* 1954; *Tsotsi,* 1954]. Tabata did not believe that people in the reserves could be mobilised through a slogan of nationalisation: from their perspective the state's trusteeship of the land was tantamount to nationalisation. For Tabata, who represented a left pole within the AAC, organising around the right to buy and sell was not necessarily antithetical to socialism. As Averbach earlier, Tabata saw the achievement of such a right as the pivot of a permanent revolution, in that a legal right to buy land without the means to do so could never satisfy popular land hunger and that this realisation would drive people beyond capitalism. Any new division of land enacted by a democratic Parliament would reflect the balance of class forces at that time and could not be stipulated beforehand (Interviews with Tabata and Gool, 1987 and Alexander, 1987).

Paradoxically, the other position, articulated by Hosea Jaffe and the majority of the Anti-CAD, also assumed a high degree of African peasant consciousness. Because the Ten Point Programme was a minimum programme, Jaffe argued, Point 7 implied a democratic redivision of the land rather than a maximum socialist demand of collectivisation. Redivision meant the expropriation of large landowners, with abolition of white control of land and of exploitative practices like speculation and landlordism, and the allotment of land to smallholders on an equal, per family basis. Although in Jaffe's interpretation Point 7 did entail the right to buy and sell land, a right which would satisfy an aspirant black bourgeoisie, this would not be able to satisfy the land hunger of most blacks. In this respect, Jaffe subordinated the right to buy and sell to the need for an equitable redivision of the land. Undoubtedly also influenced by Averbach's 'tribal proletariat' concept, Jaffe assumed that migrant workers or 'peasant-workers' would return to the land, opt for individual titles to non-marketable land and apply the technical and co-operative practices learned in their urban worksites to agricultural production [*Jaffe*, 1953: 24–6].

From outside the NEUM, K.A. Jordaan, a former member of the now defunct FIOSA, argued that the agrarian question was not the sub-soil of a South African revolution, as it had been in other revolutions, because the majority of the people did not look to land for their subsistence. South Africa's democratic struggle differed markedly from classical peasant-based democratic revolutions because most South Africans had been uprooted, and those still on the land were a proletarianised reserve labour force. Unlike classical democratic revolutions in which the bourgeoisie had been able to satisfy popular democratic demands, albeit in a delayed, top–down manner, South Africa's white bourgeoisie, Jordaan maintained, could not satisfy the democratic demands of the black majority; indeed, democracy might even undermine capitalism in South Africa, whose development has been premised on the lack of democratic rights.

Point 7, Jordaan argued, contained elements which, from the point of view of capitalist development, were both progressive and backward. It did not address social relations on the land after the initial reallocation of land; thus it sidestepped the class nature of the future state [*Jordaan*, 1959: 32–3]. Underlying the AAC's demand for the right to buy and sell land, Jordaan continued, was the aim of creating a yeomanry, modelled on Stolypin's scheme in pre-revolutionary Russia. But industrial South Africa lacked the large peasantry upon which to develop a yeomanry: the bourgeoisie relied on the superexploitation of proletarianised reserve-dwellers and would never allow sufficient numbers to withdraw from the labour market to develop as independent farmers.

To call for the development of a small stratum of black capitalist farmers or peasants in South Africa's conditions, as the AAC did, was not historically progressive from the point of view of the working class, even if it accorded with the laws of capitalist development. But the Anti-CAD's call to break up and redistribute large, productive capitalist landholdings using a quantitative yardstick was economically unviable and utopian, assuming that Africans had a prior land claim and would abandon industrial employment for small-scale agrarian cultivation. Jordaan suggested that nationalisation would allow the continuation of large, mechanised farms conducive to agricultural productivity, enabling a gradual transition to collectivisation [1959: 34–8].[20]

To what extent did the NEUM debates on the agrarian question engage with the prevailing social realities in the countryside? As Jordaan pointed out, both sides subordinated large-scale production to smallholder posses-sion, effectively ignoring not just the issue of economies of scale on already mechanised farms but the possible interests of the agricultural proletariat. If the Anti-CAD's conception of an equitable distribution of land amongst the entire rural population was impractical from that point of view, it was also utopian in its belief that such farming would necessarily take place on a household basis, given the extent to which rural households had been broken up, even then, and agricultural cultivation had become predominantly female.

On the other hand, if the AAC's aim was to link up rural and urban struggles through migrant labour, then why, in addition to addressing the struggles to forestall proletarianisation, did the AAC not also concern itself with the landless reserve dwellers, often the most militant on the mines, or more broadly with labour tenants, who might not envision their access to land in terms of the right to buy and sell? As Claassens' research [1991] shows, many labour tenants still stake their land claims on their families' long-term occupancy, disdaining the concept of legal ownership. Even in the reserves, that right did not always strike a chord. Ralph Bunche, an African-American social scientist visiting South Africa in the late 1930s, recounts that one of his Durban informants, Reverend Abner M'timkulu, described

> ... Zulus as not interested in the franchise because it is foreign to their experience; their thinking is entirely in terms of *land* and *more land* – they think that if they can get more land their problems will be solved. But they aren't interested in buying any land – they think it must be *given* to them – because they say the land belonged to their fathers and they wish it to be given back to them [Bunche Collection; emphasis in original].

Amongst Trotskyists, then, solutions to the agrarian question ranged from various schemes for smallholder possession to large-scale nationalisation as a prelude to collectivisation. Can the position that Africans, tired of trusteeship, would resist nationalisation, be reconciled with the position that nationalisation was compatible with widespread rural proletarianisation and productive economies of scale? The former position emphasizes subjective aspirations of some reserve-dwellers; the latter, objective conditions both in parts of the reserves and on white farms. What both positions missed is that the highly differentiated and rapidly changing rural population made any rigid solutions to the agrarian question very difficult to maintain in the late 1950s. In that respect, these opposing views might have been temporarily reconciled through practical recognition that a specific socialist solution to the agrarian question would depend on the variety and balance of class forces in town and countryside at the time of a social revolution. Yet, if these opposing positions on the agrarian question could have been temporarily united under the banner of 'Land and Liberty' in a manner which left open the path to socialism, how can the intensity and animosity of the NEUM's disputes on the agrarian question be explained?

The intensity of the theoretical disputes masked the political crisis facing all socialists which related to the theory–practice problem. Fuelling the disputes were two practical problems. First, the question of whether to organise in the reserves on the basis of a classically democratic or an explicitly socialist programme, a problem which became more acute after the passage of the Suppression of Communism Act in 1950, which pushed the entire socialist movement underground. Secondly, the question of whether to actively support armed struggle in the Pondoland uprising against state repression. Despite their fierce theoretical disputes, neither socialist tendency nor the NEUM nor the ANC supplied arms requested by Pondoland militants during their uprising.[21] In the NEUM, the internal pressure which this created within its core, the Workers' Party, led to its organisational split. Only with the banning of political opposition to apartheid following the Sharpeville massacre and the ensuing nationwide uprising, did socialists begin to seriously address the issue of armed struggle and attempt to conceptualise it in relation to rural insurgency.

CONCLUSION

These experiences of South African socialists indicate the interrelationship of political theory and practice. Despite the symbolic significance of land for most blacks and the massive land hunger of the rural majority, only a minority of socialists, whether Communists or Trotskyists, gave their theoretical or practical attention to rural mobilisation. In the late 1920s and 1930s, when socialists began to consider the agrarian question more seriously, they worked with abstract and polarised notions of a peasantry and a rural proletariat which were derived from earlier European experiences and debates and which overlooked the salience of gender in African rural cultivation [Lenin, 1974; Banaji, 1990]. However, South Africa's migrant labour process had its own distinctive characteristics. The deliberate state policy to stabilise reserve-based migrant labour as a permanent social class went counter to capitalism's historical tendency to link proletarianisation with urbanisation. It also went counter to popular aspirations, both those of the most proletarianised reserve dwellers, mainly men, who spent most of their working lives in industrial areas, struggling over working conditions at their places of employment, and those with peasant aspirations who needed adequate access to land.

From the late 1930s through the 1950s, empirical developments, coupled with their own practical efforts in the reserves, compelled socialists to revise the abstract concepts with which they had initially analysed the rural population, although they did not grapple with the implications of changing gender relations in the reserves. To a striking extent the common observations of socialists organising in the reserves from the late 1930s through the 1950s overrode their sectarian political divisions. But the divergent socialist tendencies which permeated the South African Left in the late 1920s and 1930s coloured theory and practice. Generally, Communists were less concerned with theory but stronger in practical work while the theoretical insights generated by Trotskyist analyses and debates were not systematically applied to their work in the reserves. This dichotomy impeded the work of socialists in rural areas and the development of socialism as an effective movement. This is a significant and complex factor in the recovery of the history of the South African Left.

NOTES

1. Scholarship on South Africa's agrarian question has been bifurcated between a structural political economy approach concerned with the impact of apartheid on class structure and rural development [Wolpe, 1972; Levin and Neocosmos, 1989; Weiner and Levin, 1991; Mabin, 1991; Marcus, 1989] and a social history approach [Beinart and Bundy, 1980; Keegan, 1986a, 1986b; Hendricks, 1990: 9–11] compares these approaches. Alternative developmental models have envisioned either a society based on articulating modes of production in which continued proletarianisation in the rural areas is expected to give a working class thrust to the national struggle or a neo-classical populism premised on small-scale rural capitalism.

2. As Dobb [1963: 2–3] notes, definitions of concepts influence the principles according to which we select variables for study, form hypotheses and develop analyses and interpretations of history and politics. To analyse historical and, hence, changing phenomena with a fixed and abstract definition might obscure their development; thus the need to continually reevaluate and modify abstract definitions by reference to history. By questioning the construction of Marxist models and concepts, Marxism as a methodology which attempts to illuminate and explain patterns of social development can be strengthened [Burawoy, 1989].

3. The peasantry is a class of agrarian producers which possesses its means of production; it includes labour-tenants and sharecroppers who rent or obtain access to land owned by other people in exchange for labour, crops or cash. Unlike feudal lords or the bourgeoisie and proletariat, it is not specific to a particular mode of production. Its possession of the means of production is a defining feature across pre-capitalist and capitalist periods; the discontinuity comes from the transformation of the relations of surplus extraction which, under capitalism, increase the threat of proletarianisation. During feudalism, surplus production was transferred directly to the lord under threat of coercion. In capitalism the process is more complex. Typically surplus is extracted through the market but landlords may extract surplus crops or labour services and the state may extract surplus through taxation, agricultural pricing schemes or extra-economic means (see Hilton [1978] and Dobb [1963: 1–32] on class). Most Africanists identify peasants as rural cultivators who control their means of production, who are generally organised in subsistence-producing households, who produce a surplus for other classes, extracted by rent or taxes, and who possess a distinct peasant culture which nonetheless is related to the broader social culture. According to Klein peasants engage in both subsistence and market production, which distinguishes them from pure subsistence cultivators, on the one hand, and capitalist farmers, on the other [Klein, 1980: 9–13; also Isaacman, 1990: 1–2]. However, the differentiation and fragmentation of the household under capitalism, seen in extreme form in South Africa due to the migrant labour system, suggests that peasant production cannot adequately be understood in terms of household production.

 4 Conventionally, peasants have been defined as male heads of households [*Wolf,* 1966: 61].
   Wolf [1961: 20–21] notes five types of peasant production systems, including fallowing
   systems which use hoes or digging sticks and which are common in African female farming
   areas, but adds that he does not discuss this type because of its limited influence. Feminist
   analyses have pointed to the role of female labour in household-based peasant production,
   which is particularly significant in sub-Saharan Africa, including South Africa [*Jackson,*
   1978: 25–31; *Walker,* 1990: 173].
 5. Ntantala [1992: 2] refers to the 'one-family one-lot' system which British colonialists
   introduced in the Idutywa district in the Transkei after the mid-nineteenth century as an
   incentive for African settlement. Because each family unit was given a title deed to a lot, she
   points out, polygamists were able to accumulate large landholdings. On the death of the title-
   holder, land went to the senior heir, thereby precluding younger sons from acquiring land.
 6. Pass laws, or influx and efflux controls, regulated the movement of African male labour to
   and from reserved areas and date from the nineteenth century. The government tried to
   extend passes to African women in the 1950s, and from 1963 they had to carry passes.
 7. Walker [1990: 173] notes that women cultivators reorganised agricultural production in
   response to these changing conditions. Through inter-cropping they achieved a more
   intensive use of land, and they switched from labour-intensive crops like sorghum to the
   production of maize which, though higher-yielding, was more susceptible to drought.
 8. Hendricks [1990: 152] argues that the state's minimal efforts to promote a stable middle
   peasantry in the confined and depleted reserves meant that ' ... the idea of creating a stable
   middle peasantry ... .itself was still-born'.
 9. Luxemburg argued that antagonistic class interests within nations prevented any collective
   national will and bourgeois leadership of a national movement could divert the proletariat
   from its own class struggle [*Davis,* 1976: 13–15, 27–9; *Luxemburg,* 1976: 150–51]. Lenin,
   by contrast, believed that in so far as the bourgeoisies of oppressed nations which had not yet
   completed their democratic revolutions fought for the right of national self-determination,
   they had a progressive potential. With the October 1917 Russian Revolution, Lenin's
   solution, expressed in the slogan, 'the right of nations to self-determination', that is, the right
   of oppressed nations to choose and agitate for political self-determination through
   independent statehood, became paradigmatic [*Lenin,* 1971a: 41–5, 1971b: 101].
10. Unevenness characterises social development generally, but is accentuated under capitalism
   because of the system's potential for rapid growth in response to specific investment
   opportunities. Combined development refers to the compressing of different stages of
   capitalist development. For example, industrial development in economically backwards or
   newly developing countries may outpace that in earlier industrialised countries, like Britain,
   because it is financed by massive investment with access to the latest techniques. See Trotsky
   [1977: 27*ff.*].
11. Between 1932 and 1934 the CPSA had briefly resurrected the Native Republic thesis, with
   conflicting interpretations. The dominant position saw the Native Republic as a workers' and
   peasants' government but Lazar Bach and L.L. Leepile called 'For Independence and Soviet
   rule and for the voluntary unification of the free Native Republics – Basuto, Bechuana,
   Swazi, Zulu, Xosa etc. into a Federation of Independent Native Republics', [*Umsebenzi,* 5
   May, 1934: 1; *Simons and Simons,* 1983: 473]. This minority thesis was a response to
   attempts to incorporate the British Protectorates into the Union of South Africa; nonetheless,
   most socialists rejected it on the grounds that it would reinforce national fragmentation. In
   this context, the WPSA initially thought that Trotsky's argument reflected a mechanical
   application of the Soviet model of national self-determination, which in South Africa, they
   believed, would reinforce sectional divisions. Interview with Dudley, 1988.
12. Thus, in the first years of the All African Convention, formed in 1935 to fight the state's
   attempts to curtail African voting rights, both left-wing Communists and Trotskyists
   concurred on the need to boycott the proposed Native Representative Council. Communist
   Johnny Gomas felt intellectually closest to the Trotskyists, even though he disdained what he
   saw as their lack of grass-roots activity. Fanny Klenerman, who joined the Johannesburg
   WPSA after being expelled from the CPSA, nonetheless helped distribute the CPSA's organ,
   Umsebenzi. Alpheus Maliba, who originally worked with expelled Communist T.W. Thibedi

in the short-lived Communist League of Africa, joined the CPSA in 1936, but still asked Trotskyists to publish one of his pamphlets.

13. The neglect of the rural proletariat evoked considerable criticism by Trotskyists outside the NEUM. See Ernstzen [1950: 11–12]; Mettler [1957: 18–19]; Jordaan [1959]; Interview with Jordaan, 1987.

14 The WPSA sold *The Spark* on the mines, and its ephemeral Johannesburg organ, *Umlilo Mollo*, contained a number of letters from mineworkers and metal workers. Fanny Klenerman [n.d.] noted in her memoirs that miners came to some of the WPSA's public meetings.

15. During the period between the disbanding of the CPSA in 1950 and the formation of the South African Communist Party (SACP) in 1953, Johannesburg Communists organised a discussion club to consider issues of theory and strategy. The lectures and discussions concerned primarily the nature of capitalist development and the national question in South Africa. Only one lecture, by Dr Z. Sanders [1953] addressed the agrarian question.

16. Reflecting the CPSA's changed policy towards the NRC in the 1940s, Maliba later campaigned unsuccessfully for a seat in the NRC [*Basner,* 1993: 122].

17. In the Transkei, for instance, the original function of the *Makhuluspani* (Big Team) was to raise funds and punish thieves. But in the late 1950s it ' ... "changed its tactics and began to threaten chiefs and headmen whom it regarded as collaborating too closely with the Government. The establishment of Bantu Authorities, in particular, saw an increase in its activities"' (Hammond-Tooke quoted in *Beinart and Bundy,* 1980: 307).

18. Mayer [1978: 16] writes: 'Formerly a woman had the exclusive right to cultivate any land she had once turned over and her prescriptive right to cultivate was inherited' and he quotes Monica Wilson that '"traditionally, every married woman was entitled to a field, and rights over fields were the property of women rather than of men"'. Mayer argues that male control of land rights developed in two stages. In the late nineteenth century the introduction of the plough, used with cattle, gave men a far greater role in agriculture than previously. In the twentieth century the squeezing of land for Africans led both African male elders and white administrators in the reserves and bantustans to curtail women's rights to land.

19. Within the Congress Alliance there was no comparable controversy on the agrarian question in the 1950s. The Freedom Charter's clause on the agrarian question read:

> The land shall be shared among those who work it! Restriction of land ownership on a racial basis shall be ended, and all the land redivided among those who work it, to banish famine and land hunger; The state shall help the peasants with implements, seeds, tractors and dams to save the soil and assist the tillers; Freedom of movement shall be guaranteed to all who work on the land; All shall have the right to occupy land wherever they choose; People shall not be robbed of their cattle, and forced labour and farm prisons shall be abolished.

The main division within the Congress Alliance and within the ANC in the 1950s was over the national question. This concerned the Freedom Charter's second clause, 'All national groups shall have equal rights'.

20. More recently, Jordaan [Interview 1987] questioned whether the failure of collectivised agriculture in the USSR, Tanzania and Mozambique negated the viability of collectivisation for South Africa. Unlike those cases, he argued, South Africa's relative industrialisation would preclude the need for state-driven primitive socialist accumulation based on exploiting the peasantry. Moreover, state policy had prevented a private property tradition amongst blacks, in contrast to Europe's long tradition of private possession or ownership, suggesting that resistance to collectivisation would not be as great in South Africa as in other countries.

21. For the NEUM's response to the request for arms see *South Africa: An Analysis of the Political Situation in South Africa and the Nature of the Struggle for Liberation* [late 1961], Borthwick Institute, University of York and Drew [1991: 474–505]; for the ANC, verbal communication from Howard Barrell, St. Antony's College, Oxford, 4 April 1992.

REFERENCES

Alexander, Neville, 1986, 'Aspects of Non-Collaboration in the Western Cape 1943–1963', *Social Dynamics*, Vol.12, No.1, pp.1–14.

All African Convention (AAC), 1948, *Minutes of the All African Convention*, author's possession.

Banaji, Jairus, 1990, 'Illusions about the Peasantry: Karl Kautsky and the Agrarian Question', *Journal of Peasant Studies*, Vol.17, No.2, Jan., pp.288–307.

Basner, Miriam, 1993, *Am I an African? The Political Memoirs of H. M. Basner*, Johannesburg: Witwatersrand University.

Beinart, William and Colin Bundy, 1980, 'State Intervention and Rural Resistance: The Transkei, 1900-1965', in Martin A. Klein, ed., *Peasants in Africa: Historical and Contemporary Perspectives*, Beverly Hills and London: Sage, pp.270–315.

Bradford, Helen, 1988, *A Taste of Freedom: The ICU in Rural South Africa, 1924–1930*, Johannesburg: Ravan.

Brass, Tom, 1991, 'Moral Economists, Subalterns, New Social Movements, and the (Re-) Emergence of a (Post-) Modernised (Middle) Peasant', *Journal of Peasant Studies*, Vol.18, No.2, Jan., pp.173–205.

Bunche, Ralph, Bunche Collection, Special Collections, University Research Library, University of California, Los Angeles.

Bundy, Colin, 1988, *The Rise and Fall of the South African Peasantry*, Second Edition, Cape Town and Johannesburg: David Philip and London: James Currey.

Bundy, Colin, 1987, 'Land and Liberation: Popular Rural Protest and the National Liberation Movements in South Africa, 1920–1960', in Shula Marks and Stanley Trapido (eds.), *The Politics of Race, Class and Nationalism in Twentieth-Century South Africa*, London and New York: Longman, pp.254–85.

Bunting, Brian (ed.), 1981, *South African Communists Speak: Documents from the History of the South African Communist Party 1915–1980*, London: Inkululeko.

Bunting, S.P., 1928a, 'First Address to the Sixth Comintern Congress', Moscow, 23 July, Bunting Papers, Department of Historical Papers, University of the Witwatersrand Library.

Bunting, S.P., 1928b, 'Address of 20 August 1928', Sixth Comintern Congress, 38th session, Moscow, 4, Bunting Papers, Department of Historical Papers, University of the Witwatersrand Library.

Burawoy, Michael, 1989, 'Two Methods in Search of Science: Skocpol versus Trotsky', *Theory and Society*, 18, pp.759–80.

Chaskalson, Matthew, 1987, 'Rural Resistance in the 1940s and 1950s', *Africa Perspective*, New Series, 1, 5 and 6, Dec., pp.47–59.

Claassens, A., 1991, 'Contemporary Land Struggles in Rural Transvaal', *Antipode*, Vol.23, No.1, pp.142–57.

Communist League of South Africa (CLSA), 1935, 'We Smash this Bogey', *Workers' Voice*, Vol.1, No.3, Oct., p.9.

Davis, Horace, 1976, 'Introduction: the Right of National Self-Determination in Marxist Theory – Luxemburg vs. Lenin', in Horace B. Davis (ed.), *The National Question: Selected Writings by Rosa Luxemburg*, New York and London: Monthly Review, pp.9–45.

Delius, Peter, 1993, 'Sebatakgomo and the Zoutpansberg Balemi Association: the ANC, the Communist Party and Rural Organisation, 1939–1955', *Journal of African History*, Vol.34, pp.293–313.

Dobb, Maurice, 1963, *Studies in the Development of Capitalism*, New York: International.

Drew, Allison, 1991, 'Social Mobilisation and Racial Capitalism in South Africa, 1928–1960', Ph.D., University of California, Los Angeles.

Ernstzen E., 1950, 'The Last Ten Years of the Liberatory Movement', *Discussion*, Vol.1, No.2, Dec., pp.6–13.

Everatt, David, 1991, 'Alliance Politics of a Special Type: the Roots of the ANC/SACP Alliance, 1950–1954', *Journal of Southern African Studies*, Vol.18, No.1, March, pp.19–39.

Ganyile, Anderson Khumani, n.d., 'Notes on the Pondo struggle against Bantu Authorities: The Back-ground to Resistance', typed ms., 38 pp., Ruth First Collection, Institute of

Commonwealth Studies, University of London.

Hendricks, Fred, c. 1986, Lecture to the South Peninsula Educational Fellowship, Cape Town.

Hendricks, Fred, 1990, 'The Pillars of Apartheid: Land Tenure, Rural Planning and the Chieftancy', Ph.D., Uppsala University.

Hendricks, Fred, 1993, 'Capitalism and the 'Agrarian Question' in South Africa', Paper presented to the Marxist Theory Seminar, University of the Western Cape, 13 May.

Hendricks, Fred, 1995, 'Is There a Future for a Black Peasantry in South Africa?', *Comparative Studies of South Asia, Africa and the Middle East*, Vol.XV, No.1, pp.41–57.

Hilton, Rodney, 1978, 'Introduction', in Rodney Hilton (ed.), *The Transition from Feudalism to Capitalism*, London: Verso, pp.9–30.

Hirson, Baruch, 1977, 'Rural Revolt in South Africa: 1937–1951', paper presented at the Institute of Commonwealth Studies Postgraduate Seminar, *The Societies of Southern African in the 19th and 20th Centuries*.

Hirson, Baruch, 1986, 'The Making of an African Working Class on the Witwatersrand: Class and Community Struggles in an Urban Setting, 1932–1947', Ph.D., Middlesex Polytechnic.

Hofmeyr, Willie, 1983, 'Rural Popular Organisation Problems: Struggles in the Western Cape, 1929–1930', *Africa Perspective*, pp.26–49.

Hofmeyr, Willie, 1985, 'Agricultural Crisis and Rural Organisation in the Cape: 1929–1933', M.A. dissertation, University of Cape Town.

Hooper, Charles, 1989, *Brief Authority*, Cape Town and Johannesburg: David Philip.

Hyslop, Jonathan, 1986, 'Teachers and Trade Unions', *South African Labour Bulletin*, Vol.11, No.6, June–July, pp.90–97.

Hyslop, Jonathan, 1987, 'CATA and CATU: The Politics of African Teachers' Organisations in the Cape, 1948–1968', unpublished ms.

International Communist League (B.-L.), 1935, 'Afrique du Sud: Sur quelques questions tactiques; Remarques du Camarade Dubois', *Bulletin Interieur de la L. C. I.*, no.2, May.

International Communist League (B.-L.), 1936, 'Afrique du Sud', *Service d'Information et de Presse de la L.C.I. (B.L.)*, no.4, 20 July, pp.27–8.

Isaacman, Alan, 1990, 'Peasants and Rural Social Protest in Africa', *African Studies Review*, Vol.33, No.2, Sept., pp.1–120.

Jackson, Sam, 1978, 'Hausa Women on Strike', *Review of African Political Economy*, 13, May–Aug., pp.21–36.

Jaffe, Hosea, 1953, 'The First Ten Years of the Non-European Unity Movement', excerpts from a lecture delivered in December to the Cape Flats Educational Fellowship, in author's possession.

Johns, Sheridan, 1976, 'The Birth of the Communist Party of South Africa', *The International Journal of African Historical Studies*, IX, No.3, pp.371–400.

Jordaan, K.A., 1959, 'The Land Question in South Africa', *Points of View*, Vol.1, No.1, Oct., pp.3–45.

Keegan, Timothy, 1986a, 'The Dynamics of Rural Accumulation in South Africa: Comparative and Historical Perspectives', *Comparative Studies in Society and History*, Vol.28, No.4, pp.628–50.

Keegan, Timothy, 1986b, *Rural Transformations in Industrialising South Africa: the Southern Highveld to 1914*, Braamfontein: Ravan.

Kies, Ben, 1943, *The Background of Segregation*, Cape Town: Anti-CAD.

Klein, Martin A. (ed.), 1980, *Peasants in Africa: Historical and Contemporary Perspectives*, Beverly Hills, CA and London: Sage.

Klenerman, Fanny, n.d., unpublished memoirs, Department of Historical Papers, University of the Witwatersrand Library.

Lenin Club, 1934a, *Workers of South Africa Awake!*, British Library, London.

Lenin Club, 1934b, 'Draft Thesis: The Native Question (Majority)', Cape Town, typescript.

Lenin, V.I., 1971a [1914], 'The Right of Nations to Self-Determination', in V.I. Lenin, *Critical Remarks on the National Question; The Right of Nations to Self-Determination*, Moscow: Progress Publishers, pp.39–97.

Lenin, V.I., 1971b [1916], 'The Socialist Revolution and the Right of Nations to Self-Determination (Theses)', in V.I. Lenin, *Critical Remarks on the National Question; The Right of Nations to Self-Determination*, Moscow: Progress Publishers, pp.98–111.

Lenin, V.I., 1974, *The Development of Capitalism in Russia*, Moscow: Progress.

Levin, Richard and Michael Neocosmos, 1989, "The Agrarian Question and Class Contradictions in South Africa: Some Theoretical Considerations', *The Journal of Peasant Studies*, Vol.16, No.2, Jan., pp.230–59.

Lewis, Jack, 1984, 'The Rise and Fall of the South African Peasantry: A Critique and Reassessment', *Journal of Southern African Studies*, Vol.11, No.1, Oct., pp.1–24.

Lodge, Tom, 1983, *Black Politics in South Africa since 1945*, London and New York: Longman.

Luxemburg, Rosa, 1976, 'The National Question and Autonomy: the Right of Nations to Self-Determination', in Horace B. Davis (ed.), *The National Question: Selected Writings by Rosa Luxemburg*, New York and London: Monthly Review, pp.101–56.

Mabin, Alan, 1991, 'The Impact of Apartheid on Rural Areas of South Africa', *Antipode*,Vol.23, No.1, pp.33–46.

MacMillan, W.M., 1919, *The South African Agrarian Problem and Its Historical Development*, Johannesburg: Council of Education, Witwatersrand.

MacMillan, W.M., 1949, *Africa Emergent: A Survey of Social, Political and Economic Trends in British Africa*, Harmondsworth: Penguin.

Mageza, A., 1944, 'Louis Trichardt Tragedy', *Inkululeko*, 25 Nov., p.4.

Mantzaris, E.A., 1987, 'Radical Community: the Yiddish-speaking Branch of the International Socialist League, 1918–1920', in Belinda Bozzoli (ed.), *Class, Community and Conflict: South African Perspectives*, Johannesburg: Ravan, pp.160–76.

Marcus, Tessa, 1989, *Modernising Super-exploitation: Restructuring South African Agriculture*, London: Zed Books.

Mayer, Philip, 1978, *Wives of Migrant Workers, Volume III, Migrant Labour: Some Perspectives from Anthropology*, Grahamstown: Rhodes University.

Mbeki, Govan, 1964, *South Africa: The Peasants' Revolt*, Harmondsworth, Middlesex: Penguin.

Mettler, R. [Baruch Hirson], 1957, 'It is time to awake!', unpublished ms., Nov., Carter-Karis Microfilm Collection, 2:DA 13:84/9.

Mon, A. [M. N. Averbach], 1944, 'The Colour Bar and the National Struggle for Full Democratic Rights', *Workers' Voice*, Theoretical Supplement, Vol.1, No.2, Nov., pp.7–10.

Mon, A. [M. N. Averbach], 1945, 'A Comment on Trotsky's Letter to S.A.', *Workers' Voice*, Theoretical Supplement, Vol.1, No.3, July, pp.6–11.

Moodie, T. Dunbar, 1986, 'The Moral Economy of the Black Miners' Strike of 1946', *Journal of Southern African Studies*, Vol.13, No.1, Oct., pp.1–35.

Natal University College, Department of Economics, 1949, 'The National Income and the Non-European', Chapter XIV, in Ellen Hellmann (ed.), *Handbook of Race Relations in South Africa*, Cape Town, London and New York: Oxford University, pp.306–47.

New Unity Movement (NUM), 1989, 'A Tribute to Leo Sihlale', *New Unity Movement Bulletin*, Vol.3, No.2, July, p.16.

Non-European Unity Movement (NEUM), 1948, Minutes of the Non-European Unity Movement Annual Conference, December, author's possession.

Ntantala, Phyllis, 1992, *A Life's Mosaic: the Autobiography of Phyllis Ntantala*, Cape Town: David Philip and Bellville: Mayibuye.

Ntsebeza, Lungisile, 1988, 'Divisions and Unity in Struggle: The ANC, ISL and the CP, 1910–1928', B.A. Honours dissertation, University of Cape Town.

Nzula, A.T., Potekhin, I.I. and A.Z. Zusmanovich, 1979, in Robin Cohen, *Forced Labour in Colonial Africa*, London: Zed Books.

Plaatje, Solomon, 1987, *Native Life in South Africa* (edited by Brian Willan), Burnt Mill, Harlow, Essex: Longman.

Roux, Edward, 1929, 'What is the I.L.P. doing in South Africa?', *Labour Monthly*, Vol.11, No.2, pp.90–6.

Roux, Edward, 1930, 'The Recent Events in South Africa', *Labour Monthly*, Vol.12, No.1, Jan., pp.54–7.

Roux, Edward, 1949, 'Land and Agriculture in the Native Reserves', Chapter VII in Ellen Hellmann (ed.), *Handbook on Race Relations in South Africa*, Cape Town, London and New York: Oxford University, pp.275–91.

Roux, Edward, 1964, *Time Longer than Rope*, Madison, WI: University of Wisconsin.

Roux, Edward, 1993, *S.P. Bunting: A Political Biography*, New Edition. Cape Town: Mayibuye Books.

Sanders, Z., 1953, 'Aspects of the Rural Problem in South Africa', lecture delivered to the Johannesburg Discussion Club on 1 December, 1952, *Viewpoints and Perspectives*, Vol.1, No.1, 21 Feb.

Scott, James, 1985, *Weapons of the Weak: Everyday Forms of Peasant Resistance*, New Haven, CT: Yalem University Press.

Simons, Jack and Ray Simons, 1983, *Class and Colour in South Africa, 1850–1950*, London: IDAF.

Socialist League of Africa, 1961, 'South Africa: Ten Years of the Stay-at-Home', *International Socialism*, 5, Summer, 5–15.

[Society of Young Africa] (SOYA), [c. 1954], 'Land and National Oppression', Lecture, typescript, 16 pages, incomplete, author's possession.

Southall, A.J., 1978, 'Marxist Theory in South Africa until 1940', M.A. dissertation, University of York.

Stalin, Joseph, 1940, *Leninism*, London: Lawrence & Wishart.

Stein, Mark, 1978, 'Max Gordon and African Trade Unionism on the Witwatersrand, 1935–1940', in Eddie Webster (ed.), *Essays in Southern African Labour History*, Johannesburg: Ravan, pp.143–57.

Tabata, I.B., 1945, *The Rehabilitation Scheme: 'A New Fraud'*, Cape Town: All African Convention (WP).

Trotsky, Leon, 1974, 'On the South African Theses: to the South African Section', *Writings of Leon Trotsky: 1934–35*, New York: Pathfinder, pp.248–55.

Trotsky, Leon, 1977, *The History of the Russian Revolution*, Vol.I, London: Pluto.

Trotsky, Leon, 1982, 'The Permanent Revolution', [1930] in Leon Trotsky, *The Permanent Revolution and Results and Prospects*, London: New Park.

Tsotsi, W.M., 1953, 'The Path of Liberation: Being the Presidential Address delivered at the Conference of the All African Convention held in December 1953', Lady Frere: SOYA.

Tsotsi, W. M., 1954, 'Address on the National Situation', Anti-CAD Conference.

Turok, Ben, n.d., *The Pondo Revolt*, Congress of Democrats, author's possession.

Van der Horst, Sheila, 1949, 'Labour', Chapter V in Ellen Hellmann (ed.), *Handbook on Race Relations in South Africa*, Cape Town, London and New York: Oxford University, pp.109–57.

Walker, Cherryl, 1990, 'Gender and the Development of a Migrant Labour System c.1850–1930', in Cherryl Walker, ed., *Women and Gender in Southern Africa to 1945*, Cape Town: David Philip; London: James Currey, pp.168–96.

Weiner, Daniel and Richard Levin, 1991, 'Land and Agrarian Transition in South Africa', *Antipode*, Vol.23, No.1, pp.92–20.

Wilson, Francis, 1972, *Migrant Labour*, Johannesburg: South African Council of Churches and Spro-Cas.

Wolf, Eric R., 1966, *Peasants*, Englewood Cliffs, NJ: Prentice-Hall.

Wolf, Eric, 1987, 'On Peasant Rebellions', in Teodor Shanin (ed.), *Peasants and Peasant Societies*, Oxford: Basil Blackwell, pp.367–74.

Wolpe, Harold, 1972, 'Capitalism and Cheap Labour-Power in South Africa: from Segregation to Apartheid', *Economy and Society*, Vol.1, No.4, pp.425–56.

'8,000 Natives Disappear from Reserve', 1950, *The Friend*, 29 Dec.

'Communists Hold First Rural Conference', 1944, *Inkululeko*, 15 April, p.5.

'Chief Mopeli Blames Native Trust for Unrest in Reserve', 1950, *The Friend*, 5 Dec.

'Dealer's Evidence Before Commission', 1950, *The Friend*, 7 Dec.

'May Day 1944: Nation-wide Celebrations', 1944, *Inkululeko*, 20 May, p.5.

'Successful Transkei Conference', 1944, *Inkululeko*, 30 Oct., p.4.

INTERVIEWS

Neville Alexander, Cape Town, Aug. 1987.
R. O. Dudley, Cape Town, Feb. 1988.
K. A. Jordaan, Harare, Dec. 1987.
I. B. Tabata and Jane Gool, Harare, Dec. 1987.

The Politics of Land Reform in South Africa after Apartheid: Perspectives, Problems, Prospects

RICHARD LEVIN and DANIEL WEINER

INTRODUCTION: DEMOCRATIC TRANSITION AS UNFINISHED BUSINESS

Transforming existing land and agrárian relations presents the new democratic South African government with one of its major challenges. Colonial land dispossession and apartheid forced removals lie at the heart of the repressive regime which the national liberation movement sought to overthrow. A decisive transformation of land and agrarian relations is thus intimately bound up with the construction of a new democratic order in South Africa. Expectations in rural areas are very high, and the 1994 election results reveal that with the exception of Natal, there was a massive ANC vote in provinces with a predominantly rural constituency.[1] This offers a major challenge to the ANC, as its capacity to deliver will weigh heavily in future elections, as was the case in the November 1995 local government elections.

The commitment to undertake a national programme of land and agrarian reform is likely to be severely constrained by numerous political and economic concerns. This study identifies a variety of political considerations which will constrain or enhance the possibilities for meaningful land and agrarian reform. These are essentially linked to the balance of political forces as they manifest themselves in the process of democratic transformation and are expressed in the nature of the political transition itself, as well as in the character of local organisation, the role of civil society, the constitution of the new government and its bureaucracies, and

Richard Levin and Daniel Weiner, Department of Sociology, University of the Witwatersrand, Johannesburg, South Africa and Department of Geology and Geography, West Virginia University, Morgantown, West Virginia, USA. The authors would like to acknowledge the John D. and Catherine T. MacArthur Foundation, whose generous research grant assisted in generating information used in this study. This is an original study which draws on ideas and joint work undertaken with Sam Mkhabela, Ray Russon and Ian Solomon; the authors are grateful to Henry Bernstein for his extensive comments on earlier drafts.

the changing disposition of the ANC as the leading force within a national liberation movement whose immediate past history is one of mass action and socio-political contestation.

The trajectory of the South African liberation struggle as it evolved in the 1980s was guided by the aspiration towards an all-encompassing moment in which the apartheid regime would be overthrown and defeated and a new democratic government installed. It was characterised by a combination of mass mobilisation, political trade unionism and armed propaganda. Frequently it was assumed by various components of the Mass Democratic Movement (MDM), which emerged at the end of the 1980s, that the new order would exhibit features of both democracy and socialism. The MDM was constituted by a broad alliance of organisations, and was multi-class in character, bound together by a joint commitment towards national democratic struggle.

The de Klerk reforms of 1990 signalled that the balance of political forces had reached a stalemate. While the MDM struggles under the aegis of the ANC succeeded in isolating the apartheid regime globally, rendering the system unworkable on the home front, and undermined economic confidence, militarily the regime remained firmly in control. This meant that the overthrow of the apartheid regime as once envisaged by the ANC would not occur. At the same time, with the collapse of existing socialism in eastern Europe, and the emergence of pro-democracy movements elsewhere in Africa, it became clear to the apartheid regime that it could no longer continue ruling in the old way. With the backing of the global superpowers, the de Klerk regime opted for a negotiated solution to the political crisis. This support was in line with a shift amongst imperialist powers to support the replacement of (some) authoritarian regimes by elected governments under pressure to implement and thus legitimised, the macroeconomic adjustment programmes demanded by neo-liberalism.

A key question about the political conditions which will favour or retard possibilities of significant land reform concerns the character of the transition to democracy in South Africa. Two understandings of political transition are briefly presented here.[2]

A neo-liberal theory of political transition has emerged which parallels the neo-classical economic strategies adopted by international financial institutions. This theory argues that to be orderly, transitions need to be managed through a process of elite pacting. It partially reflects the reality that apart from the major bourgeois revolutions and the socialist revolutions in Russia and China, few transitions to democracy have emerged out of a decisive rupture whereby an existing regime is overthrown through revolutionary insurrection. They occur rather through processes where current ruling power blocs are able to maintain a large degree of control over existing organs of social power, including state apparatuses and private property [*Adler and Webster*, 1994].

In contexts of extreme conflict and contestation such as South Africa, accommodation is reached through the fear by both parties of the imminence of civil war which could prove mutually and individually damaging. Under these conditions, reformers within the authoritarian power bloc and moderates within the democratic opposition form an alliance through a process of elite bargaining [*Przeworski*, 1991]. In so doing, they distance themselves from extremists in their respective camps: the reformers from the hardliners, and the moderates from the radicals. The result of this is an elite-pacted democracy in which politics becomes the preserve of politicians and bureaucrats, and is divorced from the mass of the people. The alliance between moderates and reformers brings about a form of democracy which to a large extent preserves the existing status quo through an inevitable social and economic conservatism.

This pessimistic neo-liberal theory of political transitions mirrors actual transitions, particularly those in Latin America. At the same time, it leads to a politics of the inevitable (a pessimistic structural inevitability), in which the role of human agency and popular movements is disregarded [*Adler and Webster*, 1994].

A different understanding of transition is found in views of political change in South Africa as generating an agenda of structural or radical reform [*Saul*, 1993]. This places democratic popular movements at the centre of the transition, arguing that the long-term structural transformative goals of struggle must be continually articulated by popular movements. Short-term achievements in the form of government reforms must not be seen as ends in themselves, but rather as essential stages in a long term process of structural transformation. Each individual reform is seen as part of an ongoing process of opening up the political space for agitation for further reforms.

This is important in terms of building consciousness amongst the members of a popular movement, because in order to succeed radical structural reform must be rooted in popular initiative, such that short-term achievements strengthen the capacity of a popular movement to further advance its struggles. The key ingredients of a structural reform programme are mass mobilization, participation and popular impetus. In order for the thesis of structural reform to adequately guide the transition process in South Africa, the role of the ANC alliance – the MDM – both present and future, becomes critical. A weak ANC outside of government and parliament is likely to lead to demobilisation, with political transformation dominated by political elites within the state. Under these conditions, politics and government remain isolated from the majority of the people who increasingly revert to extra-parliamentary action in order to achieve their political objectives.

In the case of South Africa, it is also important to understand that the nature of the state and its executive under the interim constitution and government of national unity (1994–99), makes it difficult for the ANC to achieve the objectives laid out in its Reconstruction and Development programme (RDP). This will be even more true if the ANC attempts to realise RDP aims through state action alone, through an exclusive focus on restructuring the state apparatuses and institutions. The state cannot simply be transformed from above, but needs to be changed through a combination of action from above and below. This underscores the critical importance of sustained popular organisation to exert the kinds of pressures from below that compel parliamentarians and government bureaucrats towards structural reform.

The relevance of this discussion of transition theory is apparent for the politics of land and agrarian reform. If transition in South Africa is limited by an elite pacted democracy, prospects for significant land and agrarian reform are remote. One reason is that entrenched powerholders will maintain the capacity to shape the content and institutional form of land and agrarian reform. Furthermore, the character of elite-pacted democracy is such that government becomes increasingly detached from the people and systematically aims to neutralise the scope and organisational capacity of popular movements. On the other hand, a 'democratic structural reform project' provides the minimum conditions for implementation of the ANC Alliance's RDP.[3]

The role of popular organised formations is critical to the realisation of the long term transformative goals envisaged by the RDP. The precise character and scope of the transition in South Africa is presently hotly contested terrain. It contains elements of both an elite pact and structural reform which is possible since both are forms of capitalist transition. While structural or radical reform within the context of national democratic struggle can lay the basis for socialist transition, it is not in itself socialist in character. Indeed this kind of project runs the risk of slipping into populism characterised by discourses of 'people's capitalism' which attempt to conceal petty bourgeois forms of nationalism and state-directed accumulation. Institutional transformation is certainly a central element of structural reform, but cannot be achieved solely by and within the state: it must be complemented by systematic and sustained popular democratic forms of organisation, involving locally specific forms of class and popular alliances.

Within the context of national democratic struggle, alliance politics has become a central feature of South African national liberation practice, but inadequate attention has been devoted to the class nature of these alliances, and the role of the working class. The 49th ANC Conference Resolution

'On Strategy and Tactics', echoing earlier ANC positions states that: 'We are not simply transferring unchanged power structures from one elite to another' and that 'Owing to its strategic location and capacity, the main social motive force for transformation is the working class' [ANC, *Report on the 49th ANC National Conference Decmber 1994*: 22]. However, there is little evidence in current political practice within the ANC–COSATU–SACP alliance of a commitment to working class leadership. On the contrary, the transition in South Africa has been dominated by emergent bourgeois forces of the historically oppressed black majority. In the rural areas, this has seen the rise of a new dominant alliance of petty bourgeois forces in provincial legislatures and state bureaucracies and an emergent petty capitalist class including incipient kulaks. These class forces, often in alliance with chiefs, are emerging at the expense of farmworkers, labour tenants, worker-peasants and allotment holding wage workers, although in electoral terms at least, these class forces remain allied under the broad framework of the ANC.

PROBLEMS IN POLITICAL ORGANISATION

Rural Resistance and Organisation

National liberation and land struggles have been closely linked in the broader African context. In South Africa, the founding of the African National Congress in 1912 was influenced in no small measure by the proposed land bills which culminated in the 1913 Land Acts. Land and rural struggles in the 1940s and 1950s were also important in transforming the ANC into a broad-based national movement, culminating in the declaration of the Freedom Charter in 1955. Overt and hidden resistance to apartheid rule in the rural areas continued through the 1960s and 1970s, although armed propaganda was rarely carried out in rural contexts. During the period of mass mobilisation of the 1980s, rural organisation and struggle picked up markedly. Nevertheless, the negotiated settlement at the World Trade Centre in Kempton Park which brought about democracy in 1994, was inspired far more by the urban mass struggles and political unionism of the ANC-led Congress alliance than by rural interests. This reflects an ideological bias in the development of strategies and tactics of national resistance rather than the absence of potential bases of rural resistance. Mass campaigns of the 1950s suggested the possibilities of a national political programme in the countryside as Zeerust, Sekhukkhuneland, Zululand, Pondoland and the Transkei manifested stiff rural resistance to apartheid legislation (see Drew in this volume). The national liberation movement, under the aegis of the ANC failed, however, to develop an analysis and strategy of rural resistance and organisation. This is because its leadership cadre and guiding ideology are predominantly drawn from the urban petty-bourgeoisie and proletariat. As Bundy [1984: 28] noted in his analysis of rural resistance between 1920 and 1960:

> Despite the realities of resistance and unrest in the countryside, the nationally organised movements – physically located as they were in the urban centres, ideologically concerned either with the vanguard role of the proletariat or with wringing political concessions for the 'modernising' section of the black population, structurally ill-equipped to respond to the inchoate and murmurous patterns of peasant resistance – failed to lead (or follow) them.

The absence of a major commitment to rural struggle by the national liberation movement is mirrored by a gap in the literature on rural struggles and resistance. Mbeki's work [1964/1984], drawing on his engage-ment in rural organising for the ANC in Pondoland, provides an account of peasant uprisings in the Eastern Cape in the 1950s. Bradford [1987] accounts for the growth of the ICU in the 1920s, while Delius [1990] examines the role of migrants in rural resistance in the Northern Transvaal in the 1950s. These attempts to uncover key episodes of collective and organised resistance show how an analysis of processes of production and reproduction can provide a framework for more systematic understanding of forms of rural resistance and struggle. There is little doubt that in South Africa, as elsewhere in Africa, struggles between rural labour and forces bent on extracting surpluses in the form of labour, rent, taxes and food were central episodes in the political and social history of the country. This provides the focus for historians concerned with exploring the concepts of 'everyday' or 'hidden' forms of peasant resistance, and con-stitutes the core of Beinart and Bundy's [1987] studies of the Transkei and Ciskei areas of the Eastern Cape. These analyses illustrate how rural men and women developed their own weapons of resistance through work slowdowns, pilfering, sabotage, dissimulation and flight. One should note, however, Isaacman's [1993: 236] qualification that analyses of everyday or hidden forms of resistance can 'distort or render meaningless the notion of resistance itself', when 'used crudely or taken out of context', particularly when these daily acts are seen as individualised and localised rather than constitutive of collective or broad-based resistance.

Struggles for power and political space involve grappling with local power dynamics and organising within the context of a specific balance of forces. Competition for power and space around issues of land and water has been a continuous struggle for Africans in rural South Africa in a context of limited resources for, and severe repression of, rural political organisation.

State Repression in Rural Areas

To enforce its policy of native 'homelands' and to disable forces of opposition and resistance, the apartheid state generated structures of domination and oppression within the bantustans. The first structure was that of direct coercive suppression of political activity through the South African Police (SAP), the South African Defence Force (SADF) and their bantustan surrogates. A second structure of oppression involved the attempt to legitimise domination through the homeland governments themselves. By erecting puppet regimes headed by African leaders, the South African state attempted to legitimise its control over African subjects. The bantustan governments have been indicted for their authoritarianism and corruption, and their failure to deliver basic services to their inhabitants. They also sponsored their own political parties to oppress the national liberation movement; in many cases, these parties demanded membership from civil servants and others.

A third structure of repression centred on the tribal authorities and the chieftaincy. The Bantu Authorities Act (1951) and the Bantu Laws Amendment Act (1952), in conjunction with the earlier Native Administration Act (1927) gave the South African State President power to appoint, depose, define the jurisdiction of, and limit or extend the powers of, individual chiefs and their headmen and councillors. This included chiefs' power of land allocation, judicial proceedings and general regulation. In fact, the Native Administration Act of 1927 established the Governor General as the 'supreme chief of all Natives in the Provinces of Natal, Transvaal and the Orange Free State': he was endowed with 'traditional authority' to control the African inhabitants of the land. In the same way as the SAP and the SADF were used to close down the space for political activity, there are numerous examples of repression by chiefs. The reformulation of their 'traditional' powers allowed chiefs to control land allocation as well as to collect a variety of taxes and to impose levies on their subjects. They used their *indunas* (headmen) as informers, and they themselves were informers to the police. It was also not uncommon to find chiefs holding positions in bantustan governments such as minister of finance or even commissioner of police.

A fourth structure of repression centred on the emergence of vigilantes at the beginning of the 1980s. These vigilantes operated 'either with the passive connivance of the homeland authorities or under their direct instruction' [*Haysom*, 1986: 55]. Vigilantes operated in both urban and rural areas. In the bantustans, they became notorious in KwaNdebele, the Ciskei and KwaZulu. In the case of KwaNdebele, the rise of vigilantism was directly linked to popular resistance in Ekangala and Moutse to incorporation in KwaNdebele.

Over and above these various forms of repression in the bantustans, other forms of repression characterised social relations on white farms and forest plantations, where workers often faced outright violence, and were denied rights to organise.

Repression and Resistance

Repression has had a profound effect on the nature and scope of popular organisation and resistance. It impacted heavily on the prospects of political mobilisation in a context characterised by scarce resources for organisation. As noted, in the urban areas, political organisation and resistance has been more pronounced, and of greater weight in the national liberation struggle in the last three decades or so. Apart from the ideological lacunae of the leadership of the liberation movement, it must be recognised that organisation and resistance require a certain level of infrastructure and communications to be effective and sustainable. Rural areas have a more limited capacity for organising because of the logistical constraints of scarcity of telecommunications and electricity, in addition to the funds required to sustain a movement and its participants. This was the case historically in South Africa and remains so.

A further constraint on political organisation is the existence of divisions and cleavages within rural society. Aninka Claassens [1991] has written about two communities in the south-eastern Transvaal that have resisted forced removals. In identifying conditions favouring successful organisation in these two communities she finds that: 'The Driefontein and Kwa Ngema stories show how the various opportunities for tactical manoeuvrability differ and how local resistance grows out of local tradition and style. Often the forms that resistance takes appear unexpected and inappropriate to outside eyes. Yet it is only issues which are meaningful and dear to people's hearts and seize their imagination that galvanise community participation'.[1991: 144]. South Africa's rural areas are fragmented ethnically and differentiated along the lines of class, gender, generation and lineage. Such divisions hamper the possibilities for sustained organisation and collective action. Churches, which have on the whole played a broadly supportive role in the liberation struggle, are subject to sectarian disputes and often divide rather than unite villagers.

Without romanticising the role of the United Democratic Front (UDF), it can be argued that during the 1980s, the first steps towards rural organisation within a broad national project were undertaken. Furthermore, UDF-linked organisations relied on local initiative, due to the implementation of successive states of emergency and the resultant dispersion of political leadership. Organisation revolved around local issues with youth in the lead. This meant that education often took precedence over other basic demands for land, water and electricity. The central role of youth in the struggle has its parallel in Zimbabwe, where Kriger [1991: 27] suggested that participation by youth in the guerilla struggle transformed generational relations. '"Youth" used their power which they acquired from their duties in the support organisations to challenge parents' authority and control over their lives. The opportunity to alter oppressive constraints imposed by elders on their daily life ... provided an important impetus that helped sustain "youth"s' participation in the guerilla war'. It is clear that the youth played a central role in the development of rural organisation and resistance in bantustans in the 1980s, including their resistance to oppressive patriarchal relations.

The unbanning of the ANC in 1990 had a profound impact on the political landscape in the countryside. While it provided the oppressed majority with a tremendous boost in confidence, it also recast emergent forms of organisation from below into more centralised structures of organisation from above. The unbanning of the ANC also led to the consolidation and reorganisation of the 'civic association' structures (or civics) which emerged within the UDF. These emerging bodies often differed sharply with the ANC over the role and status of the chieftaincy. However, neither the ANC nor the civic movement has adequately addressed the land question within local political arenas.

The ANC and Its Rural Constituency

The euphoria which accompanied the unbanning of the ANC soon gave way to frustration, as local ANC activists battled to sustain the momentum of mobilisation. UDF organisation involved local people in local civic issues, while the ANC's priorities rested in building national and regional structures to lead the final phase of the liberation struggle. These problems were sometimes compounded by the substitution of local UDF leaders by new ANC leaders, highlighted in an interview with a civic activist and leader from Mpumalanga:

> During the days of the UDF, it was easy for people to understand the struggle. Activity such as stay-aways, barricading etc involved people on the ground and made sense to them. When it came to the new politics, people lost interest ... When we started, our struggle involved activity, but during the period of the unbanning, people began to lose interest in politics. They no longer wanted to participate ... The UDF encouraged the formation of civics which were led by the youth and teachers. After the unbanning, there was a lot of confusion amongst the civic organizations because the programme of the ANC and UDF was not the same. We had expected that the ANC officials would come from the UDF and this brought confusion because the

UDF people couldn't relate to the ANC. The UDF had encouraged grassroots activity. Even football clubs had a voice in the UDF. The ANC structure and understanding of democracy were different as civic structures were not high on the ANC agenda and the civic momentum during the UDF period could not be taken forward. The disappearance of the UDF crippled civic organizations because the ANC was now looking strictly to political issues and not looking to civic related issues and this weakened them (*Interview*, Makushu, 12 Dec.1993).

Existing structures and agendas were altered through the introduction of a new leadership cadre, which diverted political energies and priorities from local issues towards the imperatives of building a national ANC. While much energy flowed into the establishment of regional offices, insufficient attention was devoted to developing the mechanisms necessary to maintain a mass-based organisation with strong regional, sub-regional (or district) and local structures. The result is the development of a politics which has led to political demobilisation:

There had been a culture of local participation in development, but this ended once the UDF stopped organising. Now, people wait for the ANC. It has taken the struggle away from grassroots initiatives. Concentrating on the transition is different to concentrating on local demands; as a result, people have become demobilised … Furthermore, ANC branches are not strong. There are no issues for people to organise on a local basis. The only issue is trying to ensure Mandela's victory in April, but that doesn't help at all with development. During the time of the UDF, people were organised on local political issues relating them to national ones and that is not happening any more. People are not encouraged to take up local issues (*Interview*, Makushu, 12 Dec. 1993).

The unbanning of the ANC thus allowed it to move into the local spaces created by UDF structures, and to divide those spaces between itself and the civics or other community-based organisations.

In some provinces, such as Mpumalanga, the Northern Province and the Eastern Cape, the contrasting positions on the chieftaincy between the ANC and the civics is an ongoing source of tension. The civics are generally opposed to the chieftaincy, while the ANC in these provinces, in line with the national position, has reached accommodation with chiefs. In certain cases this may have led to the preservation of the chieftaincy in a context where its powers were being eroded through popular initiative.

The Tribal Authority and Land

Historically, chiefs have played a central role in the allocation of land in South Africa. The search for new systems of land allocation and tenure will have to involve an analysis of the historical role of tribal authorities. Despite a groundswell of opposition to the institution of the chieftaincy within certain localities, the ANC has tended to vacillate on the question of the future role of chiefs. In the interests of alliance building, this vacillation gave way to cautious support for 'progressive chiefs', as coalitions were formed in the negotiations period with the Intando Yesizwe party of KwaNdebele, Inyandza of KaNgwane, the UPP of Lebowa and with the bantustan regimes of Venda and Transkei. The Patriotic Front electoral alliance has strengthened the hands of chiefs eager to consolidate their hold over land allocation.

The power of chiefs to allocate use rights to land is attributed to 'tradition' and 'customary' law, but it is now widely recognised that concepts of 'tradition' and 'custom' are historically produced and transformed within particular power relations [*Hobsbawm and Ranger, 1983; Levin, 1990*]. The colonial state period in Africa, often in the interests of promoting indirect rule, sought ways to reinforce the rule of 'tribal chiefs' in pursuit of political stability. The question of land control was central to these reconstituted relations as Bassett [1993: 6] points out:

> Consonant with the policy of indirect rule, the state sought to maintain the political authority of chiefs and other elites whose status was partly based on their power to allocate use rights to land in 'their territory'. The fact that the state often concocted this land-controlling power indicates that colonial authorities played an important role in the creation of customary tenure.

It has been argued that the evolution of 'customary' land laws was shaped by European colonists concerned to impose mangeable systems of property on African societies. In the absence of private property, ownership was conferred upon presumed political entities occupying particular areas. Colson [1971: 197] argues that the search for 'owners' of land

> ... encouraged the confusion of sovereignty with proprietary ownership and the creation of systems of communal tenure which came into being with precisely defined rules ... The newly created system was described as resting on tradition and presumably derived its legitimacy from immemorial custom. The degree to which it was a reflection of the contemporary situation and the joint creation of colonial officials and African leaders, more especially of those holding political office, was unlikely to be recognised.

The notion that the chief was a custodian or trustee of land is partially a colonial creation, produced by the search for a system of customary land tenure. Writing on pre-colonial Zimbabwe, Ranger [1993: 356] argues that 'if the idea of chiefly "trusteeship" was largely a myth, so too was the idea of chiefly 'ownership' of land', and that the practice of "'traditional communal tenure" grew up in a sort of rural power vacuum during early colonialism'. In the context of the Northern Sotho of South Africa, Letsoalo [1987: 20–1] argues that

> ... the chief ruled (controlled or administered) the land. He controlled it in the sense that he allocated the land. Once a tribal member had asked for land and had been given it, then the control by the chief ended ... By implication, allocated land was the tribesman's – he owned it. The chief was *mongmabu* (the highest authority in the land) but the man given the land owned it, because the link between the land and the individual tribesman was stronger than the link between the land and the chief ... Misunderstanding of the 'functions' of the chief and the cultural obligations of tribal people have led to the many allegations that the chief controlled the land of the tribesmen.

These arguments undermine any simplistic notions of communalism and communal tenure applied to the South African bantustans. Such notions are based on the presumption of an egalitarian pre-colonial society grounded in relations of reciprocity, with unequal relations largely the product of subsequent external interventions of capital and the colonial state. This view is partly a product of Africanist interpretations of history, but is also a more general feature of nationalist discourses prominent in moments of transition through national liberation struggles. While 'reciprocity' undoubtedly has existed historically, and continues to exist, this is largely governed by the imperatives of the reproduction of the powers of the chieftaincy and carries with it relations of patronage and domination, often characterised by their repressive content. Writing on the Northern Sotho, Delius [1983: 52] observes that:

> While much emphasis has been laid on the redistributional role of chiefs in this and similar societies, there is a danger that ideology is mistaken for practice. An example of the way in which rulers fostered the image of themselves as benefactors rather than extractors is provided by the missionary observation in the 1860s that while all gifts were presented to chiefs in private and in secret, chiefly beneficence was always given the maximum possible display. Redistribution was, however, a reality, both as an ideology and because chiefs, in part, invested accumulated wealth in relationships

of clientage and maintaining popular support. There was, however, no simple reciprocity between giving and receiving, and chiefs presided over a complex system of redistribution which served to sustain chiefly power.

In South Africa today, institutions of chieftaincy, and its continued role in land allocation, are obscured by myths and ambiguities around concepts of 'traditional' communalism and reciprocity. In the context of land dispossession and forced removals, the South African state sought ways to secure control through 'traditional' rule in the native reserves. The Native Administration Act of 1927 modified and consolidated the system of tribal courts and tribal law. Some modifications undermined the powers of the chiefs by placing them under the jurisdiction of a 'White Supreme Chief', who was empowered to rule by proclamation, and appoint, suspend or dismiss chiefs. Despite the protests of chiefs, articulated in a convention held in Bloemfontein in 1928, Government Notice No.2252 of 21 August 1928, further limited and constrained the powers of chiefs. Nevertheless, the right to control land allocation within the reserves continued to be vested in chiefs.

The inauguration of apartheid in 1948 saw greater powers designated to the chieftaincy, formalised in the Bantu Authorities Act of 1951 and the Bantu Laws Amendment Act of 1952, which made chiefs and headmen salaried government officials. They were charged with responsibility for the first tier of local government and empowered to continue allocating land. The new laws also provided for the deposition and installation of chiefs by government authorities if it were felt that their performance was unsatisfactory. Increasingly, chiefs became instruments of the apartheid regime in its onslaught against opposition and its obsession with control of the rural population. During the initial period of Bantu Authority rule, chiefs who resisted the new legislation were deposed and replaced by appointees of the state [*Yawitch*, 1981]. This period was also characterised by a more systematic enforcement of 'betterment' measures involving land rehabilitation and stock control, provoking an intensification of resistance in the 1950s.

Little has been written on the chieftaincy in the 1960s and the 1970s, but with the development of bantustan administrative infrastructure, chiefs became part of the bantustan system. In an interview with Chief Khumalo of Malekutu in the Nsikazi district of KaNgwane (22 March 1993), who is also the former Minister of Police in KaNgwane, he stated that it was essentially apartheid legislation and the promulgation of the Promotion of Bantu Self-Government Act of 1959, which led the chieftaincy under the ambit of the Tribal Authority to become a repressive institution in the 1960s. By the 1980s, chiefs were firmly entrenched, but the rise of the UDF and the development of civic organs began to challenge their legitimacy and hegemony in rural areas.

Control by chiefs over land allocation continues to constitute the fundamental material basis of their power, and as Haines and Tapscott point out, is also the 'most crucial mechanism for the interplay of corruption and control' [1988: 169]. There is widespread recognition of this in rural villages and a growing resentment of how chiefs, through bantustan tribal authority structures and their control over the allocation of land, have become increasingly oppressive and corrupt. The redefinition of customary law and propensity towards corruption have steadily eroded the legitimacy of the chieftaincy. In many localities, community members are forced to pay levies and taxes to the chief, including a fee to cover the costs of ploughing the chief's farm.

The purpose of chiefly extra-economic coercion would appear to be twofold: on the one hand to develop accumulation strategies, on the other hand to facilitate ongoing reproduction of its hegemony. These practices are contradictory, however, since they generate corruption and thus serve to delegitimise the chieftaincy. Antagonism towards chiefs is often ambiguous, however, and directed more towards individuals rather than the institution of chieftaincy. Nevertheless, in most provinces, there is fairly extensive rejection of chiefs maintaining their land allocation functions and a pre-ference for these functions being vested in new democratic local government structures.

The introduction of Houses of Traditional Leaders within new provincial administrations is likely, in cases, to reinforce the role of the chieftaincy in land allocation. This has led to bitter struggles at a local level in particular provinces where the chieftaincy had been rolled back. In the Eastern Cape, for example, where the UDF was more active in rural areas than in other parts of the country, attempts to introduce a House of Traditional Leaders has provided a theatre of struggle between the Congress of Traditional Leaders of South Africa (CONTRALESA) and the South African National Civic Organisation (SANCO). Since 1990, SANCO has entrenched itself in rural areas in the province, and in the former Ciskei in particular the allocation of land to rural residents has become a prerogative of SANCO leaders. CONTRALESA leaders have expressed fear that the Local Government Transition Act and the introduction of Transitional Local Authorities would undermine their authority. In the Eastern Cape chiefs called for SANCO to be barred from rural areas and prevented from canvassing support. SANCO leaders, however, observed that such a move would deny rural people freedom of association, while Secretary General Penrose Ntlonti asserted that 'SANCO will remain in rural areas to ensure people-centred development and grass roots participation in all aspects of civil society' (*Weekly Mail and Guardian*, 2– 8 Dec. 1994, p.12).

While the alliance between the ANC and 'progressive' chiefs reflects a pragmatic politics of building electoral support, civics have often clashed with chiefs for control over rural political space. Nevertheless, there is little evidence of a coherent ANC or civic programme around the land question. Part of the problem appears to lie with the leadership that has misread the importance of land in the social reproduction of rural people, and has not organised systematically around land issues.

The ANC and the Land Question

Despite the central role which forced removals and land dispossession have played in the historical development of colonialism and apartheid, land has not featured strongly very highly on the ANC's agenda; it tends to be relegated to the background of the strategic agenda. This is partly a result of particular conceptions of development in South Africa in which the role of industrialisation and the creation of a working class are the major priority, with little recognition that agrarian questions include the relationships between industry and agriculture, and town and country.

The mass-based struggles of the 1980s, led by the UDF under the broad aegis of the ANC, gained momentum through widescale rejection of the PW Botha reforms, including the establishment of the Tri-cameral Parliament. They were advanced at a local level through a primary focus on education and urban civic issues. School boycotts and rent boycotts became the stuff upon which rebellion was fostered. The result was an unprecedented mass uprising of national proportions which was sustained through the mid-to late 1980s, but which was most advanced in urban areas. Nevertheless, there was also a revival of rural struggles. In some localities such as the Border corridor in the Eastern Cape, village-based Residents' Associations emerged in a highly politicised environment, and some affiliated to the UDF while resisting their scheduled removal or incorporation into the Ciskei [*Grahamstown Rural Committee*, 1991: 137–8].

Nevertheless, the UDF and the MDM which succeeded it, were unable to raise the level of rural organisation to constitute a revolutionary challenge to the bantustan system which the majority of rural people are subject to. At the same time, the trade union movement under the aegis of COSATU was unsuccessful in its efforts to make a serious impact on the organisation of farmworkers, and concentrated on food processing and allied industries. In rural areas, residents' associations and youth congresses became the major vehicles of organisation and resistance, rather than peasant associations or structures with the potential of combining political struggle with production and reproduction. The youth-based culture of resistance of the 1970s and 1980s while spreading to the countryside, also underestimated the land question as a mobilising issue, and generated politics which often alienated older villagers because of its somewhat rhetorical and in cases coercive approach. While the ANC's rallying cry of 'Render the Country Ungovernable' struck a sympathetic chord in the rural areas, the assaults on tribal authorities which this led to in particular areas, were insufficiently linked with the land question. Thus the possibility of articulating and organising a political demand for reform within the bantustans during this period was lost.

Following the unbanning of the ANC, it moved quickly to establish a National Land Commission and Regional Land Commissions. These structures were reasonably democratic, although inadequately linked to the local level. They were responsible for early policy work, through the 1991 ANC National Conference in Durban, to the National Policy Conference held in Johannesburg in 1992. In the wake of the policy conference, however, the National Land Commission began to disintegrate. One problem identified at the Durban Congress was the absence of a distinct department within the ANC dealing with land and agricultural affairs. Despite the recommendations made by the National Land Commission, it was effectively dissolved in 1992 and subsumed under the department of economic planning as the land and agriculture desk. The head of the National Land Commission was assigned the portfolio of agriculture, while an appointment was made in 1993 to fill the vacant land portfolio. Steps were taken in the latter half of 1993 to revive the National Land Commission with its regional structures, but by then, links with local level structures were even more tenuous. A progressive, albeit contradictory policy guideline exists, reflected in the land reform position of the RDP. Nevertheless, the place accorded to private property rights in the ANC's own proposed Bill of Rights, as well as other concessions, indicate that the aspirations of rural people around land have been subordinated to other priorities, despite a large demonstration by rural people outside the World Trade Centre (where the transition from apartheid was being negotiated) in September 1993. The attempt by NGOs in the National Land Committee to facilitate the formation of a rural social movement at the Community Land Conference in Bloemfontein in February 1994, is a further mirror to the ANC's failure to take the land question sufficiently seriously.

Another major problem with existing ANC land policy and the RDP is persisting uncertainties around the character and weight of civil society and the role of popular participation. At least at a rhetorical level, there is a central commitment to a democratic programme of change: 'The Government must proactively assist civil society to gain access to information and to participate effectively in the consultations required for a "people-driven" RDP. Equally, civil society must ensure that the resources of Local and

Provincial Governments are rapidly re-organised and redirected' [*RDP White Paper*, 1994: 53].

However, successful 'participation' is contingent upon the existence of democratic structures and, minimally, the development of a strategy of long-term social transformation or structural reform. This implies a commitment towards creating the political spaces to develop such an agenda and a strong civil society. Civics are key structures for a future democratic development programme, but their experience in the post-1990 period is highly uneven, and they have often relied heavily on the ANC for their organisational growth. In many instances, they have not yet developed clear democratic procedures and practices. There is a tradition of South African political thought which believes that the movement form is a far more effective construct for representing the interests of civil society than political parties, and that the ANC in particular, as the leading force in the Government of National Unity, represents the state 'side' of the state/civil society dichotomy [*Fine*, 1992]. In the broader African context, prospects of democracy have frequently been undermined by the merging of state and party. In the short run in South Africa, the transitional constitution precludes this possibility through the creation of the Government of National Unity (GNU). The GNU has already demonstrated its fragility on a number of occasions, but its existence does prevent the ANC from 'becoming the state'. The overwhelming mood at the ANC's 49th National Conference in Bloemfontein in December 1994 was to do away with the GNU in five years time, but it also resolved to strengthen the Alliance with COSATU, the SACP and SANCO, and to maintain its movement form: 'The ANC's crucial role as a ruling party needs to be carried through effectively and professionally. This role should reinforce, not undermine, the ANC's continuing role as a broad movement with grass roots structures, capable of organising and mobilising the broad mass of our people' [*Report on the 49th ANC National Conference December 1994*: 22].

At the level of resolution at least, there is thus a recognition within the ANC of the role of its structures as organs of civil society. Indeed, and if democratically organised, political parties as Fine [1992] has argued, are probably the most effective mediators between civil society and the state. Moreover, the ANC's central programme, the RDP, remains a programme of the Alliance which retains a broad movement form. The ANC thus maintains a dualistic movement/political party form.

This is why the ANC is well placed to take forward a programme of participatory policy, planning and development, provided that its structures are democratically organised from local through regional to national level. There are two obstacles to this in practice. The first is that the ANC leadership has virtually moved *en bloc* into Parliamentary structures, and has shied away from strategising specifically around the question of the ANC's respective roles 'inside' and 'outside' of Parliament. Secondly, as we have shown, the legal emergence of the ANC in 1990 led to the erosion of nascent democratic grassroots structures now subordinated to the priorities of a national political project of negotiated transition and 'reconciliation'. It is for this reason that the formation of a broad-based rural social movement needs to remain on the agenda.

Civil Society and the Transition

At its 49th Congress, the ANC resolved to remain a national liberation movement, despite its formal registration as a political party. In theory, this implies that the ANC, as the leader of the mass democratic movement, is ideally placed to take the lead in rural organising: to support popular democratic organisations in the countryside, and to build a progressive democratic *national* programme around the activities of these organisations. It also implies, that as an organisation with a movement form, the ANC should actively intervene in the terrain of civil society, and mediate between popular organs of civil society and the state. Of course, an ideological commitment to retaining a movement form may not be matched by practice, and the ANC may conduct its affairs like any other bourgeois political party, with its central focus on elections and parliamentary institutions.

Moreover, it must be stressed that the state/civil society relationship is contradictory. As the leading force in the government of national unity, the ANC is likely to find itself 'representing' the state in conflictual relationships with rural (and urban) people. It is also possible that the parliamentary /governmental component of the ANC will find itself in conflict with the extra-parliamentary ANC and MDM. These contradictions are inevitable, however, and indeed necessary if the ANC is truly committed to building democracy. The best mechanism of accountability and most secure way of building democracy is to have a strong extra-parliamentary ANC, to which elected representatives in the legislature and executive remain accountable.

The NLC's Community Land Conference of February 1994 was an historic occasion which provided rural representatives with the opportunity of articulating for themselves demands around land. The event was also a milestone in which civil society flexed its muscles and sent a clear signal to the ANC that it was devoting insufficient attention to rural issues. The need for a rural social movement was articulated in Bloemfontein, and will remain on the future agenda. In the light of the NLC's apparent reluctance to take the lead in forming such a movement, there is little likelihood of a *national* social movement emerging solely through grassroots initiative. It is here that the ANC could take a leading role, by beginning to articulate and organise around rural land issues.

NGOs have played an important support role in the anti-apartheid struggle and are currently reassessing their role. Historically, rurally oriented NGOs have tended to focus on 'black spot' victims of forced removals, labour tenants, bantustan consolidation victims and to a limited extent, farmworkers. The bantustans have on the whole received insufficient attention, and could become an important focus for future NGO work. Current thinking within the NLC favours a shift away from restitution issues towards land access and redistribution. This would be welcome and would take the NGOs into the bantustans where there is a massive need for capacity building. This could lead to a collaborative relationship with the state as well as with grassroots organisational initiatives by structures of the MDM, through a programme of democratic public action.

Trade unions also have a greater role to play in the countryside and need to extend their organisational capacity significantly. The organisation of farmworkers is of fundamental importance. Access will be easier than in the past but the task of organising farmworkers will remain organisationally and logistically difficult. Nevertheless it is crucial that farmworkers and labour tenants be brought into an inclusive participatory process of land reform, including identifying local priorities. In the rare cases where white farmers demonstrate an interest in promoting land reform, they too should be included.

There is also a role for white farmers' organisations, although their existing unions are a highly contested terrain (especially by formations of the Afrikaner right in the Free State and Transvaal). The South African Agricultural Union (SAAU) was historically closely linked with the development of apartheid, but includes elements keen to deracialise the land question. This has involved, *inter alia*, attempts to coopt the National African Farmers' Union (NAFU) in a search for black landowning allies. NAFU tends to represent wealthier segments of the black rural population and the potential for cooption is high. Nevertheless, NAFU or segments of it, or alternative new farmers' associations, could align themselves with popular organisations and position themselves within the MDM. Local black farmers' unions could have an important role in building rural participatory democracy, since their organisation is linked to production and its social relations.

There is a host of organisations of civil society, including political organisations, civics, NGOs, trade unions and farmers' unions. The development of a democratic process of land reform will require national as well as local initiative and action.

DEMOCRATIC LAND REFORM: PROCESSES AND PRACTICES[4]

An elite-pacted transition has the potential to create serious tensions between ANC leadership and its various constituencies. The demobilisation of an historically mass-based organisation is taking place as policy debates are subsumed by the politics of elite bargaining. As a result, any process of reconstruction will be fraught with difficulties. Key land reform questions are debated with relatively little incorporation of local community knowledge and expertise. If structural reform is to take precedence over elite pacting, then an alternative political process must be created, centred on genuine popular participation articulated at the national, regional and local scales.

Such an alternative needs to take seriously the role of 'communities' as particular ideological and political constructs in South Africa. It is the forms taken by apartheid repression (of all blacks), which made formations of community, and indeed people, possible in the South African context. Despite the role of the organised trade union movement and rhetoric about working class leadership, insufficient attention has been paid to the fact that people in various communities experienced apartheid repression differently due to class and other social differences. As ideological constructs, 'the people' and 'the community' tend to conceal both class differences and 'contradictions amongst the people'. The outcomes of popular struggles have different effects for different social classes, contingent on which class leads a popular movement. In the era of post-apartheid reconstruction, new forms of class alliance have emerged through processes of bourgeois elite pacting, as noted earlier. The alternative processes presented below thus depend on worker peasants, allotment holding wage workers, rural proletarians and marginalised women playing a central political role.

Currently, the Department of Land Affairs (DLA), in line with the RDP, distinguishes between land restitution to the victims of forced removals, and land redistribution to meet the land needs of rural people through a demand-led land reform process. The department has set in place a series of initiatives which centre on the establishment of a land reform pilot programme to 'kick-start' the redistribution component of its programme (see also Murray in this volume). Indications are that in this particular phase of the programme, better organised communities will be prioritised. Nevertheless, the department is committed to a participatory process (*Department of Land Affairs*, 1994). Local participation needs to be facilitated through local and community development forums where land committees/interest groups can be established. Such forums are part of the RDP strategy, and a major challenge is to ensure that their constitution is democratic and can facilitate broad-based participation. The RDP provides for the establishment of state (RDP commissions) and parallel civil society structures (development forums). Provincial and regional land reform co-ordinating structures will have to be set up by the DLA through provincial RDP commissions, and link in with local, regional and provincial development forums. This process needs also to link interactively with national-level policy formulation: to articulate national land policy objectives locally, while helping to communicate local needs and capabilities to the centre. This will require the investment of resources in authentic capacity building at the provincial level. Success will depend largely on a genuine commitment towards the strengthening of organs of civil society, particularly development forums, which will enable land allocation structures to work closely with the DLA.

The establishment of democratic land committees at the local level must lay the basis for the articulation of provincial and regional policy and projects. The ideal organisational forms for this are workshops whereby locally mandated delegates participate in the formation of provincial and local development forums. Provincial delegates could then take the process forward to the national level. Specifically, a locally-based participatory strategy which is articulated at the provincial and national levels, could involve the following steps:

(1) Local level meetings to initiate the participatory process

These meetings are intended to facilitate the establishment of interim land committee structures to initiate the process of identifying key local land reform issues, while also discussing provincial and national policy proposals. These initial local level meetings would also be used to establish structures for the implementation of a baseline socio-economic survey and intensive interviewing, as well as to begin the process by which local people are involved. The (magisterial) district may not provide the appropriate scale to initiate this, as districts are products of apartheid geographies that a land reform programme will attempt to erode.

(2) Research, Report-back and Mental Mapping Workshop

This workshop entails a report-back on the findings from the survey and intensive interviews. These provide the context for mental-mapping exercises and the initial formulation of policy ideas. The base-line survey, intensive interviews and mental-mapping aim to generate valuable information on the historical geography of forced removals, the levels of agricultural land demand, envisioned future farming systems, perceptions of who should benefit from land reform, where and how land should be obtained for a land reform programme, and the desired mechanisms through which land should be allocated. This workshop is also intended to identify individuals to work with regional co-ordinators on the drafting of policy documents and preliminary ideas for specific projects to be discussed at the next workshop.

(3) Policy Formulation Workshop

This workshop will present draft policy documents for discussion, and elicit feed-back on specific ideas for land reform projects and programme implementation. The potential popularity of policies and projects will be discussed and evaluated through a matrix ranking exercise which attempts to stratify responses by gender, age and class. Delegates will be elected to take mandated positions on policy and projects to a regional meeting.

(4) Provincial Consolidation Workshop

Depending on the requirements of a particular province, this workshop could be held initially at a regional (that is, sub-provincial) level, where elected, mandated delegates would then take forward proposals to a provincial workshop.[5] At these workshops, elected representatives discuss national land reform policy and agree on an agenda for the implementation of popular projects in the local level. Participation by (national) DLA officials at provincial-level workshops, is essential. A central objective of the provincial consolidation workshop is to initiate a process whereby local-level participatory research, results and policy ideas can be translated into specific land use plans which are technically, politically, ecologically and socially sound.

The process as outlined above is fraught with potential difficulties and is likely to be highly contested. The most serious problem will be the identification by communities of land which is not available for redistribution. Given the fact that communities are not homogeneous, competing local claims and aspirations will surface (as the case studies by Cousins and Murray in this volume demonstrate). The process also necessitates strong and committed leadership at the provincial and regional scale which is allocated sufficient resources to mediate and communicate local and national level objectives.

CONCLUSION

The Ministry of Land Affairs has moved rapidly to implement land restitution. The Restitution of Land Rights Act, 1994 was legislated in Parliament in November, providing for the establishment of a Land Claims Commission and a Land Claims Court. In media briefings which followed the legislation of the Act, however, both State President Nelson Mandela, and Land Minister Derek Hanekom were at pains to assure white farmers that the Act would not imply expropriation of their land, and that if in isolated cases white farmers would have to leave their land, they would be fully compensated. In a television interview, Minister Hanekom emphasised that the Act was 'symbolically terribly important'. Black rural people, of course, desire more than symbolism, and the likelihood of the majority of them receiving land through the land claims process is remote.

In the meantime, the Land Affairs Ministry is pressing on with its redistribution programme. The initial phases of this programme are being developed through a Pilot Land Reform Programme which will be implemented over a two-year period in each province, and expanded over time. This programme, in the first instance, will be funded by the RDP to which donor contributions are being sought, while in the longer term it will be funded through the line budget of the DLA. The Chief Directorate of Land Reform was established within the department following the repeal of the Land Acts by the de Klerk regime, but has done relatively little work since then. However, this directorate is now placed at the heart of the Land Affairs Department. The DLA acknowledges that 'grand plans developed in a hurry and imposed from above have seldom worked anywhere' [*Department of Land Affairs*, 1994: 2], and has therefore

> expended considerable time on ensuring the participation of a wide range of groupings both inside and outside of goverment in the design of the Programme to ensure the incorporation of diverse insights and experience. The expressed land problems of rural communities and the solutions they have suggested over many years of land struggles have particularly been taken into account in the Programme's design. The Department of Land Affairs has taken these lessons to heart in embarking on a pilot initiative as a kick-start measure for a wider process of land transfer. It is hoped that through a limited number of initiatives that reflect the full diversity of conditions and land needs ... further lessons will be learned to ensure that the land needs of disadvantaged groupings are met in the most effective ways [*ibid.: 3*].

In embarking on such a strategy, the DLA is to some extent postponing the development of a comprehensive national programme, hoping that such a programme will evolve out of the various initiatives that arise, and that further reforms will provide a 'more enabling environment'. This is a risky course of action: while perhaps meeting the aspirations of those involved in pilot projects, it will not fulfil the land needs and demands of the majority. While the DLA claims to be engaged in a participative process, the 'pilot strategy' is a technicist approach, which emphasises productivity, output, market return and similar criteria. The conception of the pilot projects emphasises institutional reform, but does not seriously consider the strategic political conditions under which social transformation takes place.

A successful national land and agrarian reform programme which is articulated at the provincial and local levels will require serious commit-ment and transparency by government organs of the new democratic state. It also requires a political project of structural reform and rejection of an elite-pacted transition process. A commitment to a programme of structural reform on the part of the ANC requires extra-parliamentary struggles to complement parliamentary endeavours, in order to achieve its objectives.

Establishing a progressive role for the state is a key challenge for a democratic South Africa. In the case of land and agrarian reform, the ANC as the dominant political force within the Government of National Unity, and through its Minister of Land Affairs, needs to play a central role in articulating a democratic land reform strategy that will link local, regional and national scales of action. With land as a national competency, there are no provincial land ministries. Agriculture at national level, and in six out of nine provinces, is controlled by National Party ministers. In the absence of provincial ministries and structures, the national land ministry will be ineffective without the counterweight of an organised ANC outside of parliament. At the same time, the DLA remains staffed by civil servants of the old regime. Some of these may be willing to adopt the rhetoric of the RDP in order to preserve their positions, while their bureaucratic practices remain unchanged. Others may be more obstructionist, forcing the minister and his new cadres to waste valuable time in neutralising and edging them out of office.

The outlook since the April 1994 election is not encouraging. The ANC-led government's commitment to 'National Reconciliation', while necessary given the balance of forces, is increasingly serving class interests of capital and the black bourgeoisie, as Arnold Sibanda [1988] suggested happened in Zimbabwe. The ANC's Land Affairs Minister, Derek Hanekom has argued that: 'A viable rural economy will benefit everyone. Reconciliation lies in communication and understanding of the issues. We are working for maximum co-operation between advantaged and disadvantaged communities and there are exciting cases of willing sellers and buyers' [New Ground, Spring 1994: 21]. This optimistic perspective is likely to become increasingly tempered by the contradictions of rural social relations. The interests of 'advantaged' and 'disadvantaged' communities are generally diametrically opposed. The Labour Tenants Bill (1995), which seeks to give land rights to labour tenants through assisted purchase illustrates this. The Bill is anything but radical, but has been vigorously opposed by organised white agriculture which has demonised Hanekom in the process.

Despite the commitment by the new government and its Land Affairs Minister to a market led strategy of land reform, there appears to be little willingness on the part of white agriculture to contribute to the process. Minister Hanekom's suggestion of a modest one per cent agricultural land tax was greeted with derision by organised white agriculture, and the SAAU congress held in October 1994 resolved to boycott such a move if implemented. Hanekom has urged white farmers to give landless people the hope of access to land, warning of more radical policy measures which the ANC would have to implement if it faces re-election in 1999 having delivered little land: 'If there are still millions of people who remain landless ... they will insist that more drastic measures are taken – and that we want to avoid' [*The Star*, 21 Oct. 1994].

There is little chance, however, of elite-pacted transitional politics delivering substantial land through the market to apartheid's rural victims. Market-based solutions on their own cannot resolve the land question since poor peasants and rural proletarians will remain marginalised, as articulated by a villager in Lebowa:

> There is no way we can remain poor in our native land. For instance, let us say that Mr Mahlangu has a pair of shoes and at night I come and steal it. If the owner identifies his shoes, even if there are slight changes made to them, do you expect him to pay for the changes that have been made? I do not think this is possiible because I have acquired ownership through illegal means. We are not going to compensate them for stealing our land [*Interview*, Marite, 19 January 1993].

Such sentiments, if articulated forcefully and channelled politically, will increasingly force the ANC to recognise that the interests of white agriculture and those of the black rural masses -farmworkers, labour tenants, worker-peasants, allotment holding wage workers and the rural proletariat in the former bantustans- are irreconcilable. This is particularly true in a context where, at a national level, the ANC is caught between the needs and aspirations of its support base, and alliances forged in the interests of 'reconciliation' and 'nation-building'. While private property and land rights are a sacred cow not only for erstwhile foes of the ANC, but increasingly for its emergent bourgeois leadership too, the contradictory character of rural social relations, and the challenge of rural organisation and struggle, will reassert themselves in the agenda of social transformation.

NOTES

1. Rural here refers to the former bantustan areas (including peri-urban settlements), white farming areas and rural towns.
2. Clearly an alternative socialist perspective on transition needs to be developed. The South African Communist Party (SACP), the major organised socialist force, has not developed such a vision.
3. The RDP was formulated by the ANC and its allies, the Congress of South African Trade Unions (COSATU) and the SACP.
4. This section draws extensively on Levin and Weiner [1994].
5. In the case of the Eastern Cape, for example, which brings together the Transkei, Border and Ciskei, regional workshops would be appropriate, whereas in the Western Cape, Gauteng and Mpumalanga, they may not.

REFERENCES

Adler, G. and E. Webster, 1994, 'Challenging Transition Theory: The Labour Movement, Radical Reform and Transition to Democracy in South Africa', University of Witwatersrand, History Workshop, 13–15 July.

African National Congress, 1992, *Ready to Govern: ANC Policy Guidelines for a Democratic South Africa*, Johannesburg (adopted at the National Conference 28–31 May).

African National Congress, 1994, *The Reconstruction and Development Programme*, Johannesburg: Umanyano Publications.

African National Congress, n.d., *Report on the 49th ANC National Conference, Bloemfontein 1994*, ANC Department of Information and Publicity.

Bassett, T.J., 1993, 'The Land Question and Agricultural Transformation in Sub-Saharan Africa', in T.J. Bassett, and D.E. Crummey (eds.), *Land in African Agrarian Systems*, Madison, WI: University of Wisconsin Press.

Beinart, W. and C. Bundy, 1987, *Hidden Struggles in Rural South Africa*, Johannesburg: Ravan

Bradford, H., 1987, *A Taste of Freedom: The ICU in Rural South Africa, 1926-1930*, New Haven, CT: Yale University Press.

Bundy, C., 1984, 'Land and Liberation: The South African National Liberation Movements and the Agrarian Question, 1920s–1960s', *Review of African Political Economy*, 29.

Claassens, A., 1991, 'Contemporary Land Struggles in Rural Transvaal', *Antipode*, Vol.23, No.1.

Colson, E., 1971, 'The Impact of the Colonial Period on the Definition of Land Rights', in V. Turner (ed.), *Colonialism in Africa 1970–1960, Vol.3, Profiles of Change: African Society and Colonial Rule*, Cambridge: Cambridge University Press.

Delius, P., 1983, *The Land Belongs To Us*, Johannesburg: Ravan Press.

Delius, P. 1990, 'Migrants, Comrades and Rural Revolt: Sekhukhuneland 1950–1987, *Transformation*, 13.

Department of Land Affairs,1994, *Land Reform Pilot Programme*, Programme Overview, Oct.

Fine, R., 1992, 'Civil Society Theory and the Politics of Transition in South Africa', *Review of African Political Economy*, 55.

Grahamstown Rural Action Committee (GRC), 1991, 'Between a Rock and a Hard Place: Forced Removals and the Bantustans in the "Border Corridor" of South Africa', *Antipode*, Vol.23, No.1.

Haines, R. and C.P.G. Tapscott, 1988, 'The Silence of Poverty: Tribal Administration and Development in Rural Transkei', in C. Cross and R.J. Haines (eds.), *Towards Freehold? Options for Land and Development in Black Rural Areas*, Cape Town: Juta.

Haysom, N., 1986, *Mabangalala: The Rise of Right-Wing Vigilantes in South Africa*, Occasional Paper No.10, Centre for Applied Legal Studies, University of the Witwatersrand.

Hobsbawm, E. and T. Ranger (eds.), 1983, *The Invention of Tradition*, Cambridge: Cambridge University Press.

Isaacman, A.F., 1993, 'Peasants and Rural Social Protest in Africa', in F. Cooper, F.E. Mallon, S.J. Stern, A.F. Isaacman and W. Roseberry, *Confronting Historical Paradigms: Peasants, Labour and the Capitalist World System in Africa and Latin America*, Madison, WI: University of Wisconsin Press.

Kriger, N., 1991, 'Popular Struggles in Zimbabwe's National War of Liberation', in P. Kaarsholm (ed.), *Culture and Development in Southern Africa*, London: James Currey.

Letsoalo, E., 1987, *Land Reform in South Africa: A Black Perspective*, Johannesburg: Skotaville

Levin, R., 1990, 'Is This the Swazi Way?', *Transformation* 13.

Levin, R. and D. Weiner, 1993, 'The Agrarian Question and Politics in the New South Africa', in *Review of African Political Economy*, 57.

Levin, R. and D. Weiner, 1994, 'Towards the Development of a Participatory Rural Land Reform Programme in a Democratic South Africa', in Levin and Weiner (eds.) [1994].

Levin, R. and D. Weiner, 1994, *Community Perspectives on Land and Agrarian Reform,* Final Report Prepared for the John D. and Catherine T. MacArthur Foundation.

Mbeki, G., 1984, *South Africa: The Peasants Revolt*, London: International Defence and Aid Fund for Southern Africa (first published 1964).

Przeworski, A., 1991, *Democracy and the Market: Political and Economic Reforms in Eastern*

Europe and Latin America, Cambridge: Cambridge University Press.

Ranger, T., 1993, 'The Communal Areas of Zimbabwe', in T.J. Basset. and D.E. Crummey (eds.), *Land in African Agrarian Systems*, Madison, WI: University of Wisconsin Press.

RDP White Paper Discussion Document, 1994, CTP Printers, Cape Town.

Saul, J.S., 1993, *Recolonisation and Resistance in Southern Africa in the 1990s*, Trenton: Africa World Press.

Sibanda, A., 1988, 'The Political Situation', in Stoneman, C. (ed.), *Zimbabwe's Prospects*, London: Macmillan.

Yawitch, J., 1981, *Betterment: The Myth of Homeland Agriculture*, Johannesburg: Institute of Race Relations.

The Political Economy of the Maize *Filière*

HENRY BERNSTEIN

THE APPROACH OF *FILIÈRES VIVRIÈRES*

The term *filière* appeared in the Journal of Peasant Studies for the first time recently, in a review of literature on agricultural restructuring by David Goodman and Michael Watts [1994: 36, 39, 44 n 50]. In this article, a *filière* approach is used to investigate the dynamics of the maize industry at the end of apartheid, and to explore its legacy to the new political dispensation in South Africa. First, it is useful to introduce the *filière* approach, and to illustrate its relevance to the case of the South African maize industry, before analysing the latter in more depth and detail.

The method of *filière vivrières* (food commodity chains) is to investigate the various stages – and their interconnections – in the journeys of food commodities from farmer's field to consumer's plate. The principal stages of such journeys, as outlined in this study, are (i) how the conditions of production are established, (ii) farm production, (iii) marketing, (iv) processing, (v) distribution, and (vi) consumption.[1]

The original inspiration of the *filière* approach (in French industrial economics) was to uncover and analyse price formation in the journey of a commodity from raw material to final product, through its various stages of physical transformation (processing, manufacturing), transport, storage and so on. This is often expressed as the distribution of the value added of the final product among the various activities (and agents) that contributed to its production and realisation.[2] This can be a useful exercise, despite assumptions that (a) the stages/transformations of the commodity carry it through a series of quite distinct and separate markets and market transactions, (b) each market is simply an aggregation of exchanges between individual sellers and buyers of commodities. Even if one questions such limiting (and indeed reified) assumptions of conventional economics, empirical findings about price formation along the chain can provide valuable data to an alternative approach and form of analysis.[3]

The alternative pursued here is to combine the *filière* approach as a

Henry Bernstein, Department of Anthropology and Sociology, School of Oriental and African Studies, University of London, Thornhaugh Street, Russell Square, London WC1H OXG, UK.

research tool with analysis of the social relations and institutions that structure economic life and markets (and how they change historically). In short, a form of analysis informed by political economy (rather than a conventional economics premised on the maximising behaviour of individual agents in ideally competitive markets). This use of *filières vivrières* has been developed by a group of researchers at CIRAD (Centre de coopération internationale en recherche agronomique pour le développement) in Montpellier [*Benz et al.,* 1994], whose thematic and methodological concerns converge with those of certain anglophone political economists of food systems [*Bernstein and Leplaideur,* in press].[4] The distinctive features of the research programme (a set of perspectives, methods and questions) suggested by this approach can be outlined under several (connected) headings.

First is the focus on 'real markets' as distinct from the formal modelling of abstract markets in economic theory [*Mackintosh,* 1990; *Hewitt de Alcantara* (ed.), 1992]. 'Real markets' here does not denote an (inevitable) empirical deviation from the theoretical abstraction of perfectly competitive markets. Rather, it denotes a particular *object of analysis,* whose characteristics and dynamics are established *theoretically* as well as empirically through investigating the specific forms of social relations and institutions that constitute real markets – and their differentiated agents – in particular places at particular times.[5]

Second, this conceptualisation of 'real markets' – as a particular object of analysis investigated through social relations and institutions – focuses attention on questions of *power* in understanding how markets work; more precisely, the sources, exercise, and effects of unequal market power in the relations between differentiated agents. The latter encompasses not just the conventional functional differentiation of producers/consumers, sellers/ buyers, but the *social differentiation* of class and gender, and how it defines the characteristics of particular categories or groups of producers/consumers, sellers/buyers, in given markets.[6]

A third, connected, point is that markets are imbued with politics as well as economics, in ways that subvert the conventional distinction of markets as (properly) an autonomous sphere of economic behaviour and its rationality, and politics as a sphere of behaviour exogenous to markets but which may (improperly) 'intervene' in, 'interfere' with, or 'distort' market mechanisms. Challenging this conventional distinction are the perceptions, first, that markets have (variant) political, institutional and legal conditions of existence that affect their functioning, and second, that (differentiated) market agents pursue forms of collective action, to influence those conditions and to strengthen their market power by other means.

This links further, and closely, to a fourth issue: that of different, and contested, notions of market 'regulation'. The conventional view of regulation restricts it to legislative, policy and administrative measures that affect the structure and performance of markets. In neo-liberal ideology regulation is seen, on a priori grounds , as harmful to competition, hence efficiency, which generates the blanket policy prescription of 'deregulation'. An alternative view is that regulation is a generic feature of markets, referring to how they are structured by different forms of power and control in both their conditions of existence and their 'internal' functioning – and, of course, by how these elements interact. This generates a very different perspective on policy issues, now conceived in terms of better *vs* worse forms of regulation rather than 'less' *vs* 'more' regulation.[7]

This brief review of aspects of the 'real markets' perspective provides a necessary but not sufficient introduction to the rationale of the *filières vivrières* approach and its research programme. In principle, the above observations apply to the investigation of any given (single) market. The next step is to carry them forward to consideration of *filières* that (typically) involve, and connect, a sequence of transactions in different markets.

A first question is whether markets that correspond to the various stages of a *filière* are indeed separate and autonomous from each other. One issue for investigation is whether key agents operate in two or more stages/ markets of the *filière,* in what ways and with what effects. One manifestation of this is the debate about interlinked or interlocked markets (for some combination of land, labour, credit, crops) in South Asia [e.g., *Crow,* in press; *Janakarajan,* in press; *Olsen,* in press]. Examples from the South African maize *filière* (see Table 1) include maize farmers (in production; in marketing through the majority representation of their organisation NAMPO in the Maize Board); and, more importantly, the major summer grain cooperatives (in credit and input supply; maize purchase, handling and storage; maize milling and feed manufacture; distribution).

A second question is whether, and how, there are aspects of the functioning and regulation of any given *filière* that can only be grasped by considering it as a *whole* (rather than as a sequence of discrete stages and transactions). With reference to maize in South Africa, this can be illustrated by the (historic) form of regulation exercised by the Maize Board through its single-channel marketing authority, determining buying and selling prices and managing exports and imports. This example conforms to the conventional, and narrow, conception of regulation noted earlier, which has restricted (most) debate of 'reform' of the maize industry to alternative measures of 'deregulation'.

However, there is a characteristic tendency of agriculture in modern capitalism – the increasing domination of *filières* by corporate (agribusiness) capital in strategic locations upsteam and downstream of farming [*Bernstein,* 1994a] – that raises research questions linked to the second, broader, conception of regulation. In the case of maize in South Africa, it can be argued that the demise of the control scheme, that is, 'deregulation', may reveal – and enhance – forms of ('private') regulation of the maize *filière* by an alliance of the major grain co-operatives and corporate capital in milling and feed manufacture (see further below). More generally, the scale and strategies of agribusiness capital (not least in food processing and distribution) generate new forms of globalisation (and regulation) of *filières vivrières,* the significance of which can only be grasped by examining such *filières* in their totality (see the brilliant analysis by Friedmann [1993]).

A third question (or set of questions) posed at the level of the *filière* as a whole, concerns how the structuring of the connections between its various activities – farming, trade, processing, consumption – affect livelihoods and welfare. This is perhaps more evident at the point of consumption, given the importance of food to human welfare and reproduction, and the association of poverty with diets inadequate in quality and/or quantity. Such highly charged questions as who eats what? how much? how often? how do they acquire their food? remind us of the destination of the *filière* in consumption, of issues of food security as an indispensable condition of well-being [*Drèze and Sen,* 1989], and that answers to these questions in any empirical study will reflect, *inter alia,* the functioning of *filières:* what they make available to whom, where, in what ways, on what terms.

Beyond this central importance for consumption of food staples, the nature and organisation of *filières vivrières* also bear on livelihoods through the generation of employment and income opportunities, whether in wage labour (its conditions of employment, work and remuneration) or self-employment (petty commodity production in food farming, trade, processing, transport). This is relevant to most of the principal branches of food production in South Africa, marked by the legacies of the racial ordering of land ownership and labour regimes in farming, and by a high degree of capital concentration in many activities in their *filières.*[8] In short, food security as a strategic concern in the restructing of South African agriculture raises issues on the supply side of *filières,* and its linkages, as well as on the demand (or needs) side [*Bernstein,* 1994b].

A fourth set of issues about connections between the activities/stages of *filières* concerns the investigation of relations of exchange and distribution as well as those of production (in farming, processing). Here *filière* research raises questions about the extent and nature of determination of particular activities/agents by others at different points in the chain. These questions resonate those about power in real markets noted earlier, but extend their focus to links between activities and groups of agents located in different stages of the *filière.* One example would be those situations in which merchant capital (sometimes combined with processing capital) is able to

TABLE 1

THE MAIZE *FILIÈRE* IN SOUTH AFRICA AT THE END OF APARTHEID

ACTIVITIES/ FUNCTIONS	MARKETS/REGULATION		
	INSTITUTIONS	AGENTS	ASSOCIATIONS
1. Supplying Conditions of Production			
LAND	Apartheid laws and. apparatuses	• (white) land buyers/sellers	(SAAU etc.)
LABOUR	Apartheid laws and apparatuses	• Labour buyers/sellers (white capitalists/ black workers)	(SAAU etc.)
INPUTS	(Industrial protection)	(Production and/or distribution)	(SAAU etc.) SAMPI/NAMPO
– Seed		• Corporate capital • CCs (Sensako,Saffola) • PCs	
– Fertiliser	(Competition Board)	• Corporate capital • PCs (distribution and mixing)	FSSA FAC of SAAU
– Chemicals (pesticides, herbicides)		• Corporate capital • (TNC affiliates) • CC (Sentrachem)	AVCASA
– Machinery	Industrial Protection: (ADE)	• Corporate capital (TNCs) • and franchising through PCs, CCs (Boeresake, Vetsak)	
– Petroleum products		• Corporate capital (and Total – SAAU) • PCs in distribution	FLC of Cooperative Council
FINANCE	DOA Land Bank	• PCs • Commercial banks	(SAAU)
OTHER SERVICES e.g. Research Extension. Insurance	MB	• PCs • CCs (Setraoes, Sentraboer)	
2. Production	(MOA/DOA) (MB)	• Farmers • Workers	NAMPO (SAAU, TAU, OFSAU) (unions, political organisations)
3. Marketing			
– Buying	MB (NMC)	• PCs • Independent millers	Cooperative Council (SAAU)
– Storage	MB	• PCs • CC (Uniegraan) • Independent millers	Cooperative Council (SAAU)
– Selling	MB	• PCs • Independent millers	Cooperative Council (SAAU)

TABLE 1 (cont.)

ACTIVITIES/ FUNCTIONS	INSTITUTIONS	AGENTS	ASSOCIATIONS
– Transport		• Spoornet (railways)	
– Exports/Imports	(MB)		
4. Processing			
– White maize (maize meal)	(MB)	• Corporate capital • PCs • CC (Amaizco) • Individual capital • Workers	NAMM TU (FAWU)
– Yellow maize (Animal feeds)	(MB)	• Corporate capital • PCs • Workers	AFMA TU (FAWU)
5. Distribution			
– Maize meal	(MB)	• Manufacturers • Wholesalers (corporate, individual) • Railers (corporate, individual) • Workers	TU (SACCAWU)
– Yellow maize		• Manufacturers (corporate, PCs)	
6. Consumption			
– Maize meal		• Mostly (poorer) black consumers	
– Yellow maize		• Animal producers – poultry – cattle, sheep	YMCO SAPA SAFA

KEY

ADE	African Diesel Engine	OFSAU	Orange Free State Agricultural Union
AFMA	Animal Feeds Manufacturers Association	PC	Primary Cooperative
AVCASA	Agricultural and Veterinary Chemicals Association of South Africa	SAAU	South African Agricultural Union
CC	Central Cooperative	SACCAWU	South African Commercial, Catering and Allied Workers Union
DOA	Department of Agriculture		
FAC	Fertiliser Advisory Committee	SAFA	South African Feedlot Association
FAWU	Food and Allied Workers Union		
FLC	Fuel Liaison Committee	SAMPI	South African Maize Producers Institute (1966-1980)
FSSA	Fertiliser Society of South Africa	SAPA	South African Poultry Association
MB	Maize Board		
MOA	Ministry of Agriculture	TAU	Transvaal Agricultural Association
NAMM	National Association of Maize Millers	TNC	Transnational Corporation
NAMPO	National Maize Producers Organisation (from 1980)	TU	Trade Union
		YMCO	Yellow Maize Consumers Organisation
NMC	National Marketing Council		

control, directly or indirectly, the nature of farming and its possibilities of accumulation and technical change [e.g. *Harriss*, 1990].

Finally, the *filières vivrières* approach – again exemplified by the work of the CIRAD *équipe* – also highlights questions of sociological and cultural dynamics that may shape the forms and functioning of particular *filières*. One kind of example is the role of kinship and its idioms in the economic organisation of petty commodity production in food cultivation, processing and trade [*Moustier*, 1994]; another is the part of Islamic brotherhoods in the domestic and international market strategies of large rice merchants in Guinea [*Leplaideur et al.*, 1990]; yet another is how cultural forms and meanings enter the organisation of trade and consumption [*Moustier*, 1993; *Rival*, in press].

Some analytical components in 'mapping' the structure of a *filière*, are illustrated in Table 1. This outline is structured in two ways: by the various sequential stages of the commodity chain, as summarised at the beginning of this study, and by four columns/headings – activities/functions, institutions, agents, associations -which summarise information about each stage of the *filière* and its constituent parts.

The first column – activities/functions – sets out what is done at each stage of the *filière*. Evidently these activities will not be identical for all *filières vivrières*, nor will the types of agents who perform them. Starting with activities enables identifying where two or more activities are performed by the same agent, and assessing its significance (activity combinations of mercantile enterprises in India are stressed by Harriss-White [in press]).

Depending on the relative complexity of any *filière* in relation to research and/or policy objectives, the schema (starting with activities/functions) could be more or less elaborated or abbreviated and simplified. For example, the marketing function in the outline contains a number of different activities, which could be amplified in much greater detail. In terms of other considerations noted earlier, and on the argument that the maize *filière* has distinctive forms of regulation as an integrated commodity chain (see below), even the summary outline suggests that a virtually exclusive focus on marketing arrangements (as in the current 'reform' debate in South Africa) misses some key issues for any significant restructuring.

The second column – institutions – comprises, but also extends, the conventional understanding of regulation, that is, laws, state departments and other apparatuses and their functions, parastatal bodies and enterprises, policy instruments and policies specific to the *filière* in question and more generally (including at the macroeconomic level). There are examples of each of these, that should be self-evident, in the outline.

Two further points: I have restricted the use of the term 'institutions' to state constituted bodies and practices for the sake of convenience, and to maintain the distinction with non-state forms of organisation and practice. Second, the conventional sense of 'regulation' does indicate some important questions (even if unable to provide adequate answers, in part through missing out, hence failing to investigate connections with, economic and market regulation in the broader sense). Another preoccupation with (conventional) regulation in the neo-liberal ascendancy centres on forms of interaction between state agents and market agents encouraged by particular statutory arrangements – again an important issue, if not amenable to satisfactory investigation within the conventional analytical framework (see Harriss-White [in press]).

Institutions are put in the second column, as they establish (as noted earlier) state derived (statutory and other) conditions of particular markets and their functioning, ie influencing how activities are performed by agents in those markets. This is not to say, of course, that all statutory conditions are observed by all market agents, who may individually or in combination (associations, in the fourth column) pursue ways of evading or seeking to change those conditions, with greater or lesser success; nor that statutory conditions are implemented or enforced by state agents in relation to all market agents at all times. Again, the neo-liberal insistence that state regulation generates practices of rent-seeking, corruption, evasion and so on, often merits investigation (consider the apartheid state, for example), if not acceptance on deductive grounds, but has to be related to the politics of regulation, and widespread rigging, that are part of the 'normal' dynamics of markets, and to which neo-liberalism turns a blind eye.

The classification of market agents in the case of the maize *filière* is twofold: in social terms of capital and labour and in functional terms of producers and consumers. Capital is divided into corporate capital, individual capital (most farmers, some independent millers, wholesalers and so on), and the distinctive form of capital of the grain cooperatives. Also, of course, capital appears as 'consumer' as well as producer: millers 'consume' unprocessed maize, feed manufacturers milled yellow maize, livestock producers animal feeds, and so on. Workers, and the propertyless in general, appear as consumers only of final products – maize meal, and animal products incorporating maize based feeds.

Petty commodity producers (see above and note 8) are virtually absent because of the nature of this particular *filière*, and are probably represented mostly by (smaller) independent retailers. The double classification of agents as capital/labour and producers/consumers, and its connections, have additional content from South Africa's racial order (mostly white capital/ black labour). Consumers of maize meal could be further identified in terms of inter-class and intra-class (occupation, income, gender, urban/rural) differentiation.

The final column – associations – refers to organisations of 'public action', that is, 'purposive collective action, whether for collective private ends or for public ends (however defined)' [*Wuyts et al.,* 1992]. Hardly surprisingly, it is the range, number, specialisation – and *power* – of such associations of capital that are the striking feature of this last column. They are organisations of public action 'for collective private ends', many of which had official representation in apartheid state institutions, and/or quasi-official access to and influence over policy making. The extent to which these channels of the politics of the maize *filière* and its constituent activities and markets, change with the new political dispensation, and how, remains to be seen.

In explaining the classification employed in the sketch map of the maize *filière* of activities/functions, institutions, agents, associations, and illustrating its uses, I have (unavoidably) omitted much of the conditions of existence of any given *filière* in its wider political economy (locally, nationally, internationally), and of the kinds of sociological and cultural dynamics indicated earlier. Possible difficulties in using the *filière* approach are outlined next.

One issue, just signalled, is that the advantages of the *filière* approach in cutting a particular 'slice' from larger economic organisms to examine under the analytical microscope, may have corresponding disadvantages if we lose sight of the entitites from which the 'slice' is extracted, how and where it fits into, and is shaped by, other elements of those entities.[9]

The location of given *filières* in the wider political economy, and its effects, is not the only issue here. There is another possible difficulty in that (at least some) key agents in the *filière* are not wholly specialised producers/ consumers of the commodity in question. Greater or lesser degrees of specialisation/diversification will characterise farmers, processors, traders and so on, both as (differentiated) categories of agents and as individual decision makers, and affect their strategies in producing and using the definitive commodity of the *filière* in relation to other options available to them (opportunities of, and constraints on, accumulation or simple reproduction).[10]

This leads to a more specific issue in using the *filière* approach. In its strict application, it identifies a clearly defined final product (by its *use value* in consumption), then works back along the chain of its production and realisation as a commodity (both use value and exchange value). For example, does maize constitute a single *filière,* or do its two principal final products in South Africa – maize meal and animal feeds – require the analysis of two distinct *filières* (of white and yellow maize respectively)?[11] This example suggests an initial common activity – maize farming (barely differentiated by production conditions of white and yellow varieties) –

eventuating in distinct *filières* (from processing onwards) of distinct final products with separate markets.

Having sketched these salient features and issues of the *filières* approach, I present next a conventional view of the maize *filière* in South Africa before pursuing an analysis based in political economy.

THE STORY OF A MAIZE *FILIÈRE* I

An extensive elevated plateau deep in the interior of a large country is the main area of cultivation of the country's principal grain, maize. Between 3 and 3.5 million hectares are planted to maize each year on large, mechanised farms; 4,000 to 5,000 farmers provide most of the market for a population of some 40 million people. The size of harvests is highly dependent on rainfall and subject to severe annual fluctuations. Average maize yields even in a reasonable year are about one-third of those in the world's leading producer and exporter, the USA.

There are two distinct uses and markets for maize: white maize is milled to produce meal, the staple food of a large proportion, probably the majority, of the country's population; yellow maize is used to make animal feeds. Maize is marketed through a statutory single-channel marketing scheme operated by the Maize Board. The principal function of the Board is to determine the buying and selling prices of maize for each marketing season following the harvest, but it does not handle maize. This is done by its agents, above all the big cooperatives in the main growing areas. These cooperatives own most of the grain silos, channel credit to many maize farmers, and also supply them with inputs (seed, fertiliser, machinery, fuel). They are also involved in milling (maize meal) and animal feed production.

Corporate companies in milling and feed manufacture are the biggest customers of the Maize Board. Millers sell to supermarket chains and to wholesalers who supply independent, mostly small, retailers from whom the majority of consumers, especially in the non-metropolitan areas of the country, buy their maize meal. Feed manufacturers sell their products to the country's chicken and feedlot industries.

This *filière* has a number of interests and actors. Maize farmers have a strong producer organisation with majority representation on the Maize Board. The cooperatives are a distinctive form of business enterprise, run by professional managers and engaged in additional activities upstream and downstream of crop marketing. The Maize Board negotiates between various interests in the *filière*, subject to government policy which it has to implement.

Just as farmers are interested in higher producer prices and returns, industrial users of maize are interested in paying lower prices, although this is more strategic for feed manufacturers than for millers. The former compare the Board's selling prices (and associated costs such as transport) with the prices of other domestically produced grains (for example, feed wheat) and world market prices of yellow maize. Millers, in effect, have an assured market for maize meal in the absence of strong competition from substitutes, and there is no significant international trade in white maize to provide an alternative to domestic supply. (Other relevant but less central actors in the maize *filière* include the banks which lend to the Maize Board, co-operatives, and farmers; agricultural input production and distribution companies; the state railway company which transports maize; producer organisations in branches whose fortunes are affected by trends in the maize industry, for example, in other grains and in cattle).

The *filière* sketched is characterised by a high degree of regulation, especially the statutory control of marketing with administered prices. The historical origin of this control scheme reflected concerns to secure stability of supply and of prices, including the effect of stable prices for farmers' incomes. More recently, the effectiveness of single-channel marketing in meeting these concerns has been increasingly questioned in the context of a general government commitment to greater 'market orientation'. This is manifested in the gradual withdrawal of various forms of subsidy and support to maize farmers, and to the Maize Board and the marketing system it operates.

For the Board, the main change has been in the mode of calculating producer or buying prices: from de facto 'cost plus' prices to prices based on projected market realisation. A key element of the latter is a downward sliding scale according to the extent that harvests exceed domestic demand of 6.5 million tons. This is to cover the costs of storage, and especially of losses on exports of maize surplus to requirements (costs previously met by the government). With the introduction of the new system of price determination, there has been a growing gap between the Maize Board's buying and selling prices, to the dissatisfaction of both farmers (who realise a smaller share of the final price of maize and maize products) and feed manufacturers (especially on the coast), who believe that they could import yellow maize more cheaply than buying it from the Board.

Policy debate centres on the abolition of statutory marketing and price determination, together with import liberalisation (replacing physical controls with tariffs, in any case now required by GATT). The argument for such 'deregulation' is that competition will generate greater efficiency not only in marketing but also in farming and processing, with net gains to the economy, including to the consumers of maize products.

This version of the story does not mention South Africa, nor does it need to – it simply absorbs the 'problems' of South African agriculture and their 'solutions' in a generalised discourse of 'regulation' and 'deregulation'. The sources, forms and effects of market regulation and reform, and their contestations, carry no imprint of the distinctive trajectory of capitalist development in the context of South Africa's 'racial order' (to use the expression of Greenberg, [1980]). Nothing of the latter is evident in this first version of the maize story, which employs the discourse of the protagonists of its 'deregulation' debate: an all-white debate about the organisation of an all-white industry. A different version confronts relations of production and power, how they are embedded in institutions that structure markets, and in terms of which alternative conceptions of restructuring markets – that is, alternative modes of regulation – can be posed.

THE STORY OF A MAIZE *FILIÈRE* II

A different version of the maize story is located in the context of the distinctive development of capitalism in South Africa, with its principal and extreme features of combined class exploitation and national oppression (outlined in the first essay in this volume). Key to the maize bonanza years of the 1960s and 1970s were the provision of cheap finance to farmers (at negative real interest rates), and guaranteed market sales at 'cost plus' prices, supported by various subsidies. These measures underwrote mechanisation, the adoption of improved varieties and heavy applications of chemical fertilisers, and the expansion of maize planting (including on marginal soils, notably in the western Transvaal); the construction of modern silos and bulk handling facilities by the co-operatives; and the disposal of surplus maize in good harvest years.

It is frequently observed that these mechanisms of regulation stimulated concentration both in farming and throughout the agricultural sector. The latter is understood here as encompassing (a) all the linkages of farming backwards (to chemical, seed and machinery production, and to finance) and forwards (to marketing, processing, distribution), (b) how these linkages shape farm labour processes and technology, and (c) how they affect, and are affected by, government policies [*Bernstein*, 1994a]. On one hand, concentration in farming, and/or its subordination to corporate capital (agribusiness, food industries), represents a general trend in contemporary capitalism. On the other hand, in South Africa it also bears the particular imprint of agricultural regulation under apartheid, not least as the bonanza gave way to an incipient crisis in the maize *filière* from the early 1980s (see below). In the familiar dynamic of capitalism, crises prepare the way for restructuring, for new forms of regulation and conditions of accumulation, that also accentuate previous tendencies to concentration.

Growing concentration in farming, in marketing (via the grain co-operatives), and in processing (milling and feed manufacture), are evident in South Africa in the decades before 1980 and since then. The total number of white farm units declined from (approximately) 104,000 in 1960 to 70,000 in the early 1980s and 59,000 in the late 1980s. In the mid-1980s six per cent of white farms generated about 40 per cent of gross farm income (see further Marcus 1989, on concentration). There is also a trend, through takeovers and amalgamation, to fewer and bigger grain cooperatives. Today six co-operatives account for the great bulk of marketed maize, of which two 'giants' stand out: the Central West Transvaal Coop at Klerksdorp, and the Eastern Transvaal Coop at Bethal. The high degree of concentration of milling and feed manufacture in corporate enterprises has been attributed to the system of licensed sales operated by the Maize Board, which favours the biggest buyers of maize [*Smith*, 1981]. However, these enterprises are also subsidiaries of the handful of conglomerates that dominate the South African economy. According to Dor [1992], Premier Milling (Liberty) accounts for 20 per cent of all maize meal, and Tiger Foods (Barlow Rand) for 25 per cent of maize meal and a remarkable 50 per cent of animal feeds; other big corporate concerns include Tongaat-Hulett (Anglo-American) and Foodcorp (Sanlam). To extend the illustration further downstream: just one poultry company, Rainbow Chickens, uses half a million tons of yellow maize annually, that is, 15 per cent of total domestic market sales.

Before considering the points of pressure, and more recent emergence of crisis in the maize industry, how does the *filière* (and its location within the wider political economy) affect the black population of South Africa? And which types of people within it? There is not the space here to elaborate on the complex social differentiation of the black population – its ubiquitous (if not uniform) divisions of class and gender, its urban-rural differences (and connections) – but we can briefly consider the positions of blacks as maize farmers, workers, and consumers.

Black farmers also grow maize but we do not know how many, how much, where, or in what ways. This reflects the general lack of reliable data on demographic, social and economic conditions in the (former) bantustans, where roughly half of the black population (of 30 million) live in an area equivalent to one-sixth of the land fenced by white farms. Lack of knowledge of their conditions of life is itself a product of apartheid. For example, in an extensive recent report on the maize industry [*Willemse et al.*, 1993] which contains 27 tables of data, there is just one table on maize farming in the bantustans (on areas planted to maize in 1988!).

Blanket 'guestimates' hover around a (conveniently round) figure of 10 per cent of the bantustan population that derives any significant element of its livelihoods from its own farming. Most of these farmers are women cultivating 'sub-subsistence' plots for household food provisioning. The smaller numbers of petty commodity producers are mostly men engaged in more specialised cash crop farming, combined with growing food for household consumption and possibly local sales as well. The only more substantial black maize farmers, of whom there is some systemic evidence, are in parts of (former) Bophuthatswana bordering the western Transvaal [*Stacey*, 1992].[12] Their activity has been constrained by both the exactions of a bantustan state agricultural scheme, and the need to sell their crop through the Northwest Transvaal Coop in Lichtenburg, on inferior terms to those of its (exclusively) white farmer members.

Maize production in the bantustan areas is of concern to the established interests of the maize *filière* (especially the Maize Board and millers) only to the extent that a good harvest increases the (limited) scale of self-provisioning, thereby reducing demand for industrially processed maize meal.

Black workers are the majority of the labour force on the farms, and in maize handling, storage, milling, manufacture, and distribution. The massive reduction in black farm labour families on maize farms from the 1970s was noted earlier, but can not be quantified. Farm workers on the highveld have barely been reached by trade union organisation, if at all, although there have been efforts to provide them with legal representation in some cases of dismissal, eviction and physical assaults by employers. Trade union organisation of other black workers – notably through FAWU (Food and Allied Workers Union) – has proceeded much further, if unevenly so, in both the big co-operatives (grain handling, storage, milling) and in corporate enterprises in maize processing and distribution [*Labour Research Service*, 1988].

Income distribution in South Africa, hence the distribution of entitlements and levels of consumption, follows the contours of its 'racial order', as one would expect. The 1991 household census indicates that blacks (75 per cent of the population) earned 25 per cent of total income. However, income distribution within the black population is the most unequal of the four 'population groups' (black, coloured, Asian, white), and increasingly so. The Gini coefficient of black income distribution rose from 0.47 to 0.62 between 1975 and 1991; in 1991 the poorest 40 per cent of households in the total population earned just four per cent of total income [*Whiteford*, 1994].

This is relevant as maize meal is the staple carbohydrate of poor (rather than all) black people, especially those in the bantustans, who are mostly (and for the majority, entirely) dependent on sources of supply other than their own farming and any locally supplied markets. These sources of supply are maize meal (and other foods) conveyed by migrant workers, 'commuters', and urban relatives, or distributed through (typically small) black retail shops, or maize sold directly into bantustan areas by neighbouring white farmers in contravention of marketing regulations and to realise higher prices than those offered by the Maize Board (a practice said to have increased in recent years). While there is no systematic evidence, retail prices of maize meal in bantustan rural areas are higher than in metropolitan areas, so that many of the poorest people pay more for their staple food.

It seems almost superfluous to add that consumers of maize meal have lacked any effective representation of their interests in the Maize Board (or other institutions of the *filière*), in contrast to millers and both producers and consumers of animal feeds. The only successful action on behalf of consumers was through the anti-VAT (value-added tax) campaign of COSATU (Congress of South African Trade Unions) in 1992. This was the drought year when food price inflation escalated beyond an already high rate of general inflation. As the government introduced VAT, the strongly supported trade union campaign succeeded in getting maize meal and some other basic foods exempted from the new tax provisions.

Finally, it is interesting to note that sales of maize meal have increased in recent years. While this is partly due to rapid black population growth, the Maize Board also claims credit for its advertising and promotion campaigns for maize products. However, it seems likely that increased sales also reflect growing poverty and the inability to purchase such alternatives as wheat products and rice. A revealing indication is what happened in the wake of the harvest failure of 1992. The Maize Board ordered that maize meal contain a mixture of white maize and at least 50 per cent (imported) yellow maize. On previous occasions consumers' aversion to this type of mixture was reflected in sharply reduced sales of maize meal; that this did not occur in 1992 and 1993 further suggests the extent of poverty in constraining consumer 'choice'.

From Bonanza to Crisis

The story of the maize *filière* can now be extended to the emergence and growth of crisis from the early 1980s. This account provides a basis for then returning to the current debate over 'deregulation' of maize marketing signalled earlier.

The conjuncture of the early 1980s combined a number of developments within the maize *filière* and its wider setting, and their interactions. First, in 1980 NAMPO (National Maize Producers Organisation) was established as the exclusive commodity organisation for maize recognised by the SAAU and the government. NAMPO derived from SAMPI (South African Maize Producers Institute), whose origins and history provide the one striking exception to the earlier generalisation about NP (and *Broederbond*) domination of the institutions of 'organised', that is, white, agriculture. Indeed, SAMPI was founded in 1966 explicitly to contest the NP machine politics of the Maize Board, and the SAAU and its provincial and commodity organisations, drawing on an ideological heritage of frontier populism and its 'rugged individualism' in the northwestern Orange Free State and adjacent areas of the western Transvaal [*Marais*, 1991].

Once established, NAMPO took control of the Maize Board to pursue its project of the aggrandisement of 'King Maize', as one might call it (on the analogy of 'King Cotton' in the history of the southern USA). The overt agenda of this project was to obtain better prices and other conditions for maize farmers, but there was also a more hidden, and highly ambitious, agenda: to establish the control of NAMPO over key linkages in the *filière* (for example, fertiliser supply, management of exports), and to make 'King Maize' dominant in the institutions and politics of 'organised' agriculture as a whole (and in competition with the powerful forces of the red meat industry).

Coinciding with SAMPI's, now NAMPO's, long plotted capture of the Maize Board, South Africa's white farmers produced their biggest ever harvest of 14.4 million tons in 1981, much of which had to be exported at great loss subsidised by the government. This highlighted a growing tension in the regulation of the maize *filière*. From 1980–85 NAMPO pursued its grandiose project, partly within and through the Maize Board, in increasing conflict with the government. In 1985 the Minister of Agriculture refused to raise the buying price of maize, and NAMPO members of the Board resigned. The 'reformism' of the NP regime of P.W. Botha now included a commitment to greater 'market orientation', including phasing out subsidies to farming and other moves in the direction of 'deregulation'. The rapid inflation of maize prices during NAMPO's reign at the Maize Board had also antagonised big business (because of its effect on wage struggles) and, according to Marx [1992: 149–50], contributed to a new surge of militant black politics.[13]

Moreover, in 1982 the Conservative Party (CP) was formed by a split from the NP in protest against its 'reformism'. The CP immediately attracted strong support in the maize heartlands of the OFS and Transvaal, where it went on to capture control of the provincial agricultural unions and to intervene in the leading grain cooperatives. In short, the internal politics of the system of agricultural regulation shifted radically, while the electoral base of the NP had broadened and no longer relied on rural constituencies. Without elaborating on that politics, my view (from my own research) is that the positions of NAMPO did not simply reflect the extreme Afrikaner party allegiances of the highveld [*Charney*, 1987], despite their shared social geography.

NAMPO had overreached itself in 1985. Following internal realignments, it returned to the Maize Board in 1987 with a still strategic but suitably more modest vision of the maize industry, and the place of farmers in it. NAMPO negotiated its re-entry with a package of measures centred on the new system of price determination by projected market realisation (noted earlier), together with rules that now prohibited the Maize Board from deficit financing of its operations. On its side, the government wrote off the accumulated debt of the Board's stabilisation fund (some R400 m), and financed an incentive scheme (proposed by NAMPO) to convert marginal maize land to grazing.

While NAMPO has remained adept at securing whatever sources of subsidy are still available to maize farmers, the general level of government support to agriculture declined significantly in the 1980s. In the 1960s and 1970s, mechanisation and expansion of maize farming was financed largely with soft credit from the state Land Bank channelled through the grain cooperatives, whose share of total farm debt increased from eight per cent in 1970 to 23 per cent in 1980. The enormous growth of farm debt that followed (from R867 million in 1980 to R16 billion in 1990) was financed more by the commercial banks, whose share increased from 21 per cent to 31 per cent while that of the Land Bank/co-operatives remained constant.

The massive farm debt of 1990 indicates an 'accumulation crisis' in agriculture, that is, a structural crisis of profitability and liquidity, exacerbated but not created by the cyclical effects of drought [de Klerk, 1991]. Simultaneously with the gradual replacement of concessionary by commercial credit, the terms of trade for maize farmers declined as input costs rose more rapidly than the Maize Board's buying prices, especially since the institution of the new pricing system in 1987. The problems of maize farmers, and the pressures on their historically entrenched position in the filière, were compounded further by a mounting political offensive for more comprehensive 'deregulation'. This is discussed in the next section, which also considers how the co-operatives and corporate milling interests positioned themselves in the 'transition' from 1990 to 1994.

Before that, it is worth noting the paradox by which many maize farmers were granted a stay of execution by the drought of 1991–2. The government of F.W. de Klerk, now immersed in the constitutional negotiations to end apartheid, granted a 'drought relief' package of over R3 billion in 1992–3, mostly directed to cushioning farmers' debts to the co-operatives. There were two strategic reasons for this. The first was to reproduce existing property rights and relations beyond the end of apartheid, by preventing foreclosures and maintaining prices in the land market to obstruct any land reform programme of a future ANC government. The second was to strengthen the capital assets of the cooperatives (see further below).[14]

As a result, a larger area was planted to maize in 1992–93 (3.5 million hectares) than in 1991–92 (3 million hectares), with a harvest of some eight million tons: 1.5 million tons above the point at which the sliding scale of buying prices, pegged to domestic market requirements of 6.5 million tons, starts to operate. The disarray in the maize industry (including pressure from corporate millers) was reflected in the Maize Board's inability to agree prices for the 1993–94 marketing season, so that prices were set by the cabinet. In 1993, maize farmers again extended their planting (to perhaps 3.9 million hectares) in a bid to realise the most of their last maize price of the apartheid era. Together with very good rains, this produced a harvest of 12.1 million tons, the largest since 1981. But the NP government declined to set prices for the maize marketing season that began on 1 May. The new ANC-led government, elected in South Africa's first non-racial general election at the end of April 1994, now had to decide how to deal with this bumper crop, as well as confronting strategic issues of restructuring the maize *filière* in future.

Regulation through 'Deregulation'

The crisis in the maize *filière* at the end of apartheid is not symmetrically distributed (no crisis ever is), but affects in particular (weaker) maize farmers (as noted), the weaker of the grain co-operatives, the Maize Board itself, and consumers of maize meal. I come back to these and other actors in the *filière* in considering the campaign for 'deregulation' of the maize market.

The notion of 'deregulation' embodies a conception of markets located in a continuum of greater to lesser 'regulation', with an idealised fully 'free' and competitive market at the latter end of this continuum. The English language sense of 'regulation', as conventionally employed here, means legislative, policy and administrative measures affecting the structure and performance (competitiveness, 'efficiency') of markets. The key assumption is that regulation is 'external' to markets (or how markets should be), and their proper function of price formation through the (unhindered) operation of demand and supply.

Such notions dominate debate concerning market reform (and agricultural restructuring more generally) in South Africa, where all major agricultural commodities have been subject to different types of control schemes under the Marketing Act, with maize the most important case of single channel marketing. As implied earlier, the last phase of apartheid saw a gathering and combative campaign for the 'deregulation' of agricultural markets, that brought together big business interests, some 'renegade' producers organisations (for example, beef and dairy farmers), and (white) consumer groups. The case for 'deregulation' has been articulated by various business leaders and economists, proclaimed by the business press (notably the *Financial Mail*), and endorsed in recent government reports [*RSA*, 1992a; 1992b] and by the World Bank [1993].

Given that the historic rationale of South Africa's modes of agricultural regulation was to support white farmers, calls for 'deregulation' have a powerful ideological resonance at the end of apartheid. To dismantle such structures is to promote both efficiency and equity: efficiency for the standard reasons noted, equity by removing barriers to entry and entrepreneurship by those 'disadvantaged' under the 'racial order'. The universality of citizenship in the new constitution is to be matched by liberating markets from (racial) particularism, extending their promise of free, competitive activity to all. As the World Bank has put it, the 'guiding principle [is] political and economic liberalization' (cited by Williams [1993: 2]): the road to freedom and prosperity in South Africa is charted through 'deregulation'. As in the ideological framework of structural adjustment elsewhere in Africa, (virtually) all stand to gain, with the only losers those who have benefited from the rents and other unwarranted gains of state economic regulation [*Bernstein*, 1990].

This conception contains a crucial assumption that 'deregulation' is the only credible solution to the problems of any given system of regulation. A broader sense of 'regulation' noted earlier (and more common in French than English language usage) refers to how markets are structured by different and particular forms of power and control. Those forms are both economic and political, can be generated inside markets as well as outside them, and often dissolve the conventional conceptual boundaries of what is 'endogenous' and 'exogenous' to markets. This usage incorporates the recognition that 'regulation' is an intrinsic, and indeed constitutive, element of markets in the real world and how they function.

The primary objective of 'deregulation' of the maize market in South Africa is abolition of the statutory powers of the Maize Board, opening up the organisation of trade to entrepreneurs, and price formation to demand and supply. A reformed Maize Board is an option: to act as a buyer (of last resort) at floor prices, to monitor imports to prevent unfair dumping, to provide market information and analysis. These are the recommendations of the Kassier Committee of Inquiry into the Marketing Act, which suggested that deregulation 'should ensure that sufficient supplies of food at afford-able and internationally competitive prices are available at the household level' [*RSA*, 1992b: xii].

Will it? The removal of assured sales at uniform prices, together with the ending of financial support to white farmers, would squeeze out econo-mically weaker maize producers. In other respects, however, the Maize Board presides over, rather than underpins, the maize *filière*, in which the current scale of concentration and power would persist, or grow, following the abolition of statutory controls. First, of course, bigger and stronger maize farmers may continue to expand their scale of operations, as in the past. Second, the big grain co-operatives had been preparing for the abolition of the statutory controls of the Maize Board, and for the (eventual) demise of apartheid, since at least the mid-1980s. The basis of the co-operatives' strategy is their near monopoly control of the infrastructure of bulk handling and storage of maize in the highveld, and its principal thrust to enhance their capital formation independently of the historic association with the Land Bank and Maize Board (see further below).

As already noted, corporate milling and feed manufacture interests, and also food wholesaling and distribution through supermarket chains, are characterised by a high degree of concentration. (Metro, the largest food wholesale company in South Africa, that supplies most black retailers, is owned by Premier Food Industries, one of the corporate giants of milling.) Even agricultural economists favouring market 'deregulation' have stressed that 'it should be accompanied by a simultaneous deconcentration exercise in the [food] manufacturing, distribution and retail industries. This would in some way [*sic*] avoid further price increases and a further increase in the producer-retail price gap. It is therefore necessary to introduce strong anti-trust and monopoly legislation' [*van Zyl and Kirsten*, 1992: 179]. While 'deregulation' thus seems to involve the enactment and/or more effective implementation of certain measures of regulation, the World Bank is sceptical of their effectiveness (and desirability?):

> An active anti-trust policy is 'likely to prove difficult' given the 'financial leverage' of 'existing conglomerates' and the likelihood that divested subsidiaries will remain in the hands of one or another of those institutions. All that remains is to 'promote changes in the economic environment' by regulating statutory (ie government, HB) monopolies and restrictive barriers to entry and prosecuting restrictive practices [*Williams*, 1993: 16, summarising *World Bank*, 1993].

These observations and prescriptions offer less assurance of food supply 'at affordable and internationally competitive prices' to South Africa's poor than Professor Kassier's committee suggested market 'deregulation' would provide. Moreover, they contain a further assumption that competition is intrinsic, and indeed 'natural' to markets, which deliver the goods unless obstructed from doing so. The principal source of obstruction is government action ('regulation' in the conventional sense), which is – conveniently enough – also the most easily identified and remedied. A secondary source of obstruction may be (illegitimate) 'manipulation' of sales and prices through concentration of market shares, collusion among (major) market actors, and so on. The former is the primary target of 'deregulation'; the latter represents a slight complication, a footnote to the main story (of getting the state out of the market), and can be addressed by measures to prevent restriction of competition. This attenuated notion of 'competition policy' reflects the abstract, residual and naturalistic underlying view of the inherently competitive, hence 'efficient', market; at best, it promises the most frail of defences against the increasing concentration of both co-operative and corporate capital, and of their mutual accommodation.

Postscript: Developments in 1994–95

The maize prices for the 1994–95 marketing season were announced in early June 1994 (more than a month after the usual start of the season), having been decided by three Ministers of the new Government of National Unity: those for Agriculture (the same NP Minister as before the election), and for Land Affairs and Trade and Industry (both ANC). The Maize Board's sale price for white maize remained the same as the previous year, with a slight reduction in the price of yellow maize (a token concession to the feed manufacturers and consumers). But the buying price increased significantly, exceeding the expectations of NAMPO and against the recommendations of both the feed industry and the LAPC (Land and Agriculture Policy Centre, an ANC established 'think tank'). The maize farmers got their end of apartheid 'dividend' after all, and at whose expense?

Concerning the future of the Maize Board: the Kassier Committee that recommended the deregulation of agricultural commodity markets at the end of 1992 (above) was followed by AMPEC (Agricultural Marketing Policy Evaluation Committee), in which 'organised' (that is, white) agriculture was strongly represented. The first of AMPEC's (delayed) reports appeared in early 1994, its chairman noting that 'each of the 29 members disagreed with parts of the report' (*Finance Week*, 3–9 Feb. 1994). After the election, in June the Minister of Agriculture appointed a (much smaller) Maize Facilitating Committee, whose proposals the next month resumed the process of 'edging to deregulation', in the words of the *Financial Mail* (22 July 1994). Thereafter the Minister announced the formation of a Technical Working Group to Revise the Marketing Act, consisting of eight Afrikaners (from the inherited nexus of 'organised' agriculture) and two blacks 'representing' small farmer and consumer organisations – 'new role players in agriculture', as the official discourse has it (Department of Agriculture press release, 26 Sept. 1994).

On one hand, the form of such procrastination is familiar from the stonewalling long practised by 'organised' agriculture. On the other hand, it occupies another three years (from the appointment of the Kassier Committee in June 1992 to the start of the 1995–96 maize marketing season), during which the key agents of the *filière* continued to reposition themselves, above all the big grain co-operatives, as described earlier. It is likely that the Maize Board will finally lose its statutory powers in 1995, broadly along the lines proposed by Kassier in December 1992 (and supported by the milling industry, animal feed users, the World Bank *et al.*). This ostensibly historic 'deregulation' will be enacted when other, more potent forces have secured the conditions of their (private) regulation of the market. *Plus ça change, mais ... .*

CONCLUSION

> 'The hidden monopolies and controls that exist in agriculture by virtue of the control linkages between agricultural credit, marketing, commercial co-operatives, the Land Bank and the SAAU, must be broken up to enable new farmers to enter the sector' [*ANC*, 1992: 33–4].

This statement, from the Policy Guidelines generated by the ANC National Conference in May 1992, indicates a keen sense of issues of regulation in its broad sense, as used in this paper. In practice, the principal policy thrust of the new government, continuing that of the last government, is on marketing reform: 'deregulation' as narrowly (and misleadingly) conceived.

It could be considered that the emergent system of regulation, suggested above, manifests simply the 'normal' trajectory of corporate agribusiness. However, this does not grasp the special place of the grain cooperatives in a new system of regulation, and how it serves their strategic project.[15] On one hand, they employ familiar methods of agribusiness: takeovers and amalgamations, diversification and increasing vertical integration, futures trading in the new South African Futures Exchange, and so on. Perhaps the most striking symbolic expression of this is the recent conversion of the giant East Transvaal Cooperative (OTK) to a private company under the provisions of the 1993 Co-operatives Amendment Act.

On the other hand, and unlike more conventional agribusiness, the co-operatives are *regionally* based entitities, with highly ramified linkages throughout the spatial economy of the highveld and a distinctive connection with white landed property and farming. That the strategic aim of the grain cooperatives is to reproduce the historic white domination of the rural highveld can be illustrated briefly by several instances of recent changes, the significance of which has gone largely unremarked.

First, the Amendment Act of 1993 allows co-operatives to buy land, which they can use to maintain white control of land as economically pressured farmers (including those indebted to the co-operatives) sell up.

Second, the Act also allows cooperatives to greatly expand their business with non-members. While this was partly a retrospective legitimation of existing practices, it accompanied a new wave of expansion of co-operative activity in neighbouring black rural areas. As the ramshackle agricultural development corporations in the northern bantustans started to collapse altogether after 1990, the cooperatives moved in to sell inputs (and consumer goods, including the staple maize meal) to black farmers and other rural people. Third, and connected with this, the co-operatives now present themselves to provincial governments as agents to design, deliver and manage agricultural development projects in the former bantustans, that is, as standard bearers of the Reconstruction and Development Programme.[16]

What then of the Co-operative Council, a – or the – principal component of the SAAU, hence the political bloc of 'organised' agriculture? How can it accommodate key organisations of white supremacy in highveld agriculture that no longer have the legal status of co-operatives (as the former OTK)? The answer is that the Council has reconstituted itself as the Agricultural Cooperative Business Chamber (ACB) which is able to maintain the membership of 'companies established by co-operatives transforming themselves into companies but remain (*sic*) under the control and ownership of farmers and co-operatives'.[17]

What this means is that the ACB incorporates the same forces and organisations (despite changes in names and legal status) as the old Co-operative Council; it continues *de facto* as the political bloc of white agricultural interests. In short, the forms of business organisation, methods and practices – and the system of regulation they seek to establish and control – are both vehicle and cover for the reproduction of white landed property and agrarian power in the highveld.

NOTES

1. These stages are most appropriately distinguished as *activities* or *functions* (see further below). According to the nature of the farm product, and the technology and labour process of its production, different types and degrees of first stage processing may take place on farm as well.
2. See, for example, Dor [1992] for a calculation of the composition and distribution of the consumer rand of maize meal in South Africa.
3. In practice, of course, it may be very difficult to measure price formation and value added along the chain because of commercial secrecy as well as for technical reasons; this applies *a fortiori* when such data are used to assess the 'efficiency' of markets through which the commodity passes and the rates of profit of agents in those markets. See the controversy in South Africa around the BTT (Board of Tariffs and Trade) report on the price mechanism in the food chain [RSA, 1992a] that 'exonerated' the big food distribution companies, to the scepticism of the trade unions and food consumers, and indeed of another government report published in the same year of galloping food price inflation [RSA, 1992b].
4. As so often in social science the *filières vivrières* approach developed at CIRAD represents a

new synthesis or application of existing ideas, which does not detract from its value. A fine example of a *filière* type analysis, *avant la lettre,* is Boesen and Mohele's [1979] study of tobacco in Tanzania that links 'the political economy of a commodity producing peasantry' with the organisation of the world market in tobacco and global manufacture of tobacco products.

5. This is an important point, if a somewhat clumsy formulation. Conventional economists of any sophistication know that real world markets are likely to be 'imperfect' to some degree or other, for some reason or other. The notion of *'degree'* of imperfection, of course expresses deviation from the abstract norm of perfect competition, and is thus a mode of characterisation rather than a means of explanation. The latter involves conventional economists in identifying the reasons for (varying degrees of) market imperfection as deviation from the abstract norm. This may be because there is too little of some things (for example, information), too much of others (for example, transaction costs; concentration of market shares by a few big market 'actors'), or illegitimate 'interference' with market mechanisms (eg through collusion in market sharing and/or price fixing; and above all through government regulation).

6. For illuminating indications of how market power can be operationalised in empirical investigation and analysis, see Harriss-White [in press].

7. I am grateful to Maureen Mackintosh (personal communication) for this point.

8. The work of the research group at CIRAD in Montpellier includes studies of *filières* in which a dynamic petty commodity production dominates, or has a substantial share in, production, processing and/or trade, for example, of rice in northern Ghana [*Samuels et al.,* 1992] and of vegetables in several African cities [*Moustier,* 1993].

9. How the maize *filière* fits into the broader political economy of South Africa is suggested below. The underlying methodological stance of this study is that South Africa necessarily manifests both the essential features, dynamics and contradictions of the capitalist mode of production and the historically specific forms of property, production, power and social struggle through which capitalism has developed there. In this respect I would distance myself from Goodman and Watts [1994], whose reponse to what they consider determinist views of the tendencies of (globalising) capital in agriculture is to invoke a (virtually unlimited?) diversity of forms (including the particularities of *filières*). This seems to resonate a post-modernist aversion to 'totalisation' (what was once called a holistic analysis), that avoids the dialectical challenge of grasping both the general tendencies of capital and its historically specific forms, embracing the latter and repudiating the former (there is no forest, only trees). An expression of this is the contrast between their estimation and mine of the work of Friedmann [1993], which concerns not just the substance (and importance) of her argument but the nature and style of the theoretical project that produced her findings..

10. This formulation is perhaps biased towards the features of petty commodity production and small capitalist enterprise. The terrain of corporate capital is different in that it incorporates activities that are highly specialised organisationally (for example, milling companies) and technically (massive grain mills) within highly diversified conglomerate holdings, an illustration of the concentration and centralisation of capital respectively.

11. A question put to me by Richard Pearce and Philip Raikes in personal communications.

12. There are also some big African maize farmers in the eastern highveld. At a meeting with the Northern Region African Farmers Union (NORAFU) in Pietersburg in April 1995, one committee member told me that he has 247 ha under maize which yielded over 5,700 bags of grain in that year's harvest.

13. Marx [1992: 245] records a worker he interviewed in Soweto in 1988 as saying 'Mealie (i.e. maize) meal is politics here. We have no other politics.'

14. The R3.4 billion paid out by the government to white agriculture in 1992–93 was covered by an IMF loan, another item in the legacy left by apartheid to constrain a new democratic government; see Padayachee [1994].

15. The following briefly summarises some of the findings of a substantial study by Amin and Bernstein [1996], which we hope to publish as a monograph in due course.

16. The image-building offensive to establish their place in the 'new' South Africa is exemplified in the special supplement on *Agricultural Co-operatives* to the *F & T Weekly,* 22 Oct. 1995, especially the article titled 'Geared to the RDP' (p.30).

17. Supplement to *F & T Weekly*, 22 Oct. 1995, p.33. The tortuous formulation reflects the complex formal (legal) and informal (political) manoeuvres through which OTK converted itself into a particular form of private company. These manoeuvres are explained in Amin and Bernstein [1996]; underlying them is a combined strategy of consolidating the property rights of existing members and management in the assets of OTK, closing entry to any new members (that is, black farmers and other entrepreneurs), and allowing for expanded capital formation by a future listing of the new company on the Johannesburg Stock Exchange.

REFERENCES

Amin, N., and H. Bernstein,1996, *The Role of Agricultural Co-operatives in Agricultural and Rural Development*, report for the LAPC, Johannesburg.

ANC (African National Congress), 1992, *Ready to Govern: Policy Guidelines for a Democratic South Africa*, Johannesburg: ANC.

Benz, H. et al., 1994, *Methodes d'analyse des rapports sociaux dans les échanges vivriers en Afrique at en Asie du Sud*, Montpellier: CIRAD.

Bernstein, H., 1990, 'Agricultural "Modernisation" and the Era of Structural Adjustment: Observations on sub-Saharan Africa', *Journal of Peasant Studies*, Vol.18, No.1.

Bernstein, H, 1994a 'Agrarian Classes in Capitalist Development', in L Sklair (ed.), *Capitalism and Development,* London: Routledge.

Bernstein, H., 1994b, 'Food Security in a Democratic South Africa', *Transformation* 24.

Bernstein, H., Crow, B., Mackintosh, M. and C. Martin (eds.), 1990, *The Food Question*, London: Earthscan.

Bernstein, H. and A. Leplaideur (eds.) (in press), *Exchange Relations and Food Provisioning. Studies from Africa and South Asia*, London: Macmillan.

Boesen, K. amd A.T. Mohele, 1979, *The 'Success Story' of Peasant Tobacco Production in Tanzania*, Uppsala: Scandinavian Institute of African Studies.

Bundy, C., 1979, *The Rise and Fall of the South African Peasantry*, London: Heinemann.

Charney, C., 1987, 'The National Party, 1982–1985: A Class Alliance in Crisis', in W.G. James (ed.), *The State of Apartheid*, Boulder, CO: Lynne Reiner.

Crow, B. (in press) 'Class and Seasonal Differences in Exchange Conditions in Rural Bangladesh', in Bernstein and Leplaideur.

de Klerk, M, 1985, 'The Labour Process in Agriculture: Changes in Maize Farming in the 1970s', *Social Dynamics*, Vol.11, No.1.

de Klerk, M, 1991, 'The Accumulation Crisis in Agriculture', in Gelb (ed.) [1991].

Dor, G., 1992, 'The Politics of Food', *New Ground* 8.

Drèze, J., and A. Sen, 1989, *Hunger and Public Action*, Oxford: Clarendon.

Friedmann, H., 1993, 'The Political Economy of Food: A Global Crisis', *New Left Review* 197.

Gelb, S., (ed.), 1991, *South Africa's Economic Crisis*, Cape Town: David Philip.

Goodman, D., and M. Watts, 1994, 'Reconfiguring the Rural or Fording the Divide?: Capitalist Restructuring and the Global Agro-Food System', *Journal of Peasant Studies* 22(1).

Greenberg, S.B., 1980, R*ace and State in Capitalist Development: South Africa in Comparative Perspective*, New Haven, CT: Yale University Press.

Harriss, B., 1990, 'Another Awkward Class: Merchants and Agrarian Change in India', in Bernstein *et al.* [1990].

Harriss-White, B. (in press), 'The Politics of Market Systems: Neglected Dimension of *Filières,* with a Case Study from West Bengal', in Bernstein and Leplaideur (in press).

Hewitt de Alcantara, C., (ed.), 1992, *Real Markets: Social and Political Issues of Food Policy Reform*, special issue of *European Journal of Development Research*, Vol.4, No.2.

Janakarajan, S. (in press), 'Exchange Relations as Power Relations: A South Indian Case Study', in Bernstein and Leplaideur (in press).

Labour Research Service, 1988, *Milling: Sector Review for the Food and Allied Workers Union*, Salt River: Labour Research Service.

Leplaideur, A. *et al.,* 1990, *Quelques premières informations sur l'économie du riz en Guinée Conakry,* Montpellier: CIRAD.

Mackintosh, M., 1990, 'Abstract Markets and Real Needs', in Bernstein *et al.* [1990].

Marais, A.H., n.d. (1991?), *SAMPI. Stryd om Autonomie Spesialisasie in die Mieliebedryf 1966–1980*, Bothaville: NAMPO.

Marcus, T., 1989, *Modernizing Super-Exploitation: Restructuring South African Agriculture*, London: Zed Books.

Marx, A., 1992, *Lessons of Struggle: South African Internal Opposition, 1960–1990*, Cape Town: Oxford University Press.

Moustier, P., 1993, '*An Evaluation of Urban Food Supply in Africa: Case Studies of the Vegetable Filières Supplying Brazzaville, Bangui and Antananarivo*', draft Ph.D. thesis, University of London: Wye College.

Moustier, P., 1994, 'Rèflexion autour du cas du commerce légumier à Brazzaville', in Benz *et al.* [1994].

Olsen, W (in press) 'Competititon and Power in Local Markets: A South Indian Case Study', in Bernstein and Leplaideur.

Padayachee, V., 1994, 'Debt, Development and Democracy: The IMF in Post-Apartheid South Africa', *Review of African Political Economy* 62.

Rival, L. (in press), 'Locating Power in Markets: Anthropological Contributions to the Study of Food Trading', in Bernstein and Leplaideur.

RSA (Republic of South Africa), 1992a, *An Investigation into the Price Mechanism in the Food Chain*, Pretoria: Board of Tariffs and Trade.

RSA, 1992b, *Report of the Committee of Inquiry into the Marketing Act*, Pretoria: Department of Agriculture.

Samuels, F., Leplaideur, A. and B. Harriss, 1992, *Changing Agrarian Structure and Petty Commodity Production in the Northern Region of Ghana*, Montpellier, CIRAD.

Schrire, R., 1992, *Adapt or Die: The End of White Politics in South Africa*, New York: Ford Foundation.

Smith, P.M., 1981, *An Overview of the South African Maize Milling Industry*, University of Cape Town, Graduate School of Business, MBA Research Paper

Stacey, G., 1992, 'The Origins and Development of Commercial Farmers in the Ditsobotla and Molopo Regions of Bophuthatswana', University of Pretoria, Department of Agricultural Economics, MSC dissertation.

van Zyl, J. and J. Kirsten, 'Food Security in South Africa', *Agrekon*, Vol.31, No.4.

Whiteford, A., 1994, 'The Poor Get Even Poorer', *Weekly Mail*, 11–17 March .

Willemse, J., van Rensburg, G., Takavarasha, T. and J. van Zyl, 1993, *Agricultural Marketing: Maize*, Johannesburg: Land and Agriculture Policy Centre.

Williams, G., 1993. 'Setting the Agenda: A Critique of the World Bank's Rural Restructuring Programme for South Africa', unpublished paper, cited with author's permission.

World Bank, 1993, *South African Agriculture: Structure, Performance and Implications for the Future*, Washington, DC: World Bank.

Wuyts, M., Mackintosh, M. and T. Hewitt, (ed.), 1992, *Development Policy and Public Action*, Oxford: Oxford University Press.

Labour Organisation in Western Cape Agriculture: An Ethnic Corporatism?

JOACHIM EWERT and JOHANN HAMMAN

INTRODUCTION

South African commercial agriculture, perhaps more than any other sector of the economy, has always had a poor labour image. Especially in the days of apartheid-style influx controls, the labour regime on white-owned farms was said to be little short of despotic and ultra-exploitative. If anything had changed at all in recent decades, it was that this kind of 'super-exploitation' had been 'modernised', both in a technological and in a social sense [*Marcus*, 1989].

While few would disagree with this broad view, it is also true that macro-analyses of farm labour in South Africa largely failed to illuminate the particular dynamics and texture of labour arrangements in specific sectors of commercial agriculture. One of the sectors suffering from this kind of 'underexposure' is the fruit and wine industry of the Western Cape. Largely unnoticed by analysts and activists alike, labour arrangements on fruit and wine farms have undergone a quiet evolution over the last ten to fifteen years. Unmistakable changes in the way workers are recruited on the rural labour market, fitted into a formalised structure of work organisation and dealt with politically, have shifted these farms from the traditional low-wage, paternalist regime to a juncture where neo-paternalist relations are set to move into one of two directions: either a phase of increasing confrontation and adversarial bargaining or a situation where the paternalist legacy is transformed into a corporatist arrangement under which workers 'share' with farmers in decision making and even in ownership.

It is the central argument of this paper that the restructuring of labour

Joachim Ewert, Department of Sociology, University of Stellenbosch, 7600 Stellenbosch, South Africa; and Johann Hamman, Centre for Rural Legal Studies, 156 Dorp St., 7600 Stellenbosch, South Africa. The authors would like to thank Terence Fife and Antoine van Niekerk, both from the Centre for Rural Legal Studies, Stellenbosch, for their assistance in the fieldwork part of the study. They are also grateful to Simon Bekker, Albert van Zyl, Jerry Eckert, Gavin Williams and Henry Bernstein for their constructive comments on earlier drafts of the study. It was first presented as a paper at the 'Agrarian Questions' congress, held at the University of Wageningen, Wageningen, the Netherlands, 22–4 May 1995.

organisation on wine and fruit farms has less to do with the political transition in South Africa or the recent extension of labour legislation to agriculture,[1] than with a new competitive orientation on the part of leading farmers and managers in the Cape fruit and wine industry, the sanctions and boycott campaign against South African export goods and the potential 'threat' of the unionisation of farmworkers, which were the major forces behind the restructuring process starting in the early 1980s. However, given their subtle and cumulative nature, these changes only became apparent in more recent times.

MODERNISING WHAT? THE UNEVEN TRANSFORMATION OF LABOUR ORGANISATION IN AGRICULTURE

Before the 1990s prevailing debates about agricultural transformation in South Africa gave almost no hint that a new approach to labour had been emerging on Western Cape fruit and wine farms. The reasons for this neglect are not hard to find. First, the majority of studies did not focus on this region at all, but concentrated on the maize and wheat of the highveld and sugar in Natal. Secondly, the main concern of these studies was the transformation of squatting, share-cropping, labour tenancy and similar arrangements into capitalist relations of production. For instance, in two seminal articles Mike Morris [1976; 1977] argued that by the early 1930s wage labour on farms had become diffused to such an extent that white landowners no longer derived a substantial surplus from 'direct feudal rent (i.e., as a labour rent for the land he [the African farmworker] tilled)'; they derived it instead 'indirectly through the appropriation of the surplus value embodied in the agricultural commodities [the African farmworker] produced' [*Morris*, 1976: 304]. Even so, labour tenancy lingered on and it was only by the mid-1970's that the transformation to capitalist relations of production had been completed: ' ... [L]abour tenancy in South African agriculture had to all intents and purposes been abolished and farm labour was stabilised' [*Morris*, 1977: 71]. Thus, presumably, relations between landowner and farmworkers in the northern regions of South Africa had been brought in line with those in the Western Cape where, after the abolition of slavery in the 1830s, capitalist relations had been in existence for more than a century [*Scully*, 1987; *Bradford*, 1990].

One of the major forces behind the elimination of the labour tenancy system, it was argued, were changes in agricultural labour processes in the wake of the dramatic expansion, mechanization and scientification of farming operations after the Second World War. Tractors, mechanical harvesters, herbicides, pesticides, fungicides, chemical fertilisers and automatic irrigation were introduced on a big scale [*de Klerk*, 1984; *Budlender*, 1984]. As a result, the overall volume of agricultural production increased threefold in the three decades after 1945 [*Greenberg*, 1980]. This tendency towards increased mechanisation continued unabated before the mid-1980s saw the onset of a deep agricultural crisis [*de Klerk*, 1991: 222–4].

It was during this shift to large-scale, mechanised production, that spokesmen of the more progressive sections of the white farming establishment began to propagate a new orientation towards farm labour. Mechanisation, they argued, required a smaller, better-trained and better-paid force of regular workers. From about 1970 onwards, the South African Agricultural Union (SAAU) urged farmers to raise wages and improve conditions in order to remain competitive in the labour market. A resolution at the Union's 1973 congress put the future labour strategy in a nutshell: 'Our policy is for farmers to employ a hardcore of well-paid, well-housed and well-fed workers who live on the farms with their families. These workers are then supplemented by organised teams for seasonal work' [*Lipton*, 1986: 98].

However, the response on the part of farmers was uneven. By the mid-1970s case studies from different sectors presented a varigated pattern: in the maize and wheat growing regions, for instance, mechanisation continued unabated, but so did underemployment [*Wilson et al.*, 1977: 27; 195]. In the main citrus producing area of the Western Cape, on the other hand, time seemed to stand still. There the all too familiar syndrome of paternalism, violence, dependency and poverty was still firmly in place [*Theron*, 1976]. By contrast, the fruit-producing district of Elgin/Grabouw was starting to feel the effects of real restructuring. Unlike the process in maize, modernising forces did not stop at technology, but were busy redefining the labour market, as well as management : coloured[2] workers were deserting the farm for better opportunities in nearby towns, only to be replaced by African contract workers from the Eastern Cape. Together with this tendency, one contemporary observer noticed 'the emergence of a seperate management class, with professional qualifications in agriculture and commerce'. This, in turn, was accompanied by 'the inevitable tendency to view workers as impersonal labour units' [*Petersen*, 1976: 1–2].

As part of a more fundamental restructuring process, Marcus [1989: 91] argues, this trend towards the 'individualisation' of labour had become fairly widespread by the end of the 1970s. Where the rationalisation and formalisation of labour organisation came in the wake of changes in farm ownership and a more managerial approach to labour, it caused ruptures in farmworkers' consciousness as shaped by the paternalist regime.

However, all of this was seemingly less true for regions like the Western Cape, where the main unit of labour was still the (coloured) family. Here the outstanding feature of the restructuring process was twofold: in response to labour shortages caused by the general movement of coloured workers into the towns, farmers started to recruit African male migrants on a bigger scale and to employ an increasing number of coloured female workers on a permanent basis [*Marcus*, 1989: 92–3, 101].

The former trend was to become less and the latter more pronounced during the 1980s: the abolition of the Coloured Labour Preference policy in 1986[3] accelerated the in-migration of African people into the Western Cape and reduced the necessity for recruiting contract labour; the full-time integration of farmworkers' wives became a conscious strategy of the 'Farm Management Movement' launched at the beginning of the decade. Starting with the privatisation of the old marketing body for the fruit industry (that is, the Decidious Fruit Board) the new-look 'Unifruco' switched from a control to a growth orientation and urged its farmer members to adopt modern management concepts and a greater quality awareness.[4] In this quest Unifruco was aided by the Co-operative Winegrowers Association (KWV), the National Productivity Institute (NPI), the National Training Institute (NTI) and the SAAU.

Close on the heels of, and not unconnected to the revamping of the marketing agency, came the establishment of the 'Rural Foundation' in 1982. Basically a brainchild of key figures in the farming and university community of Stellenbosch, it embarked on an extensive program of 'social development' of farmworker communities – firstly in the Western Cape and later also in other parts of the country. Funded by the government, overseas donors and farmers themselves, its programmes were mainly geared towards the improvement of productivity and the improvement of the industry's negative labour image in the face of looming anti-apartheid sanctions. The latter were at their most effective during the period 1986–89, but, if anything, the loss of markets in the USA and Scandinavia made fruit and wine farmers even more cost conscious and the marketing effort more efficient. By the end of 1989 Unifruco was already 'coping' with sanctions.[5]

How these forces had combined to change the face of labour organisation in the Western Cape, became apparent after a decade of 'rural reform'. By the early 1990s, social development on Rural Foundation farms exceeded the objectives the Foundation had set for itself six years earlier: for instance, the fertility rate, the rate of teenage pregnancies and the infant mortality rate had all declined significantly [*Groenewald*, 1993: 11–12]. Research on four fruit farms in the Elgin area found a marked improvement in living standards, an increased emphasis by management on trying to improve workers' productivity and a definite shift away from the emphasis on coercive methods of control. Instead, management tried to encourage workers' consent by, amongst other measures, introducing liaison committees and a low-level version of worker participation. As a result, the relationship between management and workers appeared to be far more amicable [*Mayson*, 1990: 284–6, 271].

That appearances can be deceptive or that the situation on the Elgin farms might be less than representative, was born out by another micro-study, this time undertaken in the Stellenbosch district [*du Toit*, 1993]. It clearly illustrated that the farm management movement was not without its own internal contradictions and dislocations. By paying lip service to ideals of rural reform, while simultaneously insisting on their 'parental' authority, managers were undermining paternalism itself. Together with the spread of literacy, the influence of radio and television and of the nearby town or city, these contradictions had created the opportunity for farmworker unions to gain a foothold on the farm. As a result, the study concluded, 'the Western Cape today is the scene of a three-cornered hegemonic contest between tradional paternalist farmers, the new proponents of "human resources management" and the beginnings of a militant farmworkers' union' [*du Toit*, 1993: 317].

Contradictory and uneven, the pictures presented by the two micro-studies give a hint as to how labour organisation in the greater Western Cape may have changed since the early 1980s. However, being individual case studies in design, and not neccessarily representative of the region, they leave a number of questions unanswered: to what extent has the 'farm management movement', as manifested on the Elgin farms, become diffused in the wider region? Has it changed farmers' strategies of recruiting labour? What has happened to labour processes and skill requirements? Has work organisation become more formalised and bureaucratic? How far advanced is unionisation in the Western Cape and has it, together with the general franchise, made workers more assertive and relationships more adversarial? It is questions like these which existing studies have so far failed to answer adequately. At the same time, they provide the rationale for our own survey.[6] The information gathered in the course of our fieldwork is analysed against the backdrop of the economics of fruit and wine farming in the area.

EXPORT OR DIE: THE ECONOMICS OF FRUIT AND WINE FARMING IN THE WESTERN CAPE

Deciduous Fruit

If fruit farmers are amongst the socially more progressive sections of white farming, it is also because they can afford to pay. Undoubtedly, the Cape fruit industry is the success story of South African commercial agriculture. Its exports represent 40 per cent of South Africa's total foreign earnings from agricultural products [*Unifruco*, 1993]. Although it occupies no more

MAP

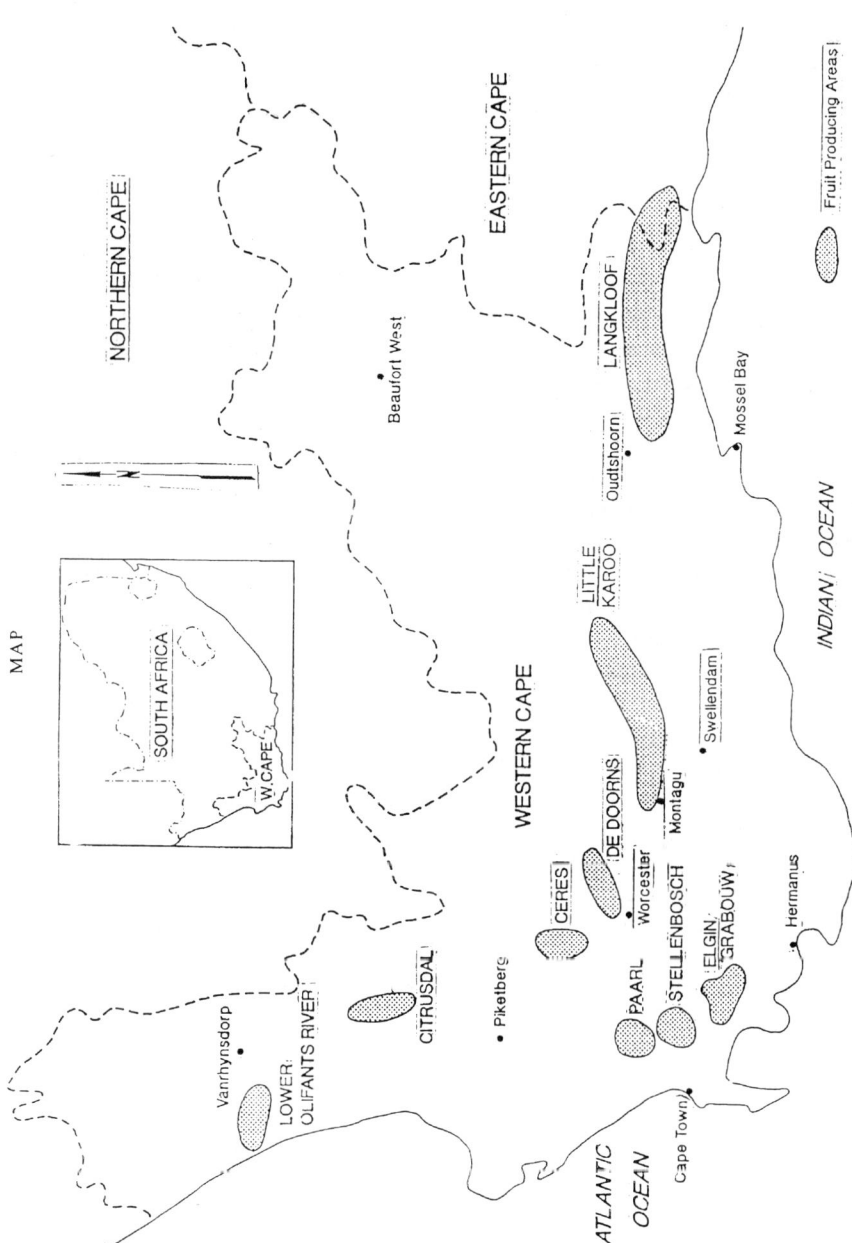

than one per cent of agricultural land in the Western Cape, deciduous fruit production makes by far the largest single contribution to the value of agricultural output in the region, accounting for about one quarter [de Klerk, 1992: 1].

It is generally accepted by analysts that the future prospects of the South African fruit industry look promising. Since the lifting of sanctions in 1990, the industry has shown strong, consistent growth. Except for a slump in 1993 (R1 359m)[7] earnings have shown a consistent rise, reaching a record high of R1,901 m in 1994,[8] which represents approximately 500 per cent growth since 1984 (R359 m) or 2300 per cent growth since 1974 (R82 m).[9] The bulk of South African export fruit goes to the European market where, in contrast to other agricultural products, it gains low-tariff access because of its seasonal advantage. In 1993 its market share was estimated at 37 per cent of all deciduous fruit imported into the EU during the November–July season [Unifruco, 1993]. In relation to its main competitors, Chile and New Zealand, South Africa enjoys the comparative advantage of relative closeness to the European market. To this the industry has added a reputation for quality and reliability. Although Chilean fruit has a bigger share of the European market (60 per cent), it is generally of a lower quality. South African stone fruit of the same grade fetches 50 per cent more than the Chilean product, grapes approximately 25–30 per cent more, and apples and pears 10 to 15 per cent [Cape Times, 18 Feb. 1994].

As indicated by the figures above, the Cape fruit industry continues to expand at a fast rate. New plantings are taking place, not only in the traditional areas but also in others such as Piketberg and Swellendam – despite a high initial capital outlay of R35,000 per hectare and a long gestation period. On average, fruit trees take four years to produce and about 15 years to break even [de Klerk, 1992: 2–3]. 'Easy peeler' citrus is relatively new, but expanding rapidly in the Paarl/Stellenbosch area (where it is often part of a mixed farming strategy, the other main components being vegetables and wine grapes). In recent years the industry has been given an extra boost by a considerable increase in consumer demand – both local and overseas – for fruit juice/concentrate. This trend is expected to continue.

In the latest development, the marketing organisations of the deciduous fruit and citrus industries have joined forces to co-ordinate their operations on overseas markets. Known as CapeSpan International, this merger is expected to lend further momentum to already expanding markets in Eastern Europe and the Far East.

Given the rate of expansion, analysts have predicted employment in the industry to grow, perhaps by as many as 3000 jobs a year [de Klerk,1992: 7]. Right now the industry provides work for approximately 330,000 people at peak season [Unifruco, 1993]. On average, total labour costs (cash wages plus social expenditure like medical aid and so on) make up 35 per cent of fruit farmers' running costs.[10] Although they insist that they cannot afford to spend more on labour, this must be seen in relation to their own expectations regarding a 'satisfactory' profit. Exact figures are not known, but according to a Unifruco source[11] Cape fruit farmers are not prepared to live with the lower profit margins of their Chilean counterparts.

Wine

The state of the wine industry is not nearly as healthy and vibrant as that of fruit. In 1992, the annual value of wine grapes produced in the Western Cape was estimated at 15 per cent of the total value of agricultural output in the region – making it second to deciduous fruit, but only at about half the value of the latter [*de Klerk*, 1992: 13].

Unlike their counterparts in the fruit industry, most wine farmers are domestically oriented. Until recently the industry was tightly controlled by a central body, the co-operative KWV. Some two years ago plantings were deregulated, but a basic floor price per tonnage is still set by the KWV. Analysts suspect that the controlled price is being set at higher levels than market value and that this reduces competitiveness [*de Klerk*, 1992: 15]. At the same time, the measure lends protection to a considerable number of wine farmers who produce lower-quality grapes for conversion into distilled and low-priced wines. This situation continues to exist, despite the fact that the domestic market has shown hardly any growth for years.

For export farmers, however, conditions have improved dramatically since sanctions were lifted in 1990. In 1991 as much as 20 per cent of production – compared to roughly 10 per cent in previous years – was earmarked for exports. In 1993 the country exported a total of 2.8 million cases of wine. For 1994 the projected sales were 5 million and in 1995 this figure is expected to grow by at least 20 to 25 per cent (*Cape Times*, 18 Feb. 1995).[12] The main beneficiaries of the export boom are those co-operative or estate wine cellars which, unlike the domestically oriented farmers, have built a reputation for quality wines and geared themselves to newly-accessed overseas markets.

The prospects of the industry depend to a large extent on its ability to build on the export successes of the last five years. The international market for wine is highly competitive and unlike fruit, there is no seasonal advantage. To sustain a reasonable growth rate, the industry as a whole will have to face difficult structural changes: a more market-related output pricing structure; investment in new cultivars; a much improved and expanded marketing capability and a more efficient use of existing resources [*de Klerk*, 1992: 17].

At this stage the wine industry employs around 50,000 people at peak season. Traditionally, the majority of wine farmers have had a worse labour image than their colleagues in the fruit industry. Low wages, poor housing and the infamous 'tot' system[13] made them easy targets for the sanctions and boycott campaigns in Europe and the United States. However, as we discovered in our field work, the situation in this sector has not remained static either. While 'domestic' wine farmers remain generally less progressive than the fruit farmers, export-oriented wine farms have introduced a labour dispensation which has kept pace with the innovations in the fruit sector. Conditions on 'traditional' wine farms being what they are, they have become targets for emerging farmworker unions. Being less profitable than either their export-oriented colleagues or the average fruit farmer, they are bound to resist organising drives.

LABOUR ORGANISATION IN WESTERN CAPE AGRICULTURE:
CURRENT PATTERNS AND TENDENCIES

Farming Strategies

As can be expected market conditions in the different sectors are reflected in farmers' strategic thinking. From our survey it became clear that most farmers or management teams had a definite farming strategy – if only in the sense of a particular thrust or a set of objectives. In the majority of cases the latter were expressed in unambiguous financial terms.

After visiting some 42 farms/agribusinesses, we could basically distinguish three broad strategies: (1) diversification, (2) expansion or (3) a combination of the two. Without exception, the fruit farmers of the Grabouw/Elgin and Ceres districts are either expanding or planning to expand their apple, pear or plum orchards – in one case by as much as 100 hectares per year. The bulk of the fruit produced on these farms is destined for export. In the Ceres area, some of the farms have also diversified into vegetables; not, in the first place, to spread the risk, but because natural conditions are ideally suited and because vegetables fetch excellent prices on both foreign and domestic markets.

The size of the fruit/vegetable farms included in the survey varied between 45 and 1,500 hectares. As could be expected, this enormous variation was also reflected in turnover figures. Calculated as an average over a three-year period (1992–94), turnover varied between R27,000 and R33,000 per ha. In this most wealthy farming sector of South African agriculture, a 'satisfactory profit' is defined as 23 per cent on turnover or 12 per cent on capital (average figures). In order to achieve this, the large farmers/businesses emphasised 'the optimisation of farming skills', 'the development of human resources' and 'the critical management of labour'.

In the equally lucrative table grape sector, the farming strategy was frequently defined as 'maximum profits'. For one young, up-and-coming farmer this meant that he simply had 'to be better than the rest'. For another, that, in addition to well-known cultivars, he was moving into new and special cultivars that could be marketed very early. On these farms, where table grapes were sometimes supplemented by citrus or fruit, the average turnover was R40,000 per ha. A 15 per cent return on capital or 30 per cent on turnover was regarded as a 'satisfactory profit'.

Diversification was the strategy that characterised the majority of wine farms in our sample. For the last ten to twenty years in the Stellenbosch, Paarl and Lower Olifantsriver districts this has meant a progressive reduction of vineyards in favour of crops such as vegetables, fruit, citrus, raisins and sultanas (the latter limited to the Lower Olifantsriver region). This shift has been necessitated by a stagnant domestic market for average quality table wines and a chronic overproduction of some 20–25 per cent. In Stellenbosch and Paarl wine farmers try to compensate for the low-profit (albeit low-risk, due to guaranteed minimum prices) vineyards by branching out into export citrus and/or vegetables. On the Vredendal-Lutzville axis in the Lower Olifantsriver district, farmers have downscaled their dependence on markets for grapes by converting part of the crop into raisins or sultanas and by planting tomatoes as well as table grapes. In this district farms are small (38 ha on average) but yields relatively high due to its favourable agro-climatic conditions. This factor, plus a history of poor labour relations, has prompted a number of farmers to pool resources and mechanize hitherto labour-intensive farming operations.[14] Five out of six farmers interviewed had shown a profit the previous year. The average turnover per hectare over the previous three years was approximately R16,000.

Rather than diversify, all three estate cellars visited in the Stellenbosch area attempt to sell as much as possible of their high-quality table wine on overseas markets. Over the last three years the average turnover was R1,75m. There are fears that the initial rush for South African wines in the post-sanction era may be over, and that this is happening in an increasingly competitive global market for better wines [*Platter*, 1993]. For the moment, however, all three owners expect their sales to increase.

The Labour Market

Whatever constraints fruit and wine farmers face, a shortage of labour is certainly not one of them. Not one of the 42 farmers/managers interviewed stated that they experienced problems in keeping their permanent labour force at the size desired. Farm work may have the lowest status of all occupations in the eyes of the coloured community, but this is more than compensated by a number of other labour market factors, including high unemployment, a fast-growing pool of landless people in the former 'homelands' of the Eastern Cape, and massive migration from there to the Western Cape. The processes at work have resulted in a considerable oversupply in the regional labour market. One of its manifestations is the inevitable squatter camp or 'informal settlement' that accompanies almost every established town in the rural Western Cape. It is not surprising then that almost no farmer went out to actively recruit workers for the permanent labour force. The majority came to the farm looking for work or was drawn from the seasonal labour force.

As it is, not that many vacancies arise amongst the permanent labour force. Turnover is relatively low if one considers that, on average, 55 per cent of the workers interviewed had been employed for longer than five years on their current farms. A significant, albeit lower, average percentage had been in the farmers' employ for more than one generation. Wages may be low and hours long if compared to jobs in the non-agricultural sector, but most of the workers interviewed can not vote with their feet as they have only an average 6.7 years of schooling and their farming skills are difficult to sell in the urban labour market. Of permanent workers interviewed, 91 per cent are children of farmworkers and have known nothing but farmwork all their lives. When they leave a farm, they mostly find work on a farm in the same district or in a neighbouring one. For now, at least, the rural labour market in the Western Cape is very localised. However, this may change: the majority of farmers did not expect their employees' children to follow in the footsteps of their parents. Higher school qualifications and the children's expectations would make them leave for the towns and cities. Only after a fruitless search would the occasional job seeker return to the farm.

When farmers did express concern about the labour market, it was about recruiting the 'right quality' of worker. When asked what the 'right quality' means, three personality traits were mentioned repeatedly: reliability, sobriety and a willingness to learn. A handful of farmers also complained that truck and tractor drivers were scarce and that skilled artisans ('specialist workers') and white managers were hard to come by. The latter, said one Paarl table grape farmer, 'is the biggest labour problem in the industry'. As a result, an increasing number of middle-managerial posts are filled by coloured supervisors and foremen.

Farmers/managers were less selective when it came to seasonal workers. In five of the six districts at least half of the farmers interviewed recruited seasonal labour from local squatter settlements. In the Lower Olifantsriver valley, with its history of below-average wages and poor labour relations, local people are reluctant to take on seasonal work. As a result, farmers drive 200 km or more to economically depressed areas like Namaqualand or the Karoo to secure the necessary labour. In the major fruit-growing regions of Grabouw/Elgin and Ceres, farmers still recruit a fair number of African men from the Transkei, although to a lesser extent than in the past.[15] Other farmers satisfy their seasonal labour needs by employing workers from a neighbouring farm (made possible by a complementary harvesting cycle) or by drawing on the labour of farmworkers' wives (where they are not already expected to work full-time).

If the seasonal or peripheral labour market shows no definite segmentation by race or gender, the same can not be said of the permanent labour force. One finding that stands out from the survey, is that Africans have not even begun to penetrate the core of permanent workers on these farms. Apart from the single-digit numbers of Africans employed on eight of the farms surveyed, the permanent labour force is coloured and increasingly female. Even if one were to count those African men on 11-month contracts as permanent, this is limited to a handful of farms and they do not enjoy the status or benefits of permanent employees.

The reasons for the racially homogeneous and increasingly feminine character of the labour core are not difficult to unearth. On fruit and wine farms where labour costs (individual plus social wages) constitute anything between 28 per cent and 50 per cent of running costs, employers have devised new strategies of 'getting more out of their labour'. On two-thirds of the farms visited this has resulted in the full integration of farmworkers' wives into the permanent labour force. The farmer incurs the costs of building and maintaining a crèche, to release women for full-time wage employment, making a more efficient use of overhead capital in the form of worker housing. From the workers' point of view, this arrangement has the advantage of almost doubling the household income.[16] This feminisation of the core has occurred at the cost of other workers and does not imply an absolute increase in the size of the labour force. On the contrary, on every farm the number of permanent workers per hectare has remained constant or declined due to an increase in productivity. What this means, of course, is that despite their labour-intensity, the number of jobs in the fruit and wine industries is decreasing in relation to area under cultivation. New employment opportunities only arise with the expansion of acreage. This bestows a position of relative privilege on core farmworkers – especially on those employed on export farms, where they earn above average wages, receive social benefits and live in reasonable housing. These farmworkers are no longer the rural underclass. That position has been taken over by the rural poor who live in shanty towns and form part of the seasonal labour market.

Division of Labour and Work Organisation

When seasonal workers enter Western Cape farms they come face to face with an internal labour structure. Depending mainly on the size of the farm and the attitudes of the owner, this internal structure is characterised by more or less elaborate features. On smaller farms, where most workers perform a whole range of tasks, a horizontal division of labour is almost non-existent. Whatever job/wage hierarchy does exist is arbitrarily decided upon by the farmer, hardly ever justified and largely taken as given. At the bottom are the majority of general farmworkers with the tractor and truck driver occupying the next two rungs on the job ladder. If the farm happens to be of a fair size, a coloured foreman or two and a white farm manager normally complete what is a straightforward structure of authority. However, this picture changes significantly when it comes to the bigger farms and agri-businesses mainly geared to the export sector. Sheer numbers (ranging from 270 to 800 workers) compel the owners to jettison direct, personal control in favour of a system based on specialised expertise and impersonal organisational rules. On these kinds of farms there is normally a horizontal division between the production, finance, personnel, mechanical maintenance and packing departments. In addition each division is vertically differentiated. Production, for example, normally consists of two to three layers of management with the supervisor, specialist worker, truck and tractor driver (spraying specialist), irrigation expert and general worker completing the hierarchy in descending order. On some farms the category of general worker has been further differentiated into several grades, for example, 'fieldsman I, II and III', according to skills and experience. In those cases where the farming complex is not company but family owned, ultimate control rests with family members – whether as senior managers or as directors who have little to do with the day-to-day running of the enterprise.

While a performance orientation pervades the export farm and the spirit of paternalism is on the retreat, gender and racial divisions of labour remain firmly entrenched in Western Cape agriculture. On wine, citrus and vegetable farms, women are mainly employed to harvest and to perform 'light' auxiliary tasks like the trellising of vines. Packing of table grapes, citrus, vegetables or fruit, is almost exclusively reserved for women. Men refuse consistently to perform certain tasks (for example, spacing the branches of fruit trees) which they regard as 'women's work'. Although women are increasingly sought after as pruners, the best-paid jobs on farms remain the domain of men.

Whatever divisions exist between (coloured) men and women, these are largely set aside when it comes to maintaining solidarity *vis-à-vis* 'outsiders', that is, Africans. Almost without exception the coloured farm-workers interviewed did not regard Africans as part of the 'farm family'. Even those who expressed less social distance and showed a more accom-modating response, were reluctant to work under an African supervisor or have African workers as their next-door neighbours. In their answers, coloured workers (mostly men) emphasised differences of language, religion, culture, lifestyle and even styles of working in order to explain their attitude. Tales of individual African workers who had been integrated into the coloured farm community or married into it, were few and far between and outnumbered by ugly accounts of social ostracism.

Many of the observations and reservations of coloured workers corresponded to the views of farmers themselves. Stressing the importance of communication, and the feelings of coloured workers, farmers said it would be 'inviting trouble' to employ a substantial number of African men living permanently with their wives and children on the farm. Not only would it result in ethnic friction, but it could also mean inviting the union vanguard onto the farm, as African workers are often perceived as more militant and inclined towards collective action. The upshot of this shared consciousness between white owner and coloured farmworker is that Africans, where they are employed, are mostly hired on a seasonal basis, work in separate gangs, are housed separately and live separate social lives. In short, modernisation on the bigger export farms may have all but swept away paternalist relations, but gender and racial divisions of labour remain strong features of the organisation of farm work.

Wages, Working and Living Conditions

Historically, farmworkers were excluded from labour laws, their employment conditions being governed by the common law contract of employment, which provided no protection against unscrupulous employers. In 1993 the Basic Conditions of Employment Act (BCEA) was extended to farmworkers, providing them with legal protection for the first time in South African history.

When interviewed on this issue, most of the farmers (regardless of sector) alleged that the *de facto* situation on the farm with regard to working hours had basically been in line with the Bill by the time it became law. However, a number also admitted that the Act had put a sudden stop to work on Saturday mornings. When criticising the BCEA, they stressed that it was too rigid regarding the seasonal change in daylight time and that it took too little account of the particular conditions existing on individual farms. As a result, a fair number had elicited the 'consent' of their workers in order to adapt the Act to local circumstances.

Our survey showed that, for a 48-hour week, permanently employed men get paid R95 on average. For approximately 42 hours' work permanently employed women receive R74. On average, seasonal workers earn the same as the latter. Looking at the fruit industry alone, the average cash wage per week for permanent male workers amounted to R117. Piece work systems are prevalent in both the wine and fruit industries, and during harvesting permanent workers are also paid according to piece work rates. Payment in kind (that is, food) has virtually disappeared and the cash part of the wage is by far the most important component of farmworkers' remuneration.

Although it is doubtful whether cash wages have increased much, if anything, in real terms over the last ten years,[17] farmers' wage bills almost double when spending on social development and benefits are taken into account. Contributions to transport costs, medical care, pension funds and funeral benefits are fairly generalised throughout both sectors. The upgrading of on-farm housing has also improved standards considerably, with most cottages having been electrified with piped water available inside or close by. However, even on some of the most progressive farms toilets are still outside and bathtubs are few and far between. On the other hand, community halls have sprung up on a whole number of farms as part of the 'community development' drive in the 1980s and 1990s.

Labour Relations

In contrast to the social side of farm life, developments with regard to labour relations have been much more uneven. On the smaller farms (especially in wine) paternalism has proven to be a hardy plant – albeit one with considerable mutations. The passing of the Agricultural Labour Act in January 1994 has set limits to farmers' arbitrary exercise of power and has facilitated the formalisation of the employment relationship. For example, written employment contracts with permanent employees had been signed on 74 per cent of farms visited (very few seasonal workers were covered in this way). Disciplinary and grievance procedures (often though, in the form of 'farm rules') were in place on 60 per cent of the farms. On 64 per cent of the sample farms, a so-called liaison or community committee had been established. As the name suggests, the main purpose of these committees is to serve as a channel of communication between farmers and workers and to deal with community issues. In some cases they also discuss 'work-related' issues and committee members are consulted on the hiring, retrenchment and promotion of workers. In a number of cases the same committees are also used as forums to explain the workings of the farming enterprise. However, after interviewing workers, it also became clear that in a number of cases the committee existed in name only and was for all practical purposes defunct. Where they did function, they had no say regarding wages and working conditions. These, like employment contracts and 'farm rules', were in most cases determined unilaterally by the farmer. Having no negotiating power regarding wages and working conditions, it stands to reason that these committees do not feature at all when it comes to questions of investment, other financial matters or technology.

It is the medium-sized and bigger farms in the fruit industry that have gone beyond this neo-paternalist model of labour relations. Forced to formalise in the wake of expansion, four big agri-businesses in our sample epitomise the industrial model of organisation in agriculture. With its rational-legal structure of authority, it frees workers from the kind of personal web that is still part of life on the neo-paternalist farm. At the same time, enterprise size and the formal nature of its relationships generate a kind of alienation and collective consciousness that makes workers on these farms most prone to unionisation. Not surprisingly, big agri-businesses have become the bridgehead for trade union activity in Western Cape agriculture. Unlike workers on neo-paternalist farms, where relatively few of those interviewed had had contact with a union, workers employed on corporate farms and in packing sheds had signed up in considerable numbers.

The most active farmworkers' organisation in the region, the Farm and Rural Workers Support Association (FRWSA), claims a membership of 18,000, 4,000 of whom are paid-up, in the Western Cape. The organisation has a presence on 26 wine and 50 fruit farms, mostly in the Stellenbosch and Grabouw districts. Other unions in the sector are the Food and Allied Workers Union (FAWU) – primarily focused on the processing plants, but also present in Stellenbosch and Grabouw – and the National Union of Wine, Spirits, Farm and Allied Workers Union. The latter has a foothold primarily in wine cellars, but has also penetrated some wine farms. In February this year, COSATU (Congress of South African Trade Unions) launched its farmworker union, but so far it has made very little headway in the Western Cape. Lack of funds and of organisational capacity appear to be major obstacles.

Strikes, recognition agreements and collective bargaining on a number of corporate farms in the Western Cape have irrevocably destroyed the paternalist spirit and replaced it, predictably, with low-trust, adversarial relations. However, there are a handful of medium-sized, family-owned farms in the fruit industry which are spearheading a different, corporatist route. On two farms in the Elgin/Grabouw-Villiersdorp area and on one in the Citrusdal valley, the ethos is one of 'participatory management': work teams have a high degree of autonomy and worker representatives co-decide on production, technology and financial issues. Epitomising the new corporatist spirit is the 'Whitehall' farm in Elgin where permanent (mostly coloured) workers have acquired a 50 per cent share with capital borrowed from an independent development agency and a commercial bank (*Weekly Mail*, 13–20 Jan. 1995). Here, where workers are co-owners of the farm, relations are markedly different from those at the Fordist-type agri-business a few kilometres away or on the neo-paternalist farms in the neighbouring winelands. The decision-making arrangements within the workers trust are such that all decisions have to be ratified by 70 per cent of the shareholders. The process makes provision for all workers to be informed about all aspects of any decision. After operating for one year an increase in production has already occurred. Whitehall family members ascribed this to the motivation of the workers, resulting from the introduction of the share scheme. Apparently, the acquisition of business management and negotiating skills on the part of workers is another major benefit of the project [McKenzie, 1995: 9–10] Progressive and mutually advantageous as it may be, it remains to be seen how many farmers are prepared to follow this pioneering example.

CONCLUSION

In 1995 labour organisation in Western Cape agriculture looks decidedly different from what it was ten to 15 years ago. Social development indicators for farmworker communities have improved, the core labour force is smaller and has become more feminised. On the other hand there is a growing pool of casual, seasonal labour in rural towns and squatter camps, supplied by thousands of proletarianised Africans from the former bantustans in the Eastern Cape who have come to this region in search of jobs and a better life. So far, however, they have not succeeded in penetrating the core labour force in any significant way. At the same time, their presence as readily available seasonal labour has made African migrant contract labour less important than in the 1970s.

Ironically, the novel presence of a great number of African work seekers in the rural labour market of the Western Cape is facilitating an ethnic alliance between permanent coloured farmworker on the one hand and white owner on the other – at a time when paternalist relations have all but disappeared in the wake of a decade or more of rural modernisation. As we suggested, the latter was not set in motion by state pressure, worker resistance or even benevolence on the part of fruit and wine farmers. Rather it was the quest for more growth and higher productivity, international boycotts and sanctions, and the possibility of unionisation which lay behind the movement for rural reform. In the event it also gave birth to new tensions and contradictions.

Whether neo-paternalist or thoroughly formalised, relations on the farm have become less deferential and more conflictual than in the past. However, if more than the present handful of fruit farmers were to cross the threshold of equity-sharing and co-decision-making, we could witness the emergence of a firm ethnic alliance between white owners and core coloured workers on Western Cape farms. By implication this would also mean a 'deeper' segmentation of the rural labour market along coloured-African and permanent-seasonal lines. If, on the other hand, farmers are not prepared to meet rising expectations, the ongoing erosion of coloured workers' neo-paternalised-cum-ethnic consciousness is bound to gather momentum and usher in a phase of labour unrest, possibly forging worker solidarity across ethnic and labour market divides.

NOTES

1. The Basic Conditions of Employment Act (BCEA) was extended to agriculture on the 1st May 1993. Amongst other provisions, it sets a maximum work week of 48 hours, guarantees two weeks' paid holiday per year and makes provision for 30 days' sick leave spread over three years. The Agricultural Labour Act promulgated on 17 January 1994, incorporates the BCEA, makes provision for collective bargaining and protects farmworkers against unfair dismissal.
2. 'Coloured' refers to descendents of unions between white settlers, khoi-khoi, imported slaves and African people since the colonisation of the Cape in the mid-seventeenth century. Close to 80 per cent of coloured people in South Africa live in the Western Cape.
3. As part of the larger array of apartheid controls over the movement of people, the coloured labour preference policy stipulated that no employer in the larger Western Cape could hire an African, unless he/she could reasonably prove that no coloured person could be found to fill a particular vacancy. In addition, Africans were subject to a number of other legal and administrative controls regulating their residence in urban areas.
4. This insider account was given by Fred Meintjies, chief PRO at Unifruco, the fruit industry's marketing organisation. Personal communication, Aug.1995.
5. Fred Meintjies, personal communication, Aug. 1995.
6. The survey sample included 42 farms in six different districts of the Western Cape wine, fruit and citrus region, namely, Grabouw/Elgin, Stellenbosch, Paarl, Ceres, Citrusdal and Lower Olifants River. Due to resource limitations, three other important districts, Hex River (table grapes) Little Karoo and Langkloof, could not be included. Lack of access to the fruit industry's membership list, meant that a genuine representative sample could not be drawn. Instead, we used the 'snowball' method in order to gain access to farms. Despite these limitations, we tried to ensure that farms of different sizes, ownership structures and labour management systems were included in the sample.
   On each farm we conducted one lenghty, semi-structured interview with the farmer-owner or with a senior manager. In addition, we conducted a similar interview with at least one farmworker. For the selection of the latter, we were almost totally dependent on the owner/manager, with the result that senior workers and supervisors are over-represented in the worker sample, thus the worker response is likely to have a conservative bias. Although the situation has improved considerably, access to farms remains difficult.
7. One Pound sterling exchanges against approximately six Rand.
8. Figures provided by Niel Hugo, Unifruco economist, personal communication, Jan. 1995.
9. Figures provided by Fred Meintjies, personal communication, Aug. 1995.
10. Figure calculated from our survey data.
11. Niel Hugo, personal communication, June 1995.
12. Calculated in terms of volume, exports have increased from 23,090,052 litres in 1991 to 50,891,808 litres in 1994. Personal communication, Anelise du Toit, KWV head office in Paarl, Aug. 1995.
13. The 'tot' system refers to the practice of paying farm labourers in alcohol. Wine was dispensed up to six times a day, thereby creating a permanently intoxicated and alcohol-dependent work-force.
14. In this region we came across a handful of farmers who had pooled resources to acquire

grape and tomato harvesting machines.

15. On some of our sample farms in the Grabouw/Elgin area African seasonal workers had been replaced by coloured workers from the Karoo or the local area. This had occured because of negative experiences on the farmers' part. For example, contract workers had used the farm as a stepping stone on the way to metropolitan Cape Town and 'deserted' shortly after arrival. In two other cases they had tried to stage a strike for higher wages. At a major agri-business in the Ceres area, management is considering the scrapping of single sex housing on the farm and replacing the contract workers involved with local job seekers. In this case, the sentiment is not necessarily anti-contract worker, but management does not want to incur the capital costs involved in the conversion of single male housing into family homes.

16. One could of course argue that, had the wives not worked full-time on the farm, farmers would have to nearly double the male worker's wage in order for the latter's family to reproduce itself. Viewed from this perspective, the feminisation of the permanent labour force means that the farmer is getting two workers for the price of one.

17. In 1985 the average weekly wage for general farmworkers in the Western Cape was calculated at approximately R40 [*Groenewald*, 1985] taking into account a substantial amount of payment in kind. Although this represented a 100 per cent increase over the previous five year period, it fell short of the minimum existence level for a family of five. Since then nominal wage increases have been eroded by an average inflation rate of 12 per cent, conservatively estimated.

REFERENCES

Bradford, H., 1990, 'Highways, By-ways and Culs-de-Sac: the Transition to Agrarian Capitalism in Revisionist South African History', *Radical History Review*, Vol.46, No.7.

Budlender, D., 1984, 'Agriculture and Technology: Four Case Studies', *Second Carnegie Inquiry into Poverty and Development in Southern Africa*, Paper No.23.

de Klerk, M., 1984, 'The Labour Process in Agriculture: Changes in Maize Farming during the 1970s', mimeo.

de Klerk, M.,1991, 'The Accumulation Crisis in Agriculture', in Stephen Gelb (ed.), *South Africa's Economic Crisis*, Cape Town: David Philip.

de Klerk, M., 1992, *Prospects for Commercial Farming in the Western Cape*, Economic Trends Research Group, Working Paper No.11, University of Cape Town.

du Toit, A., 1993, 'The Micro-Politics of Paternalism: Discourses on Management and Resistance on South African Fruit and Wine Farms', *Journal of Southern African Studies*, Vol.19, No.2.

Greenberg, S.B., 1980, *Race and State in Capitalist Development*, Johannesburg: Ravan Press.

Groenewald, C.J., 1985, 'Loonpeile vir Plaaswerkers' ('Wage Levels for Farmworkers'), unpublished paper, Department of Sociology, University of Stellenbosch.

Groenewald, C.J., 1993, 'Social Development of the South African Agricultural Labour Force', paper presented at the Conference on Comparative Research on Welfare States in Transition, 9–12 Sept.1993, Oxford, England.

Lipton, M., 1986, *Capitalism and Apartheid: South Africa 1910–1986*, London: Wildwood House.

Lipton, M., 1993, 'Restructuring South African Agriculture', in Merle Lipton and Charles Simkins (eds.), *State and Market*, Johannesburg: University of Witwatersrand Press.

McKenzie, C., 1995, 'Alternative Relations of Production in Western Cape Commercial Agriculture', unpublished paper.

Marcus, T., 1989, *Modernising Super-Exploitation: Restructuring South African Agriculture*, London: Zed Books.

Mayson, D., 1990, 'The Rural Foundation, Management, and Change on Fruit Farms: A Case Study of Selected Farms in the Elgin Area', unpublished Masters dissertation, University of Cape Town.

Morris, M., 1976. 'The Development of Capitalism in South African Agriculture: Class Struggles in the Countryside', *Economy and Society*, Vol.5, No.3.

Morris, M., 1977, 'State Intervention and the Agricultural Labour Supply Post-1948', in Wilson *et al.* (eds.) [1977].

Petersen, A.J., 1976, 'Changes in Farm Labour in the Elgin District', unpublished paper presented at the Farm Labour Conference, University of Cape Town.

Platter, J., 1993, 'The Wine Industry: A. Scenario', *Wynboer*, Dec.

Scully, P., 1987, 'The Bouquet of Freedom: Racial and Economic Relations in the Stellenbosch District, 1870–1900', unpublished MA thesis, University of Cape Town.

Theron, J., 1976, 'Farm Labour in the Citrusdal Valley', unpublished paper presented at the Farm Labour Conference, University of Cape Town.

Unifruco, 1993, *The Cape Fruit Industry in Perspective*, Bellville.

Wilson, F. *et al.* (eds.), 1977, *Farm Labour in South Africa,* Cape Town: David Philip.

Livestock Production and Common Property Struggles in South Africa's Agrarian Reform

BEN COUSINS

INTRODUCTION

Recent research on livelihoods in those parts of South Africa under forms of communal tenure has pointed to the central importance of the local natural resource base in sustaining rural households [*Levin and Weiner,* 1994; *LAPC,* 1994]. This is true despite the much larger amounts of household income derived from migrant worker remittances, state pensions, and other non-rural sources, than are derived from local production and direct provisioning from the natural environment. Studies of water resources [*Forster,* 1994; *Woodhouse,* 1994], woodlands [*Gandar and Christie,* 1994], communal grazing land [*Scholes,* 1994], and wild foods and medicinal plants [*Cunningham,* 1985] have explored the use of these resources within multi-faceted systems of provision. It is likely that they are particularly important for the poorest rural households [*May et al.* 1995].

A second dimension of natural resource use in rural South Africa is the political/institutional. Customary controls on resource use have been undermined by the imposition of authoritarian forms of local governance [*Cross and Haines,* 1988; *de Wet,* 1991; *McAllister,* 1992], and the creation of strong, democratic institutions of local government is widely seen as fundamental to the emergence of viable resource management regimes [*LAPC,* 1994]. A third dimension is the ecological: stress on livelihoods has in turn contributed to stress on the resource base, and signs of environmental degradation have led to fears that current patterns of land use and resource utilisation are not sustainable [*LAPC,* 1994].

At present all three dimensions are subject to uncertainty, as a result of: (a)

Ben Cousins, Programme for Land and Agrarian Studies, School of Government, University of the Western Cape, P. Bag X17, Bellville 7535, South Africa. This study is based on two conference papers, which were presented to a workshop on 'Community Perspectives on Land and Agrarian Reform' in Johannesburg in March 1994, and to the 'Agrarian Questions' Congress in Wageningen in May 1995. Thanks to staff of the Transvaal Rural Action Committee (TRAC), the Association for Rural Advancement (AFRA), and other National Land Committee affiliates for information on livestock and rangelands disputes, and to Andrew Ainslie for data on the Mid-Fish River Basin and for useful comments on an earlier version.

incomplete knowledge and understanding of the economic, political, institutional and ecological processes which have brought about the observable patterns described in the literature; (b) uncertainty as to how these patterns and processes will be affected by government policies and programmes – such as the Reconstruction and Development Programme (RDP) – which attempt to restructure rural social relations through redistribution of land and the creation of democratic forms of rural local government. Past neglect of black rural social and ecological realities by researchers has contributed greatly to the former; the inherently fluid and contingent nature of the current conjuncture is the primary reason for the latter.

In relation to land reform, there are signs that rural people are becoming impatient with the slow pace of implementation of programmes for land restitution, redistribution and tenure reform. Land invasions are threatened in a number of districts; in others there is tension and conflict over land claims and boundary disputes; labour tenants are organising large protest marches and lobbying for government support; and negotiations between contending parties are taking place on these and related issues in many parts of the country. Land struggles of one kind or another are thus a central feature of the post-apartheid era.

Some of these struggles are over access to and control over land in general; others are directly concerned with common pool resources such as water, woodlands and grazing. This article focuses on contemporary conflicts over livestock and rangeland resources, and suggests that the roots of these struggles lie not only in the inequitable distribution of land due to past policies of segregation and apartheid, but also in the multiple functions of livestock within complex livelihood systems, and their role in the dynamics of social differentiation. Data and perspectives from livestock and rangelands research in both South Africa itself and in other parts of Africa are referred to when relevant.

The political and institutional dimensions are central to any discussion of common property regimes, and theoretical perspectives from the wider literature are brought to bear on the specificities of South Africa. Several distinct axes of struggle over common property are identified, and the complex interactions between the economic, ecological and political/institutional dimensions are explored in two detailed case studies from the Eastern Cape and Kwazulu-Natal. These provide general lessons for the political economy of common property regimes within South Africa's agrarian reform.

CONCEPTUAL ISSUES: COMMON PROPERTY MANAGEMENT

Common Pool Resources and Property Regimes

Common pool resources are those which are used or can potentially be used by more than one agent, either simultaneously or sequentially, and where exclusion from the resource is difficult or costly to achieve [*Ostrom,* 1986]. Different kinds of institutional arrangements to manage such resources are feasible, and there is debate on the question of which is most appropriate: a private market, or state ownership and regulation, or what is known as a common property regime.[1]

In the latter a defined user group limits access by outsiders and defines rules for resource use by insiders. Proponents of common property point to the existence of viable, longstanding institutional arrangements of this kind in many parts of the world, in relation to the utilisation of many different kinds of common pool resources – for example, water, forests, wildlife, fisheries, and grazing land [*National Research Council,* 1986; *McCay and Acheson,* 1987; *Bromley and Cernea,* 1989; *Bromley,* 1992]. Most commentators agree that a fourth alternative, open access, characterised by the absence of any distinct group of owners or users with defined rights and duties, is least desirable because it does not allow for any form of planned management. Nevertheless, the literature describes many situations where common property or state property arrangements have broken down and open access obtains – giving rise to the gloomy prognosis sometimes known as 'the tragedy of the commons' [*Hardin,* 1968].

Swallow [1990: 3–4] summarises the differences between common property and open access as follows: in a common property regime: (1) no single individual has exclusive rights to the use of the resource, (2) group members have secure expectations that they can gain access to future use of the resource, (3) there are functioning membership criteria, (4) there are communally-defined guidelines for resource use, and (5) there is an enforcement mechanism for punishing deviant behaviour. Relatively few African rangeland situations appear to satisfy all the conditions for common property, and conditions (4) and (5) appear to be the most problematic [*Swallow,* 1990: 22].

Lawry [1990: 5], distinguishes between a 'minimum' definition of common property and those arrangements needed to regulate more intensive use of resources. A 'minimum' definition is met where group membership rules are well defined and non-members are excluded from common resources. Lawry suggests that these arrangements have often been adequate when pressure on resources was not excessive, but that intensified controls and their enforcement become necessary with population growth, technological change, national economic integration and the decline in the political legitimacy of local institutions. However, the evolution of more intensive common property regimes is problematic given these conditions: 'fundamental changes in rural economies' have led to an erosion of the 'social and economic bases for collective control of individual use' [*ibid.,*

24; see also Swallow, 1993: 16–17].

Where common property rules break down or fail to evolve to fit changing conditions, then several outcomes have been observed: one may be increased resource degradation as the property regime slips towards open access [*Vedeld,* 1992: 8], another is 'spontaneous enclosure' or privatisation [*Behnke,* 1988; *Graham,* 1988], yet another is the capture of the commons by groups of commercial producers [*Lawry,* 1990: 18; *White,* 1992: 51] who may pursue private accumulation strategies in the name of community development [*Cousins,* 1992b: 68]. None of these is particularly attractive as a 'solution' to problems of common property management.

This suggests that attempts to achieve a better fit between contemporary social, economic and political conditions and modified common property arrangements are worth pursuing. Where groups of resource users are asserting their desire to seek such solutions, as appears to be the case with many communities claiming land in South Africa, then the case for doing so is even stronger. However, a number of critical issues will need to be confronted.

Critical Issues in Common Property Regimes

(i) The definition of user groups: At minimum common property regimes define who is allowed access to resources and who is excluded, and membership criteria must therefore be clarified, including the rights and duties of absentee members of rural communities or other groupings. The question of whether or not membership of the user group is compulsory must also be confronted. Oakerson refers to these as 'entry and exit rules' [1986: 17]. The size of the user group is critical [*Wade,* 1987; *Ostrom,* 1986], since transaction costs are lower in smaller and more cohesive groups. As Murphree [1993: 7] observes, ' ... a communal resource management regime is enhanced if it is small enough (in membership size) for all members to be in occasional face to face contact, enforce conformity to rules through peer pressure, and has a long standing collective identity'.

It is important to have a clear understanding of socio-economic structure and its effect on resource use [*Ostrom,* 1986; *Peters,* 1986; *Cousins,* 1992b]. A heterogeneity of interests within user groups presents potential difficulties [*Lawry,* 1990], although potential conflicts between uses of a resource (for example, between cropping and grazing of wetland areas) and between different categories of users (for example, commercial versus subsistence producers) can be defused through negotiation. The 'capture' of common property regimes by powerful elites is a potential problem [*Lane and Moorehead,* 1995: 131].

(ii) Resource management rules: Operational rules govern the way that a common pool resource is used; these involve the definition of jurisdictional

boundaries, and the partitioning of resource use ie. limiting where, when and to what degree resources can be exploited by group members, as in a grazing rotation [*Oakerson*, 1986]. Ostrom [1986: 611–13] suggests a number of other considerations in relation to common property rules: rules should be clear-cut and unambiguous, so that all members can know and agree upon them; the fewer rules there are the more likely it is that they will be followed; rules should be clearly enforced by officials, and will be more effective if backed by the imposition of mild social sanctions.

(iii) Innovation and 'traditional' institutions: The question of combining elements of 'customary' common property regimes with emergent formal institutions is important because the former often persist in one form or another and remain meaningful to rural communities. Some aspects of production are still organised through such aspects of social organisation as kinship networks (for example, sharing access to draught animals – see Muchena [1989]; McAllister [1992]). Customary institutions for regulating resource use are often kinship-based, are also territorial in nature, and may be combined with formal institutions set up by the state (for example, grazing scheme committees) in hybrid or 'mixed' institutions [*Swift*, 1995: 4–5; *Cousins* 1989: 349]. These institutions may prove appropriate for three aspects in particular: defining group or 'community' membership; resolving conflicts at the local level and defining sanctions for rule infringements; and defining rules for resource management based on local knowledge.

(iv) Institutional hierarchies: There is a need to consider the 'nesting' of local institutions within larger structures [*Ostrom*, 1986: 612], and to think through relations between levels within a hierarchy of institutions and organisations dealing with natural resources [*Swift*, 1995]. Lawry argues that the state has a definite role to play in creating the conditions for effective local management, through ' ... clarifying group territorial rights, adjudicating boundary disputes, and providing technical assistance to local groups attempting to intensify management' [*Lawry*, 1990: 23]. State policies can also help improve the economic incentives for collective action for example, through offering preferential marketing rights to groups managing common pool resources. More importantly, government can assist in enforcing resource management rules which have broad local support but cannot be made effective because community authority is not in itself strong enough. This has been termed a 'co-management' approach.

Swift [1995] offers a contrasting emphasis on the need to 'roll back the frontiers of the state' in pastoral regions in Africa, suggesting that an important principle to follow in institutional development is that of subsidiarity that is, ' ... administrative tasks should be carried out as near to the level of actual users of resources ... as is compatible with efficiency and accountability'. The advantages are potential gains in efficiency, savings in administrative costs, and the possibility of ' ... a more flexible institutional response to the management needs of a dynamic ecosystem' [ibid.: 158–9]. This perspective is an important reminder that co-management arrangements should aim at defining an enabling, facilitative and back-up role for the state rather than one which replaces or undermines local institutional capacity.

(v) The policy and programme environment: To support the evolution or establishment and effective functioning of common property regimes, an enabling policy and programme environment is needed. This will involve creating an appropriate legal framework, giving legal identity to common property arrangements which evolve at the local level but without imposing rigid and restrictive structures. It should also make available support services which assist communities and groups to design their own appropriate institutional arrangements, using a facilitative and processual approach, and provide appropriate rule enforcement procedures at higher levels in the institutional hierarchy to back those which prove ineffective at lower levels. To constrain the possibility of elite capture, external authorities should hold a brief for democratic processes which guarantee the rights of the less wealthy and powerful (including women and youth) to an effective say in decision making, and this may be included as one dimension of the enabling legal framework. Conflict resolution within and between user groups, through negotiation, mediation or arbitration, will be another role for external bodies.

LIVESTOCK PRODUCTION AND ECOLOGICAL DYNAMICS ON COMMUNAL RANGELAND IN AFRICA

Where extensive livestock production is a central component of livelihood systems, as in large parts of Southern Africa, there are distinct economic and ecological advantages to common property institutions. There are several reasons for this.

Firstly, livestock herds within village economies are often multi-purpose in character and yield high rates of economic return per hectare when all their functions are valued. The economic value of livestock output from communal herds in Africa is often much higher than that from commercial ranches [Barrett, 1992; Behnke, 1985a: de Ridder and Wagenaar, 1986; Jackson, 1989; PDN, 1992; Scoones, 1992].

Secondly, for multi-purpose herds high stocking rates make economic sense, and optimum stocking rates in these systems will be higher than those in single purpose (for example, beef) production systems; furthermore, these high stocking rates may well be ecologically sustainable. This is because livestock herders pursue 'opportunistic' strategies, based on mobility, to optimise their use of the variability of African rangelands [*Sandford*, 1983]. Variability occurs over both space and time, and at both the macro-scale (for example contrasts between clay veld savanna and sand veld savanna, or 'sweetveld' and 'sourveld'), and at the micro-scale (for example, between riverine areas and toplands). There is seasonal variation in forage availability, and interannual variability in the amount of rainfall occurring in different parts of a landscape. Rangeland environments are thus 'patchy', and an accumulating array of evidence has shown how pastoralists and agro-pastoralists in Africa make use of this patchiness to sustain high stocking rates [*Fry and McCabe*, 1986; *Scoones and Wilson*, 1989; *Scoones*, 1990; *Oba*, 1992].

Thirdly, environmental variability means that high stocking rates will be facilitated by a property regime which allows flexible access to different habitat patches within rangelands by numerous individually-owned herds that is, within a common property regime.

Fourthly, ecological dynamics in arid and semi-arid rangelands with particularly high rates of variability in rainfall may be *non-equilibrial* in character that is, driven by episodic events such as droughts or fires, and thus ' ... the condition of [a] grazing system at any particular time is determined more by the chance occurrence of non-biological events than by interaction between the biological components of the system itself' [*Behnke and Scoones*, 1993: 9; also *Ellis and Swift*, 1988; *Westoby et al.*1989]. In these systems opportunistic strategies involving a great deal of mobility require a regime of property rights which provides ' ... security of tenure while permitting flexibility of use patterns' [*Behnke and Scoones*, 1993: 30].

These emerging perspectives on African communal rangelands have several implications for policies and programmes promoting common property regimes. One is that external interventions to force down stocking rates against the will of livestock owners will be resisted and are both unnecessary and unlikely to succeed. Authority over such matters should be left to local institutions. Recognising the spatial heterogeneity of rangeland resources implies that herd movement as a management strategy should be accepted and facilitated, rather than suppressed, and herders be encouraged to co-ordinate movement and agree on access to key rangeland resources at different times of year and in different years. The possibility of conflict over such access must be recognised, however, (particularly in drought years – see Oba [1992]) and institutional mechanisms designed for negotiation, mediation and conflict resolution.

Spatial heterogeneity occurs at different scales (at local, regional and national levels), and its nature varies with agro-ecological zone. The extent of herd mobility will thus also vary between years and between zones; the implication is that a hierarchy of institutions will be needed to negotiate and co-ordinate access and help resolve conflicts [Swift, 1993], and that this probably calls for the involvement of government agencies and state legal authorities. Thus 'co-management' models will probably be appropriate, even when the importance of building strong local institutions is affirmed [*Lawry*, 1990].

The distinction between equilibrial and non-equilibrial systems has important tenure implications. In the former there is direct feedback between animal numbers and vegetation states, successional processes can be identified, and conventional notions of carrying capacity are relevant [*Behnke and Scoones*, 1993: 12]. *Exclusive* forms of common property are appropriate, in which boundaries between user groups are clearly defined and enforced, and management rules take into account the internal heterogeneity of resources important for herd mobility at the local level [*Scoones, 1989; Cousins, 1992b*]. In non-equilibrium situations 'opportunism' will be more important as a strategy, and *non-exclusive* forms of tenure will be more appropriate. These allow co-ordinated access to the heterogeneous patchwork of resources at a larger scale, within a framework of a great deal of temporal variation.

AXES OF STRUGGLE OVER COMMON PROPERTY

This discussion of critical issues in common property regimes in general, together with a consideration of central aspects of African livestock systems on communal rangelands, helps define certain potential axes of struggle over common property arrangements. These will be useful in analysing the South African case study material presented below. Struggles may take place over:

(i)   *gaining rights to the use of common pool resources*: as when access to traditional commonages has been lost through dispossession or legislation, and re-establishment of legitimate access is sought;

(ii) *defining the membership of the user group which has rights (and corresponding duties)*: this may be contentious in situations of high social and physical mobility, or where dispossession took place decades ago (both relevant in South Africa);

(iii) *defining and defending the boundaries of territories within which common pool resources exist*: exclusion is a central feature of common property, but is often disputed by groups or individuals without rights of use. Boundary disputes are common, but may result in negotiations over temporary use arrangements. Non-exclusive and co-ordinated access forms of tenure may be more appropriate in drier areas, but reaching agreement on timing and rates of utilisation is often difficult;

(iv) *agreeing on operational or management rules for resource use*: since rules may involve limitations on use, or contributions of labour or cash for maintenance of the resource, they may well be contentious within the user group, particularly when the group is heterogeneous in its composition;

(v) assignment and use of authority for rule enforcement: policing and the imposition of sanctions is required to maintain the integrity of the property regime, and contestations over the legitimacy of the agents with these responsibilities may occur;

(vi) relationships with external authorities: disagreements often occur between user group members and external agents with responsibilities or powers in relation to resource management, and are exacerbated when issues such as stocking or offtake rates are at stake.

As described below, struggles along many of these axes are evident in the South African countryside at present.

LIVESTOCK PRODUCTION AND RURAL LIVELIHOODS IN CONTEMPORARY SOUTH AFRICA

How important is livestock production off communal rangelands within the livelihood strategies pursued by rural black South Africans, and what is its character? This section reviews contemporary studies[2] of livestock and rural livelihoods, and discusses these region by region.[3] A conceptual model of livestock production is then presented which attempts to capture some key characteristics while taking account of the wide degree of heterogeneity displayed.

The Multiple Functions of Livestock

Kwazulu: Researchers in different regions have come to contrasting conclusions concerning the most important function of stock in black rural areas, but few have attempted an analysis of the livelihood system as a whole. One exception is Tapson [1990; 1991], who analysed national cattle herd statistics for Kwazulu as well as 1983 survey data for the Ogwini and Mabedlana areas. These show that there is a great deal of activity into and out of herds, and that total offtake exceeds that of a commercial ranch herd.

However, sales for cash are a minor component, more important being consumption activities such as slaughter, *lobolo* (bride-wealth), and mortality. Herdowners who were interviewed identified milk supply as the single most important reason for keeping cattle. Offtake in the form of *lobolo* exceeded sales or slaughter, but slaughter rates were ten times higher than sales rates, and in 77 per cent of cases slaughter took place 'for custom or celebration'. This ensures a regulated supply of meat without waste. Tapson identifies mortality as a consumption variable, using the argument that holding on to animals that may die is a rational decision to insure against risks of herd loss. He also argues, although without presenting data on its incidence, that loaning (*ukusiza*) distributes benefits through the community, that the prestige this confers on owners is itself a good, and that borrowing animals for ploughing involves reciprocal obligations.

Tapson concludes that cattle in Kwazulu represent non-human wealth which is consumed by households, ie, they are high value Z-goods, and perform the functions of cash, savings, consumer durables, equity and property investments. The most valued output is milk, and if anything the Kwazulu herd is a dairy herd rather than a beef herd. The objectives of herd owners are to improve the yield of consumable products, and to increase the size of the 'investment portfolio' for security. Tapson finds that cattle were not valued as draught animals by his respondents, and argues that survey data which revealed that 68 per cent of herds had less than two draught oxen (when four are generally needed for ploughing) support this view. However, this ignores borrowing or hire of draught animals and combining oxen from different herds to form a ploughing team, and respondents' views may have reflected the fact that draught is a self-evident value [*Tapson*, 1990: 158]. Tractor ploughing services were also subsidised by the Kwazulu Government at the time (Tapson, personal communication). Nevertheless, the possibility of an absolute shortage of draught oxen in the survey areas should not be discounted.

Gandar and Bromberger [1984] report that in Mahlabatini District in 1981, where 81 per cent of households owned at least one head of cattle (although 71 per cent owned 10 or less), sales were negligible and slaughter rates were also low. They emphasise the importance of milk production, estimating output at 550 litres per annum per household; at local prices the value of milk production was higher than that of egg and crop production combined, and it was of particular importance to households in drought years. Crop output was generally poor in this district, with 92 per cent of households not able to produce the minimum household requirement. Cattle were an important store of wealth, the value of the average cattle holding (8.35 head) being equivalent to the average household cash income over 2.5 years. Draught power was another key function of cattle, but there was a shortage of draught power overall, and herds were too small to provide both replacement and a full range of subsistence needs. Half the households in the sample also owned small stock, mainly goats. Remittances and pensions were the most important sources of cash income in the area, and constituted 60 per cent of total income.

Colvin [1985] investigated cattle marketing, and interviewed 480 sellers of cattle at 20 auction venues, mainly in northern Zululand. Almost without exception these sales arose from 'compelling economic circumstances that *forced* owners (in spite of the long term disadvantages) to sell one or more head ... [for] pressing subsistence needs'. He identifies marked regional variations in levels of sales: 85 per cent of recorded sales in Kwazulu are in only three of its 26 magisterial districts, where sales are held at frequent intervals and auctions are well attended.

Auerbach *et al.* [1991] explored the demand for draught power from oxen and from tractors in two areas, Nhlangwini and Biyela. In Nhlangwini draught animals were involved in the cultivation of fields, either alone or in combination with hand hoes and tractors in 85.4 per cent of cases. Average ownership of oxen per household was 1.2 oxen. In Biyela, where average ownership of oxen was 1.9 head, 82 per cent of those who ploughed their own fields did so with oxen, and 62 per cent of those who hired contractors used oxen for ploughing. Taking observed ploughing performance into account, in relation to arable land under cultivation there was an excess of animal draught power available in these locations, which did not suggest a significant potential market for the services of tractor contractors. These data suggest that draught is an important function of cattle in many areas.

Transkei: In the Shixini area in the Transkei Heron [1990] analysed the impact of cattle holding on crop production in a sub-ward where 73 per cent of adult males were migrants in South Africa. Although remittances were the principal form of income, agricultural production for home consumption was also important for people, and continued to be organised partly through co-operative arrangements such as work parties and 'ploughing companies'. There was a shortage of cattle and implements, and since tractors were scarce, 62 per cent of households obtained access to draught through the 'ploughing companies'. Unlike the work parties these were organised through kinship networks, and 92 per cent of members were related to the head of the company. These were usually the people who contributed most cattle and implements, and who thus ploughed at optimum times. Partly for this reason, and partly due to increased supplies of manure, maize yields were positively correlated with stock holdings, as was the area of land cultivated.

Heron points out that a factor influencing rural production is phase in the domestic developmental cycle, although he agrees with Spiegel [1982] that this needs to be analysed in relation to structural factors in the wider political economy (see also Murray 1981). If we relate this to livestock, cattle may be more important for production in the years in which a young migrant is building up a rural household base, but 'retirement fund' attributes may be more crucial in later years when children are establishing their own households (see Ferguson [1990] for Lesotho).

Beinart's [1992] review of Transkei data stresses the continuing relevance of the multiple functions of cattle ('investment, bridewealth, draught and milk'), but also the shifts in relative importance of different functions over time – for example, possibly a decline in draught provision as tractor ploughing has spread. However, he cites a study in the coastal Bizana district where most households still had access to land and were effective food producers; here almost all ploughing was done by oxen [ibid.: 185]. No clear overall picture emerges, but evidently there is a great deal of regional variation in respect of the importance of draught power provision by livestock. Beinart also points to the class formation processes in homelands which result in businessmen and civil servants investing part of their earnings in agriculture (and, by implication, in herds of livestock).

Gazankulu: The relative importance of livestock functions probably varies with the distribution of stock and the class identity of livestock owners, as illustrated in Ritavi 2 in Gazankulu in the 1980s. Van der Waal [1991] describes a typical 'homelands' scenario where 'development ... seems to function primarily in the interests of the state, members of the emerging upper middle classes (businessmen, government officials and tribal leaders), metropolitan industrialists and a white farmer'. Agricultural projects in the district included large scale government run plantations (sisal, citrus, etc.), a maize project and irrigation scheme for the 'better farmers' (0.17 per cent of the population, mainly those with access to capital such as the chief and his relatives, businessmen, etc.).

Within Tiekieline settlement in Ritavi 2, differential access to wages, the main form of cash income in this labour reserve, was partly reflected in possession of cattle. Here 203 cattle were owned by 15 men (out of a total of 79 'economically active' men and 108 such women), and a further 203 were owned by two businessmen from outside the settlement. One of these was a relative of the chief, and his cattle had exclusive access to 200 ha of fenced grazing and an irrigation dam. In this situation the meagre dryland cropping engaged in by residents was not well integrated with cattle keeping – ploughing was done by donkeys, or by hiring in plough teams and (in 1988/89) government tractors for those few who could afford the payments. Cattle in this situation appeared to function mainly as a source of savings (small herd owners) or investment (larger herds).

Fischer [1987] describes the class-biased nature of a livestock development scheme in another part of Gazankulu, in the Seville settlement in Mhala district. Former labour tenants on Seville farm were subject to betterment planning in the 1960s, and between 1971 and 1981 had 1000 ha of their communal grazing allocated to a commercial cattle development scheme. Membership requirements (six brucellosis-free animal units) excluded almost all residents, and by 1985 the scheme had not yet reached its target of twenty members; more than half of the 120 cattle on the scheme were owned by one man. For this minority the commercial functions of cattle were prominent.

The other residents (in a total of 60 households) were restricted to 600 ha for residential, arable and grazing land for their 205 cattle and 204 goats, which were themselves distributed in a highly skewed manner. Only five households owned more than ten cattle, and three owners between them owned 52 per cent of all cattle. Only the largest herd owner sold animals regularly; the majority kept cattle for draught provision, investment and security. Cattle sales were often an emergency measure when other savings were exhausted or when school fees were urgently needed. Goats were an alternative investment for similar purposes. The importance of cattle for draught power provision in Seville is emphasised by Fischer. Cultivation was restricted after a drought in which cattle died or were weakened, 'since only expensive tractor power was available', and virtually all households resumed cultivation when cattle numbers rose again after residents had used other income to invest in animals. As in the Transkei, stockless households gained access to draught through joining ploughing teams and contributing their labour.

Lebowa: Vink [1986] provides data on the skewed distribution of livestock in Lebowa in 1984/85, when only 29.2 per cent of all rural households owned any animals at all, and 34.4 per cent had access to only residential land. Only a fifth of all rural households had access to all three traditional land rights (arable, grazing and residential). Owners of small cattle herds (<9 head) constituted 18 per cent of rural households and owned between a third and a half of all cattle, averaging 4.1 cattle each. Owners of large herds (>9 head) constituted four per cent of rural households and owned between a half and two-thirds of all cattle, averaging 18.6 cattle each (or 38.72 if two exceptional cases are included). Large herd owners had significantly higher incomes and net worth than other groups.

Other studies cited by Vink show that large owners were drawn from the ranks of tribal leaders, elders, and councillors, and probably also from homeland businessmen. According to Vink, tribal leaders had gained political power within the homeland and were using their control over the allocation of land rights to entrench their own privileged position. Take-off from all herds through commercial sales was low (less than 7.5 percent), and Vink concludes that the motives of large herd owners was not primarily to earn cash income from cattle, but to seek the benefits of investment, milk and meat supply, prestige and the maintenance of tribal customs. High stocking rates on Lebowa's rangelands are ascribed to a 'tragedy of the chiefs' rather than a 'tragedy of the commons'.

Bophutatswana: Does the relative importance of different livestock functions vary with agro-ecological zone? Data for the Dryharts area of Taung district in the former Bophutatswana, quoted by Schmidt [1992] shows that offtake from sales in 1989 was 6.8 percent, much higher than the 0.8 per cent for Kwazulu herds reported by Tapson [1991]. Sales and slaughter together increased offtake to 10.35 percent. Although Schmidt does not report the annual rainfall in Dryharts, it is presumably in a dry (possibly semi-arid) zone, and relatively high take-off may reflect a greater emphasis on sales of stock. Unfortunately Schmidt also does not make any mention of cropping, and it is thus difficult to evaluate his informants reported 'reasons for keeping cattle', in which there is no mention of draught. Despite the resulting ambiguity Schmidt's results are interesting: milk consumption is rated as most important, with emergency sales (that is, savings) in second place. Schmidt's analysis emphasises the rationality of storing wealth in the form of cattle, both for savings and investment purposes, with the added advantage of increased prestige, and provides insight into one reason why stocking rates in the area are so high (245 per cent of recommended rates).[4]

Also for Bophutatswana, Groenewald and Du Toit (1985) surveyed 511 cattle owners, and report sales figures of over ten per cent in certain districts. Ninety per cent of respondents said that they obtained milk from their herds, and 27 per cent that they sold milk. Over 70 per cent sold meat or cattle – a much higher proportion than reported elsewhere. Another possible factor influencing livestock functions is herd size. In this survey sales from herds of twenty or less were lower (33–53 per cent of respondents) than from larger herds of 20 or more (80–100 per cent of respondents). Colvin [1985], however, cites evidence from communal land herds in Swaziland that offtake was highest from small cattle owners (less than 17 head) in the lowveld and highest from larger herd owners (17 or more head) in the highveld (data taken from Low and Fowler [1980]). He argues that lowveld owners rely more on sales of cattle to meet their basic needs than do highveld owners, who have greater access to crop income and wage earnings, and that higher selling rates from small herds arise from the greater proportional effect of forced sales to meet essential needs. There is thus contradictory evidence on the effect of herd size on importance of function (see also Vink [1986: 132]).

Livestock and Social Relationships

These studies provide evidence on the skewed distribution of livestock within rural communities, and the growing proportion of stockless households. Some examine the social relationships that provide these households with access to animals for important functions such as draught – see Heron [1990] and Fischer [1987]. McAllister [1986] describes these arrangements, and the central role of livestock in social life in general, in Shixini ward in the Transkei, where 'betterment' had not yet been implemented:

> People give and receive stock on loan, pay for various services (such as that of the diviner or herbalist) with stock, make and receive stock prestations, *nqoma* (lend or put out) their cattle to other homesteads, are involved in bridewealth transactions, help each other meet bridewealth obligations, etc. Homesteads group their cattle together for herding purposes, and combine them in ploughing groups [*ibid.*: 472–3].

McAllister cites evidence that one of the effects of the relocation of households entailed by 'betterment' planning has been to disrupt such relationships (for example, in one area *ukunqoma* was no longer practised). It is therefore not clear to what extent these arrangements survive or have been modified in the numerous rural communities subjected to 'betterment' or other forms of forced resettlement.

Although he does not provide quantitative data, Tapson [1991] stresses the continuing importance in Kwazulu of lending (*ukusiza*), reciprocal obligations when draught animals are borrowed, and redistribution of benefits through the sharing of meat from slaughtered beasts. Tapson's survey also revealed the extent of *lobolo* exchanges involving cattle in Kwazulu – these were the largest single type of transaction, and payments and receipts accounted for 4.2 and 5.8 per cent of the total herd in the survey. Even larger numbers of animals had been committed for future payments – 11.2 per cent of the herd was recorded as debits and 12.7 per cent as credits [*ibid.*: 11].

Not all studies agree that these kinds of practices survive. Karaan *et al.* [1993] report a survey finding in Lebowa that nearly half the respondents rated the 'commercial' function of livestock to be the most important, followed closely by 'wealth', with very few rating ploughing, rituals, bridewealth or prestige as important.

Few studies have taken gender relations into account. An exception is

Ferguson [1990], whose analysis for Lesotho probably has great relevance for South African rural areas where migrant labour has also been a dominant feature. In this view men and women have different interests with regard to livestock-as-retirement-fund. Men build up the mystique of livestock ownership in order to protect their stored assets for the future, but women attack this mystique to assert their claims for cash to meet the immediate needs of the household, which is their domain of responsibility. Although male and female interests clearly do not conflict in respect of ownership of stock as such, and older women share a direct interest with older men in the high levels of bridewealth which the mystique helps to maintain, Ferguson suggests that the cultural definition of livestock as a particular kind of property generates contestation at both the ideological and the immediate economic level. This can lead to tensions within the household around decisions on whether or not to sell an animal. Recently the Rural Women's Movement has made demands for women to be allowed to make decisions about livestock and to have access to land for grazing and cattle posts [*TRAC,* 1993]. This is an indication that gender struggles may assume a growing importance in rural South Africa in future, and are another factor that may influence the social and economic role of livestock.

Summary

Livestock production in black rural areas today continues to be multi-purpose in character, but which functions are important depends on a number of factors. One influence is agro-ecological zone: livestock sales for cash may be more important in dry areas with poor cropping potential than elsewhere. Another is the economic profile of the region: using cattle for draught power is less important in areas where tractor services are available and affordable, and more important where they are not and where land availability makes cropping a viable option. A function of cattle which is important in most areas is milk production for home use. Livestock continue to be a useful form of savings (or 'store of wealth') for migrant workers, but phases in the 'developmental cycle' of the household must also be taken into account. Herd size and composition influence the decision to sell, but there is contrasting evidence from different regions on whether or not large herd owners have a greater propensity to sell animals for cash. Many studies report that sales are occasional, driven by an immediate need for cash for the household, and often of an 'emergency' nature.

The role of stock is also influenced by the class identity of the owner. Livestock ownership is highly skewed in most areas, is often correlated with higher levels of crop production and with higher levels of income from non-rural sources, and is thus a reasonably reliable indicator of social differentiation. Class formation processes in the former homelands have probably led to a concentration of a significant proportion of livestock in the hands of an elite composed of 'traditional' leaders, bureaucrats and businessmen, some of whom manipulate the communal tenure system for their own benefit.

Transactions between households involving livestock (for example, bridewealth payments, loaning, and co-operative arrangements for ploughing) are found in many areas, but their importance probably varies regionally. Prestige is still associated with high levels of ownership of stock, but again this is probably variable, and cultural context may be relevant. Although not yet researched, the outcome of gender struggles over household decision making is another factor influencing the uses of livestock.

LIVESTOCK AND RURAL LIVELIHOODS: A CONCEPTUAL MODEL

On the basis of both historical accounts and contemporary research a conceptual model of livestock production and rural livelihoods is offered in Figure 1. The model outlines a number of key aspects to be taken into account in analysis: (i) the range of possible functions that livestock can play, singly or (more usually) in combination with each other, and the value of livestock production when this range is taken into account; (ii) sources of variation in the relative importance of livestock functions (for example, by agro-ecological region, socio-economic class, economic profile of the region and so on).

The model can be used as a framework for both analysis and planning, and provides a checklist of key aspects to be taken into account. The analysis presented here suggests that anything less than a 'holistic' or integrated view of livestock production is likely to underestimate its importance in rural livelihood systems, and to overlook important objectives held by livestock owners. The model also assists analysis of the heterogeneity of livestock producers, both between regions and within local populations, a factor which will be critical in planning land redistribution and development programmes.

LAND USE AND RESOURCE MANAGEMENT

This section discusses three questions: are the high stocking rates found in black rural areas sustainable, or are they headed for ecological disaster? How do livestock herders actually make use of rangeland to sustain high densities of livestock populations? And is there a shortage of grazing land for rural households with livestock or attempting to enter into livestock production? All three are relevant in relation to emergent regimes of communal rangeland management and the axes of struggle identified above.

FIGURE 1

LIVESTOCK PRODUCTION AND RURAL LIVELIHOODS: A CONCEPTUAL MODEL

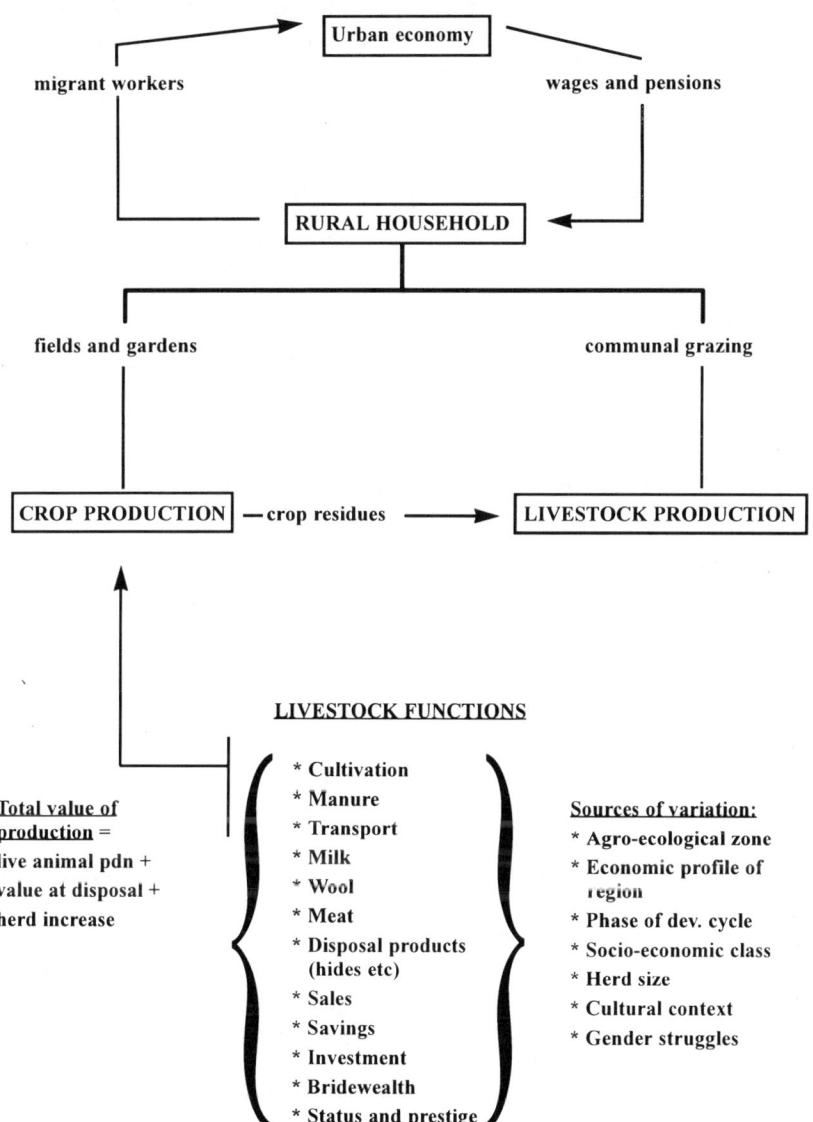

Stocking Rates and Ecological Sustainability

Many studies report high stocking rates on communal rangeland in black rural areas, often two or three times the recommended rate, or what is said to be the 'carrying capacity' of the land. Examples include Lyne and Niewoudt [1991] for Kwazulu; McKenzie [1984] for the Transkei; Barrowman and Klug [1982] for Vulindlela in Kwazulu; Gandar [1991] for Cornfields in Natal; Schmidt [1992] for Dryharts in Bophutatswana; and Vink [1986] for Lebowa. These data have given rise to a concern for ecological sustainability, seen to be threatened by serious 'overgrazing' (see citations in Tapson [1991]), and the perceived problem has often been linked to the underlying system of communal tenure [*Boonzaier et al.,* [1990].

Two recent reviews of the South African literature on stocking rates and sustainability have come to rather different conclusions. For Kwazulu, Tapson [1990; 1991] argues that warnings of ecological collapse due to overgrazing and consequent soil erosion have been made for 50 years, over which time a decline in primary productivity would have surely led to a decline in stock numbers and an increase in stock mortality. Data from a 15-year time series (1974 to 1988) shows an increase in stock numbers from 1.27 million to 1.515 million and a declining trend in mortality. Tapson also argues for the relevance of analytical models such as Walker's [1980] which propose that heavily grazed veld displays qualities of 'resilience' (in which stress may lead to considerable change but a return to an equilibrium state is still possible), albeit at the expense of stability. In support he cites McKenzie's [1982] research in the Transkei, which showed that grasslands grazed at twice the recommended rate contained an abundance of climax species and had a high basal cover, and Danckwerts and Stuart-Hill's [1988] work on the recovery of semi-arid grassveld after drought. On the basis of research findings Tapson questions the reliability and usefulness of standard tools for determining stocking rates (for example, the Veld Condition Score technique), and he also cites work on erosion [e.g. Venter *et al.,* 1989] which calls into question the view that heavy grazing leads to serious soil losses.

Shackleton's recent [1993] wide-ranging review of the literature covers some of the same ground as Tapson, but extends these arguments to communal grazing in moist (>800 mm annual rainfall), mesic (600–800 mm) and semi-arid (<600 mm) zones. Have grasslands changed as a result of constant high stocking rates? Shackleton concludes that in terms of both species composition and basal cover, a variety of research results demonstrate that moist and mesic grasslands show little change, but that some changes were evident in semi-arid zones – although here rainfall had an overriding effect whatever the stocking rate. In respect of herbaceous primary productivity there is meagre and sometimes contradictory evidence, but again moist and mesic grasslands appear little affected. For all three criteria there was little difference according to the grazing system (for example, continuous vs rotational) used (see also Hoffman [1988] for the Karoo). Are the observed changes irreversible? Again, Shackleton cites research findings which demonstrate the resilience of heavily grazed communal rangelands, which often recover rapidly after drought or periods of rest. He concludes that either communal range is extremely resilient, or that recommended stocking rates (from 50 per cent to 25 per cent of those actually found) are too conservative.

Land Use and Local Knowledge

The two reviews cited make occasional reference to research elsewhere in Africa, and it is important to note that there is a growing literature in support of their conclusions [*Behnke and Scoones*, 1993]. This research also suggests that herding practices and local knowledge systems are central issues in the sustainability debate [*Fry and McCabe*, 1986; *Scoones and Wilson*, 1989; *Oba*, 1992; *Scoones*, 1995].

Behnke and Scoones [1993: 13] show how mobility can increase the overall carrying capacity within a region which incorporates a wide range of seasonally variable carrying capacities in different zones. This assumes a pattern of predictable environmental fluctuation. A similar argument is made by Sandford [1983: 33–6] for situations where stock movement takes place in response to unpredictable rainfall fluctuations, disease outbreaks, borehole breakdowns and range fires. In the former case pastoralists often follow regular transhumant routes (as is practised for example in southern Matabeleland in Zimbabwe, Botswana, Lesotho, and Maasailand); in the latter movement is more contingent and depends on herdowners preserving access to fallback areas.

There appears to have been relatively little detailed research on how grazing resources in South Africa's black rural areas are actually used, or on local knowledge of rangeland ecological dynamics. For the Transkei, however, McAllister [1986] has indicated that in Shixini ward in Willowvale district the informal leaders of sub-ward 'sections' (the senior men), may close areas of grazing to allow grass to recover, and use of grazing in areas controlled by sections other than one's own is allowed only after permission has been sought. One of the effects of Betterment planning, according to de Wet [1991], was to impose a rigid division between residential, arable and grazing land which 'deprived people of flexibility of land usage which was previously ecologically adaptive'. For the arid and semi-arid zones, Archer [1993] has described seasonal transhumance in the Richtersveld, and Cousins

[1995] reports that a community-based grazing management plan is being developed in Leliefontein on the basis of local knowledge and practices. These are indications that herders in South Africa, as elsewhere, pursue opportunistic strategies in their use of rangeland resources and that they base these on a fine-tuned understanding of their environments.

A Shortage of Grazing Land?

If communal grazing lands are not necessarily over-stocked (from the point of view of ecological sustainability), they are perhaps *under*-stocked from the point of view of rural households. As pointed out above, there are large numbers of stockless households in most black rural areas, and many herds are small and cannot supply critical functions such as draught power. At the same time, stock numbers in regions such as Kwazulu [*Tapson*, 1991] and Transkei [*McKenzie,* 1984; *Beinart,* 1992] have been relatively stable for some years, and may have reached some kind of ecological limit (perhaps understood as 'ecological carrying capacity'). Here livestock populations may be regulated by density-dependent factors acting on birth and death rates, but limited by density independent factors such as climatic variability [*Scoones* 1993; *Tapson,* 1991]. The implication is then that stockless households attempting to use increased income from formal or informal employment to invest in livestock of their own are constrained by the fact that grazing land is in short supply. Hence broadened access to multiple-function livestock benefits (other than by expanding existing arrangements between households which spread the distribution of those benefits), depends on improved access to rangeland resources, which must be included in land redistribution programmes.

LOCAL INSTITUTIONAL FRAMEWORKS IN RURAL SOUTH AFRICA

Rangeland resources are exploited by herders who move their animals across variable terrain, at different scales, and take account of both regular and irregular fluctuations in resource availability over time. However, local institutional frameworks create a context of both constraints and opportunities for individual herder decision making. In rural South Africa these are currently in flux for a number of reasons: the precise character of rural local government is yet to be decided; the role of 'traditional' authorities in formal structures of governance is unclear and contested; and legal frameworks for various forms of communal tenure are under review. This section briefly outlines the key issues in question.

Rural Local Government

South Africa's interim constitution makes provision for three levels of governance (national, provincial and local), within a quasi-federalist system in which significant powers in most sectors are devolved to provincial governments. The division of powers and responsibilities between national and provincial levels is encountering many difficulties (for example, in relation to budgeting and development planning); with respect to agrarian reform it is highly problematic since land is defined as a national 'competency' but provinces have responsibility for agriculture. Local government is also a provincial competency, and the possibility exists of a variety of arrangements emerging in different parts of the country.

Most debate thus far has centred on local government for urban areas, and *rural* local government has received relatively little attention. Proposals for rural local government include those by McIntosh [1994], and Lund and Wakelin [1993]. These suggest a fourth tier of governance – a primary local authority, as a sub-unit of district councils. To be effective local government must be representative, accountable, with a viable fiscal base, and overcome the legacies of fragmented, centralised and un-coordinated administration inherited from the apartheid past [*McIntosh,* 1994]. This suggests significant support from central or provincial government for capacity building at local level, as well as financial support given the relatively weak economic base of most rural areas. Of particular importance is the delineation of the powers and functions of district councils and the primary bodies, with significant implications for management of common pool resources. By November 1995, when the first democratic local government elections took place, these implications had not yet been explored in any meaningful way (but see Westaway [1994] for a speculative discussion in the Namaqualand, Northern Cape context).

Traditional Leaders and Local Institutional Frameworks

The role of traditional authorities (chiefs and headmen) in an emerging democratic order is a controversial and highly contested issue in South Africa today. A key issue is their land allocation powers. The subordination of customary authorities to repressive state apparatuses, combined with corruption and repression, has undermined the legitimacy of these institutions [*Hendricks,* 1992]; (Levin and Weiner, this volume). Central to the mechanisms through which chiefs have maintained their power has been their control over land [*Haines and Tapscott,* 1988]. Levin and Mkhabela [1994] provide a detailed case study of these processes in the Northern and Eastern Transvaal Lowveld. One example of corruption [*ibid.,* 225] involves the dispossession of communal pasturage by the chief in order to secure private grazing for his own herd of cattle.[5] Chiefs have also used their salaried employment, privileged access to land and livestock, and coercive extraction of levies and taxes to engage in 'accumulation from above', and have thus been central to processes of social differentiation.

The key question is what formal powers are accorded to 'traditional' leaders in emerging local government structures, and whether these include authority over land allocation, land use and related development planning. Also in question is their role in natural resource management. One possibility is that chiefs play an advisory role only, and sit on local councils or land boards in an *ex officio* capacity. The ANC has been somewhat ambivalent on these issues, and the outcome is by no means clear. The Congress of Traditional Leaders of South Africa (CONTRALESA), which is allied to the ANC, is arguing for the retention of land allocation powers by chiefs. In some areas, such as the Eastern Cape, there is conflict between CONTRALESA and organisations such as the South African National Civics Organisation (SANCO), which argue that local government structures must consist only of democratically elected representatives.

Legal Frameworks for Communal Land Ownership

The RDP [*ANC,* 1994] commits the new government to 'development of new and innovative forms of tenure, such as Community Land Trusts, and other forms of group land-holding', and asserts a need to recognise and protect a diversity of tenure forms. Some communities acquiring land through a restitution claim (for example, the Mfengu in the Eastern Cape) or through a state-supported redistribution process (for example, Cornfields-Tembalihle in Natal – see below) have taken ownership through Trusts established under existing legal models, but these are widely acknowledged to be problematic in their complexity, administrative requirements and inaccessibility to poor communities.

The new Department of Land Affairs is initiating a national programme to promote tenure security, and some progress has been made in the drafting of a framework for legislation on communal ownership of land. This aims to be both facilitative and regulatory in an attempt to reconcile public interests and the narrower private interests of communities and individuals. It attempts to be flexible in relation to legal structure, land usage, rights and forms of tenure, and forms of governance, and to allow for a continuum of alternative models. The proposed Act would create a new type of institution known as a 'Communal Property Association'.

There is an urgent need for a more appropriate legal framework for communal tenure. The policy framework for the Pilot Land Reform Projects recently announced in all nine provinces requires groups acquiring land to be legally constituted entities, and it is not yet clear what forms this may take. More generally, the proposed framework would appear to have the potential to facilitate the emergence of viable common property arrangements. However, significant support needs to be provided for the collective decision-making processes leading to the establishment of a Communal Property Association (for example, through offering facilitation, mediation and advice services) if this potential is to be realised.

COMMON PROPERTY STRUGGLES: CASE STUDIES

Data supplied by affiliates of the National Land Committee (NLC) indicate that struggles over communal grazing and other common pool resources are widespread. Livestock and grazing are at the centre of disputes between commercial farmers and evicted labour tenants in the Eastern Transvaal (see also *Land Update* 33, 1994) and in Natal (*New Ground* 19, 1995). Grazing land formerly owned by the South African Development Trust (SADT) is claimed by competing groups in the Queenstown area of the Eastern Cape, and the dispute has remained unresolved since 1990. Similarly, four different communities in Namaqualand are claiming rights to grazing land on state owned farms along the Orange River. Also in Namaqualand, residents of the arid Richtersveld area were granted controlled access to the newly proclaimed Richtersveld National Park in 1991; they are adhering to agreed stock limitations, but have not yet been granted access to adjacent state land as also agreed as part of the settlement. In the Transkei residents of Dwesa and Cwebe have invaded neighbouring coastal nature reserves which they claim were forcibly taken from them in the 1950s, and have begun to harvest shellfish and fuelwood and to graze their cattle. They were recently granted controlled access by the provincial government, but are pursuing their claim and state that they wish to develop the reserves as tourist enterprises (*Land Update* 36, 1995). This section analyses two cases where detailed information is available.

Cornfields – Tembalihle[6]

In Natal, two freehold communities which have large populations of freehold plot owners and tenants have recently bought land from neighbouring white farmers under Act 126 of 1993,[7] which makes provision for a government grant covering 80 per cent of the land price, plus a subsidised loan. Disputes over common pool resources have been a major feature of relations between black and white landowners, and it was these that prompted negotiations over land acquisition.

In both Cornfields and Tembalihle the population is highly dependent on urban migrant remittances and state pensions, and on livestock to a lesser extent. In late 1989 a survey in Cornfields revealed that there was a 'considerable degree of income inequality', with 30 per cent of sample households receiving an income of R400 per month or less, but 20 per cent earning R1,000 per month or more, and another four per cent earning more

MAP 1
CORNFIELDS AND TEMBALIHLE

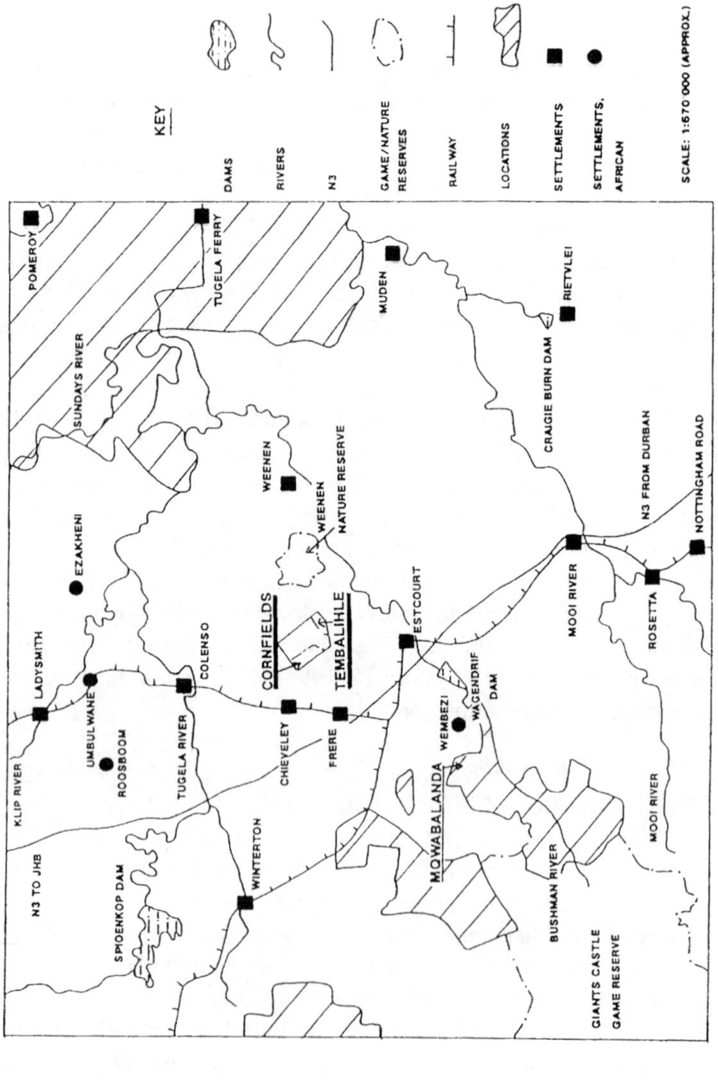

KEY

DAMS

RIVERS

N3

GAME/NATURE
RESERVES

RAILWAY

LOCATIONS

SETTLEMENTS

SETTLEMENTS,
AFRICAN

SCALE: 1:670 000 (APPROX.)

POMEROY

TUGELA FERRY

SUNDAY'S RIVER

MUDEN

RIETVLEI

CRAIGIE BURN DAM

WEENEN

WEENEN
NATURE RESERVE

N3 FROM DURBAN

EZAKHENI

CORNFIELDS

TEMBALIHLE

ESTCOURT

MOOI RIVER

NOTTINGHAM ROAD

LADYSMITH

COLENSO

ROSETTA

UMBULWANE

ROOSBOOM

TUGELA RIVER

CHIEVELEY

FRERE

WAGENDRIF
DAM

MOOI RIVER

KLIP RIVER

WINTERTON

MOWABALANDA

WEMBEZI

BUSHMAN RIVER

N3 TO JHB

SPIOENKOP DAM

GIANTS CASTLE
GAME RESERVE

than R2,800 per month [*Bromberger,* 1991: 21]. Some 60 per cent of the sample owned cattle or goats or both, but only 36 per cent had cattle (with a mean herd size of seven). Landowners owned about three times as many cattle as tenants and nearly twice as many goats [*Gandar,* 1991: 39]. Only one family in ten cultivated fields. Gandar estimated that cash earnings from agriculture amounted to an average of only R4 per month per household, and the amount of meat provided was small. Milk, draught power and manure were not assessed. Nevertheless, 80 per cent of respondents said they regarded themselves as belonging to 'farming families', and, (male) farmers at meetings 'were emphatic that they regarded themselves as stock farmers'; in addition 'they were adamant that they would not reduce their herds and said that access to grazing is one of their most urgent needs' [*Gandar,* 1991: 41].

Both communities are surrounded by white farms and were designated as 'black spots' in the 1970s and threatened with removal (see Map 1). With the assistance of an NGO (the Association for Rural Advancement, AFRA) removals were successfully resisted and the communities were officially 'reprieved' in 1990. However, evictions of labour tenants from white farms in the district in the 1960s and 1970s have resulted in rising populations and extreme pressure on the local resource base. By the 1990s there were about 4 000 people living on 593 ha in Cornfields, and about 2,700 people living on 242 ha in Tembalihle [*AFRA,* 1993].[8] Residents began to rely heavily on neighbouring white farms for their grazing, water, firewood and thatching grass. This led to cattle impoundings by white farmers, heavy fines and pound fees, arrests of women collecting wood and water, and claims for damages by community members. In times of drought the tensions threatened to spill over into violent conflict.

In the early 1990s white farmers in the district launched a Biosphere initiative which aims to establish a conservation and ecotourism area on 56,000 ha, and eventually encompass 150,000 ha. Cornfields and Tembalihle fell within the proposed Tugela Biosphere Reserve. To resolve the ongoing conflicts, and provide a more secure context for the Biosphere, farmers agreed in 1993 to negotiate with the two communities for the transfer of some of the surrounding farms, provided that they would be adequately compensated. By 1994 agreement had been reached to transfer 8,500 ha to the communities at a cost of around R6 million (about 90 per cent of market value). In terms of Act 126 the state has agreed to pay 80 per cent of the costs, residents have raised 5 per cent as a down payment, with the other 15 per cent as a loan from the state. The guidelines accompanying the Act require groups acquiring land to set up a legal body or 'community government structure', to assume responsibility for payment of the balance of the purchase price, and also to control livestock numbers, manage grazing land, and manage other 'development initiatives' by the group (for example, the use of clay, firewood, etc.).

Negotiations between community representatives (assisted by AFRA), white farmers and officials of the Department of Land Affairs have been accompanied by an intense process of internal debate and decision making within Cornfields and Tembalihle. In September 1993 a Participatory Rural Appraisal (PRA) exercise was carried out in the two communities by AFRA staff and others. This included discussions in different wards on the questions of form of ownership and on criteria for membership, as well as developing a community profile and investigating local resources and land uses [*AFRA*, 1993; *Midnet*, 1994: 22–3]. There was general agreement that land should be held communally, and that all current residents should become joint 'owners'. Elected committees within both communities then initiated debates on whether or not to purchase under Act 126, and eventually this was agreed to. Another PRA exercise in December 1993 investigated local opinions on the precise definition of membership, on the rights and obligations of members (with a particular focus on common pool resources), on financial contributions to make the five per cent down payment, and on the restrictions imposed by the Act (for example, complying with recommendations made by the Department of Agriculture with regard to stocking rates). Also debated were the responsibilities, powers and composition of the committee to be elected to manage the affairs of the new landholding body, and whether or not the existing committee should fulfil some or all of these new tasks.

All these proved to be controversial issues, and it was difficult for residents to reach agreement. This was partly because of the diversity of potential members: both present and absentee landowners (that is, title deed holders), tenants on existing land, labour tenants on farms to be purchased, other labour tenants, and those members of the communities who agreed to be removed by the state in 1988. The rights of unmarried women was also controversial. Questions of grazing rights and the regulation of stock numbers by an elected committee, but subject to recommendations made by state officials, were particularly difficult, and decisions on these were deferred to a later date. The representivity of the existing committees, comprising mostly older men, has been a sensitive issue. Social differentiation, contrasting opinions on key issues, and power plays by opposed interest groups have been problematic aspects for the NGO (AFRA) which has attempted to play a facilitative role in the process.

In January 1994 a decision was made to form a landowning trust in each community, and in the next few months more meetings were held to formulate the deeds of Trust and develop criteria for choosing Trustees. Here the issue of the role of tenants and of women as particular interest groups again aroused heated debate; both groups were eventually included as potential Trustees, but only two women were elected to the Trust. Difficult questions of detail (for example, on regulations for the use of common pool resources) were left for communities to formulate into by-laws at a later stage as their management systems developed.

Trusts were formed in May 1994, and ownership of the farms changed hands in early 1995. In September 1994 AFRA, other service NGOs and the committees jointly investigated land use planning options in both communities, and the issue of stock limitation was again debated by different groups. There appears to be support amongst some community members for stocking rate regulations, and a livestock tax has been suggested as a possible mechanism. No by-laws governing resource utilisation have been formulated to date. The boundary between land to be taken possession of by Cornfields and that by Tembalihle is unclear in one locality, and negotiations on this issue continue. In Tembalihle there is an ongoing dispute between households which have paid their full contribution to the purchase of the farms and those which have not, and this conflict may be the underlying reason for damage to fencing which demarcates grazing areas.

The Mid-Fish River Basin[9]

The mid-Fish River Basin in the Eastern Cape displays in a particularly stark form many of the characteristics of rural South Africa which are likely to make resolution of common property struggles difficult. It is located at the boundary between the former Ciskei homeland and white-owned commercial farmland, and comprises a complex mosaic of contrasting land tenure and land use systems (Map 2). These are the result of a long history of conquest, white settlement and development, black impoverishment, out-migration, resistance and land struggles over the past 150 years in what was originally known as the frontier zone, and subsequently as the Border region. Also important is the agro-ecology of the area. In general it is semi-arid and marginal for cropping: rainfall is low and unreliable (400 mm to 500 mm), high rates of evaporation and run-off further reduce the availability of water, and droughts are common. Soils are shallow, infertile and erodible, slopes are steep, and the natural vegetation is dominated by woody shrubs of low value as forage.

Livelihoods, land use and tenure systems: In 1835 a parcel of 'neutral' territory east of the Fish River was ceded to 'loyal Fingos' (Mfengu) who had fought alongside the British; under the 1913 Land Act this was scheduled as Fingo's Location. The rest of the area was successively allocated to white settlers and their descendants on either side of the Fish

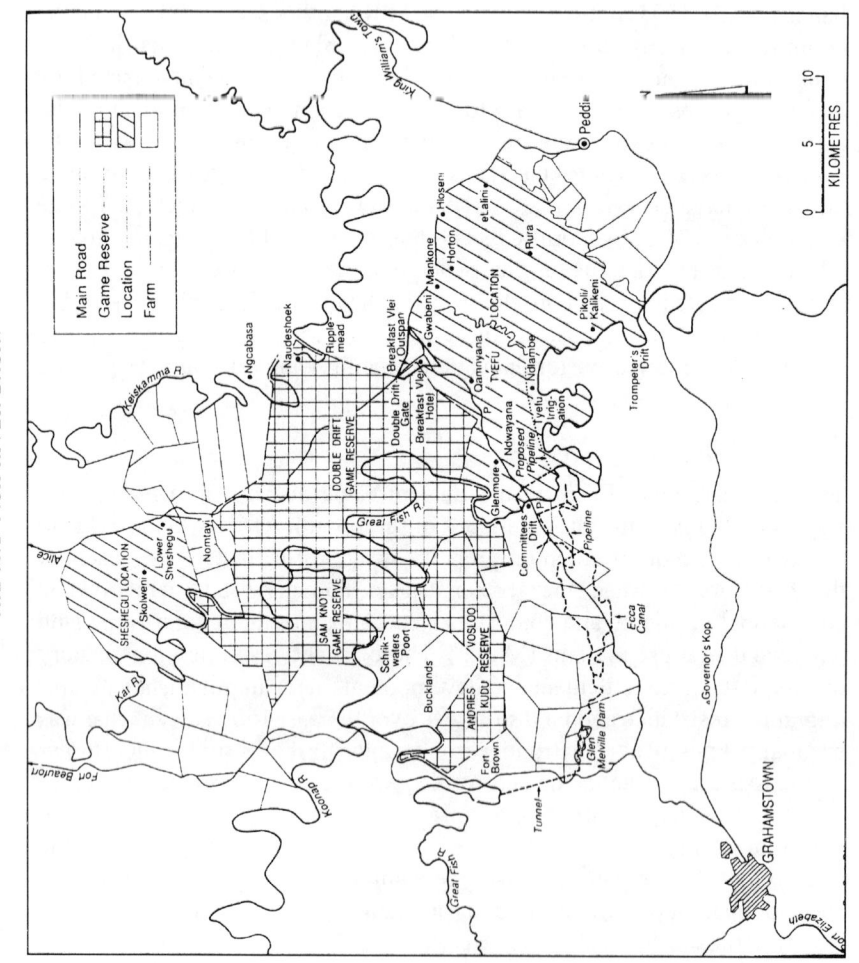

MAP 2

THE MID-FISH RIVER BASIN

River. In the run-up to Ciskei's 'independence' in 1982 the white-owned farms to the east of the river were bought up by the South African government and incorporated into the Ciskei, either as 'released' farms or into the L.L. Sebe Game Reserve. From 1979 the state began to forcibly remove people from so-called 'black spots' in the Eastern Cape to the area, and the 'rural township' of Glenmore, consisting of 4,500 people, was established on a released white farm adjacent to the Fish River. At present the area contains four distinct units of settlement, tenure and land use:

(a) The 'released' farms are either held by civil servants from the former Ciskei government under leasehold tenure (mainly for extensive livestock production), or are unused. They contain forage resources which are better than average for the zone, but the legitimacy of the leases is now in question given the re-incorporation of the Ciskei into South Africa.

(b) There are three nature reserves, managed either by the state or by a Ciskeian parastatal. In addition to the former L.L. Sebe Game Reserve (subsequently renamed the Double Drift Game Reserve) to the east of the river, are two reserves to the west formed in the 1970s and 1980s from former commercial ranches. The reserves were generally heavily grazed prior to their proclamation, but today carry more vegetation than the surrounding farms, partly because they contain high lying areas with generally higher forage production potential than elsewhere in the zone. The reserves protect some rare large herbivores and areas of unique Valley Bushveld.

(c) White farms to the west of the Fish River, under freehold tenure, are used mostly for mohair production from Angora goats on extensive range. About 260 ha is under irrigation using water from the Fish-Orange scheme,[10] the main crop being lucerne for farmers' livestock or for sale as a cash crop. The average net white farm income in 1991 was estimated at R71,000. However, drought, depressed markets and high transport costs are severe problems. As is generally the case within white agriculture, the withdrawal of high levels of state subsidy and support is now putting the economic viability of these enterprises into question. Workers on these farms are poorly paid, and only a quarter have permanent full-time employment. Population densities on the farms are similar to those found on land in the previous two categories (about 3–6 persons/km^2).

(d) In Tyefu and Sheshegu Locations land is held under a form of communal tenure. Population densities are very high (over 70 persons/km^2), and many of the common features of Southern African labour reserves are present:

systematic underdevelopment of agriculture and of infrastructure and services, high rates of labour migration, heavy reliance on state pensions or disability grants (and remittances to a lesser degree), high levels of local unemployment, and high dependency ratios (that is, many children and old people). Agriculture is marginal as a source of income for the majority of households. Cultivation of rain-fed crops has steadily declined since the 1950s and only a few fields along the Fish River and on the plateau are still being used; these are planted mostly to maize. A minority of households cultivate home gardens. Much household labour time is spent on collecting firewood and water for domestic use. The population is highly differentiated, with markedly skewed distributions of wealth and livestock, and villages are also internally divided by gender, clan membership and political affiliation.

The most important form of crop production takes place on the Tyefu Irrigation Scheme, on alluvial terraces adjacent to the Fish River. The scheme was begun on 121 ha in 1977, using water from the Fish-Orange scheme, and expanded to 420 ha during the 1980s. Tyefu is a typical showcase bantustan irrigation scheme, achieving little success despite massive capital outlays. From its beginnings the scheme has been plagued by conflict between local residents and management, as well as by problems of economic viability given distance from markets. The Scheme is currently managed by the Ciskei Agricultural Corporation.[11] The scheme includes 33 small-scale commercial farms (4 ha), 223 subsistence food plots (0.25 ha) and 666 allotments (0.1 ha). Commercial 'tribal estate farms' are now being phased out.

Most of the land in the communal areas is used for extensive grazing of herds of cattle (27 per cent of all livestock) and sheep and goats (73 percent). However. the distribution of stock is highly skewed, with a minority (about 22 per cent of households) owning more than 90 per cent of livestock. Some livestock owners are absentee migrants who employ local˙ residents as herders. Herds are multi-purpose in character. Stocking rates are generally high but variable in response to rainfall, with populations declining rapidly in drought years but bouncing back in years of high rainfall. Rangeland is heavily grazed and Karroid dwarf shrubs have replaced more palatable grasses and shrubs, leading agricultural extension staff and botanists to describe the area as 'overgrazed and degraded'. Erosion and deforestation around villages are also seen as major problems.

In recent years high levels of unemployment in urban areas have led to a number of people returning to their rural community of origin, where they are not seen as having forfeited their rights to fields or the use of communal land. Some have gained access to pension incomes or remittances through kinship networks, others have tried to gain access to land on the irrigation scheme or sought employment on neighbouring white farms.

Despite the unpromising nature of the agro-ecology many local residents would like to remain in the area and to see economic development take place locally. High on the list of expressed needs are jobs (in local industries, civil service posts, and in the nature reserves), new infrastructure (for water supply in particular) and improved services. Land for village irrigation projects and for livestock grazing is also seen as vital; land shortages are seen as the primary cause of environmental problems, and researchers in the area have characterised the situation as one of 'land hunger'. Legitimate institutions for local governance are seen as critically important.

Institutional frameworks: The new Eastern Cape province as a whole is currently experiencing a traumatic transition to a new institutional and administrative framework, and the mid-Fish Basin is no exception. The inherited framework is highly divided and fragmented as a result of apartheid legislation, and in a state of near collapse in the case of those areas which fell within the former Ciskei. In Tyefu and Sheshegu the tribal authority system is widely rejected and regarded as an oppressive apartheid institution used to impose bantustan rule. However, village headmen continue to draw salaries, and to receive support from a minority faction. The majority favour ANC aligned residents associations ('civics'), but these are not officially recognised. Local organisations which have had some support (for example, the Lower Fish River Development Project Steering Committee) have had no statutory powers. The province has been racked by a dispute between chiefs, on the one hand, and the South African National Civics Organisation (SANCO), on the other, on the role of traditional leaders within local government.

To the west of the Fish River, institutions for the support of white farmers have functioned fairly effectively (for example, drought relief bodies, agricultural extension services, Farmer's Associations and Soil Conservation Committees). How these will articulate with other bodies within the area for purposes of administration, development planning or natural resource management is not at all clear. Currently there are no institutional structures in the zone which enable different groups to meet, negotiate, resolve conflicts or make joint decisions. Similarly, the management of nature reserves is split between the former Ciskeian parastatal and the Cape Nature Conservation authorities.

Struggles over land and resources: Common pool resources such as water, fuelwood, vegetation and grazing land are important components of the overall livelihood system of the densely populated communal areas. Given the high levels of stress of both the resource base and people, it is not surprising that struggles over these resources are strongly evident at present and promise to become even more so in the near future. These struggles are taking, or are likely to take, a number of different forms:

Land claims: residents from different villages within Tyefu and Sheshegu Locations claim that various portions of land within the area historically belonged to them. Claims based on more recent events, and which are therefore the most likely to be addressed either through land restitution or the emergence of co-management arrangements with existing owners, are made in relation to Double Drift Game Reserve and to some of the 'released' farms. One small group of households has refused to be removed from Double Drift and still graze their herds within its boundaries. Some people feel that even the white farms should also be opened up for resettlement. There is thus strong pressure mounting to extend the area under communal tenure.

Illegal land use: although fuelwood collection within the reserves is allowed (under supervision), residents of villages also hunt illegally for wild meat within the nature reserves, and graze their cattle on 'released' farms. These activities are justified in terms of perceived rightful ownership to the land.

Stock impounding: in drought years livestock from Tyefu cross the Fish River and are sent to the pound in Grahamstown (40 km distant) by white farmers. Their owners must then pay fines before the animals are released, and also incur prohibitive travel costs. Feelings on this issue run high partly because communal grazing is in short supply as a result of processes of historical dispossession.

Internal conflicts: there are currently disputes over land rights within some villages in Sheshegu Location. In the past there have been tensions over grazing land between residents of Ndwanyana village in Tyefu and those of Glenmore township, although this has abated somewhat recently. At present most communal rangeland may even be under a form of 'open access' rather than even 'minimum' common property. Given the legacy of political and other divisions within the area, initiatives to develop resource management institutions in future are likely to generate localised disputes over rights, duties and authorities. There is also the potential for disputes over land claims between different village communities within the area.

Disputes between local communities and external authorities: relations between local residents and officials of state and parastatal bodies have long been plagued by hostility and lack of trust. Betterment planning, for example, was fiercely resisted in the area and as a result never implemented. There is great potential for similar conflicts to emerge in future, given contrasting perceptions of central issues such as stocking rates and management systems. Residents are adamant that they do not want outsiders to set limits on stock numbers.

CONCLUSION: LESSONS FOR AGRARIAN REFORM

These case studies tell us something about the concrete forms which struggles over common property are taking on the ground in contemporary South Africa, and their roots in the social relations of production. Are there any general lessons to be drawn, and what are the wider implications for agrarian reform policies?

First, these case studies point to *the necessity of understanding the origins of such struggles in differentiated rural livelihood systems in which common pool resources are a vital component of production and reproduction for many households, but access to which is unevenly distributed.* Natural resource use is thus associated with structured inequalities at the local level, arising from class-based differentiation, gender relations, divisions between landowners and tenants or squatters (for example, in Cornfields-Tembalihle), and political authority (for example, privileged access for tribal authorities, as in the Eastern Transvaal villages reported by Levin and Mkhabela [1994]). This complicates enormously the task of developing viable common property management arrangements which attempt to make provision for the policy goals of equity and democratisation.

Distinguishing only between the rich (with commercially oriented herds) and the poor (with multiple function herds) runs the risk of oversimplifying the situation in many rural communities. Different kinds of producers, emphasising different functions, and possibly including some specialised single function herds or flocks, may be present within a rural community, and represent contrasting 'recommendation domains'. Heterogeneity of producers will require similarly differentiated policies and programmes, although clearly the most disadvantaged groupings will need to be given priority.

A major question is how the stockless and small herd owners can be assisted to gain wider access to livestock. Mechanisms which have been suggested (and in some cases tried out) in neighbouring countries such as Zimbabwe include credit programmes for livestock purchase [*Chinembiri,* 1989], support for local and inter-regional livestock markets [*Sandford,* 1982], and support for existing as well as innovative draught-pooling and equitable loaning new arrangements [*Cliffe*, 1986; *Scoones and Wilson*, 1989].

Secondly, *it is important to understand the economic rationale for high stocking rate systems on communal rangeland, derived from the multiple purpose character of livestock production.* A 'holistic' analysis of multi-purpose production systems suggests that rural people attach importance to their herds and flocks because of a sound assessment of their overall social and economic value. The implication is that rural livelihoods can be improved by a broadening of access to livestock and grazing land, which must therefore assume a central role in agrarian reform.

Redistribution programmes need to investigate the extent of underutilised land suitable for extensive grazing on commercial sector farms, or even wildlife areas, and possible ways for communities to gain access to it. Some of these may not involve relocation of households – lease of grazing is a well established practice, and in Zimbabwe the Model D resettlement scheme in Matabeleland was intended to provide rotational access to a former commercial ranch by neighbouring villages.[12]

Within redistribution programmes, agencies providing support services should recognise the trade-offs which commonly have to be made within agro-pastoral systems. Some of these are between different livestock functions, for example, between milk production and herd growth, or between milk production and the provision of draught [*Scoones*, 1990]. The critical decisions on these issues are made by the producers themselves, but can be usefully supported by outside agencies with insights into the character of production, or frustrated and undermined if they are not understood. Other trade-offs are in relation to land use. High potential areas with large proportions of potentially arable land present a series of difficult choices. If draught is provided by oxen then grazing land for the herds which reproduce them is required, but if affordable tractor services are available then the land may be able to support a larger number of crop producing units. In low potential areas the potential benefits from wildlife production in its widest sense (including hunting and tourism) must be weighed against those from multi-function livestock production.

In relation to both kinds of trade-offs realism demands that the full value of production, as well as all costs, be properly accounted for. There are probably a number of regional variations, in some cases due to agro-ecological differences between zones where crop production has greater potential and others where it is more marginal, which will also have to be taken into account.

Thirdly, *struggles over common property resources such as rangelands in contemporary South Africa are tending to occur along several axes simultaneously, or in close succession.* This adds to the complexity of these situations, posing problems for both analysts, policy makers and staff of implementation agencies. For example:

* In both cases discussed here a fundamental struggle is to *gain secure rights to land with common pool resources.* The overlap between a generalised struggle for land and the specifics of common property struggles, as discussed in this article, has perhaps led to a neglect of the some aspects of the latter by land activists both at local level and in support organisations.

* *Defining membership of the user group* has proved a troublesome issue in Cornfields-Tembalihle, and is likely to be so in all cases where trusts or other formal land ownership bodies are formed. In some rural communities the rights of tenants are likely to be a contentious issue, and whether or not rights are defined in terms of households or adult individuals (which allows for clear provision for gender equality) is also likely to be controversial.

* *Boundary disputes* have occurred in many cases in connection with basic land claims, but may remain a problem between different groups acquiring land or rights of access, as in the mid-Fish River basin and in Cornfields-Tembalihle.

* *Defining operational rules for resource use* has mostly been deferred to a later date in the cases described here, but is likely to prove contentious – as in the discussion of stocking rate limitations in Cornfields-Tembalihle. Controls over resource use which may have existed in the past have disappeared in many areas, and emergent common property regimes will sometimes have to innovate in the face of what may be *de facto* 'open access' situations such as that found in the mid-Fish River basin.

* *Authority for rule enforcement* has been a difficult issue in Cornfields-Tembalihle, with debates over the composition and powers of elected committees. Where there are tensions between civic associations and 'traditional leaders', as in the mid-Fish River zone, this could prove to be particularly controversial, and rule enforcement through appeals to elected authorities could well provoke conflict rather than assist resolution of disputes.

* *Relationships with external authorities and agencies* in respect of common pool resource management is likely to become problematic soon after rights to land have been secured, eg. when land use planning begins to take place and as operational rules begin to be defined. The

lack of clarity on the structure of rural local government again poses potential problems. Tensions over the issue of stocking rate regulation and other requirements of Act 126 have been experienced in Cornfields-Tembalihle. In the mid-Fish River Basin a history of tension and conflict between community members and authorities over betterment schemes, the management of Tyefu Irrigation Scheme, and access to resources within conservation areas will have to be overcome; contrasting understandings and definitions of environmental degradation and appropriate solutions could well prove controversial in such cases.

The implication here is that all the potential axes of conflict over common property need to be borne in mind by policy makers and implementation agencies from the outset, and planned for in a systematic manner. This could mean using a discourse of 'community identity' to help secure rights to land, while simultaneously promoting internal debates and negotiations between potentially opposed interest groups within 'communities'. An analysis which recognises the reality of social differentiation, in its various guises, will assist in the design of more effective interventions.

Fourthly, the protracted process of negotiations, investigations and collective decision-making within Cornfields-Tembalihle demonstrates that *attempts to develop viable common property regimes must be recognised as being time-consuming, messy and contested in character.*[13] 'Quick fix' and blueprint solutions are unlikely to resolve conflicts, and will probably favour the interest groups which currently hold power and wealth. There is an important role for outsiders (for example, AFRA in Cornfields-Tembalihle) as facilitators of local decision-making processes, but this is not an easy task in differentiated rural communities comprising opposed factions and interests. Outsiders also have their own agendas which influence their interventions, and these need to be openly acknowledged. This often becomes clear in relation to women's rights to land and livestock and their participation in community decision-making, when patriarchal institutions demonstrate their resistance to arrangements premised on the gender equity promised by South Africa'a new constitution.

In conclusion, the evidence presented here suggests that conflicts over common property are likely to become a key issue in land restitution, land redistribution and tenure reform programmes. Emerging views on common property reinforce the need for an approach which lends active support to local level processes of decision making and institution building, as is already emphasised in government policy documents such as the RDP and guidelines for Pilot Land Reform Projects. However, it is also important to stress that political and ideological struggles will be integral to such processes. As found in the case of Cornfields-Tembalihle, participatory appraisal and planning methodologies can be emancipatory if they open up a space within which previously disempowered groupings (for example, women) can articulate their views, but this space is likely to be contested. Reconstruction and development in rural South Africa will have to continue to grapple with difficult issues of political economy.

NOTES

1. This study uses the concept of 'common property' in the restricted sense defined above, and does not take it to refer to forms of common ownership in general (in which, for example, individual usufruct of residential or arable land is granted under forms of communal tenure). Bruce [1986] clarifies these distinctions in his discussion of tenure in the African context; in South Africa there is currently a tendency to conflate these differences in discussions of land rights and tenure.
2. Space precludes a review of the changing role of livestock in rural production and social relationships in the pre-colonial and colonial periods, and in the era of capitalist industrialisation; see Cousins [1994: 2].
3. These refer to the former bantustans or 'homelands' created by segregation and apartheid policies, and which since 1994 have been re-incorporated into South Africa and its nine new provinces.
4. Schmidt argues that in the long run the rising costs of keeping large numbers of animals (increased mortality and decreased milk yields caused by 'overstocking' and reduced 'carrying capacity') will outweigh the benefits, leading to a search for alternative forms of investment, and voluntary destocking. This is a dubious argument given experience elsewhere in Africa [Behnke, 1994].
5. As noted above, Vink [1986] refers to perceived degradation of communal grazing in Lebowa as a 'tragedy of the chiefs'.
6. Information supplied by the Association for Rural Advancement (AFRA).
7. The full title of the Act is the 'Provision of Certain Land for Settlement Act of 1993'.
8. Bromberger [1991: 8] estimates that in Cornfields in 1988 there were 158 landowner households and 756 tenant households, that is, a ratio of 1: 4.8.
9. Data for this section is derived from Ainslie et al. [1994].
10. Water in the Fish River is saline and from the mid-1980s water from the Orange River has been pumped in, at great expense, to dilute it and make it suitable for irrigation.
11. In many ways the irrigation scheme constitutes a distinctive tenure and land use system of its own (Ainslie -personal communication).
12. The many problems encountered in attempting to implement this particular scheme [Robins, 1992] should not obscure the possibilities generated by the underlying principle [Cliffe, 1986].
13. Thanks to Tessa Cousins for this insight.

REFERENCES

AFRA, 1991, From Removals to Development: Cornfield – Profile and History of a Rural Community, Pietermaritzburg: Association For Rural Advancement.
AFRA, 1993, 'Summary Report: Cornfields/Tembalihle: Land Acquisition Programme', unpublished report.
Ainslie A., R.Fox and C. Fabricius 1994, Towards Policies for Feasible and Sustainable Natural Resource Use: The Mid-Fish River Zonal Study, Eastern Cape, Johannesburg: Land and Agriculture Policy Centre.

204 THE AGRARIAN QUESTION IN SOUTH AFRICA

ANC, 1994, *Reconstruction and Development Plan*, Johannesburg: African National Congress.

Archer, F., 1993, *Land Tenure in the Namaqualand Rural Reserves*, Athlone: Surplus People Project.

Auerbach R.M.B., Nichol, G.D. and M.V. Gandar, 1991, *The Tractor as a Multi-Purpose Machine in Kwazulu*, Pietermaritzburg: Institute of Natural Resources, University of Natal.

Barrett, J.C., 1992, *The Economic Role of Cattle in Communal Farming Systems in Zimbabwe*, *Pastoral Development Network*, Paper 32b. London: Overseas Development Institute.

Barrowman, P.R. and Klug J.R., 1982, 'A Preliminary Survey of Livestock in the Peri-Urban Settlement of Vulindlela', in: N. Bromberger and J.D. Lea (eds) *Rural Studies in Kwazulu*, Pietermaritzburg: University of Natal.

Behnke, R.H., 1985a, 'Measuring the benefits of Subsistence versus Commercial Livestock Development in Africa', *Agricultural Systems* 16, pp.109–35.

Behnke, R.H., 1985b, 'Open-Range Management and Property Rights in Pastoral Africa: A Case of Spontaneous Range Enclosure in South Darfur, Sudan', Pastoral Development Network Paper 20f, London: Overseas Development Institute.

Behnke R.H., 1994, *Natural Resource Management in Pastoral Africa*, London: Commonwealth Secretariat.

Behnke, R.H. and Scoones, I., 1993, 'Rethinking Range Ecology: Implications for Range Management in Africa', in: Behnke, Scoones and Kervan (eds.) [1993].

Behnke, R.H., Scoones, I. and C. Kervan (eds.), 1993, *Range Ecology at Disequilibrium: New Models of Natural Variability and Pastoral Adaptation in African Savannas*, London Overseas Development Institute, International Institute for Environment and Development, Commonwealth Secretariat.

Beinart, W., 1992, 'Transkeian Smallholders and Agrarian Reform', *Journal of Contemporary African Studies*, Vol.11, No.2, pp.178–99.

Boonzaier, E., M.T. Hoffman, F. Archer and A.B. Smith, 1990, 'Communal Land Use and the "Tragedy of the Commons": Some Problems and Development Perspectives with Specific Reference to Semi-Arid Regions of Southern Africa', *Journal of the Grasslands Society of Southern Africa*, Vol.7, No.2, pp.77–80.

Bromberger, N., 1991, 'A Socio-Economic Profile of Cornfields', in: AFRA [1991].

Bromley, D.W., 1989, 'Property Relations and Economic Development: The Other Land Reform', *World Development*, Vol.17, No.6, pp.867–77.

Bromley, D. (ed.), 1992, *Making the Commons Work: Theory, Practice, Policy*, San Francisco, CA: Institute for Contemporary Studies.

Bromley, D.W. and M.M. Cernea, 1989, *The Management of Common Property Natural Resources*, World Bank Discussion Paper 57, Washington, DC: World Bank.

Bruce, J.W., 1986, *Land Tenure Issues In Project Design and Strategies For Agricultural Development in Sub-Saharan Africa*, LTC Paper 128, Madison: Land Tenure Center, University of Wisconsin-Madison.

Chinembiri,F., 1989, 'Livestock Extension Programmes and Packages in the Communal Lands of Zimbabwe', in Cousins (ed.) [1989].

Cliffe, L., 1986, *Policy Options for Agrarian Reform: a Technical Appraisal*, Harare: FAO.

Colvin, P.M., 1985, 'Cattle sales in Kwazulu. A systems based approach to an improved marketing strategy', *Development Southern Africa*, Vol.12, No.2.

Cousins, B. (ed.), 1989, *People, Land and Livestock: Proceedings of a Workshop on the Socio-economic Dimensions of Livestock Production in the Communal Lands of Zimbabwe*, Harare: GTZ and Centre for Applied Social Sciences, University of Zimbabwe.

Cousins, B. 1989, Community, Class and Grazing Management in Zimbabwe's Communal Lands', in Cousins (ed.) [1989].

Cousins, B. 1992a (ed.), *Institutional Dynamics in Communal Grazing Regimes in Southern Africa*, Harare: Centre for Applied Social Sciences, University of Zimbabwe.

Cousins, B., 1992b, *Room For Dancing On: Grazing Schemes in the Communal Lands of Zimbabwe*, Harare: Centre for Applied Social Sciences, University of Zimbabwe.

Cousins, B., 1993, 'Common Property Institutions in Land Redistribution Programmes in South Africa', background paper for Rural Restructuring Programme, Johannesburg: Land and Agriculture Policy Centre.

Cousins, B., 1994, 'Livestock Production and Agrarian Reform in South Africa', in Levin and Weiner (eds.) [1994].

Cousins, B., 1995, 'Range Management and Land Reform Policy in Post-Apartheid South Africa', paper presented at Vth International Rangelands Congress, Salt Lake City, July 1995.

Cross, C.R. and R.J. Haines, 1988, *Towards Freehold? Options for Land and Development in South Africa's Black Rural Areas*, Johannesburg: Juta & Co.

Cunningham, A.B., 1985, 'The Resource Value of Indigenous Plants to Rural People in a Low Agricultural Potential Area', Ph.D. dissertation, University of Cape Town.

Danckwerts, J.E. and G.C. Stuart-Hill., 1988, 'The Effect of Severe Drought and Management after Drought on the Mortality and Recovery of Semi-Arid Grassveld', *Journal of the Grassland Society of Southern Africa*, Vol.5, No.4, pp.218–22.

de Ridder, N. and K.T. Wagenaar, 1986, 'Energy and Protein Balances in Traditional Livestock Systems and Ranching in Eastern Botswana', *Agricultural Systems* 20, pp.1–16.

de Wet, C., 1991, 'Some Socio-Economic Consequences of Villagisation Schemes in Africa, and the Future of "Betterment Villages" in the "New South Africa"', *Development Southern Africa*, Vol.8, No.1.

Ellis J.E. and D.M. Swift, 1988, 'Stability of African Pastoral Ecosystems: Alternate Paradigms and Implications for Development', *Journal of Range Management*, 41, pp.450–9.

Ellis J.E., Coughenour, M.B. and D.M. Swift, 1993, 'Climate Variability, Ecosystem Stability and the Implications for Range and Livestock Development', in R.H. Behnke, Jr., I. Scoones and C. Kervan (eds.), *Range Ecology at Disequilibrium*, London: Overseas Development Institute.

Ferguson, J., 1990, *The Anti-Politics Machine: 'Development', Depoliticisation, and Bureaucratic State Power in Lesotho*, Cape Town: David Philip and Cambridge: Cambridge University Press.

Fischer, A., 1987, 'Land Tenure in Mhala: Official Wisdom "Locked Up" in Tradition and People "Locked Up" in Development', *Development Southern Africa*, Vol.4, No.3.

Forster, S., 1994, 'Critical Water Issues Impeding Rural Development in South Africa', draft Position Paper, Natural Resources Management Project, Johannesburg: Land and Agriculture Policy Centre.

Fry, P.H. and J.T. McCabe, 1986, *A Comparison of the Survey Methods in Pastoral Turkana Migration Patterns and the Implications for Development Planning, Pastoral Development Network*, No. 22b, London: Overseas Development Institute.

Galaty, J.G., 1993, 'Individuating Common Resources: Sub-Division of Group Ranches in Kenya Maasaailand', paper presented at Commonwealth Secretariat Workshop on New Directions in African Range Management and Policy, Woburn, UK.

Gandar, M., 1991, 'Cornfields' Natural Resources, Agriculture and Management Options', in AFRA [1991].

Gandar, M. and S. Christiek, 1994, *Commercial and Social Forestry*, draft Position Paper, Natural Resources Management Project. Johannesburg: Land and Agriculture Policy Centre.

Gandar, M.V. and N. Bromberger, 1984, *Economic and Demographic Functioning of Rural Households: Mahlabatini District, Kwazulu*, Carnegie Conference Paper No.56, Second Carnegie Inquiry Into Poverty and Development in Southern Africa, Cape Town: SALDRU.

Graham, O., 1988, *Enclosure of the East African Rangelands: Rrecent Trends and Their Impact, Pastoral Development Network*, No. 25a, London: Overseas Development Institute.

Groenewald, J.A. and J.P.F. Du Toit, 1985, 'Marketing Behaviour and Preferences of Bophutatswana Cattle Owners', *Agrekon* 24.

Haines, R. and C.P.G. Tapscott, 1988, 'The Silence of Poverty: Tribal Administration and Development in Rural Transkei', in Cross and Haines [1988].

Hardin, G., 1968, 'The Tragedy of the Commons', *Science*, pp.1243–8.

Hendricks F.T., 1992, 'Tribalism, Chiefs and Apartheid: The Case of Poto's Pondoland', *South African Sociological Review*, Vol.5, No.1, pp.58–82.

Heron, G.S., 1990, 'The Household, Economic Differentiation and Agricultural Production in Shixini, Transkei', *Development Southern Africa*, Vol.8, No.1.

Hoffman, M.T., 1988, 'Rationale for Karoo Grazing Systems: Criticisms and Research Findings', *South African Journal of Science* 84, pp.556–9.

Jackson, J.C., 1989, 'Exploring Livestock Incomes in Zimbabwe's Communal Lands', in Cousins (ed.) [1989].

Karaan, M., W. Lubbe, A. Nkosi and J. van Zyl, 1993, *Agricultural Marketing: Red Meat*, World Bank Rural Restructuring Programme for South Africa, Land and Agriculture Policy Centre.

Lane, C. and 'R. Moorehead, 1995, 'New Directions in Rangeland and Resource Tenure and Policy', in Scoones (ed.) [1995].

Land and Agriculture Policy Centre (LAPC), 1994, *Proceedings of a Workshop on Natural Resource Management in Post-apartheid South Africa*, Johannesburg: Land and Agriculture Policy Centre.

Lawry, S.W., 1990, 'Tenure Policy Toward Common Property Natural Resources in Sub-Saharan Africa', *Natural Resources Journal* 30, pp.403–22.

Levin, R. and D. Weiner (eds.), 1994, *Community Perspectives on Land and Agrarian Reform in South Africa*, Final report prepared for Macarthur Foundation, Johannesburg: University of Witwatersrand.

Levin, R. and S. Mkhabela, 1994, 'The Chieftaincy, Land Allocation and Democracy in the Central Lowveld', in Levin and Weiner (eds.) [1994].

Low, A. and Fowler ,M., 1980, *Cattle Marketing Survey: Preliminary Report*, Mbabane: Ministry of Agriculture, Swaziland.

Lund, S. and P. Wakelin, 1993, 'Administrative Requirements for Rural Restructuring: A Summary of Collected Investigations and Recommendations', in *Proceedings of Land Redistribution Options Conference*, Johannesburg: Land and Agriculture Policy Centre.

Lyne, M.C. and W.L. Niewoudt, 1991, 'Inefficient Land Use in Kwazulu: Causes and Remedies', *Development Southern Africa*, Vol.8, No.2.

Marcus, T., 1993, 'Comparative Perspectives on Land Reform', *Indicator SA*, Vol.11, No.1, pp.44–51.

Marks, S. and R. Rathbone (eds.), 1982, *Industrialisation and Social Change in South Africa*, London: Longman.

May, J., Carter, M. and D. Posel, 1995, *The Composition and Persistence of Poverty in Rural South Africa: An Entitlements Approach*, Johannesburg: Land and Agriculture Policy Centre.

McAllister, P., 1986, 'The Impact of Relocation on Social Relationships in a "Betterment" Area in Transkei', *Development Southern Africa*, Vol.3, No.3.

McAllister, P., 1992, 'Rural Production, Land Use and Development Planning in Transkei: A Critique of the Transkei Agricultural Development Study', *Journal of Contemporary African Studies*, Vol.11, No.2, pp.200–22.

McCay, B.J. and J.M. Acheson (eds.), 1987, *The Question of the Commons: The Culture and Ecology of Communal Resources*, Tucson, AZ: University of Arizona Press.

McIntosh, A., 1994, 'Towards a Rural Local Government Policy for South Africa: Options to be Considered', paper presented to a workshop on Local Government, Community Land Trusts and Land Tenure, Surplus People Project, Jan. 1994.

McKenzie, B., 1984, *Historical, Political and Sociological Factors Affecting Land Use in the Transkei Today: An Ecological Interpretation*, Carnegie Conference Paper No.307, Second Carnegie Inquiry Into Poverty and Development in Southern Africa, Cape Town: SALDRU.

Midnet, 1994, *Sharing PRA in Southern Africa*, Pietermaritzburg: Midnet:.

Muchena, M., 1989, 'The Effect of Ox Sharing Arrangements on the Supply and Use of Draught Animals in the Communal Areas of Zimbabwe – Preliminary Findings', in Cousins (ed.) [1989].

Murphree, M.W., 1993, *Communities as Resource Management Institutions*, CASS Occasional Paper Series, Harare: Centre for Applied Social Sciences; also Gatekeeper Series No.36, London: International Institute for Environment and Development).

Murray, C., 1981, *Families Divided: The Impact of Migrant Labour in Lesotho*, Johannesburg: Ravan Press.

National Research Council (NRC), 1986, *Proceedings of the Conference on Common Property Resource Management*, Washington, DC: National Academy Press.

Oakerson, R.J., 1986, 'A Model for the Analysis of Common Property Problems', in NRC., *Proceedings of the Conference on Common Property Resource Management*, Washington, DC: National Academy Press.

Oba, G., 1992, *Ecological Factors in Land Use Conflicts, Land Administration and Food Insecurity in Turkana, Kenya*, Pastoral Development Network, Paper No.33a, London: Overseas Development Institute.

Ostrom, E., 1986, 'Issues of Definition and Theory: Some Conclusions and Hypotheses', in NRC., *Proceedings of the Conference on Common Property Resource Management*, Washington, DC: National Academy Press.

Pastoral Development Network (PDN), 1992, *Newsletter No.32*, London: Overseas Development Institute.

Peters, P., 1986, 'Concluding Statement', in NRC, *Proceedings of the Conference on Common Property Resource Management*, Washington, DC: National Academy Press.

Robins S., 1992, 'The politics of resettlement and land use policy in Matabeleland South: A new model with a familiar face?', in Cousins (ed.) [1992a].

Sandford, S., 1982, *Livestock in the Communal Areas of Zimbabwe*, Harare: Ministry of Lands, Resettlement and Rural Development.

Sandford, S., 1983, *Management of Pastoral Development in the Third World*, Chichester: John Wiley & Sons.

Schmidt, M.I., 1992, 'The Relationship Between Cattle and Savings: A Cattle-Owner Perspective', *Development Southern Africa*, Vol.9, No.4.

Scholes, R.J., 1994, 'The Use of Non-Arable Land in South Africa: Processes, Problems and Possibilities', Draft Position Paper, Natural Resources Management Project, Johannesburg: Land and Agriculture Policy Centre.

Scoones, I., 1989, 'Patch Use by Cattle in a Dryland Environment: Farmer Knowledge and Ecological Theory', in Cousins (ed.) [1989].

Scoones, I., 1990, 'Livestock Populations and the Household Economy: A Case Study from Southern Zimbabwe', unpublished Ph.D. thesis, University of London.

Scoones, I., 1992, 'The Economic Value of Livestock in the Communal Areas of Southern Zimbabwe', *Agricultural Systems* 39, pp.339–59.

Scoones, I., 1993, 'Why Are There So Many Animals? Cattle Population Dynamics in the Communal Areas of Zimbabwe', in Behnke, Scoones and Kervan (eds.) [1993].

Scoones, I. (ed.), 1995, *Living With Uncertainty: New Directions in Pastoral Development in Africa*, London: Intermediate Technology Publications.

Scoones, I. and K. Wilson, 1989, 'Households, Lineage Groups and Ecological Dynamics: Issues for Livestock Research and Development in Zimbabwe's Communal Lands', in Cousins (ed.) [1988].

Shackleton, C.M., 1993, 'Are the Communal Lands in Need of Saving?', *Development Southern Africa*, Vol.10, No.1.

Southall, R., 1993, 'Introduction: Rethinking Transkei Politics', in A. Donaldson, J. Segar and R. Southall (eds.), *Undoing Independence: Regionalism and the Reincorporation of Transkei into South Africa*, special issue of *Journal of Contemporary African Studies*, Vol.11, No.2.

Spiegel, A., 1982, 'Spinning Off the Development Cycle: Comments on the Utility of a Concept in the Light of Data from Matatiele, Transkei', *Social Dynamics*, Vol.8, No.2, pp.30–40.

Spiegel, A. and E. Boonzaier, 1988, 'Promoting Tradition: Images of the South African Past', in J. Sharp and E. Boonzaier (eds.), *South African Keywords*, Cape Town: David Philip.

Steyn, G.J. and D.R. Tapson, 1993, 'Farming Systems Research and Extension (FSR/E) Approach to Livestock Development in Parts of Sub-Saharan Africa', *Development Southern Africa*, Vol.10, No.3.

Swallow, B.M., 1990, *Strategies and Tenure in African Livestock Development*, LTC Paper 140, Madison, WI: Land Tenure Center, University of Wisconsin-Madison.

Swallow, B., 1993, 'The Role of Mobility Within the Risk Management Strategies of Pastoralists and Agro-Pastoralists', paper presented at Commonwealth Secretariat Workshop on 'New Directions in African Range Management and Policy', Woburn, UK.

Swift, J., 1995, 'Dynamic Ecological Systems and the Administration of Pastoral Development', in Scoones (ed.) [1995].

Tapson, D.R., 1990, 'A Socio-economic Analysis of Small-holder Cattle Producers in Kwazulu', unpublished PhD. dissertation, Vista University.

Tapson, D.R., 1991, *The Overstocking and Offtake Controversy Reexamined for the Case of Kwazulu*, Pastoral Development Network, Paper No.31a, London: Overseas Development Institute.

Transvaal Rural Action Committee (TRAC), 1993, 'Demands for a New South Africa Adopted by the Rural Women's Movement, November 28th 1992', *TRAC Newsletter*, No.25.

van der Waal, C.S., 1991, 'District Development and Closer Settlement Economy in Gazankulu', *Development Southern Africa*, Vol.8, No.3.

Vedeld, T., 1992, *Local Institution-Building and Resource Management in the West African Sahel*, Pastoral Development Network, Paper, No.33c, London: Overseas Development Institute.

Venter, J., Liggit, B., Tainton, N.M. and G.P.Y. Clarke, 1989, 'The Influence of Different Land-Use Practices on Soil Erosion, Herbage Production and Grass Species Richness and Diversity', *Journal of the Grasslands Society of Southern Africa*, Vol.6, No.89–98.

Vink, N., 1986, 'An Institutional Approach to Livestock Development in Southern Africa', Unpublished Ph.D. dissertation, University of Stellenbosch.

Wade, R., 1987, 'The Management of Common Property Resources: Collective Action as An Alternative to Privatisation or State Regulation', *Cambridge Journal of Economics* 11, pp.95–106.

Walker, B.H., 1980, 'Stable Production versus Resilience: A Grazing Management Conflict', *Proceedings of the Grasslands Society of Southern Africa* 15, pp.79–83.

Weiner, D. and R. Levin, 1991, 'Land and Agrarian Transition in South Africa', *Antipode*, Vol.23, No.1, pp.92–120.

Westaway, A., 1994, *Plotting the Path to Popular and Viable Local Government in Namaqualand*, Athlone: Surplus People Project.

Westoby, M., B.H. Walker, and I. Noy-Meir, 1989, 'Opportunistic Management for Rangelands not at Equilibrium', *Journal of Range Management* 42, pp.266–74.

White, R., 1992, *Livestock Development and Pastoral Production on Communal Rangeland in Botswana*, London: Commonwealth Secretariat.

Woodhouse, P., 1994, 'Soils and Irrigation Systems in the Hazyview Area of the Eastern Transvaal', in Levin and Weiner (eds.) [1994].

Land Reform in the Eastern Free State: Policy Dilemmas and Political Conflicts

COLIN MURRAY

I. INTRODUCTION: THE REGIONAL CONTEXT

There are three principal elements of South Africa's emerging land reform policy. The first is restitution of land to those who were dispossessed under apartheid laws. The second is redistribution of land to those who need it. The third is tenure reform, intended to achieve security of tenure for people holding land under diverse forms of tenure.[1] The national Department of Land Affairs is primarily responsible for the policy, and for the disposition of funds from the Reconstruction and Development Programme (RDP) for its implementation. Each of the nine provinces has been allocated a substantial budget from the RDP for its Pilot Land Reform Programme, administered through a Provincial Steering Committee (PSC), a formally constituted but non-statutory body.[2] These provincial frameworks are by no means uniform in respect of their composition and representation or of their institutional capacities to plan and implement a detailed land reform programme and to respond to regional political pressures. The diverse agencies involved are 'feeling their way' in a climate of political change, uncertainty over institutional responsibilities and volatility of conflicting demands.

The absence of uniformity and the prevailing uncertainty reflect many factors. Perhaps the most important of these are a legacy of different divisions of institutional responsibility for land and agricultural matters in the past, between erstwhile 'homeland' governments and central and provincial administrations; protracted delay over the re-integration of 'homeland' government departments and agencies into their respective new provincial frameworks; corresponding confusion over the distribution of particular functions at any one time; differing histories of NGO activity and

Colin Murray, Institute for Development Policy and Management, University of Manchester, Precinct Centre, Oxford Road, Manchester M13 9GH. The author would like to thank Henry Bernstein for his constant intellectual support – if not necessarily his agreement – and for his editorial comments on the draft of this study. He would also like to thank Sienie Jankowitz, of the University of the Orange Free State, for drawing the maps.

involvement – NGOs in some regions have taken stronger initiatives in this area of policy-making than NGOs in other regions;[3] and routine conflict or strategic incompatibility between 'top-down' technocratic planning and political pressures 'from below'. Meanwhile, uncertainties have been compounded by the absence of effective structures of representation below the level of provincial government itself, a problem which may be partly resolved in due course, in some areas, by the outcome of local government elections held in November 1995.

This article offers an account of the policy dilemmas and the political conflicts associated with land reform in an area of the Free State which coincides approximately with the Pilot Land Reform District in that province (see Map 1).[4] The first element of land reform policy, that of restitution, is discussed in relation to three different land claims which reflect, in turn, three different experiences of dispossession. The second element of land reform policy, that of redistribution, is discussed in relation to conflicts over the allocation of state-owned land on the periphery of a huge relocation township, Botshabelo, which was established in late 1979 in the heyday of apartheid social engineering (see Map 2). The third element of policy, relating to security of tenure, necessarily pervades the land reform programme as a whole, although different particular questions of relative security and insecurity arise in different circumstances. Tenure questions are discussed here mainly in relation to two quite different categories of land ownership and land use in an erstwhile fragment of independent 'homeland': land privately owned by Africans and contiguous 'communal' land administered by Tribal Authorities established under the apartheid regime.

The land reform programme in the Free State has been affected by administrative re-organisation in a number of different ways. First, the regional administrative boundaries of the Department of Agriculture, which formerly related to agro-ecological regions partly inside and partly outside the province, were revised to fit the provincial boundaries. It was re-constituted as the Department of Agriculture and Environmental Affairs, and identified by the provincial government as responsible for land reform at provincial level. Secondly, the separate agricultural development agencies associated with the respective 'homelands' of Bophuthatswana and Qwaqwa (see Map 1), Agricor and Agriqwa, were integrated into the new Free State structure. These processes of re-organisation were marked by a temporary paralysis of institutional responsibility and by pervasive anxiety over actual and potential redundancies and career implications. Thirdly, a Rural Strategic Unit (RSU) was established at Glen College of Agriculture, north of the provincial capital of Bloemfontein, to advise the provincial Minister of Agricultural and Environmental Affairs on policy and to provide a strategic management capacity, although its relationship with other departmental officials is somewhat ambiguous. Fourthly, a regional office of Land Affairs was established in the province in mid-1995, with representation on the Provincial Steering Committee, and with direct responsibility outside the Pilot Land Reform District itself for responding to demands for land and for managing important aspects of financial and other support. Fifthly, a district land reform office was set up in October 1995 at Thaba Nchu, in the heart of the Pilot District. Its newly-appointed officers are paid from the Land Affairs budget, based in the established local office of Agri-Eco, formerly Agricor (Bophuthatswana), and accountable to the PSC.

Irregular but intensive research work was undertaken in the period 1993 to 1995.[5] The research area, shown in Map 2, embraces many different categories of land.

(1) The Thaba Nchu magisterial district is a former 'homeland' area, part of the independent republic of Bophuthatswana from 1977 to 1994. It comprises (i) rural areas occupied under 'communal' tenure, marked as 'State/Tribal land' on Map 2; (ii) black-owned private land, shown in the key as 'Thaba Nchu freehold farms'; (iii) two blocks of state-owned land, marked respectively as 'Excelsior Farms' and 'Sepane Farms'; and (iv) a substantial urban area, consisting of Thaba Nchu itself, the adjoining 'new' town of Selosesha and the four Bultfontein 'zones'. The first two sub-categories of land listed here are discussed in the fourth section of this study.

(2) Botshabelo is a large resettlement town on the western boundary of the Thaba Nchu district, with a population of perhaps 250,000 people in the mid-1990s. A strip of white-owned farmland to the west and south of Botshabelo, between the township and the Modder river, was purchased by the central state in the late 1980s. This land is available for redistribution: the policy dilemmas and the political conflicts that have arisen are analysed in the third section of this article.

(3) The magisterial districts which surround Thaba Nchu and Botshabelo are commercial farming areas, in which – as a result of the rigorous enforcement of land segregation policies through most of the twentieth century – landownership is almost exclusively white. The political economy of commercial agriculture is extremely important to an assessment of the prospects of successful agrarian reform, but it is not directly discussed here.[6] Brief reference, however, is made in the third section below to a small number of schemes that emerged late in 1995 to transfer portions of white-owned farmland to black farmworkers and their families.

(4) The sites of land claims discussed in the second section of this article
are also marked on the maps. Thaba Phatshwa is shown on Map 2.
Bethany and Herschel are shown on Map 1.

MAP 1

THE EASTERN FREE STATE, SHOWING MAGISTERIAL DISTRICTS IN THE
BROADER ZONE OF STUDY.

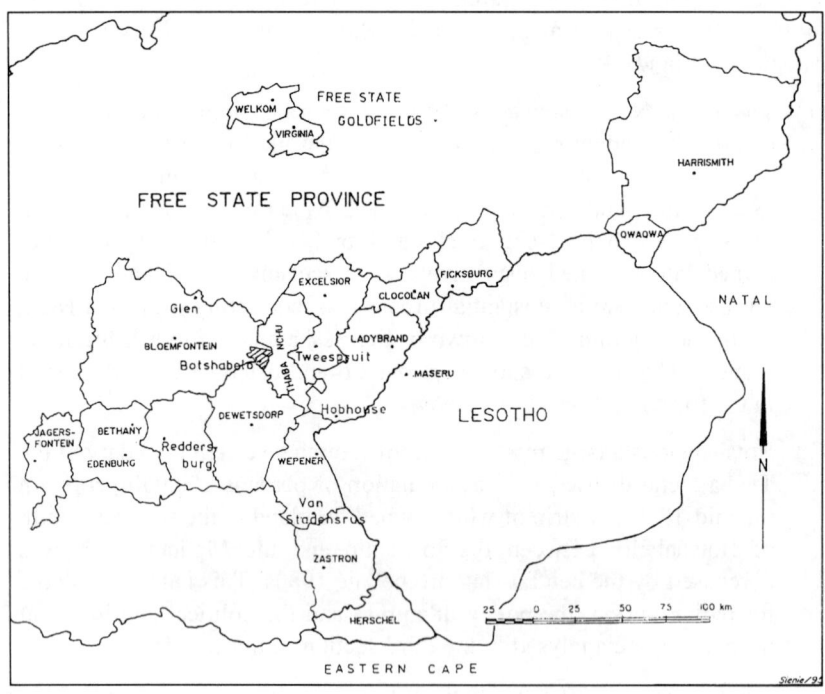

MAP 2

CATEGORIES OF LAND OWNERSHIP AND LAND USE: THABA NCHU AND
BOTSHABELO

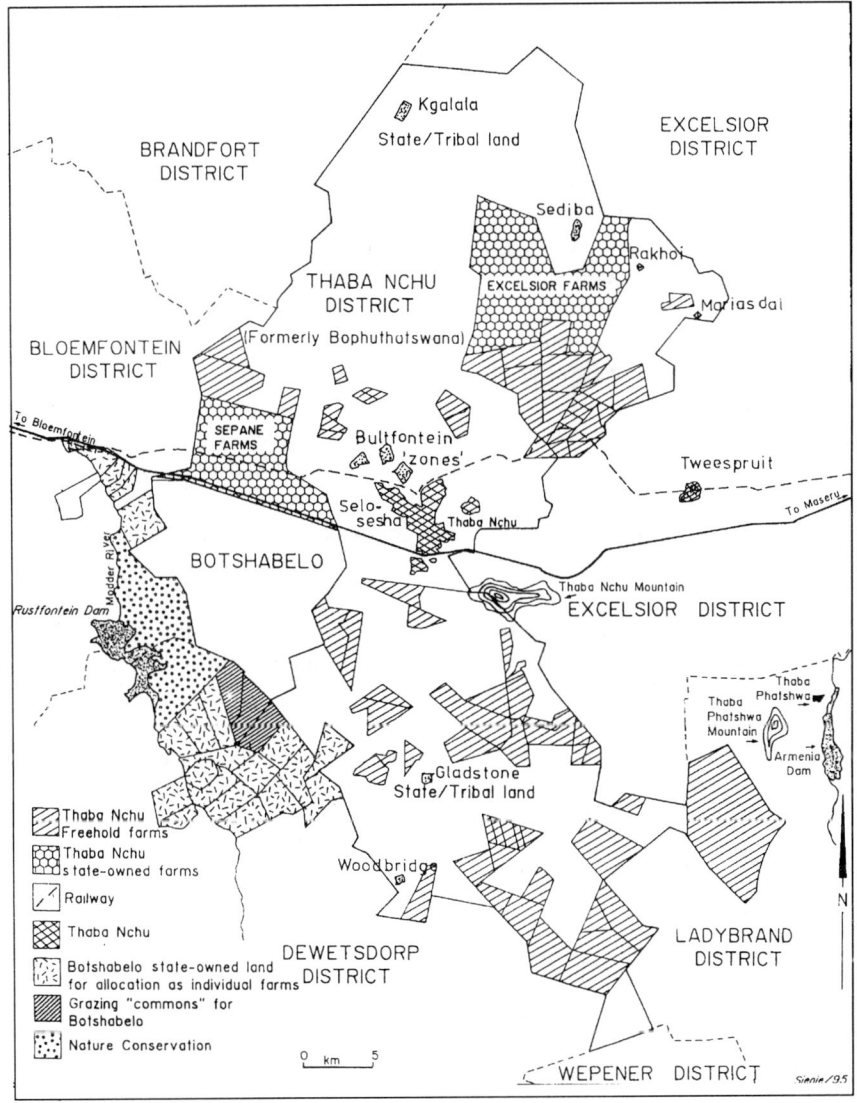

II. RESTITUTION OF LAND: THREE CLAIMS

Restitution of land is politically the most urgent element of the national land reform programme. As part of the policy of land segregation which prevailed for most of the twentieth century, many people were specifically dispossessed either of formal title to land or of long-established rights to land [*SPP*, 1983; *Platzky and Walker*, 1985]; and the ANC committed itself in its general election campaign to redress these gross injustices. One key example of such dispossession is the elimination of 'black spots': patches of land within 'white' rural areas which were owned or exclusively occupied by blacks, and whose owners or occupiers were forcibly removed, mainly in the 1960s and 1970s, in terms of the 1936 Trust and Land Act.

Such people, or their descendants, are now able to make claims for the restitution of land rights of which they were deprived in this way. The procedures are laid out in the Restitution of Land Rights Act, No.22 of November 1994. A Commission on Restitution of Land Rights and a Land Claims Court were established in terms of the Act. Its terms of reference are 'to provide for the restitution of rights in land in respect of which persons or communities were dispossessed under or for the purpose of furthering the objects of any racially based discriminatory law'. The expression 'right in land' is widely defined to refer not only to a registered title but also 'the interest of a labour tenant and sharecropper, a customary law interest, the interest of a beneficiary under a trust arrangement and beneficial occupation for a continuous period of not less than 10 years prior to the dispossession in question'. In practice, however, it is probable that the Act will be interpreted more narrowly, since the five regional Commissioners who have been appointed would otherwise be faced with an avalanche of claims. In any case, the temporal cut-off date for claims is 1913, the year of passage of the Natives' Land Act. The resolution of restitution claims is subject to the administrative and judicial procedures laid down in the Act, and falls outside the responsibility of provincial government. Provincial government departments will, however, assume responsibility for facilitating settlement or providing support in other ways for communities whose land is restored as an outcome of a successful claim.

Three land claims have been made in the area of the Free State in which research was carried out: that of the former individual owners of three fragments of Thaba Phatshwa farm (see Map 2); that of a scattered group of former inhabitants of the Bethany mission station, near Edenburg (see Map 1); and that of a remnant community of refugees from the Herschel district, Transkei, who have lived on the margins of Botshabelo township since 1986. Each of these three cases is here briefly described.

Thaba Phatshwa

In the late 1880s, after the independent Barolong chiefdom of Thaba Nchu had been annexed by the Orange Free State republic [*Murray*, 1992: Ch.1], Thaba Phatshwa farm (3,542 ha.) was registered as the private property of one of the sons of the late Barolong chief, Moroka. Between 1905 and 1922, it belonged to Jeremiah Makgothi, a teacher, court interpreter and farmer, and a prominent member of the local Barolong elite. Throughout the period of his formal ownership of the farm, Makgothi had to meet interest payments on bonds totalling £6,000. He leased parts of the farm to a local white farmer. Otherwise Makgothi worked parts of the farm himself, and the residents of the community had their own livestock and arable lands. On his death in 1922, Jeremiah Makgothi's four children each inherited portions of the farm and also of their father's debts. Two portions of the farm had to be sold to liquidate his estate. Two of his children could not extricate themselves from escalating debt, and their portions were sold in the early 1930s. One of the purchasers was their maternal uncle Moses Masisi, a successful local farmer and multiple bond-holder. From the early 1940s, three fragments of the original farm survived in black ownership. In 1938 and in 1942, since they fell within the Released Areas as defined by the Native Trust and Land Act of 1936, the remaining portions of the farm were acquired by the South African Native Trust (SANT), nominally for African occupation.

At this point, however, officials intervened to secure a different outcome, in view of the physical isolation of Thaba Phatshwa from the rest of the Released Areas in the Thaba Nchu district. A group of Afrikaans-speaking 'Coloured' people, descended from Carolus Baatje's Newlanders, had been settled since 1897 at Carolusrus, part of the farm Bofulo in the Sediba reserve in the north of the Thaba Nchu district. Relations between the Barolong and the Newlanders were strained, and the community was considered a 'stumbling block' to the development of the Sediba reserve. In 1940 the Carolusrus community was moved, with its livestock, to the ground at Thaba Phatshwa that was now owned by the Trust. Fifty-four heads of households were recorded at that time. Strong feelings quickly developed against their administration as 'Natives' under the Trust, in particular against the regime of cattle culling imposed by the Trust elsewhere in the Released Areas. In the early 1950s, therefore, a transfer was agreed by which the Department of Coloured Affairs took over administration of the Thaba Phatshwa lands belonging to the Trust, so that the remaining black-owned lands (Segogoane's Valley 665, Tshiamelo 664 and Sweet Home 667) emerged as two small 'black spots' in terms of land segregation policy. Some members of the 'Coloured' community urged action towards expropriation of these, in order to reconstitute the original farm. In the 1970s, Segogoane's Valley 665 was owned by Blanche Tsimatsima, Jeremiah Makgothi's youngest daughter; Tshiamelo 664 by three other Makgothi family heirs; and Sweet Home 667 by the estate of George Letshapa Masisi.

Under strong official pressure to leave, Blanche Tsimatsima organised the sale of Segogoane's Valley and Tshiamelo to a local white farmer in 1974. After his death in 1977, the government bought both. Meanwhile, after lengthy resistance, Sweet Home was expropriated by the central state in 1977, on the grounds that it was 'situated outside a scheduled Bantu area and a released area'. About 300 'squatters' were removed to Botshabelo. The whole of the original farm of Thaba Phatshwa was then re-integrated, as a 'Coloured' reserve [*Murray*, 1992: Ch.7].

In the early 1990s, Thaba Phatshwa was a community of about 140 households and 700 people. There were four categories of land use on Thaba Phatshwa farm. First, there were community arable and pastoral lands at the northern end of the farm, portions of which were allocated to individuals for R3/ha per annum. Some of them were leased to white farmers from across the Leeu river for growing sunflowers, etc. Secondly, Dassieshoek 666 and Mammashoek 802, both largely mountainous, were available for grazing to individuals at a monthly rental charge per head of stock. These grazing lands were considerably over-stocked. Thirdly, the farm Segogoane's Valley 665 was divided into two portions of about 250 ha each which were rented by individual members of the community, farming for themselves. Fourthly, the two farms Sweet Home 667 and Tshiamelo 664 were managed as a commercial farming enterprise by an official from Coloured Affairs (now Township Development) on behalf of the Thaba Phatshwa Council, and profits from the enterprise were committed to improvements determined by the Council such as electricity for the village houses, a water-borne sewage system and new housing. There were about 1,000 cattle and 30 sheep, the property of the Council, grazing on these farms.[7]

In 1993, a land claim was submitted to the former government's Commission on Land Allocation for the restitution of three portions of the original farm: Sweet Home 667, Segogoane's Valley 665 and Tshiamelo 664. The claim was prepared and submitted on behalf of the dispossessed Makgothi and Masisi heirs by Kabelo Tsimatsima, grandson of Blanche Tsimatsima, Jeremiah Makgothi's youngest daughter. The grounds for restitution were that Sweet Home 668 had been compulsorily expropriated as a 'black spot' in terms of the Trust and Land Act of 1936, and that Segogoane's Valley 665 and Tshiamelo 664, while not formally expropriated, had been effectively expropriated because the government had brought repeated pressure on the owners, so that they had been forced to sell out, allegedly at a lower price than would otherwise have been obtained in the open market.

The claim for restitution is fairly clear-cut, in terms of the criteria to be applied by the Land Claims Commission. But it would be extremely unjust on the 'Coloured' people of Thaba Phatshwa to be uprooted once again, and in late 1994 some of their leaders expressed vigorous opposition to the idea that some of their land might be returned to the original owners. The descendants of the Newlanders had been repeatedly shifted in the course of their history, and they were not going to move anywhere else.[8] The present claimants are all well-educated members of the middle class, who have gained their livelihoods elsewhere, essentially through other means than farming. It is implausible that, even if their claim were successful, they would actually return to occupy Thaba Phatshwa on a permanent basis. This may therefore be a case for compensation according to the alleged discrepancy between the full market value of the land, had it been freely sold by the African owners, and the price actually paid in the 1970s.

Bethany

Bethany is a farm near Edenburg, some 60 km. south of Bloemfontein (see Map 1), associated with the Berlin Mission Society. The original farm, consisting of c. 18,010 ha was registered in the name of the Society in 1881, on the basis of a land certificate issued in 1850. The mission station was established in 1834, to minister to a group of Griqua/Korana followers of Goliath Ysterbek, a sub-captain of Adam Kok, who had occupied the land. Many sub-divisions of the farm were surveyed and sold off by the Society to white farmers in the 1920s, so that Bethany farm was reduced to nearly two-thirds of its original size (11,918 ha). The present dispute is rooted in the fact of the registration of the farm in the name of the Berlin Mission Society, whereas the Bethany community – consisting of descendants of the Griqua/Korana and Setswana-speaking adherents of the mission – felt strongly that the land was theirs.

Several episodes of forced removal took place from the farm: firstly, in 1936, apparently as a result of church regulations which made residence on the land conditional on employment by the church; and in 1963, in terms of the Group Areas Act, about 1,000 people, predominantly Setswana-speaking, were relocated to Selosesha, adjoining the Thaba Nchu locations. There is an active diaspora of Bethany people in many Free State towns: Bloemfontein, Edenburg, Reddersburg, Jagersfontein, Botshabelo. Representatives of these people, particularly the Bloemfontein and Thaba Nchu groups, developed a campaign in 1993 to put pressure on the Evangelical Lutheran Church in Southern Africa, as successors to the Berlin Mission Society, not to sell the farm but to return it to the Bethany community as a whole. The church agreed to cancel the proposed sale, but the question of the return of the land to the people is still unresolved and now lies in the hands of the Commission on

Restitution of Land Rights. During 1995, pressure increased on the remaining people of Bethany, perhaps in anticipation of sale of the farm, through the appointment by the church of a new farm manager who tightened employment conditions and reduced wages in kind. The people were distressed but not well organised to resist these impositions, although they could invoke the support of the Bethany campaign group based in Bloemfontein.

Herschel

The most immediately pressing of the land claims considered here is that of the refugees from Herschel. These are a remnant of a much larger group, now reduced to only 13 families, who have been living since 1986 in very poor physical conditions, in tents and corrugated sheeting huts, on an open space not designated for residential use in the N Section of Botshabelo township. They have lost most of the livestock they originally possessed. Many other Herschel refugees have been dispersed throughout Botshabelo, and there are other remnants of this group elsewhere.

These people left the Herschel district (see Map 1) after it was incorporated into the independent Transkei in 1976. As a Sesotho-speaking ethnic minority within Transkei, they were victims of President Kaiser Matanzima's aggressive Xhosa nationalism. They were also caught up in a cynical manoeuvre by Chief Minister Mopeli of Qwaqwa, the South Sotho 'homeland' (see Map 1), to extend his own political patronage, and subsequently felt betrayed by his failure to honour promises to find some land for them in Qwaqwa. They were pushed out of Qwaqwa in 1986 and dumped in Botshabelo, where they have resolutely refused to register officially. They felt that registration on numbered residential sites implied their physical dispersal throughout the town and also the effective loss of their aspiration as a community to recover a farming livelihood. They have thus retained a strong sense of community and a strong insistence on their right to compensatory land. But the cost of maintaining their integrity, albeit as a group greatly reduced in numbers, has been their very difficult physical living conditions and also repeated bureaucratic obstructions over securing pension payments or welfare services of any kind.

The land claim that the Herschel refugees have made is clouded, firstly, by some uncertainty over the numbers of people directly affected; secondly by their efforts from time to time to invoke the remaining Sesotho-speaking people in Herschel as participants in their claim for resettlement, provoking a backlash of resentment from within Herschel itself; and thirdly by a lack of clarity over the practical interpretation of their claim to land 'as a community'. The Herschel refugees even refused the possibility opened up in 1993 by then President Bantu Holomisa of Transkei that they could return to Herschel as individuals. Yet they have also insisted on individual titles to land [*Free State RRRP*, 1995: Appendix 6]. It remains to be clarified whether private usufructuary rights to land administered on a 'communal' basis would resolve this apparent inconsistency. Their experience of harassment and dispossession, and their insistence on recovery of a farming livelihood, however, have been repeatedly and amply demonstrated.

A possible solution would be for the Free State government to authorise purchase of land in the Zastron district which adjoins Herschel, so that the refugees could be settled on land which is close to that of their original home. The cost of such purchase and settlement would have to be borne by the state. Again, this is a matter for urgent resolution by the Restitution of Land Rights Commission, through negotiation with all affected parties. This may be a case for purchase under Act 126 of 1993, which provides for assisted purchase and settlement: the community would form a Trust, which would own a farm. It is difficult to see, however, how the surviving refugees could raise even a small percentage of the likely purchase price of land in the south-eastern Free State.

These three cases are very different and require different resolutions, giving some hint of the administrative and judicial complexities which face the Commission on Restitution of Land Rights. The Thaba Phatshwa case is one of erstwhile 'black spots' which could not be effectively restored to their former owners or their heirs without disturbing the present 'Coloured' community of Thaba Phatshwa, who were also dispossessed and shunted about the country, albeit under different conditions. The Bethany case is one of church duplicity, or at least sustained prevarication, in effective collusion with the state against the remnant community of Bethany residents, and dispersed descendants thereof. The original 'Coloured' occupiers of the land were dispossessed by default through title vested in the mission, presumably as a protective device against the nineteenth-century constitution of the Orange Free State republic which committed itself to exclusively white land ownership; but the church has repeatedly sought to realise the structural advantage arising out of these historical circumstances for its own benefit rather than for the benefit of its adherents and dependents. The Herschel case is one of effective dispossession through the remorseless logic of the ethnic antagonisms of Separate Development: the refugees were a Sesotho-speaking ethnic minority in a Xhosa-dominated 'homeland'. Their claim, while extremely urgent, is also much less clear-cut than the other two claims within the terms of reference of the Restitution of Land Rights Act, since dispossession in this case was not directly an outcome of racially-based law but rather an outcome of political pressures effectively sub-contracted to an independent 'homeland' by the apartheid state.

III. REDISTRIBUTION OF LAND: BOTSHABELO STATE-OWNED
    LAND

The principal legacy of land segregation policy in South Africa through the
twentieth century was an extremely racially inequitable distribution of land.
Most of the approximately 87 per cent of the land area of the country that
fell outside the African reserves or 'homelands' is owned by whites
[*Beinart*, 1994a: 9–15]. The redistribution of land, as the most important
single element of land reform policy, refers to state-facilitated transactions
through the market that bring about a less extremely racially inequitable
distribution of land. The principles governing redistribution policy are, first,
that the state will not itself initiate transfers or indeed purchase land but,
rather, seek to respond to public demand; that there is no such thing as 'free'
land; and that 'the poor' should be able to participate as beneficiaries. Partly
as a policy compromise between these inevitably conflicting requirements,
the state is willing to subsidise the purchase of state-owned land by
individuals or groups by 'writing off' the difference between the market
value of that land and its agricultural value.[9]

State-facilitated transactions through the market may take many
different forms. Firstly, the state may encourage individual black entrepreneurs with capital resources of their own or with access to commercial
credit to buy previously white-owned land. Some transfers of this kind have
taken place in the Free State, mainly near the eastern border with Lesotho.
The entrepreneurs concerned are large-scale traders or transport operators
based in Maseru, the capital of Lesotho, who have now diversified into
farming. The number of farms transferred is small and the pattern is
necessarily haphazard, since it is the outcome of separate individual market
transactions.

Secondly, at the other extreme of the socio-economic continuum, the
state may facilitate schemes by which portions of white-owned land are
transferred to black farm-workers and their families. Through detailed
discussion perhaps with some of their own farmworkers who wish to pursue
the opportunity and are prepared to undertake the risk, some farmers are
willing to negotiate the sale of parts of their land by drawing on a state grant
of R15,000 available to qualifying households, those whose monthly
income is below a specified threshhold. Alternatively, individuals may form
a closed corporation and negotiate land purchase themselves, similarly
drawing on the R15,000 grant, with the assistance of relevant government
departments and the Agricultural Credit Board or the Land Bank. Such
transfers of private white-owned land, if at all widespread, would achieve
significant redistribution of land in the sense intended by the policy, and
they would benefit some of the poorest people. But at the present time they

also beg many questions about the motivations of the parties concerned. Are such farmers merely altruistic in seeking to encourage farmworkers to become farmers against what may be substantial opposition from other white farmers, or do they recognise long-term self-interest in adjusting to changing times? Do they seek to inflate the market price of their own land in circumstances where, without vigorous competition and without the 'artificial' boost of the state household grant, prices would stagnate or fall? Do they seek to displace their own risks of debt and over-capitalisation onto farmworkers who are ill-equipped to handle complex financial transactions for which they may now be collectively responsible? Are farmworkers indeed willing and active parties in such negotiations? All these questions remain to be resolved through practical experience. Three or four such schemes were initiated broadly within the area of study in late 1995.

Thirdly, there are significant amounts of state-owned land, which is one type of resource immediately available for redistribution. In the Free State, a swathe of state-owned land north of Qwaqwa, along the northern border of Lesotho, was poised to be sold at the end of 1995 to farmers and businessmen who had previously rented individual farms from the state, and who were able to commit some capital resources of their own. There is some question, however, whether these people properly qualify as the putative beneficiaries of land redistribution policy, who are variously described in ANC rhetoric as 'the historically disadvantaged people', 'the landless people', 'the poorest of the poor' and so on. The reason is obvious: that poor people without property cannot obtain access to commercial credit and, even if they could do so, cannot muster the capital resources necessary to embark on farming operations. There is therefore a chasm of credibility in respect of land redistribution policy: between the rhetoric, under which 'poor' people are supposed to be able to take advantage of new farming opportunities, and the reality, by which the potential purchasers who emerge are businessmen or taxi-operators or supermarket-owners. Despite the availability of the R15,000 state grants, the sale of state-owned land for purposes of redistribution policy at agricultural rather than market value, and the encouragement of alternative models of ownership and management such as closed corporations, poor people who aspire to buy farming land face enormous financial problems, firstly in bridging the gap between the purchase price of a farm and the aggregate household grant and secondly in mustering capital resources to embark on a farming enterprise.

This chasm of credibility of policy is the reason for continuing unresolved conflict over the allocation of another stretch of state-owned land, on the western and southern periphery of the huge township of Botshabelo, which is discussed in detail here. In this section I examine, first, the historical background to this extensive land purchase by the state;

secondly, the process of official planning for its disposition both before and after the election of 1994; and, third, the political conflict over the implementation of these plans. The fundamental issues concern how land situated close to such a large concentration of people can be contructively used for an experiment in land reform; and whether such an exercise is to be 'led' by the state or by local people, that is, whether or not the people of Botshabelo have been adequately represented in the decisions that have been taken.

State Purchase

Botshabelo is a huge relocation township planned in the late 1970s and sited half-way between Bloemfontein, the provincial capital of the Free State, and Maseru, the capital of Lesotho [*Murray*, 1992: Ch.6]. After 1986, when its population was several hundred thousand people, some moved to the periphery of Bloemfontein as a result of the repeal of the pass laws. Grand apartheid strategy still prevailed, however, in other respects: despite its geographical distance from Qwaqwa (see Map 1), Botshabelo was politically incorporated into the South Sotho 'homeland'.[10] When incorporation was officially confirmed in 1986, it was also announced that 12,000 ha of land would be added to Botshabelo and incorporated with it. This area consisted of a strip of white-owned farms lying between Botshabelo itself and the Modder river to the west, and stretching southwards towards Dewetsdorp (see Map 2). It was defined as Released Area, in terms of the 1936 Trust and Land Act, by Proclamation No. 26 of 1988. There were two main reasons for this purchase. The first, official, reason was that some land had to be attached to Botshabelo in order to make its political incorporation into Qwaqwa more attractive to Chief Minister Mopeli and more plausible within the framework of grand apartheid strategy which still applied in the mid-1980s. The second, unofficial, reason was that Dewetsdorp farmers and landowners had repeatedly agitated for the government to buy their land on account of the routine destruction of their farming operations that was caused by the proximity of the township. In the early 1980s farmers south of Botshabelo complained vociferously of rapidly escalating stock theft.

In the mid-1980s, Japie van Tonder's land in the area south of Botshabelo, comprising 2,350 ha, was the largest single farming unit in the area that became the Botshabelo strip. This land was bought in 1990 by the South African Development Trust, on behalf of the central state, for R1.6m. Japie van Tonder privately agreed that it was a 'good price' (c. R680/ha) and that the government had rescued them from the prospect of financial ruin. 'We were lucky that we were bought out then, before the drought came and values dropped. Since then maize prices came down, land values also. We couldn't sell privately, I tried, but no one wanted to take it on. It was impossible with all the damage. It got worse the more people went to Botshabelo.'[11]

Another major seller, Hendrik van Schalkwyk, had been farming in the district since 1946 and steadily expanded his operations over the years. In the late 1980s, he and his wife owned about five farms to the south of Van Tonder's land, amounting to nearly 2,000 ha, including seven of the small irrigated lands associated with the Papfontein irrigation scheme. In addition, he had rented several other farms in the area; and through the Agricor (Bophuthatswana) office in Thaba Nchu he rented a number of farms in the Sepane block, immediately north of Botshabelo. All these lands were used for grazing.

On their acquisition by the state in 1990, many of the farms in the Botshabelo block were leased back to their erstwhile owners. Thus Hendrik van Schalkwyk sold to the government his own land and his wife's land for over R1.69m. But he was able to continue his farming operations from his 'home' farm of Bradford, where his house was surrounded by a high security fence and patrolled by dogs. He negotiated with officials of the Department of Development Aid, within which the Trust was placed at that time, a reduced rent of R20 per ha/annum for the farms in the Botshabelo block, as opposed to the market rate of R24 per ha/annum, to allow for the high risk of stock theft. In June 1993 he reported stock losses of R1,500 to R1,800 per month. 'You can't farm up here any more', he remarked. He had already been forced to withdraw from two of the farms he rented, one of which (Schoonzicht 386) he had previously owned, and several farmworkers and their families were transported to Botshabelo.[12]

In the face of their own crisis of poverty and unemployment, the people of Botshabelo pursued diverse strategies of livelihood. Some of them cut fences and stole cattle and sheep and in these ways, probably without political motivation, they forced the retreat of large-scale commercial white farmers more surely than the sporadic murders on farms that were also taking place in the Free State and other regions of the country. As Hendrik van Schalkwyk put it in June 1993, 'we are farming backwards at a hell of a speed'. As indicated above, however, the farmers in question had already been handsomely compensated by the state. Thus they had been rescued financially from the predicament of negative equity that would otherwise, probably, have engulfed some of them by the early 1990s, as it did in other border regions such as Ciskei. White farmers who had subscribed to the political logic by which black South Africans were kept out of 'white' towns for decades, and concentrated in remote and desolate resettlement sites, had their farming operations irretrievably subverted by the ripples of unfarmability radiating outwards from Botshabelo, but were protected from financial loss by the state's need to provide more land for the nominal use of the people of Botshabelo. In some ways the problem is being transferred to farmers a little further away, who are unlikely to have their land purchased on such generous terms, and whose boundaries are ever closer to the areas of effective dense settlement.

By mid-1993, several of the farms in the Botshabelo block, together with the land in the Sepane block of Bophuthatswana, had become *de facto* an unfenced extension of the 'commons' of Botshabelo, open to uncontrolled grazing by livestock belonging to inhabitants of the township, and guarded either by family members or by paid employees. Nevertheless, some white-owned enterprises remained: they are described in Box 1. Of three observed in 1993, only one survived by the end of 1995.

Official Planning

On expiry in 1993 of the leases held by the erstwhile white owners of the farms, this stretch of state-owned land was open in principle to occupation by black farmers. Who would qualify for access to this land? A public hearing was organised at Botshabelo in May 1993 by the former government's Commission on Land Allocation (CLA), at which proposals were invited. The Farmer Development Division of the Department of Agriculture envisaged a belt of (very) smallholdings of between 1 and 10 ha. as a buffer between Botshabelo and an outer peripheral arc of 'full economic farming units'. Such an economic unit was defined as that area of land which, by combination of arable and pastoral activities, might yield a net disposable income of R15,000 per annum. Applications would be invited from men and women who wished to farm; and potential farmers would be selected by criteria relating to their capabilities, experience and financial assets. After a trial lease period, if they proved themselves, they would be able to buy the land at its agreed agricultural value. The department would offer training facilities, extension advice and financial support.[15]

The CLA made recommendations in due course which broadly endorsed the Farmer Development Division scheme. A committee was established with representation from the Agricultural Credit Board, on behalf of the Department of Agriculture, from Glen College of Agriculture, which was responsible for initial farm development, and from the local National African Farmers' Union (NAFU) branch in Botshabelo. This committee had the task of allocating land under annual leases from the Agricultural Credit Board. Twenty-one farms were identified as 'economic units' for allocation to individuals.

Pending longer-term arrangements over the disposition of the land, several annual leases were approved in late 1993. A distinctive pattern

BOX 1

WHITE-OWNED ENTERPRISES IN THE BOTSHABELO STRIP

At the eastern corner of one farm, Melville 768 (part of the original Van Tonder estate), which adjoins Botshabelo to the south-west, stood a compound protected by high electric fencing and a 24-hour armed patrol. This corner of the farm was leased by the Trust from February 1991 to Thaba Nchu Butchery and used as a vehicle repair site and a concentrated feedlot for purchased stock before transfer to the Thaba Nchu abattoir. The butchers organised training courses and employed 13 people at Melville, some resident on the farm, others in Botshabelo. By the end of 1993, however, the Melville outpost had closed.

Northwards of Melville, on a 500-morgen portion of Palmietfontein, Gert Ferreira held the western frontier of Botshabelo with guns and dogs around the clock, without which all his livestock and poultry would be 'cleaned out' immediately, as he put it. He sold oxen to people in Botshabelo for about R1,600 each, and spent most of his time defending his remaining livestock against raiders from the township. His yard was stocked with turkeys, doves and chickens. He paid R8,000 p.a. in rent for his 500 morgen, and retained an open-ended lease from the Trust on the understanding that he fulfilled an obligation as a buffer to protect the springbok on land leased to the Provincial Administration near the adjoining Rusfontein dam.[13] By October 1995, however, Gert Ferreira had left and the Palmietfontein steading was devoid of livestock. The house was occupied by a few black employees of Nature Conservation, which held the lease over the farm.

Further to the north again, adjoining the national road from Bloemfontein, another farm, Vadersgift 350, which fell within the area gazetted as Released in 1988, was owned by Sarel Henning's two sons. He had refused to sell to the Trust, holding out for a much higher price than he was offered on the basis of the value of the improvements he had made to a business that was thriving because of, not in spite of, the proximity of the township. In 1993-4 the nature of this business was advertised by a huge billboard along the roadside: Drankwinkel/Slaghuis (liquor store/butchery). It had a slaughtering capacity of 80 beef cattle and 500 sheep a month. In November 1993 the brothers Henning owned Vadersgift 350 and rented the two neighbouring farms Liefdefontein 320 and Uitkyk 435 from the Department of Agriculture. They employed 90 black people, mostly resident in Botshabelo, and 10 whites. Their livestock holdings were about 100 cattle and 2,000 sheep, about double the normal numbers because of the build-up to Christmas. All these animals had to come in to the byres on Vadersgift at night, otherwise they could not be guarded adequately. The Hennings kept ten breeding pairs of ostriches on Vadersgift as a protective buffer, because 'people are scared of them', a belief widespread amongst white farmers.[14] This enterprise remained, apparently flourishing, through 1994 and 1995.

emerges from empirical observation of access to and use of grazing land in the Botshabelo strip of state-owned land in the period 1993–94. Those who were able to place their livestock on it, either on a formal contractual basis, through the committee described above, or on an informal basis, were mainly small businessmen – general dealers, supermarket-owners, taxi-operators – or relatively well-off wage earners domiciled in Botshabelo but employed in Bloemfontein. They employed herdsmen and watchmen at their farming outposts for derisory wages. Investment in livestock was highly desirable, but highly risky also, on account of drought and vulnerability to theft.

BOX 2

A BLACK ENTREPRENEUR IN THE BOTSHABELO STRIP

Probably typical of potential applicants under this scheme was Albert Matsau, whose principal livelihood is a small store (Makholokoe General Dealer) in the D section of Botshabelo and the management of three taxis which ply the busy route between Botshabelo and the mining centre of Welkom. Matsau and his wife are Basotho who were born and brought up in the south of the Thaba Nchu district, partly on privately-owned land and partly in Trust villages where their families cultivated and reared livestock. After years of wage employment in Welkom, Albert Matsau in a 'water-pipe' company and Naomi Matsau as a domestic servant, they removed to Botshabelo in the early 1980s and established a small business there. They have two bakkies (pick-up trucks), used for transport of goods but also specifically to distribute cabbages. The family was granted a thirteen-month lease on Contest 202, a farm of 497 ha. lying along the Bophuthatswana border, from July 1993. They introduced their 20 cattle, supervised by Naomi Matsau's nephew and two casual employees based at the erstwhile white farmhouse.[16]

They had a partner, S.M. Khabuli, who was jointly responsible for the rent of R9,692.92, which worked out at R745.61 per month and R18 per ha. He was an ex-farmworker who had also established a small business, a tavern, in the K section of Botshabelo, and whose 11 cattle shared the grazing on the farm. By October 1994, after expiry of the formal lease, Albert Matsau had removed his stock to Diepwater, on the western side of the Modder river, which was part of the Botshabelo strip but lay at a much safer distance from Botshabelo itself. Khabeli remained on Contest, very uncertain what would happen.[17]

Political Impasse

The 21 farms available for individual allocation were advertised for sale in February 1994. But the perceived disparity of opportunity between the businessmen who had temporary leases, on the one hand, and the 'landless poor', on the other hand, gave rise to political anxiety over the allocation process in the immediate pre-election period. At a meeting in Botshabelo with members of the allocation committee on 8 March 1994, representatives of the Southern Orange Free State ANC Regional Executive opposed the allocations, on a number of grounds. First, a moratorium had been agreed between the ANC and the government over any further transfer of state-owned land in advance of the election of a new government in April 1994. Secondly, the land in the Botshabelo strip was alleged to be unsuitable for individual farming, because of the high risk to a viable enterprise represented by the proximity of the township, and was therefore only suitable for communal use by the people of Botshabelo. Thirdly, the government was attempting to create a buffer zone of land privately owned or leased by black farmers between Botshabelo and the white commercial farmers of Dewetsdorp.

The chair of the ANC regional Land Desk asserted that the beneficiaries should be 'the landless, poor of the poor ... not the middle-class ... people that at the moment ... this land is for'. An official of the Agricultural Credit

Board, on behalf of the allocation committee, counter-asserted that, after a public hearing where 'everyone had a chance to state their case and especially the people from the community ... ', 'this Commission on Land Allocation decided that this land must be made available for the establishment of small-scale and viable farming to people who do not own land and that is exactly what we are doing'.

The meeting was chaired by an official from Glen College of Agriculture who had responsibility for planning the farms in the Botshabelo block. Facing an impasse of mutual misunderstanding between the Agricultural Credit Board and the ANC, he reverted to the 'fundamental facts' of the carrying capacity of the veld which have governed official thinking for decades. The area could only carry 1,500 head of large stock. For a household to make a living, about 50 head minimum were necessary, which would restrict grazing to about 25 farming units. It is almost inevitable, however, that capital resources judged sufficient to start farming on a 'full-time economic' basis will have been accumulated through other activities than farming, as indicated above. These activities are unlikely to be displaced by farming on a 'full-time economic' basis. The official presumption of a division of the land into 'economic units' was therefore quite unrealistic.

An inconclusive wrangle ensued over whether or not the 'people' of Botshabelo, whoever they were, had been adequately represented in the process of consultation. The Agricultural Credit Board insisted that they had bent over backwards to ensure this. The ANC countered that 'the people that were asked to give inputs are not representative of the people'. A decision was deferred for reference back to higher levels of authority and meanwhile, it was agreed, allocation procedures that were already in hand, in the sense that arrangements for interviews of prospective farmers had been made, should not be suspended.[18] This outcome left the whole process hanging in uncertainty.

In the aftermath of the election of April 1994, the Botshabelo Transitional Local Council (TLC) flexed its political muscles by declaring that the farms belonged to Botshabelo and that people would pay rent to the TLC for access to grazing land thereon. After meetings were held to resolve this matter, the farms were re-advertised by the Agricultural Credit Board for individual allocation and prospective sale in August 1994. They were described as 'primarily suited to livestock farming with provision having been made to accommodate farmers with different needs. Carrying capacity of the farms varies from 40 to 100 head of cattle per farm.'[19]

The political impasse was not yet resolved, however. In the absence of a clear decision on the use of the land, some of it was invaded by 'squatters' determined to secure *de facto* grazing rights. Both Derek Hanekom,

Minister of Land Affairs in the national government, and Cas Human, MEC (Member of the Executive Council) for Agriculture in the provincial government, attended a crisis meeting at Botshabelo on 15 October 1994 at which Cas Human asked the people what they wanted to do with the Botshabelo block. There were complaints about the individual allocations that had been made and the rental costs imposed: people had thought they would get the land free. The official proposal, confirmed at this public meeting, was that 21 farms be sold to individual farmers so that the department could generate more money to buy more land; and that three farms be retained as commonage for the people of Botshabelo (see Map 2). The 'squatters' were not evicted, however.

A list of successful applicants was drawn up, but their names had not been made public by the end of March 1995. The exact nature and extent of financial assistance were not yet resolved, but it seemed likely that successful applicants would be able to apply to the Agricultural Credit Board for loans at eight per cent interest of amounts up to the agricultural value, as opposed to the 'free market' value, of the farm allocated.[20] It was recognised that part of the difficulty of resolving this matter in a demonstrably equitable manner lay in the estimated difference between the two values, in the light of the putative effect of the ripples of unfarmability described above on *both* values. The 'free market' value of land sold in a border area characterised by dense settlement and high levels of poverty and unemployment is vitally affected by farmers' experience of routine depredation and their expectation of such in the future. Similarly, any official estimate of the agricultural value of a particular property must take account of these practical realities that farmers face.

A great deal of technical expertise has been brought to bear from the past in the process by which state officials have planned the optimum use of this state-owned land. These plans have been pursued in a way that is largely disconnected, however, from the reality of political conflict within Botshabelo over the principles of access to and use of the land. The fundamental question in respect of this stretch of state-owned land, and in respect of other land also, is whether individual farms will be held in private tenure, fenced off, and protected against 'the people' by the whole array of forces of law and order available to the state; or whether the land will become a grazing commons for 'the people' of Botshabelo in general, which presupposes structures of regulation of access and use in which all interested parties are adequately represented (see Cousins, this volume) This question could only be resolved politically, but structures of local representation and regulation that would be adequate for the purpose did not exist through 1994–95. This is one reason why it is vitally important that legitimate and effective structures of local representation should emerge from the local government elections that took place in November 1995.

Meanwhile, the question of what should be done with the land remains vexed by uncertainty over conflicting claims by different groups and factions to represent the 'community'. A Bafutsana (Poor People's) Association was formed in August 1994. According to its chairman, it was formed by some members of NAFU (the National African Farmers' Union) who felt that they could not afford to pay monthly contributions of R25 and that most of their needs were not met. Its chairman reported that the Association applied to the Botshabelo Community Trust in October 1994 for funds with which to buy the farm Travalgar, on Botshabelo's western boundary, 'which does not belong to anyone but falls under the Department of Agriculture'.[21] In the chairman's view, land should be allocated by the magistrate because 'structures in Botshabelo are not reliable. As a community we do not trust them, they politicise everything.' He thought the conflict over use of the state-owned farms was 'caused by white people who allocated these farms to their favourite people', by which he meant MEC Cas Human's endorsement of NAFU's involvement in the planning process. Travalgar farm is already inside the formal boundary of Botshabelo township, and is unlikely for this reason to be allocated for the exclusive use of a particular group of residents. In April 1995, the chairman was displaced from office in the Association, and went off to found a new group, Matla Community, which in October 1995 was making a bid for Ramalitse farm, which lies adjacent to Travalgar but outside the formal boundary of Botshabelo. New officers emerged within the Bafutsana Association, which insisted that it was not affiliated to a political party.[22] Bafutsana claimed a membership of 260 in October 1995, of whom ten were women – a stark index of the 'invisibility' of women in respect of new opportunities of direct access to land, albeit under difficult physical conditions.

Many of the 21 farms were occupied informally through 1995 (see below), in the absence of a political resolution of the validity of these occupations or of the applications which had been made through the planning process described above. In view of the political conflict, the MEC stopped the formal allocations, and in October 1995, under a new planning regime – that of the Provincial Steering Committee responsible for the Free State Pilot Land Reform Programme – a Bloemfontein attorney was appointed as consultant, with a brief to 'establish a planning committee, comprising all stakeholders', and to 'undertake a process of consultation and mediation to ensure proper representation on the planning committee'.[23] The attorney arranged a conference of delegates of all interested groups in Botshabelo at Glen Agricultural College on 19 October 1995. A Botshabelo planning committee was elected, with representatives of the political parties, NAFU and the Bafutsana Association, the Botshabelo TLC, the

South African National Civic Organisation (SANCO), several residential sections of Botshabelo, and a group of small farmers (Kopano) on Trust land in the southern part of Thaba Nchu district who were also interested in land around Botshabelo. A chairperson was appointed, one of the fieldworkers for a Bloemfontein-based NGO, the Free State Rural Committee (FSRUC), who has considerable experience of community work and dispute resolution. The first meeting of the planning committee was held in November 1995. Its responsibilities were to initiate the process of state land redistribution in the Botshabelo area; to ensure that consensus was reached as the to best use of the land; to identify possible beneficiaries of the land through a democratic process; to facilitate the delivery of land through the Land Reform Programme; and to ensure the long-term sustainability of the land.[24]

At the meeting on 19 October 1995, neither the lawyer nor a newly-appointed official of the land reform district office at Thaba Nchu was able to reassure anxious delegates about the financial implications of the state's proposals to facilitate transfers of land. Individual households which organised themselves into groups for the purposes of land purchase and farm management would be able to take advantage of the R15,000 state grant. In most cases, however, even closed corporations of six or eight individuals and their families would not be able to muster more than a proportion of the purchase price of a farm in this way. If they were able to secure sufficient credit to cover the balance of the purchase price and to undertake necessary capital expenditure, they would be entering a commercial transaction with very formidable long-term financial implications. One of the very difficult questions of practical management which the new chairman of Bafutsana anticipated, for example, was the question of the respective monthly liabilities for service of the debt on the part of individual members of the closed corporation who brought very different levels of capital resources into the collectively-managed enterprise. One member would bring five cattle; another thirteen; and so on. Otherwise, would numbers of livestock be divided between members in a rigorously equal manner to ensure equally shared liability for regular repayments to the bank?[25] How would such a position be sustained?

This experience of conflict and impasse clearly begs an extremely important question about the politics of land redistribution in this context: what is 'the community' for the purpose? The question is particularly difficult to answer in the circumstances of Botshabelo, firstly because the inhabitants of the township have come from many disparate places and through many disparate experiences; secondly because there is no history or structure of effective representation by which outsiders can confidently judge the views of 'the people'; and thirdly because the structures of representation which emerged after the general election of April 1994, in advance of local government structures legitimated by local elections, were dominated by the pressures of competitive party political agenda. It is by no means clear that the outcome of local government elections in November 1995 will help to resolve this problem. Would SANCO, for example, continue to exert strong informal influence on the basis of its own alternative claim to represent 'the community'?

As an experiment at the front line of the provincial government's proposals for land reform, the disposition and effective use of this strip of land are a vitally important test of the credibility of such reform. There are different and sometimes conflicting criteria by which such a programme can be judged. One criterion is adequate consultation of the people directly affected by the proposals: potential beneficiaries, on the one hand, and those potentially excluded, on the other hand. Another criterion is fiscal responsibility: what mechanisms would ensure proper expenditure of very large sums of money in order to meet objectives of both efficiency and equity?

Irrespective of the resolution of the conflict over disposition of the land, the people in Botshabelo who would be able to take advantage of a grazing 'commons' are by no means 'the poorest of the poor'. Most will have a business enterprise or paid employment or a source of income elsewhere which allows them to invest in livestock. Generally, they would not be dependent on farming for a livelihood. Thus, whether the land is individually allocated and sold or whether it is opened up as a community grazing resource, the beneficiaries will be 'part-time' farmers. They will not qualify as 'very poor', not even those who informally occupied the land through 1995, members of Bafutsana (Poor People) or not. Informal occupants may, however, turn out to have nine-tenths of formal possession, in view of the odium that would be incurred by politicians at the provincial or local level who might seek to evict them in favour of a different resolution by the Botshabelo planning committee. According to an official inventory in October 1995, there were nearly 100 stock owners in occupation of these state-owned farms, with a total of 1,350 cattle, 586 sheep, 927 goats, 255 pigs and 75 horses.[26]

IV. PRIVATE AND COMMUNAL TENURE IN A FORMER 'HOMELAND'

The third principal element of land reform policy is tenure reform. The Department of Land Affairs has identified its objectives as follows:

> to ensure equal protection in law for different forms of tenure; to

improve tenancy laws to prevent arbitrary actions against tenants; to better specify and strengthen the tenure rights of people holding land under customary tenure in the former homeland areas, and to review and upgrade the administration of customary land rights; to establish an accessible legal instrument to enable land reform beneficiaries to hold land in common; to eliminate gender bias in all land-holding systems.[27]

Several bills were approved by cabinet in the second half of 1995 for placing before Parliament: the Land Reform (Labour Tenants) Bill, intended to protect surviving labour tenants – mainly in the south-eastern Transvaal and Natal – against unfair eviction; the Interim Protection of Informal Land Rights Bill, intended to freeze existing rights in respect of which no formal proof exists, pending their investigation by December 1996; and the Communal Property Association Bill, intended to provide for a group or community to hold and manage property collectively, according to agreed constitutional rules.[28] The government remains neutral over the respective desirability of private or communal tenure. In this section of the paper, I examine both forms as they have been historically established in the Thaba Nchu district, part of the former 'homeland' of Bophuthatswana, in order to determine whether there are implications for the programme of land reform as a whole.

The Thaba Nchu district has a distinctive history in the Free State [*Murray*, 1992]. It is the only district in which Africans owned private titles to land. In this district, also, were concentrated the land purchases made by the state in terms of the 1936 Trust and Land Act, to extend the amount of land available for African occupation. Eventually, the two separate reserves of Thaba Nchu and Sediba (see Map 2) were integrated into a consolidated area which became subject to a rigid regime of 'top-down' planning – known as 'betterment' and rehabilitation – through the 1940s, 1950s and 1960s. Some 40 Trust villages emerged from this process, whose inhabitants have access to land on a 'communal' basis. The meaning of this term and its implications for future land use require careful elaboration.

Finally, as part of the negotiations over the establishment of Botshabelo in 1979, two blocks of white-owned farmland, comprising approximately 15,000 ha, were purchased by the central state in the early 1980s and incorporated into Bophuthatswana in 1989. These blocks are known as the Excelsior Farms and the Sepane Farms (see Map 2). Since 1989 the two blocks have been divided into 'economic units' and leased to individual farmers who, it was intended, should reside on their rented land and derive a livelihood from it. These are not discussed here. It should be noted, however, that the re-integration of erstwhile 'homelands' into a unitary

South Africa implies a convergence of political responsibility for the administration of rural development in the Botshabelo strip and in the two state-owned blocks in the Thaba Nchu district; and some of the same dilemmas apply as analysed in the previous section.

Black Freehold Land

The Barolong territory of Thaba Nchu – about three times the size of the modern district of Thaba Nchu – was annexed by the Orange Free State republic in 1884 [*Murray*, 1992: Ch.1]. Effectively freehold titles to farms were granted to individuals who were overwhelmingly close kin or prominent political associates of the murdered chief Tshipinare. About two-thirds of the territory was disposed in this way. Much of this land, however, was alienated to whites in the late 1880s and early 1890s. In 1916, when an inventory was made by the Beaumont Commission appointed in terms of the 1913 Land Act, there were 70 African-owned farms, comprising 82,677 morgen (69,118 ha) and bonded to the amount of £56,525. In 1922 there were 91 African-owned farms, comprising 73,715 morgen (61,626 ha) and bonded to the amount of £133,707. These figures indicate three clear trends characteristic of the first three decades of the twentieth century: decreasing aggregate area, increasing formal sub-division of individual farms and rapidly deepening indebtedness [*Murray*, 1992: 101].

By 1936, Africans owned about 56,000 morgen of land in the district (c. 47,000 ha). Many African landowners, steeped in debt, had no alternative but to negotiate for the sale of their land to the South African Native Trust (SANT), which was empowered under the Trust and Land Act of 1936 to purchase land to extend the African reserves. Private black landownership in the district was therefore significantly undermined by the state provision of land for 'communal' African occupation. There was hardly any local market for land sales. When Trust purchases were completed, there was a virtual 'freeze' of the disparate fragments of land that survived in freehold ownership.

An inventory of these surviving titles prepared in 1991 in the Agricor office in Thaba Nchu showed a total of 68 farms, comprising 18,491 ha with an average size of 272 ha [*Agricor*, 1994]. Many farms are very small, and some are held in multiple ownership. Most, but not all, of the land-owners concerned are the descendants of, or otherwise related to, prominent members of the local Barolong political elite. Many of them have pursued professional, bureaucratic or commercial livelihoods and have not derived a significant income from farming their land directly. Rather, they have commonly mortgaged their land, and leased it to black tenants or to white farmers from outside the district. The land is generally under-developed. Much of it lies idle or under-used.

In historical perspective, private landownership in Thaba Nchu has been important, not as a point of departure for successful farming, but as a source of financial liquidity, through the landowners' capacity to borrow money against the security of their titles. One side of the coin of escalating mortgage indebtedness, for many, was the ultimate dispossession of their freehold land titles: many sales were enforced through bankruptcy. The other side of the same coin was educational opportunity for the sons and daughters of the landowning class. Through investment in education, they were able to consolidate a decisive advantage in respect of bureaucratic employment, professional mobility and entrepreneurial opportunity. Few of them became successful farmers. The negative explanation for this is systematic discrimination in favour of white farmers and against black farmers. The positive explanation for their relative failure as farmers is the opportunity of a secure off-farm income, albeit in narrowly restricted fields, that was opened up by access to mortgage finance. Accordingly, most of the sons and daughters of the landowning elite, and most of their sons and daughters in turn, pursued professional or bureaucratic or business careers in Thaba Nchu itself or further afield in many different parts of South Africa. Few landowners in the district today are resident on their farms.

Nevertheless, there is wide variation in the use of black freehold land in Thaba Nchu. There are a few landowners who are also successful farmers. The career of Samson Honti Seape, who did not inherit land – unusually amongst black landowners in the Thaba Nchu district – is a classic trajectory of professional employment followed by accumulation through business ventures and then investment in farming. Each successive phase was partly conditional on the previous phase (Box 3).

Seape's success as a commercial farmer is unrepresentative of the pattern of land use that prevails amongst black landowners in the district. Far more common is the leasing out of portions of land to diverse tenants, as in the example (Box 4).

Each of the 'farmers' whose activities on the land are briefly described in Box 4 below is primarily dependent on another source of income than farming: respectively, a brick-making enterprise in Thaba Nchu, selling building materials and coal in Botshabelo, state employment as an agricultural official, and running a supermarket in Botshabelo. None of them lives on the portions of land that they rent. They derive capital resources for investment in farming either directly from other income-generating activities or indirectly from them through the access to commercial credit which their other activities open up.

It is clear that rental arrangements of this kind facilitate some small-scale farming enterprises without imposing on them the very heavy burden

BOX 3

FROM TEACHER TO BUSINESSMAN TO FARMER IN THABA NCHU

Samson Honti Seape was born in 1926. He was a teacher for 22 years, from 1951 to 1972, during which period he also used his brother's farm for speculating in livestock. The family had a home base in the Mokwena location, Thaba Nchu, from which his father was absent as a migrant labourer, and his mother started a butchery at home. In the late 1960s Seape took over the butchery himself, while still employed as a teacher, and was persuaded to buy a small farm of 90 ha, north-west of Thaba Nchu town. He was able to arrange a fixed-term loan from the South African Native Trust at a low interest rate of 4.5 per cent, which he was able to repay monthly from his teacher's salary to meet the purchase price of R3,225. His farming operations were dairy cattle and cultivation of sunflowers, maize, oats and sometimes sorghum. He found he was enjoying farming; his business interests expanded in the 1970s to embrace two butcheries and two general dealers; and he was able to resign from his teaching job in 1972. From that time onwards his livelihood depended on both business and farming. He built a substantial house on the family plot in Mokwena location.

In 1979, Seape bought a large farm of 525 ha in the south of the district. He paid R27,000 in cash. The farm was in poor condition: the fences and windpump were broken, and a mud-brick store had no roof because all the corrugated sheeting had been stolen. Seape repaired all this and in 1982 he bought the neighbouring farm, also of 525 ha, for R36,780, again with one payment in cash. He now owned approximately 1,140 ha in total.

In October 1994, Seape employed six full-time workers in his farming enterprise; he had 132 cattle on the two southern farms; and extensive ploughed lands. By March 1995, he had reduced his work-force to four; he was no longer cultivating the arable lands of the southern farms, and was thinking seriously of selling. He was depressed about the prospects for agriculture generally: 'arable doesn't pay any more, because of rising costs and drought, unless you operate on a very big scale'. More specifically, he himself was old and unwell, and his six children were highly educated, geographically dispersed and unlikely to take over farming from him. On the northern farm he no longer cultivated with the diversity of the 1970s but restricted himself to fodder. He had experienced theft of crops by people who lived near his property there and complete despoliation of sorghum crops by birds [29]

of large mortgage interest repayments related to the inflated market value of agricultural land. Thus they allow some flexibility of access to land. Nevertheless, the question must be raised of whether the costs of the relative market immobility of black-owned land in Thaba Nchu are not too high to tolerate in a climate of widespread land hunger. Tenants seldom invest in improvements on a significant scale; they tend to over-stock the land, for any agreement between owner and tenant about stock limits is not easily enforced; while other land lies idle because owners or tenants cannot muster the capital resources required for farming. There are problems, then, both of under-utilisation of land and of rapid exhaustion of scarce grazing resources. Both carrots and sticks should be devised to encourage

BOX 4

DISPARATE ARRANGEMENTS

Another farm of 752 ha. in the south of the district originally belonged to one of the descendants of the old Chief Moroka. After his death, two-thirds of the farm was sold to the Trust in 1939 and became part of the lands associated with a neighbouring Trust village. The remaining third was divided between the surviving children. Four portions are presently registered in private ownership. The first portion, of 42 ha, was inherited by the eldest daughter and passed on to her adopted son, who had farmed this land directly since 1962. In October 1994 he had 35 cattle on it, of which 12 died in the subsequent drought. He employed one herdsman and two women on a part-time basis to look after his pigs. He himself lived in Thaba Nchu and derived his main livelihood from running a brickworks, after 25 years as a driver for a firm in Thaba Nchu.

The second portion, of 84 ha., was rented by a small businessman resident in Botshabelo, who in October 1994 had 20 cattle and 16 sheep on the land. He also kept pigs. A former migrant worker in Bloemfontein, he was expelled from Thaba Nchu in 1980 and moved to Botshabelo. He gave up his job in 1982 and started an alternative livelihood through selling coal and sand for plastering. He had rented the farm since 1983, and remarked specifically that people did not 'spoil' the fencing etc. in this southern portion of the Thaba Nchu district, whereas the state-owned land west and south of Botshabelo [see previous section] was routinely ravaged in this way. He employed one man at R90 a month and a 12.5 kg bag of mealie meal, and a youth at R60 a month, to supervise his livestock.

The remaining two portions, respectively of 84 ha. and 42 ha., were rented by a senior official of the Agricor office in Thaba Nchu, who was able to obtain a loan from Agribank but had his fingers burnt in the drought of 1994-5 through complete failure of his wheat crop and acute shortage of water on the farm, which led him to reduce his stock severely. Without secure employment, he would have been unable to meet his financial obligations.[30]

The widow of one of the owners of the second portion of this farm had separately inherited, together with her sister, a 140-ha. sub-division of a farm north-east of Thaba Nchu town. They had leased this to the owner of a supermarket in Botshabelo, who ceased to pay rent (R500 due half-yearly) in mid-1991. The fences on the farm had been down, so that he could claim the cost of repair against the rent, but any other improvements, such as repairing the house and the wind-pump, were his own responsibility. Despite reference of her claim to lawyers, she had been unable either to evict him or to extract rental payments from him, and in late 1995 she was contemplating selling as her only practical option, since she derived no income from her property.[31]

landowners either to become effective farmers themselves or to sell or lease to aspirant farmers with a more serious commitment to farming, even if it is only part of their livelihood.

At present, it should be noted that significant amounts of African-owned land in Thaba Nchu are leased to white farmers from outside the district who are relatively well endowed with capital resources but who find it barely profitable, because of its neglected condition, to work such land even at the reduced rents that it commands. These arrangements are inimical to the spirit of a land reform programme intended to open up opportunities for black farmers. Nevertheless, means have to be found for promoting constructive interaction between white farmers and black farmers and for taking advantage of existing skills and capital resources.

State/Tribal Land: The Trust Villages

A document drawn up in 1993–94 in the Agricor office in Thaba Nchu identifies 79,235 ha of 'State/Tribal Lands' in the Thaba Nchu district, subject to the jurisdiction of the Barolong Tribal Authority. Except for the Thaba Nchu reserve itself and a few farms excised to form the Maria Moroka (Bophuthatswana) National Park, most of the land defined as State/Tribal comprises the 40 Trust or rural villages (1,478 ha), with their associated arable lands (8,929 ha) and pastoral lands (59,957 ha.) (see Map 2). A local survey undertaken in 1991 revealed a total of 18,172 people resident in the Trust villages, of whom 2,267 – nearly half of the adults – were defined as 'farmers' by reference to the stock registration lists [*Agricor*, 1994].

After the formal independence of Bophuthatswana in 1977, the principles on which Trust or communal land in the Thaba Nchu district was administered remained those of the Trust regime. After re-planning of the Trust areas in the late 1950s, people were allocated individual portions of land of three morgen or six morgen[32] for arable use, and had access to communal grazing land which was divided into camps. Arable lands are formally allocated to individuals by the Barolong Tribal Authority, acting through the village headmen. In practice, only a few 'farmers' cultivate their own lands, mainly because they lack the resources with which to do so. In these circumstances, some Trust village lands are also rented or share-cropped by outside farmers, such as those who have rented state-owned farms in the Excelsior block, who own tractors and have spare ploughing capacity. Otherwise, Agricor used to operate projects in the Trust villages by which participants, in effect, hired Agricor to undertake all agricultural operations on their land and Agricor paid them at the end of the season after deducting costs. This system induced a culture of dependence in respect of use of the arable lands. It also entailed significant financial losses for Agricor. It was discontinued in the early 1990s. Many lands have lain idle for years.

Grazing land remains a communal resource, and is divided into separate fenced areas known as camps, access to which is supposedly regulated by rotation in order to conserve the grazing resources attached to each village. A nominal stocking rate of six hectares per unit of large stock is applied. By this measure the lands were over-stocked by 61 per cent in 1992, when 16,080 units of large stock were recorded. There is, however, marked variation in the extent of over-stocking between villages. Charges used to be levied on people who had more than six head of large stock, without apparently achieving a reduction of over-stocking. On average, people have far more livestock than can graze the limited resources without serious degradation of the veld.

According to a village profile prepared in 1993, most Trust villages have primary schools, water pipes, windpumps and taps. Cowdung, coal, paraffin and wood are used for cooking and heating. Shopping facilities are few; transport is available to Thaba Nchu by bus or taxi. Few telephones are available. In all the 40 villages, there are six permanent clinics; otherwise there is a hospital in Selosesha, adjacent to Thaba Nchu town. Amongst 110 community projects then supported to some extent by Agricor staff, knitting and crochet (40) and foodplots (24) predominated; otherwise, there were literacy classes (12), youth clubs (10) and sewing and baking clubs.

An attempt was made during 1993 by Agricor staff to discover the needs of Trust villagers, partly through the agricultural extension officers and partly through questionnaires. A wide range of needs was identified. With reference to Sediba and Gladstone, two villages which were surveyed early in 1995 as part of the Land and Agriculture Policy Centre (LAPC) research programme [*Free State RRRP*, 1995], the principal concerns were a need for more grazing land; the inadequacy of water supplies and other village services; and the shortage of employment opportunities. 'Lack of co-operation' was cited as a particular problem in Gladstone: the village has a history of political tension which relates in part to the destruction of the Trust village of Morokashoek, north of Gladstone, in the early 1980s to make way for the Moutloatsi Setlogelo dam and the Thaba Nchu Sun Hotel. Most of the thirty families from Morokashoek went to Gladstone. A division emerged between the original inhabitants of the village and the newcomers from Morokashoek, which was reflected in 'confusion' reported in the Village Development Committee (VDC) throughout the recent period of transition, which was also marked by the proliferation of new committees to deal with every aspect of social and economic development needs.

In the circumstances, it is obvious that the majority of Trust villagers are dependent for their livelihoods on pensions or employment in Thaba Nchu or Bloemfontein or, as migrants, further afield in the Free State Goldfields area or Gauteng. There are a few small local industries (for example, brick-laying, tanning of skins, carpentry) but very few opportunities for local employment, although the Thaba Nchu Sun and Naledi hotels do provide some local jobs. Of twenty households interviewed in Sediba and Gladstone as part of the LAPC land research [*Free State RRRP*, 1995, Appendix 3], 13 had an income from wages and 10 from pensions. A major source of employment in the past has been South African Railways in Bloemfontein.

Those few Trust villagers who are able to establish themselves as farmers, albeit on a modest scale, have typically spent many years as

BOX 5

A FARMER AT KGALALA TRUST VILLAGE

Ezekiel Pule, born in 1932, remembered the time of the 'strikes' which happened in 1952 when the Trust regime was introduced in the northern village of Kgalala. He was a migrant at Welkom, Free State goldfields, where he worked for 24 years for the construction firm of Murray and Roberts. In his own words (translated): 'I was a migrant staying in the hostels, I'd come home at the end of the month. My father died in 1947. I was the last of six brothers and sisters. My mother died in 1983, with about 6 to 8 cattle. I began farming only in 1988. We made half-shares with Colbert (a local white man) from 1988–94, he hasn't got a farm but he works for himself (i.e. with a tractor) out of the garages. I was given 42 morgen here by the headman by delegation from the Tribal Authority, and I have a right to that land as long as I cultivate. Others cultivate with their own cattle. I have 12 livestock. I plough other fields for cash. Some people hire out their fields. There are 15 people here with fields, but only 6 cultivating for themselves or trying to cultivate.'[33]

BOX 6

A FARMER AT WOODBRIDGE TRUST VILLAGE

Ramorena Khoathela was born in 1943 on Woodbridge farm when it was still owned by a white man (i.e. prior to its purchase by the Trust and the establishment of a Trust village there in 1949). His parents originally came from Lesotho. He passed Standard 6 after three years of boarding school in Lesotho; worked on the railways for a year; then for a company at Alberton doing tarred roads at Vanderbijlpark. At the time Sophiatown was moved, he went to work for African Explosives. 'My father died in 1974 and my mother in 1976. A year later, I came home and found 8 cattle and one horse and never worked (i.e. went out as a migrant) again. I married in 1972, my wife comes from Sasolburg. All my children are at school at Sasolburg, they stay at my brother's house. My three sisters are all in Botshabelo. My livestock now are 30 sheep, 37 goats, 27 cattle, 5 horses. We decide, as a community, how to regulate rotation between the fenced camps.'

Khoathela has been allocated a total of 40 ha arable land by the Tribal Authority. He was using 7 ha. for growing lucerne and the rest he would use to grow vegetables: some of his lands lie below the nearby Woodbridge dam and are therefore irrigated. A certificate was issued to him in 1989 as follows: 'Permission is hereby granted to Mr J. Khoathela of Woodbridge, just as he had proved himself in 3 ha of land to be a hard worker, to be borrowed [sic] an additional land of 10 ha. for the period of not less than 5 years in the said Trust land for the production of crops. The said additional land will remain under the control of the state, and if there is any change pertaining to administration thereof, the above-named farmer is no exception to the involvement'.

Khoathela remarked that he was 'the only one' from Woodbridge who was cultivating. 'Fields are empty. But people do have livestock.' He is chairman of the recently formed regional (south-west) committee of (Trust) farmers, and insisted in the interview that the future of the Trust lands should be resolved by Trust villagers themselves, not by the Tribal Authority or by educated private landowners. As a delegate to the Allemanskraal conference in October 1994 for consultation over the Free State's agriculture policy, Khoathela argued vigorously that Trust farmers should be granted stronger rights of entitlement to land, so that they could obtain access to commercial credit.[34]

migrants elsewhere in South Africa, and their links reflect this experience. The careers of two men are briefly outlined here. They were interviewed in October 1994, one at Kgalala village in the north of the district, the other at Woodbridge in the south. It may be noted that both were allocated unusually large amounts of land, suggesting substantial discretion on the part of the Tribal Authority to exceed the original nominal allocations of 6 morgen only.

Some feeling also emerged from discussions in Sediba and Gladstone [*Free State RRRP*, 1995, Appendix 3] in favour of the acquisition of title deeds in respect of residential sites and arable land, although not to grazing land which people felt should remain communal. Undoubtedly some active farmers in the Trust areas feel that they should be given stronger titles to arable land than the certificates of allocation that they hold at present, in order that they can use these as collateral in applications for commercial credit.

It is unclear, however, whether the implications of a land market – the private sale of such titles, for example, or the unequal accumulation of such titles, and the inevitable loss of entitlement on the part of some members of the next generation – were adequately discussed or resolved at the workshops in Sediba and Gladstone. If individuals own plots, either residential or arable, a market value of land will develop which will vitally affect attitudes to the buying and selling of other land. There was hostility to the allocation of land by headmen or by elected farmers' committees. Rather, according to questionnaire responses, 'the new government' should be responsible for land allocation, although how this would be done was not specified. It may be speculated that this response reflects a suspicion of established local authority and of the dominant local politics of patronage which in people's experience were bound to influence decisions over the disposition of land.

This area of uncertainty raises another fundamentally important question relating to the future administration of the Trust areas. What political authority will prevail? And how will decisions relating to the privatisation of land, or otherwise, be taken? On the one hand, the Trust villages have appointed headmen who are accountable to the Barolong Tribal Authority in Thaba Nchu, which survives the dissolution of the government of Bophuthatswana. The 'traditional' hierarchy, therefore, as established within the framework of Bantu Authorities throughout the 'homelands', remains in place. On the other hand, there has been during the period of transition a profileration of overlapping and often conflicting authorities: the local ANC committee; the civics; a new structure of elected Farmers' Committees (including, some Trust villagers felt inappropriately, some private landowners); and an older network of Village Development

Committees, sponsored by Agricor. Inevitably, there is much uncertainty and sometimes bitter conflict over the respective competences of different committees, the management of strategic priorities and the establishment of effective co-operation. The politics of 'development' in Gladstone in 1993–95 were fraught with conflict of this kind. The question of what authority is competent to manage what matters has already proved explosive elsewhere in South Africa, particularly in Transkei. The same question requires urgent political resolution in the Trust areas of the Thaba Nchu district before effective steps can be taken to resolve other practical problems such as land allocation or the particular needs expressed by Trust villagers.

In summary, the Trust villages in Thaba Nchu are administered on the basis of individual usufructuary rights to arable land and communal use of grazing land. Their inhabitants depend mainly on employment elsewhere, and on pensions. Only a few residents are successful cultivators; otherwise, arable lands are often rented by outsiders with the necessary capital resources to undertake ploughing operations. Many more residents own cattle and sheep, and pastoral lands, nominally subject to rotation and other forms of environmental regulation, are generally over-grazed. There are two fundamentally important questions relating to the future administration of land in the Trust areas. First, what structures of representation will determine this future? Will Trust villagers continue to be subordinate to headmen and chiefs within the hierarchy of the Tribal Authority, or will independent structures emerge? Secondly, would stronger individual entitlement to arable land facilitate access to commercial credit and thereby strengthen Trust villagers' farming capacity, albeit at a cost to the chiefs and headmen of the loss of some of their significant prerogative – responsibility for the allocation of land? Herein lie the seeds of much conflict in South Africa's 'communal' land regimes.

V. CONCLUSION

These case studies from the Free State represent sites of struggle over the principles and practices of land reform in South Africa as a whole. The restitution claims that have been made reflect a variety of circumstances of dispossession in the past, and their resolution requires sustained attention to the detail of those processes. The Thaba Phatshwa claim, in particular, cannot be resolved through an act of restitution to the heirs of dispossessed individuals, since a community of other 'historically disadvantaged people' – mere pawns in the great drama of dispossession that was land segregation policy in practice – was placed on the land in question.

The conflicts over redistribution of state-owned land around Botshabelo reflect a fundamental policy dilemma. Will the new state commit its resources to facilitate transfers of land within a framework of individual freehold rights, a framework that is consistent with past South African land settlement practice, with the weight of donor agency advice and with political pressure from a stratum of potential beneficiaries who, with incomes from business activities or bureaucratic or professional employ-ment, are relatively well placed to take advantage of new opportunities of access to land? Or will the state commit its resources to the much more difficult task of facilitating transfers of land within a framework of common property rights, that is consistent in some ways with black South African 'tradition' and with political pressure from other strata of potential beneficiaries who cannot afford to carry the financial burden of private purchase of land for farming purposes?

There is a variety of models of common property rights available. The most familiar in the region is the tradition of 'communal' tenure in the erstwhile African reserves, as illustrated here with reference to the Thaba Nchu district. Qualified continuity of this tradition would require a reconciliation of the historical legacy of the administrative rights of chiefs and headmen with a new insistence by land-holding communities on the resolution of land issues through democratic representation at local level. This terrain of dispute is potentially explosive. Otherwise, there are emergent forms of group ownership of land such as trusts and closed corporations, in which a balance of members' rights and obligations is constitutionally agreed, defined and written down; the legal validity of whose collective land rights is recognised both by official land registrars and by the Land Bank and other sources of commercial credit; and whose rules of operation are sufficiently flexible to allow individuals to buy or sell an interest in land in response to changing circumstances. Such forms of tenure require sustained experiment. There are important practical difficulties, of the kind identified by the chairman of Bafutsana Association in Botshabelo. But they also, perhaps, offer the best opportunity at the present time of partially bridging the chasm between the rhetoric of benefiting 'the poor' and the reality of their practical exclusion.

NOTES

1. Derek Hanekom, 'Opening Address by the Minister of Land Affairs', National Conference on Land Policy, 31 Aug. 1995; Draft Land Policy Principles, Department of Land Affairs.
2. Pilot Land Reform Programme, Introduction Manual for the Provincial Steering Committee, Free State.
3. The Border Rural Committee, for example, has taken a prominent part in shaping land reform policy in the Eastern Cape. See Beinart and Kingwill [1995] and commentary in *GroundWork*, Vol.3, Oct. 1995.

4. The Pilot Land Reform District consists of the Dewetsdorp, Thaba Nchu, Botshabelo and Excelsior magisterial districts, and parts of the Bloemfontein and Brandfort districts. It was selected because, by comparison with two other possible areas, it met many of the relevant criteria published by the Land Affairs Department; 'it is the area which has the most need in it'; and it is close to established (state) support structures.

5. This work was undertaken partly independently; partly within the terms of reference of a project sponsored by the Overseas Development Administration (ODA), UK, under its Population and Environment Research Programme, jointly with Professor William Beinart of the University of Bristol; and partly within the terms of reference of a regional study sponsored by the Land and Agriculture Policy Centre (LAPC), Johannesburg. For a report on the ODA work, see Beinart and Murray [1995]. I am grateful to William Beinart for his careful and detailed comments on those sections of our joint report which I was responsible for preparing, and from which I have drawn for this article. For a report on the LAPC work, see Free State RRRP [1995] and Murray [1995b].

6. Interested readers should refer to Beinart [1994b], Murray [1995a; 1995b], and Beinart and Murray [1995].

7. Interview, Wally Smit, Thaba Phatshwa, 21 Oct. 1994.

8. Interview, John Weymers, Thaba Phatshwa, 19 Oct. 1994.

9. The market value of land is the price actually paid by a willing buyer to a willing seller in a 'free' market. The agricultural value of land reflects the annual income that may be derived from arable and pastoral activities thereon, as estimated by agricultural officials. Market values have been generally higher than agricultural values in South Africa. However, the discrepancy between these values reflects many different variables, some of which are highly volatile in present circumstances. In respect of one farm west of Bloemfontein, for example, the vendor expected a market price of R400/ha towards the end of 1995, and put the asking price up to R700/ha on hearing that the state might help people to buy the farm. The Department of Agriculture estimated the agricultural value of the farm at R250/ha, while the Land Bank estimated the prevailing market value in the area at R286/ha.

10. This was undone later by the Supreme Court [Murray, 1992: 242–5].

11. Interview, Daniel Francois van Tonder, Dewetsdorp, 27 Nov. 1993.

12. Interviews, Hendrik van Schalkwyk, Bradford, 18 June 1993; Fonteindraai, 23 June 1993.

13. Interviews, Gert Ferreira, Palmietfontein, 16 June 1993; 6 Nov. 1993.

14. Interview, Doreen Henning, Vadersgift, 23 Nov. 1993.

15. Telephone interview, Leon Marais, Director of the Farmer Development Division, Department of Agriculture, Pretoria, 5 July 1993.

16. Interviews, Naomi Masefa Matsau, Contest, 18 June 1993; D section, Botshabelo, 5 July 1993.

17. Interviews, Samuel Mahlomong Khabuli, Contest, 27 Nov. 1993, 8 Oct. 1994.

18. Minutes of 'Botshabelo meeting: 8 March 1994'.

19. Press announcement, 26 Aug. 1994.

20. See Note 9.

21. Interview, 'Mabatho Sehlabo with K.Z. Monosi, Chairman of the Dafutsana Association, March 1995.

22. Interview, Sefakoane Makhetha, secretary of Bafutsana Association, 10 Oct. 1995.

23. Free State Pilot Land Reform, Monthly Report, Sept. 1995.

24. ibid.

25. Interview, Jonny Xhalabile, Moedersgift, 20 Oct. 1995.

26. 'Fisiese Situasie op Botshabelo Plase' [Physical Situation on Botshabelo Farms], Glen Agricultural Development Institute, Oct. 1995.

27. Land Policy: Framework Document, Department of Land Affairs, May 1995.

28. Draft Land Policy Principles, Department of Land Affairs, National Conference on Land Policy, 31 Aug–1 Sept.1995; Derek Hanekom, 'Speech by the Minister of Land Affairs'; 'What the New Land Bills Mean', GroundWork, Vol.3, No.4, Oct. 1995, pp.4–5.

29. Interview, Samson Honti Seape, Thaba Nchu, 24 March 1995.

30. Interviews, Thomas Maele, Thaba Nchu, 24 March 1995; Malesela Hyman, Botshabelo, 30 March 1995; Challa Moahloli, Thaba Nchu, 24 March 1995; Deeds Registry, Bloemfontein,

relevant Transfer Deeds (TDs).
31. Interview, 'Madibanki Setlogelo, Thaba Nchu, 10 Oct. 1995.
32. I have retained reference to morgen, instead of hectares, where this original unit of official land measurement in South Africa is still used by villagers themselves. 1 morgen = c. 0.836 ha.
33. Interview, Ezekiel Pule, Kgalala, 12 Oct. 1994.
34. Interview, Johannes Ramorena Khoathela, Woodbridge, 8 Oct. 1994.

REFERENCES

Agricor, 1994, *Thaba Nchu District: Land and Related Information*, Agricor office, Thaba Nchu.
Beinart, William, 1994a, *Twentieth Century South Africa*, Oxford: Oxford University Press.
Beinart, William, 1994b, 'Farmers' Strategies and Land Reform in the Orange Free State', *Review of African Political Economy*, No.61.
Beinart, William, and Rosalie Kingwill, 1995, *Eastern Cape Land Reform Project Pre-Planning Report*, Working Paper 25, Johannesburg: Land and Agriculture Policy Centre and Border Rural Committee, Oct.
Beinart, William, and Colin Murray, 1995, *Agrarian Change, Population Movements and Land Reform in the Free State*, report on research funded by the ODA, Aug.
Free State RRRP, 1995, *Free State Rural Restructuring Research Programme, District Study No. 2*, Appendices 1–7, April.
Murray, Colin, 1992, *Black Mountain: Land, Class and Power in the Eastern Orange Free State, 1880s to 1980s*, Edinburgh: Edinburgh University Press.
Murray, Colin, 1995a, 'Structural Unemployment, Small Towns and Agrarian Change in South Africa', *African Affairs*, Vol.94, No.374.
Murray, Colin, 1995b, *Free State Rural Restructuring Research Programme, District Study No. 2*, District Overview. April.
Platzky, Laurine, and Cherryl Walker, 1985, *The Surplus People: Forced Removals in South Africa*, Johannesburg: Ravan Press.
SPP, 1983, *Forced Removals in South Africa*, Vols.1–5, Cape Town: The Surplus People Project.

The Agrarian Question and Industrial Dispersal in South Africa: Agro-Industrial Linkages Through Asian Lenses

GILLIAN HART

While the ANC has always recognized the land question, the agrarian question as a whole has not featured centrally in the conceptualization of the national question. There is an urgent need to place the agrarian question at the centre of transformation agendas.

[*Weiner and Levin,* 1991: 40].

INTRODUCTION

In South Africa today, three crucial sets of issues are being addressed largely in isolation from one another: (1) industrial restructuring and the socio-spatial reorganisation of work as South Africa re-engages with the intensely competitive global economy, (2) the land question and agrarian reform, and (3) new systems of local governance in relation to the reconstitution of the state at the provincial and national levels. In practice, they are closely interconnected. My purpose is to illuminate some actual and possible connections, drawing both on recent research in Nothwestern KwaZulu-Natal and on comparative Asian trajectories of rural industrialisation and agro-industrial linkages.

Separate industrial and agrarian debates reflect competing and deeply problematic visions of 'the city' versus 'the countryside'. According to the dominant view, South Africa's future is metropolitan and industrial, and resources should be concentrated in major urban complexes [e.g. *Urban Foundation* 1990; *Tomlinson* 1990]. Critics of this alleged urban bias argue

Gillian Hart, Department of Geography, University of California, Berkeley, Berkeley, California 94720-4740, USA. This contribution is based on research conducted while the author held the Jill Nattrass Memorial Fellowship at the Centre for Social and Development Studies, University of Natal, Durban in 1994; the research was also supported by the National Science Foundation and the MacArthur Foundation. The industrial survey in Newcastle was conducted jointly with Alison Todes who, together with David Szanton and Henry Bernstein, has been particularly central to the writing of this study. The author also benefited greatly from discussions with many colleagues in South Africa, the US, and Europe. Ananya Roy provided excellent research assistance.

instead for a rural and agricultural strategy, and for creating peasants or small farmers wherever land becomes available through the market [e.g. *World Bank*, 1993; *Binswanger and Deininger*, 1993; *Lipton and Lipton*, 1993]. Both visions are problematic on a number of counts, not least of which are the political and social forces (or lack thereof!) that underpin them. Articulated most forcefully by the Urban Foundation, metropolitan vision in practice veers towards a corporatist coalition between metropolitan capital and certain branches of organised labour from which large segments of South African society are excluded.[1] That the small farmer vision has been spearheaded and defined in large part by the World Bank in predictably technicist terms underscores the lack of an organised coalition from within rural society around the land question, as well as the limits on redistribution imposed by what Levin and Weiner (this volume) call an 'elite-pacted settlement' (see also Bernstein [1994]; Murray and Williams [1994]; Williams [1993]).

In practice the nature and extent of land redistribution will depend both on the constitution of political forces, and on the conditions of access to non-agricultural resources. Murray's case study [this volume] of the deracialisation of land markets in parts of the Free State illustrates one dimension of this point with great clarity. He shows how those black South Africans most likely to gain access to land in formerly white rural areas are strategically-placed men with resources derived from non-agricultural sources, as well as political connections. Although local officials and white farmers invoke the notion of 'viable farm units', those actually acquiring agricultural land are far more likely to devote most of their attention to lucrative non-agricultural and largely urban-based activities. Instead of a sturdy yeomanry [*Lipton and Lipton*, 1993], deracialisation of land markets is producing gentleman farmers for whom agriculture will at most be a weekend occupation.

The small farmer model set forth by the World Bank is not, in fact, one of full-time farming. On the contrary, proponents of this model claim not only that small-scale family farming is part-time in character, but that it actually *generates* non-agricultural incomes in rural regions. For example, the Bank's indicative estimates of livelihoods generated by its proposed reforms assumes a farm–non-farm multiplier of 1.6 [*World Bank*, 1993: Annex 1, p.1]. In other words, what is being asserted is that every farm livelihood will automatically stimulate additional nonfarm rural livelihoods. Small-scale family farming in this view is not only relatively efficient, but also creates the non-agricultural conditions for its own existence via the operation of agricultural growth linkages.

These claims about growth linkages from agriculture are deeply suspect. They derive from an idealised and partial reading of 'Asian successes' –

most notably Taiwan – and invoke problematic assumptions to produce multiplier estimates that in fact have very little meaning [*Harriss*, 1987a; *Hart*, 1989; 1993; *de Janvry*, 1994]. As I shall argue later, market-based land reform in South African conditions is unlikely to produce much in the way of non-agricultural linkages, particularly in relatively remote rural regions where land is most likely to become available through the market.

Ironically, the economic and political conditions for more broadly-based access to land combined with multiple non-agricultural income sources may exist in what I shall call *interstitial places* – places neither metropolitan nor deep rural. These places embody two key thrusts of apartheid spatial engineering: forced removals and industrial decentralisation. Since the 1960s, millions of black South Africans have been forcibly removed from 'black spots' (freehold areas outside the bantustans), and expelled from white-owned farms [*Platzky and Walker*, 1985], resulting in massive agglomerations of people in the former bantustans which Murray [1988] has aptly termed 'displaced urbanization.' Interstitial spaces were also the focal points of huge state subsidies during the 1980s designed to shift industry to these labour reservoirs. In addition, they are a major locus of foreign – mainly Taiwanese – investment in South Africa.

Nowadays these places are widely viewed as distasteful relics of apartheid, which will conveniently wither away once the props – most notably industrial subsidies – are pulled out from under them. In the late 1980s, large corporate interests based in metropolitan areas spearheaded a major attack on industrial decentralisation policies, contending that subsidies were wasteful, inefficient, and had stymied metropolitan growth [*Urban Foundation*, 1990; *Development Bank of Southern Africa*, 1990]. Although critiques from the left emphasised the labour-repressive, low-wage pattern of industrialisation, the identification of industrial decentralisation with apartheid spatial engineering lent additional force to the neoliberal critique. So too did the spectre often invoked of shoddy, fly-by-night operators who abused the excessively generous subsidies. As a consequence of these pressures, the Regional Industrial Development Programme was modified along neoliberal lines in 1991; subsidies were sharply reduced, and linked to output and productivity instead of inputs. The reduction in subsidies coincided, of course, with the lifting of sanctions and the wider opening of the South African economy to the icy winds of global competition.

Central to the metropolitan vision is the presumption that industry will 'bleed away' from decentralisation areas, and 'naturally' reagglomerate in major urban areas [*Rogerson*, 1994; *Wilsenach and Lichthelm*, 1993]. In fact, the 'bleeding away' metaphor appears heavily overstated. Some industries have no doubt disappeared, particularly from remote parts of former bantustans. Particularly in certain of the more strategically located decentralisation points, however, relatively labour-intensive industries are still very much in evidence. In fact, data on approvals under the new RIDP show that a substantial proportion of prospective industrialists propose to locate in former banstustans and small towns [*Wilsenach and Lichtehelm*, 1993]. These locational patterns are particularly dramatic for foreign investors; in KwaZulu-Natal, more than 90 per cent of prospective foreign investors display a preference for these interstitial spaces [*Hart*, 1995a]. In addition, as we shall see later, foreign investors have been moving into Northwestern KwaZulu-Natal without incentives. Here and in many other parts of South Africa, white local governments in conservative small towns bordering densely-populated former banstustan areas have been by-passing the national state and establishing direct links in Asia – particularly Taiwan – in an effort to entice industrialists [*Hart*, 1995a]. In short, new impulses of industrial dispersal are taking shape in the post-apartheid era.

From a broader comparative perspective, these impulses are by no means peculiar to South Africa. Since the 1970s and 1980s, tendencies towards industrial dispersal have emerged in many different parts of the world in the context of the disintegration of import substitution industrialisation and intensified global competition. The most dramatic instance is, of course, in China where the massive surge in industrial growth has come largely from rural industries.

The most obvious interpretation is that processes of industrial dispersal are driven by an inexorable capital logic in an age of hypercompetition, increased mobility of capital, the undermining of organised labour, and the 'feminisation' of the workforce [e.g. *Amin and Robins*, 1990; *Castells and Henderson*, 1987; *B. Harrison*, 1994; *Sassen*, 1988; *Standing*, 1989]. This interpretation resonates strongly with South African debates over industrial decentralisation in the 1980s. In a particularly important set of interventions, Bell [1983; 1987] maintained that the movement of labour-intensive industries into peripheral regions of South Africa was not simply the result of apartheid policies that distorted economic incentives, but was propelled in important ways by capitalists' search for lower production costs in response to increasingly competitive conditions.[2]

Emerging patterns of industrial dispersal in South Africa and beyond are unquestionably a reflection of global processes driven by intensified competition – but these processes are constituted and experienced in different ways in different local settings, and generate widely divergent distributional outcomes. Superficially similar patterns of industrial dispersal encompass *multiple trajectories* or paths of socio-spatial restructuring and agro-industrial linkages; these in turn reflect particular local histories, class forces, and social dynamics. Accordingly, the salient questions are what are the key institutional arenas and sites of contestation in any particular setting, how have they been constituted historically, what are the dynamics by which they operate, who are the winners and losers, and what are the possibilities for reconfiguring the exercise of power and conditions of access to land and other resources?

In this study I address these questions in the context of Northwestern KwaZulu-Natal, a sub-region that exemplifies the joint processes of forced removals and industrial decentralisation, and situate them in relation to comparative Asian trajectories of rural industrialisation and agro-industrial linkages. These Asian patterns do *not* constitute 'models' that can be emulated in any direct way; the central thrust of my argument is precisely that they are the outcome of historically-specific forms of struggle at multiple societal levels. They do, however, provide lenses for bringing fresh insights to bear on debates, conditions, and possibilities in South Africa.

GROWTH LINKAGES FROM SMALL-FARM AGRICULTURE?: OF
MULTIPLIERS, MIRAGES, AND MIRACLES

> International evidence suggests that farm-nonfarm multipliers vary from 1.3 for typical sub-Saharan subsistence agriculture with low population densities and undeveloped rural infrastructure to 2.2 in modern agricultural regions ... Given the South African situation, a multiplier of 1.6 was assumed. *The multiplier is 'real' rather than inflationary, given high levels of unemployment and underemployment.* It can be shown that a multiplier of 1.6 implies that for every farm livelihood created, 0.26 nonfarm rural livelihoods will also be created. [*World Bank*, 1993: Annex 1, p.1] (emphasis added).

With this seemingly scientific and incontrovertible assertion, the authors of *Options for Land Reform and Rural Restructuring in South Africa* not only inflate their estimates of the jobs created by small-farmer land reform by 26 per cent; they also assert, in effect, that small farm agriculture creates the conditions for its own existence by stimulating non-farm jobs *within rural regions*. These claims about the spatial location of non-agricultural spin-offs are crucial to the picture of small-scale, part-time family farming that the Bank is conjuring up. In the absence of locally-available jobs, some members of newly-created farm families would become long-distance migrants, and the sturdy yeoman capable of exercising stern discipline over his family's labour becomes even more of a mirage – particularly since claims about the relatively efficiency of small-scale family farming derive from assertions about superior (or is it patriarchal?) control over family labour [*Binswanger and Deininger*, 1993; *Lipton and Lipton*, 1993]. In the logical edifice of small-farmer land reform constructed by the Bank, a lot therefore hinges on the miracle of the multiplier.

The logic behind the multiplier holds that when agricultural incomes rise, farm households will spend a relatively large proportion of incremental incomes on relatively labour-intensive non-agricultural goods and services produced in rural regions; this in turn derives from the argument that small-farm agricultural growth generates not only backward and forward production linkages, but also – more importantly – *consumption* linkages. The concept of consumption linkages originates from Lee's [1971] analysis of intersectoral resource transfers and agrarian transition in Taiwan.[3] In this macro model, consumption linkages refer to the development of the home market in an endogenously-driven *national* strategy marked by close articulation between foodgrains agriculture and industry [*Mellor and Lele*, 1973].[4] More recently, the notion of consumption linkages has been redefined in *regional* (that is, sub-national terms), drawing on neoclassical trade theory. As I have argued more fully elsewhere [*Hart*, 1993], the logic of the regional model is entirely different from the original macro formulation; it is also readily compatible with neoliberal policy prescriptions

Needless to say, it is the regional, neoclassical definition of consumption multipliers that is being invoked in the South African context to assert that increases in agricultural incomes will automatically translate into rising demand for and supply of non-tradable goods and services *within* rural regions:

> Items that are rarely traded over the borders of the region of interest, and are not close substitutes with things that are traded, are nontradables, which *by definition* are demand-constrained. Growth multipliers arising from new spending come from new consumer and intermediate demands for nontradables. Because new demand for these items cannot *by definition* be met from imports, they are *assumed* to be met by increased local production [*Delgado et al.*, 1994: 1166] (emphasis added).

This statement by purveyors of quantitative multiplier estimates neatly encapsulates the assumptions they invoke. First, the supply of non-tradables in infinitely elastic – in other words, investment flows unproblematically into the production of non-tradable goods and services. Second, what is 'non-tradable' depends on how regional boundaries are defined – a definition that, as Harriss [1987a] has pointed out, is totally arbitrary. A third assumption is that increments in demand will be met by new production at constant prices; hence the World Bank's claim that in the South African case the multiplier is 'real' rather inflationary, because of high levels of rural unemployment.

In fact, quantitative multiplier estimates are simply artefacts of these arbitrary and deeply problematic assumptions, and the 'reality' claim is an exercise in obfuscation. Multiplier estimates in Asia have been in the order of 1.8 or 1.9, whereas those in Africa are only about 1.3 or 1.4 [*Haggblade et al.*, 1989; 1991]. More recently, Delgado *et al.* [1994] have jacked up African multiplier estimates by defining some staple food commodities as nontradables, and expanding the geographical area over which the multipliers are calculated while retaining the assumption of infinitely elastic supply. This maneouvre illustrates with great clarity the totally arbitrary character of the exercise [*de Janvry*, 1994; also *Harriss*, 1987a; *Hart*, 1989; 1993].[5]

The putative Asian 'successes' that are invoked to legitimate claims that small-farm agricultural growth translates automatically into non-agricultural diversification of rural regions in fact point to several crucial qualifications. First, investment does *not* flow automatically into the production of goods and services in the local/regional economy (however that is defined). This point emerges with great clarity from the Muda region of Malaysia, the primary locus of growth linkage modelling [*Bell et al.*, 1981; *Hazell and Roell*, 1983]. On the face of it, Muda presents ideal conditions for the operation of agricultural growth linkages. The installation of a massive irrigation scheme in the early 1970s was accompanied by rapid spread of yield-increasing rice technology to which even the smallest cultivators gained access, and agricultural incomes rose significantly. Yet, despite high multiplier estimates, the regional economy remained largely undiversified. Much of the agricultural surplus has flowed out of the region, a significant chunk of it into real estate in Kuala Lumpur. At the time of my research in 1987, men and young women were migrating in large numbers to work in other parts of Malaysia. These flows of resources out of the region cannot be understood in narrow economic terms. They reflect multiple institutional logics of investment, conditioned both by the region's history and by larger political-economic structures and processes [*Hart*, 1989; 1993]. In short, assumptions about infinitely elastic supply responses are deeply suspect, as are unsubstantiated assertions by growth linkage modellers that leakages of savings outside the region are negligible [also *Harriss*, 1987a].

The other exemplary case of high multipliers is the North Arcot district of Tamil Nadu in India [*Hazell and Ramasamy*, 1991]. In North Arcot, as in Muda, burgeoning consumer demand has come about not only as a result of increased incomes in rice production, but also from extremely high levels of government spending and expansion of the state sector [*Harriss*, 1987b; *Hart*, 1993]. In both cases, the pattern of commerce within the region has shifted sharply to items that are neither labour-intensive nor locally-produced. Bell *et al.'s* estimates of consumption multipliers in Muda in fact includes demand for the local services of wholesaling and retailing of goods actually produced elsewhere. Subsequent modelling exercises have attempted to specify 'local nontradables' more precisely, but the definitions remain entirely arbitrary [*Harriss*, 1987a]. Obsessed by the spurious spatiality of 'the region', growth modellers ignore question of whether the 'non-local' commodities that form a significant part of final demand are nationally-produced or imported.

A third key point is that new industrial and service sector jobs in rural regions cannot automatically be attributed to consumption or production linkages from agriculture. In North Arcot, for example, expansion of the silk industry has been a major source of increased non-farm employment, but it has virtually no local commodity linkages; Harriss's research points instead to the 'search by industrial capital for low costs of production [trading off the costs (on transport, transactions and information) of a non-metropolitan location against the cheapness of rural labour]' [*Harriss*, 1987b: 44]. Likewise, since the early 1990s industry has started moving into the Muda region but this process has no direct links to agricultural growth; rather it has been driven by Japanese and Taiwanese industrialists' search for lower wage labour and cheaper rents, and reflects the massive surge in foreign investment in the Malaysian economy more generally [*Furuoka*, 1995].

Taiwan, supposedly the prototypical case of growth linkages, demonstrates very clearly that the diversification of rural regions is not simply the consequence of agricultural growth. Taiwan has not, in fact, been subjected to regional growth linkage modelling. Explanations of rural industrialisation in Taiwan have, nevertheless, drawn heavily on the logic of agriculture-led linkages although unlike most growth modellers they stress the importance of agrarian reform.[6] The pre-eminent interpretation is that broadly-based land redistribution in the late 1940s created the conditions for dynamic smallholder agricultural growth; this in turn set in motion a synergistic and localised cycle of agricultural and industrial expansion within rural regions, driven by mutually reinforcing consumption and production linkages. According to this interpretation, the strength of consumption linkages in Taiwan stems from highly multiplicative patterns of effective demand brought about by land reform; these in turn intersected with production linkages, enhanced by policies that favoured small-scale, labour-intensive techniques of production, and by infrastructural investment in rural regions [*Ranis and Stewart*, 1987; see also *Anderson and Leiserson*, 1980; *Ho*, 1982].

While this interpretation no doubt captures some elements of decentralised growth processes in Taiwan, the periodisation of rural diversification in Taiwan cannot be explained simply in terms of agricultural growth linkages [*Hart*, 1993]. In particular, the main surge in rural industrialisation only took hold in the late 1960s. Between 1956 and 1966, the period in which agriculture was growing most rapidly, the chief increases in rural non-agricultural employment were in the services sector.

An alternative explanation is that the rather sudden increase in rural industrialisation since the latter part of the 1960s represents an 'urban push' rather than simply an 'agriculture pull' [*Shih*, 1983; *Amsden*, 1991]. During the import substitution phase in the 1950s and 1960s, industrialisation was predominantly urban. Shih [1983] shows how, with the accelerated industrialisation brought about by Taiwan's entry into export markets in the latter part of the 1960s, important industries that were originally urban based began dispersing into rural areas. Increasing costs of production in urban areas were a major driving force behind this urban-rural shift in industrial location: 'The increasingly difficult access to city land, residential congestion, and higher wages for workers in urban areas are all conditions favouring decentralised industrialisation' [*Shih*, 1983: 20]. Amsden [1991] adduces additional corroborating macro data, and a number of village studies provide direct evidence of rapid industrialisation of rural and peri-urban areas in the late 1960s and 1970s in the context of expanding export production and increasing cost pressures [e.g. *Gallin and Gallin*, 1982; *Hsia*, 1988; *Hu* 1983; 1984; *Niehoff*, 1987; *Stites*, 1982]. By the early 1980s, rapidly escalating growth of labour-intensive, decentralised industries produced the crisis of overaccumulation that propelled many of them to overseas locations – including, of course, South Africa.

As I have argued more fully elsewhere [*Hart*, 1993] the experience of Taiwan, taken in conjunction with that of other 'Asian successes' (including, very importantly, post-reform China), points very clearly to the limitations of the regional growth linkage hypothesis even in seemingly ideal conditions – namely, densely-settled, intensively-cultivated rice growing regions where state intervention ensured broadly-based increases in agricultural incomes. Growth linkage models abstract from precisely those institutions operating at multiple levels of economy and society that have shaped what are, in fact, highly differentiated outcomes.

In the context of market-based land reform in South Africa, the invocation of localised 'farm-nonfarm multipliers', legitimated in terms of this 'international experience', is particularly misleading. If anything, comparative experience suggests that the non-agricultural spin-offs from market-based land reform within rural regions of South Africa are likely to be minimal. Even if the target of redistributing 30 per cent of arable land in formerly 'white' farming areas of South Africa were to be achieved, and even if this redistribution were to reach beyond the gentleman farmers

described by Murray, the market-based character of the reform means that
newly-created black farmers would almost certainly be scattered throughout
the country. Even if they were to experience increases in disposable income
after repaying their loans, the probability that consumption multipliers would
kick in to expand local non-agricultural jobs – and therefore guarantee the
viability of small-scale, part-time family farming – is infinitesmally small. In
the most optimistic scenario, the market-based small farmer model in South
African conditions is likely to (re-)produce high levels of rural–urban
migration.

Conversely, to the extent that non-agricultural expansion is happening in
predominantly rural regions, it is being propelled by industrial dispersal that
– in the South African context – is notable for being totally *delinked* from
agriculture. Comparative Asian dynamics of industrial dispersal are
instructive for the light they shed on the peculiarities of this delinked
process in South Africa.

RURAL INDUSTRIALISATION IN THE ERA OF INTENSIFIED GLOBAL COMPETITION: COMPARATIVE ASIAN DYNAMICS

One of the peculiarities of late twentieth century capitalism is the dispersal
of labour-intensive industry into predominantly rural regions. Efforts to
interpret these and other processes of socio-spatial restructuring are
typically cast in terms of the 'flexibility debate' [*Gertler*, 1992], in which
those who emphasise the ceaseless quest by fast, lean capital for cheap,
unorganised labour [e.g. *Sassen*, 1988; *B. Harrison*, 1994] are pitted against
those who envision the emergence of post-Fordist communities of flexibly
specialised small firms bound together by ties of co-operation, trust, and
'collective efficiency' [e.g. *Sabel*, 1989; *Storper*, 1990; *Schmitz*, 1990].
Instruments wielded by both sides in the debate are in fact quite blunt. That
industry shifts to lower cost locations obviously reflects a broad capital
logic in a context of intensified competition, but explains very little about
the forms and dynamics that take hold in particular settings – invocations of
institutional 'embeddedness' by some authors notwithstanding. Flexible
specialisation is a construction somewhat akin to growth linkages, in which
the Third Italy plays much the same role as Taiwan.[7] Both formulations
conjure up an ideal-typical institutional form, from which they then deduce
dynamic processes.

Rather than pursuing the flexibility debate, it is far more instructive to
focus on the multiple, nonlinear, divergent *trajectories* through which
industrial capital in numerous guises encounters and intersects with agrarian
conditions constituted through particular local histories together with
broader processes of agrarian transition, industrialisation, and urbanisation.

Agro-industrial 'linkages' in this processual sense are forged through struggle, contestation, negotiation, and acquiescence in multiple, overlapping institutional arenas at different levels of society and economy – in which, as we shall see, gender features prominently.[8]

Although a detailed account is obviously beyond the scope of this paper, I shall try to highlight some key dimensions of rural industrialisation in Taiwan, China, and Malaysia that bear directly on interpreting what is happening in South Africa, and on rethinking agrarian reform.[9] In terms of South African debates over industrial decentralisation, all three are instances of 'spontaneous decentralisation' [Bell, 1983], in the sense that the shift of labour-intensive industry to lower cost rural locations reflects the imperatives of accumulation in the context of intensified global competition. Yet there are wide variations in the processes through which rural industries have taken hold, as well as their organisational forms and distributional outcomes. Different Asian trajectories of rural industrialisation illustrate how these varying forms are constituted both through the politics of place [Pred, 1989; Massey 1993], and through the macro dynamics of agrarian transition.

I shall focus mainly on Taiwan, both because it has become an exemplary case of growth linkages and flexible specialisation, and because Taiwanese investment is a major feature of the South African setting I shall describe below. In the preceding section we saw how the main surge in rural industrialisation in Taiwan took place in the late 1960s and 1970s, in the context of expanding export production and escalating urban cost pressures. A central feature of Taiwanese rural industrialisation is that it emerged endogenously from within rural society, rather than through direct foreign investment as in Malaysia and the southern coastal regions of China. At the same time, rural industrial processes are intricately connected with urban-industrial complexes:

> As Taiwan felt the effects of the worldwide oil crisis in 1974, and later faced increasing competition from other third world countries, hundreds of small urban factories closed. Many laid-off workers returned to their native villages. Taking advantage of manufacturing techniques learned in city factories, these returnees set up factories which tended to be very small in scale, family-owned, and labor-intensive. These factories tended to require very little capital, minimizing start-up costs and operating expenses in may ways. For example, since most families had at least a small plot of land due to land reform, the factories could be set up on family land adjacent to, or even inside, the family house for extremely little cost. They could rely upon unpaid family labor and the much lower rural labor rates of

part-time farmers. In addition, as many as 65 percent of these factories remained unregistered, thus escaping taxation and regulation. Finally, being less subject to regulation they could manufacture with even less regard for the natural environment than their urban counterparts. These small manufacturing concerns were an integral part of the larger industrialized economy, tied by personal and informal relationships to larger factories through subcontracting work, or to urban buyers [*Buck*, 1995: 24].

These familial forms of accumulation and labour control are inflected through culturally and historically specific gender and kinship relations, in which senior males exercise considerable (although not unilateral) power through control of inherited and acquired property [*Greenhalgh*, 1994]. Inherited property – notably land – is owned by the male descent line as a whole, with fathers holding family property in trust for their sons who have rights of petition at the time of partition in terms of customary law. Property acquired through industrial activity is under the discretionary control of senior males, and provides them with tremendous leverage in intra-familial negotiations [*ibid.*]. At this level 'agro-industrial linkages' are articulated through gendered relations of property and power, which are central to understanding the speed with which industrial activity took hold in the Taiwanese countryside, and the forms it has assumed.[10]

Gender is crucial to the dynamic of accumulation in a number of other ways including, of course, labour discipline and the capacity of parents to appropriate the earnings of children – particularly daughters.[11] The inability of Taiwanese industrialists to exercise gendered control over the female workforce in South Africa is, as we shall see, one of the key reasons why Taiwanese investment operates so problematically in that context.

Agro-industrial linkages in Taiwan have been forged through historically-specific power struggles at other societal levels including, very importantly, relations between peasants and the state. The Guomindang state coalition, which fled to Taiwan from China in 1949 following their defeat by the communist forces, effectively excluded indigenous Taiwanese from access to the state, at least until the late 1970s. Land reform, implemented by the US occupation forces in the late 1940s and early 1950s, not only brought about relatively egalitarian land distribution; it also removed the indigenous landlord class from the countryside, and provided the newly-constituted state with direct control over peasant production and surplus extraction from agriculture that helped to finance the early stages of import-substitution industrialisation [*Amsden*, 1985; *Gold*, 1986]. One of the key attractions of rural industry for the indigenous Taiwanese peasantry is that it is less subject to official regulation than agriculture, and offers an avenue of escape from state scrutiny [*Niehoff*, 1987; also *Greenhalgh*, 1994]. By the same token, that indigenous Taiwanese rely so heavily on kin and community networks to mobilise capital, labour, and information is at least in part a reflection of their relations with the state.

Taiwanese industrialists have tried to sidestep the central state in other contexts as well. In the southern coastal provinces of China where most foreign direct investment is concentrated, Hsing [1995a; 1995b] describes how Taiwanese investors have established direct, personalistic connections with local government officials in rural areas, rather than going through the central state. As we shall see below, in small South African towns adjacent to former bantustans, white local government officials have sought to bypass the national state and entice foreign investors who are predominantly Taiwanese. In quite unintended ways, these personalistic strategies have meshed with a Taiwanese *modus operandi* that grew out of a peculiar set of historical conditions. Although Taiwanese industrialists in both China and South Africa have forged close relations with local governments in predominantly rural regions, industrial dynamics are in practice dramatically different [*Hart*, 1995a].

Foreign investment in China is concentrated in two provinces; in many other regions of the country, investment has emerged endogenously from within rural society. On the surface, rural industrialisation in post-reform China appears very similar to that in Taiwan; in many areas, huge numbers of tiny factories nestle in fields of rice and other crops, as well as in small towns. Since the mid-1980s, much of the extraordinary growth in industrial production in China has been concentrated in villages and small towns where wages and other costs of production are significantly lower than in the main urban areas. What makes much of Chinese rural industrialisation particularly compelling and distinctive is that the initiative for rural industrialisation has come directly from local governments, acting in effect like diversified corporations and, at least in formal terms, the majority of rural non agricultural enterprises are collectively owned. These TVE's (township and village enterprises) account for about 75 percent of China's rural industrial output, and 60 percent of rural industrial employment; they employ somewhere in the vicinity of 112 million people, and since 1990 have absorbed about 70 percent of annual net additions to the rural labour force [*Bowles and Dong*, 1994: 57–62].

Ironically, it was a study by the World Bank [*Byrd and Lin*, 1990] which first recognised that TVEs represent a remarkable institutional innovation, combining collective ownership with market discipline – somewhat along the lines of Bardhan and Roemer's [1992] theoretical model of market socialism. TVE's confront fierce market competition, although they do have preferential access to some inputs [*Nee*, 1992]. The bulk of profits of TVEs are controlled by local governments, and are to a large extent disbursed in local circuits – both in productive reinvestment, and in social services [*Oi*, 1992]. Available research on TVEs makes clear that they are enormously varied, as are interpretations of them. Although discussion of these debates and the evidence they adduce is obviously beyond the scope of this paper, the TVE phenomenon in its various guises is a powerful demonstration of the multiple forms and trajectories of rural industrialisation in the late twentieth century. TVEs are the product of Chinese history, and obviously cannot be replicated in any direct way. They are, however, an illustration of institutional innovations that open up access to resources in ways that enable resources to be used more productively – a point that is of paramount importance in contemporary South Africa.

While these and other Asian examples of rural industrialisation in the context of intensified global competition illustrate the diversity of institutional forms and distributional outcomes, they also share a key common element – namely, the shift of industry to lower cost rural locations was in each case preceded by redistributive measures in the agrarian sphere. In Taiwan, as we saw earlier, land reform endowed the peasantry with key resources from which they moved into industrial activity. China has also gone through phases of land redistribution that culminated in broadly-based access to land from which rural industrialisation has developed. In a process quite analogous to that in Taiwan, the Chinese Communist state instituted land reforms in the early 1950s that broke the power of landlords and facilitated surplus extraction from agriculture [*Selden and Ka*, 1993]. Since 1978, decollectivisation of Chinese agriculture and the emergence of the 'household responsibility system' has brought about a highly egalitarian distribution of land rights among (although not within) households [*Selden*, 1993; *McKinley and Griffin*, 1993]. In the Muda region of Malaysia where, as we saw earlier, foreign investors have been establishing since the early 1990s, there was no land redistribution; however, most households in the' huge rice-scheme have access to some land. In addition, the state pumps massive subsidies into rice production – including free fertiliser and significant price supports – to which even the smallest landholding house-holds have access. There have, in addition, been very high levels of state spending in rural regions on education, health care, and other social services. Agricultural subsidies and other forms of state spending represent an effort to contain the political threat that the rice growing peasantry poses to the ruling coalition.

These conditions of broadly-based access to agrarian resources are, I suggest, crucial to the dynamics of industrial accumulation in rural regions, and constitute a key element of 'agro-industrial linkage'. Rural industrial workers have no formal protection in terms of unemployment, health, or other benefits; however, access to land in effect subsidises the industrial wage. Elsewhere [*Hart*, 1995c], I argue that there are parallels between rural landholdings and the state-sponsored housing systems in Hong Kong and Singapore where, as Castells *et al.* [1990] point out, housing subsidises industrial wages and has played a key role in defining the conditions of competitiveness. In societies with large and largely impoverished rural populations, however, housing cannot perform this sort of redistributive function precisely because access must be rationed. This point is brought out very clearly in China, where housing and other social welfare protections accorded to the urban proletariat in the state sector have been maintained through a form of influx control; rural industrial growth has effectively bypassed this system of urban support [*Walder*, 1995].

The subsidy to capital from retention of small property is on one level an old story that has been told in terms of articulation of modes of production [*Wolpe*, 1972], functional dualism [*de Janvry*, 1981], and similar concepts, and has figured prominently in earlier agrarian debates [e.g. *Goodman and Redclift*, 1982]. It is also, of course, deeply familiar to South Africanists. Contemporary Asian patterns of rural industrialisation reconfigure this old story in new ways, and render it far more open-ended than earlier formulations. They illustrate how the political conditions of access to land and other resources, and the social institutions and power relations within and through which resources are deployed, generate quite diverse trajectories of accumulation and class formation.

These comparative trajectories also shed new light on industrial dispersal in South Africa, and its relationship to agrarian conditions. In sharp contrast to the Asian patterns just discussed, industrial decentralisation in South Africa was closely linked with an often brutal process of *dispossession* through which huge numbers of rural black South Africans have been deprived of any form of social security. That industrial decentralisation has been intimately connected with dispossession is notably absent from the vociferous neoliberal critique. It is also missing from arguments about 'spontaneous' decentralisation. Yet, as I shall now show, it is absolutely central to understanding how industrial dynamics are playing out as South Africa opens to the global economy.

FORCED REMOVALS, INDUSTRIAL DECENTRALISATION, AND TAIWANESE INVESTMENT IN NORTHWESTERN KWAZULU-NATAL

Northwestern KwaZulu-Natal exemplifies what I earlier termed interstitial places – namely, densely populated areas that have been the locus of forced removals and industrial decentralisation. Until May 1994, Northwestern KwaZulu-Natal was a bizarre apartheid patchwork, with bits of the KwaZulu

MAP 1

AREA OF STUDY IN SOUTH AFRICA

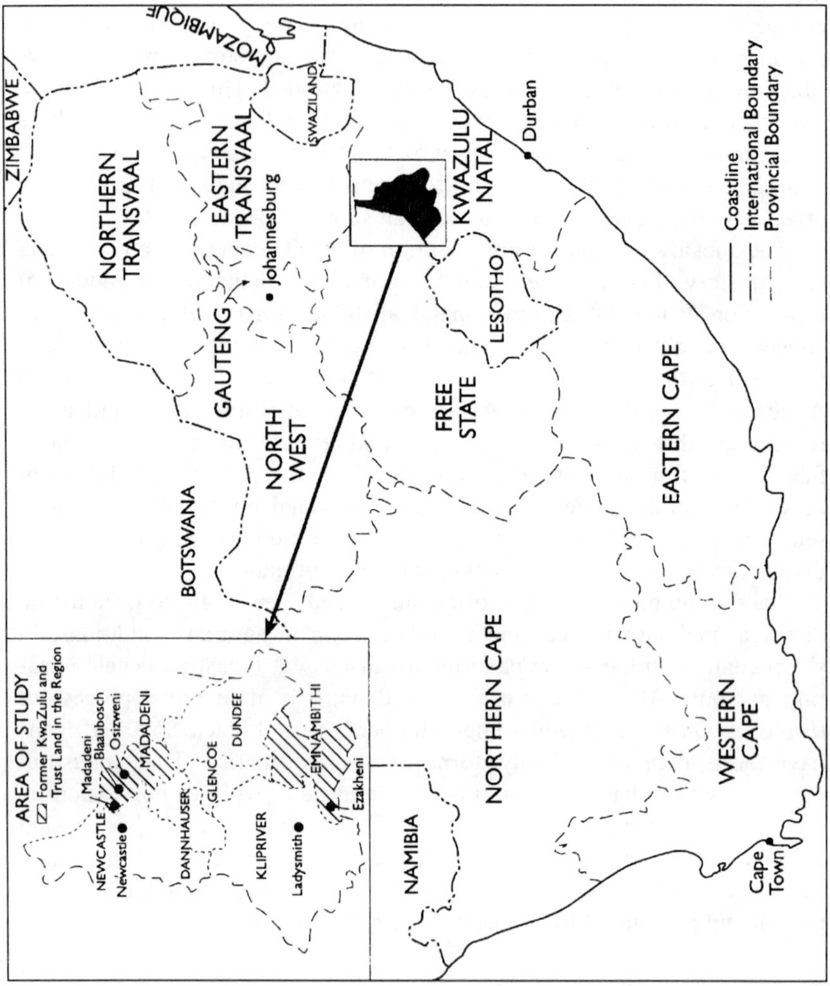

MAP 2

NEWCASTLE/MADADENI SUB-REGION

Former KwaZulu and Trust Land
Railway line
Main road
Power station
Industry
Mine

MAP 3
KLIPRIVER/EMNAMBITHI SUB-REGION

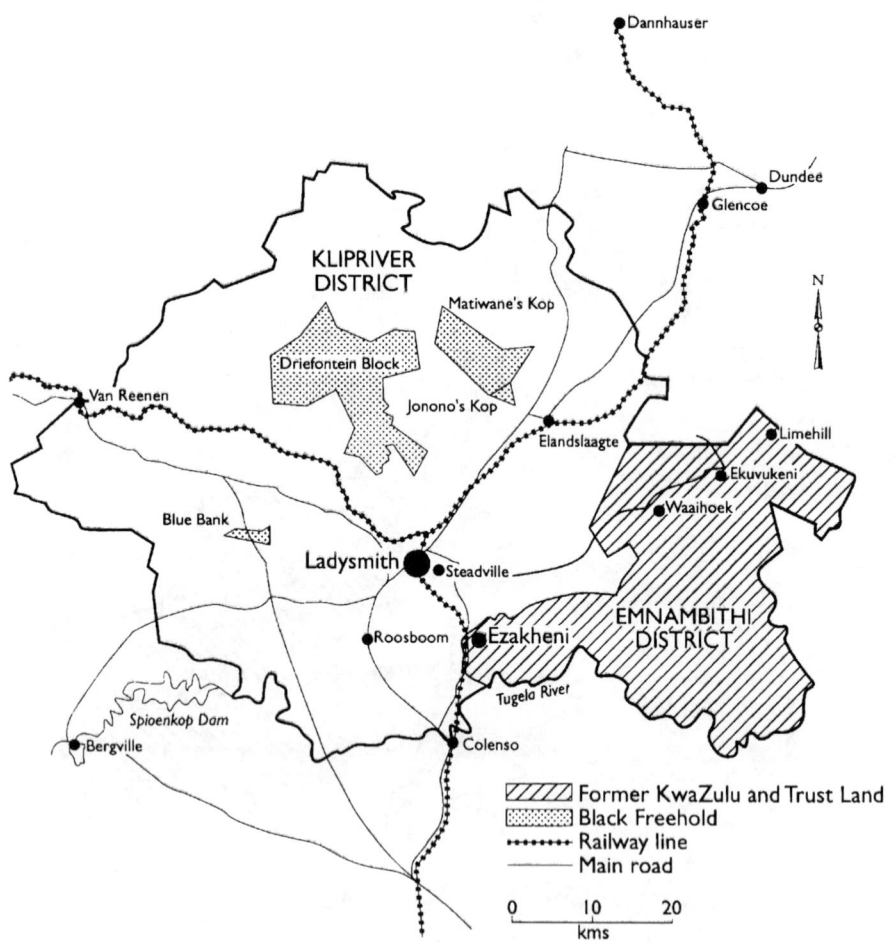

bantustan spliced into Natal (Map 1). Between 1960 and 1991, according to the censuses, the population increased from 412,000 to over a million. Yet during this period, the number of people recorded as living in those pieces of the sub-region designated as Natal fell from 343,000 (83 per cent) of the total to 294,000 (29 per cent) of the total, while KwaZulu's share of the sub-region's population rose from 69,000 (17 per cent) to 717,000 (71 per cent); the latter figure is, undoubtedly, a substantial underestimate. The large majority of the population is concentrated in large relocation townships in what was KwaZulu that are linked to formerly 'white' towns – Madadeni-Osizweni about 20 km from Newcastle, and Ezakheni which is similarly located in relation to Ladysmith; there is another large relocation complex (Limehill-Ekuvukeni) about 40 km from Ladysmith.

These relocation townships attest to the particular intensity of forced removals in this part of Natal, the cruelty of which is deeply etched into the landscape. Forced removals assumed two main forms in this region: elimination of 'black spots' or African freehold areas, and evictions of labourers and tenants from white-owned farms. Historically levels of African freehold landownership were relatively high in this area. Rural 'black spot' removals actually began in the vicinity of Newcastle in 1963, and by the early 1980s nearly half of the 'black spot' removals in Natal were in this area [*Surplus Peoples Project*, 1983]; in the vicinity of Ladysmith, however, there remain several large freehold communities that managed to resist removals. Farm evictions have been – and remain – particularly intense in this area. In addition, the region is bounded to the southeast by desperately poor, overcrowded, hardscrabble rural reserves which the American missionary Lewis Grout described in 1851 as 'fit only for the eagle and the baboon'. Farm evictions and rural impoverishment contribute to the ongoing net migration into relocation townships. For example, census figures suggest that the population of Madadeni grew at three per cent per annum compared to a natural increase of 2.3 per cent, and that about two-thirds of in-migration is by women [*Todes*, 1995a]. A survey of Madadeni, Osizweni, and the informal settlement of Blaaubosch conducted in 1992 revealed that only four per cent of households had access to rural land [*Data Research Africa*, 1993].

Dispossession and the formation of huge concentrations of population in the countryside has proceeded hand-in-hand with the constitution of these areas and adjacent white towns as industrial enclaves. Both Ladysmith and Newcastle originate from military outposts on what was the British colonial frontier in the mid-nineteenth century, and are strategically located on transport routes mid-way between Johannesburg and Durban. Until the late 1960s, their economies were based primarily on coal mining, agriculture, and public utilities. Since the 1970s, both experienced a significant – if uneven – expansion of industry during a period of decline in the South African economy more generally. In 1960, industrial employment in Ladysmith and Newcastle combined was under 4,500. By 1991 it had grown to 38,000, and had become the major sector of formal employment in the sub-region. Over the same period, Northwestern KwaZulu-Natal's share of industrial employment in the province jumped from 3.8 per cent to over 11 per cent [P. Harrison, 1994].

Industrialisation proceeded in three phases. From the post-war period until the late 1960s, large textile and clothing firms accounted for much of the industrial expansion. The second phase in the 1970s was the era of heavy industrialization, exemplified most dramatically in Newcastle where the state established a plant of Iscor, the state-owned Iron and Steel Corporation; several privately-owned heavy industries (mainly tires and machine tools) moved into Ladysmith. The Iscor-induced boom collapsed in the late 1970s, amidst a series of economic crises in the late 1970s and early 1980s in manufacturing as well as in mining and agriculture in the sub-region. The 1980s represents the heyday of industrial decentralisation under the Regional Industrial Development Program (RIDP), which provided massive subsidies to private industrialists to locate in designated 'industrial development points'; during this period, Northwestern KwaZulu-Natal garnered 29 per cent of the RIDP-subsidised projects in the province, 33 per cent of the jobs, and 25 per cent of the capital investment.

These phases coincide with shifts in macroeconomic conditions, as well as changes in national policy. Yet industrial trajectories cannot simply be read off these macro forces; in addition, they have been shaped in crucially important ways by locally-specific struggles and strategies, and intense place-based competition that goes back at least to the 1940s. Until the 1970s, direct political connections into the central state were the chief means by which white local authorities in Ladysmith and Newcastle tried to pull in industry. The 1980s saw the emergence of particularly aggressive marketing strategies by white local government officials; although these strategies were launched on the basis of resources dispensed by the national state, they operated through non-local linkages very different from the earlier direct political connections. In Ladysmith, white local officials forged a close relationship with regional authorities in the form of the KwaZulu Finance Corporation (KFC) and managed to lay claim to signifi-cant resources for an industrial estate in Ezakheni. When it became clear that the Ladysmith-KFC connection had monopolized most of the regional resources, Newcastle local officials reached directly into the global economy. They established connections in Asia (mainly Taiwan and Hong Kong), and lured approximately 65 industrialists and their families to Newcastle with a combination of RIDP incentives, as well as extremely cheap luxury houses left vacant when a planned expansion of Iscor in the 1970s failed to materialise.[12] The large reservoirs of labour created through forced removals and subsequent in-migration were, of course, a major selling point in the marketing of these places.

The sharp decline in RIDP incentives after 1991 has certainly not produced the industrial collapse that many predicted. Data supplied by the KFC for the Ezakheni industrial estate suggest that, despite some contraction after 1991, there appears to have been remarkable stability in a period of general macroeconomic deterioration in the early 1990s. According to very recent press reports, 24 more Taiwanese industrialists are poised to move into Ladysmith. An industrial survey that Alison Todes and I conducted in Newcastle in late 1994 revealed that aggregate industrial employment fell by about 16 per cent between 1989 and 1994; however, this decline came about exclusively through the contraction of predominantly male employment in heavy industries, all South African owned.[13] Employment, mainly of women, in clothing and other light industries in Newcastle actually increased by 28 per cent (that is, from just over 8,000 to 10,500) between 1989 and 1994.

This increase in employment came predominantly from Taiwanese investment. Between 1989 and 1994, the number of Taiwanese firms in Newcastle jumped from 20 to 49, and employment doubled (that is, from 2,100 in 1989 to over 4,000 in 1994); by mid-1995, several more very small Taiwanese firms had moved in. Although some Taiwanese firms closed down, a new wave of small industrialists has set up without incentives; many are former technicians who worked elsewhere in South Africa. Approximately 90 per cent of Taiwanese firms in Newcastle produce clothing, and within the clothing industry they are heavily clustered around knitwear production. In one way or another, the large majority of Taiwanese firms in Newcastle participate in the production of brightly coloured, elaborately decorated jerseys primarily for the domestic market through intricate divisions of labour and systems of subcontracting. Many of these firms are closely tied in with one another (albeit in complex and competing factional alliances), and with a large Taiwanese acrylic yarn producer in Ezakheni; this firm has in fact extended credit to small Newcastle producers to enable them to start up without subsidies.

In short, what is now emerging in Northwestern KwaZulu-Natal is a classically Taiwanese form of networked production, in which firms of different sizes have forged a variety of subcontracting and other links with one another. Taiwanese industrialists appear to be recreating in the South African countryside a logic of accumulation and forms of production organisation that are, on the face of it, very similar to those that drove rapid industrialisation in Taiwan, much of it located in rural and peri-urban areas.

Despite their evident dynamism, the networked forms of production that have taken shape in Northwestern KwaZulu-Natal are simultaneously extremely fragile. The source of fragility is not, as neoliberal critics of industrial decentralisation would have it, that they have been artificially induced by incentives; rather it is because they generate intense labour conflict that has escalated in the 1990s. With a few key exceptions, labour relations in the large majority of Taiwanese firms are deeply fraught with tension. Most Taiwanese industrialists and the women who work for them complain bitterly about one another and, particularly since 1990, few Taiwanese factories have escaped strikes and other forms of industrial action. Many Taiwanese factories have, in effect, become battlegrounds where employers, workers and increasingly trade unions, are locked in fierce and unremitting conflict which expresses itself all the way from sullen resentment to physical violence. One of the consequences of this conflict, some industrialists claim, is that they are unable to take up opportunities for exports to the United States and Europe that have opened up since sanctions were lifted. These export opportunities are particularly significant in the clothing industry, because South Africa is not subject to quotas under the Multi-Fibre Agreement.

On one level, the reasons for labor conflict are quite simple and straightforward – low wages and poor working conditions. Yet there are important insights to be gained from inquiring more closely into why networked forms of industrial organisation, which many observers regard as responsible for spectacular growth in Taiwan, operate so problematically in South Africa.

Two related sets of contextual conditions are, I suggest, particularly important in understanding how Taiwanese production networks operate in Northwestern KwaZulu-Natal. The first derives from differences in the composition of the workforce, as well as in the gendered character of relations between capital and labour. In much of the celebratory literature on Taiwanese production networks, labour quiescence and consent is simply taken for granted, or viewed as a natural concomitant of family-run business. In practice, Hsiung's [1991] research in Taiwan reveals considerable conflict between factory owners and the married women who form a major part of the workforce in small satellite factories in rural areas. Workers' resistance is, however, informal, individualised, and clandestine, and is articulated in the idiom of paternalism:

> because pre-existing family/kinship systems are intertwined with the production unit, the conflict of interest between the factory owner and waged workers often takes the form of familial disagreement. The construction of paternalism illustrates a constant struggle between

those who own the means of production and those who sell their labour ... one hidden dimension of Taiwan's economic miracle is the social construction of paternalism that fosters and sustains oppresive labor practices' [*Hsiung*, 1991: 148–9].

In South Africa, familistic forms of labour discipline derived from pre-existing relations are not only culturally unavailable; they are also precluded by the manner in which Taiwanese industrialists have been incorporated into local class-race configurations via their personalistic relationships with white local government officials, and by the way the workforce has been con-structed. As I discuss more fully elsewhere [*Hart*, 1995b], a few Taiwanese industrialists in Newcastle have sought to reconstruct paternalistic labour relations in new ways. The majority, however, resort to varying degrees of gendered and racially-charged coercion in their relations with women workers.

There is also an interesting contrast with conditions in the southern coastal regions of China, where Taiwanese industrialists also operate in a directly coercive mode. Unlike their South African counterparts, Taiwanese industrialists in China employ local men – who are typically connected to local government officials, and who aspire to become capitalists themselves – to discipline young, unmarried women workers (many of them migrants) who live in closely-monitored dormitories adjacent to the factories [*Hsing*, 1995b]. Instead of compliant young local men, Taiwanese industrialists in South Africa are more likely to confront militant union organisers. In short, the celebrated Taiwanese model of networked production rests on systems of labour coercion that are largely unworkable in South Africa.

A second, closely related set of differences derives from the very different ways workers are situated in relation to the means of social reproduction – most notably land. Not only in Taiwan, but also in China and other parts of Asia, the majority of workers in low-wage, labour-intensive rural industries belong to households with access to land. The logic of accumulation and labour mobilization in Taiwanese firms is predicated as we saw on a societal structure which, while tightly repressive and deeply oppressive of women, provides subsistence guarantees in the form of broadly-based access to land that underwrites the money wage. When Taiwanese industrialists – many of them straight out of the peasantry – came to South Africa, they encountered a workforce constituted through a particularly brutal process of dispossession. These sharp contrasts in the conditions of social reproduction defined primarily by access to land are, I suggest, central to understanding the character and intensity of labour conflict in Taiwanese firms in South Africa.

This distinction underscores the peculiar character of industrial decentralisation in South Africa – namely its close association with dispossession. Rural-urban wage disparities capture one key manifestation. Wages in places like Newcastle and Ladysmith are approximately half those in the clothing industry in main metropolitan areas of South Africa, where employment predictably is shrinking. Yet the cost of living is more or less the same [*Todes*, 1995b]; if anything, workers in Northwestern KwaZulu-Natal probably spend a larger proportion of their wages on transport than those in Durban.[14] Dispossession is also a key element of international wage disparities. The lowest female wages in Newcastle are about 90 percent higher than those paid by comparable factories in rural areas of China in nominal terms; however real wages are somewhere in the vicinity of 30 to 40 percent lower [*Hart*, 1995c].[15]

These disparities exemplify the history of agrarian transition in this region and in South Africa more generally. Agricultural growth has relied on impoverished farm workers and labour tenants; their expulsion from the land and propulsion into interstitial places like Northwestern KwaZulu-Natal constitutes the key 'linkage' between agriculture and industry in this region. That unions experience extreme difficulties in organising clothing workers to press for higher wages and better working conditions reflects not only the adamant opposition of Taiwanese industrialists, but also broader processes of labour force formation and the desperate search by huge numbers of disposed people for a modicum of economic and social security.

MULTIPLE LIVELIHOODS, INTERSTITIAL PLACES: RETHINKING AGRARIAN REFORM

> [Many black South African] households survive by structuring very careful exports of labour power to metropolitan areas, to white-owned or bantustan government farms and anywhere else which, in a circulatory pattern, provides opportunities to generate some income: not necessarily to work, but to look for work, or to trade in the informal sector. This pattern of life involves daily, weekly or other periodic travel between urban opportunities and supposedly 'rural' bases over long, expensive distances [*Mabin*, 1990: 44].

> What the rural base provides [to many black South Africans] is some security, even though inadequate, in times of unemployment and in old age. The point is that enormous investment in housing and in provision of social security, education, and health services is necessary to achieve the levels of urban renewal and development which would eliminate the need felt by many to retain a rural home.

In the interim, it might be suicidal to relinquish it [*Vaughan*, 1992: 434].

The perpetuation of multiple, diversified, spatially-extended livelihood strategies and efforts to retain a secure base is not just an apartheid hangover, destined to disappear in the context of of political and economic liberalisation. Nor are these patterns in any way peculiar to South Africa. Rather, they are a defining feature of late twentieth century capitalism, exemplifying the fiscal crisis of the nation state and its retreat from welfare provision, as well as the imperatives of flexible accumulation and global competition (see, for example, Mingione [1994] and Roberts [1994] for a discussion of these processes in Latin America). Rural industrialisation in Taiwan and China (particularly where TVEs have taken hold) represents a resolution of these tensions in the form of spatially-clustered, synergistic linkages between production and the conditions of social reproduction.

What *is* peculiar about South Africa is the degree to which the rural population has been dispossessed, both historically and through ongoing processes. Despite urban-like densities, interstitial places such as Northwestern KwaZulu-Natal have taken on the role of rural reserves. In a series of life histories that she recently gathered from residents of Madadeni, Osizweni, and the adjacent informal settlement of Blaaubosch, Alison Todes shows how these arenas of displaced urbanisation have come to operate like rural bases:

In a number of senses, Newcastle has acted in a way often described for rural areas, that is as a 'home base' from which forays in search of employment and income are made by selected members of the household. Newcastle emerged as a home base in the context of influx control when movement of families to cities was difficult and accommodation hard to find. Children were left with grandmothers while daughters worked in the city, and wives returned home on marriage – or at least after they had children. As in rural areas, pensioners retired here after working elsewhere for much of their lives. Newcastle has also acted as a place where the sick and disabled are looked after – a third of households interviewed contained sick or disabled members who had to be looked after. Although the disappearance of influx control has eased access to urban centres, lack of accommodation, violence and the absence of secure employment has meant that these patterns are perpetuated. When household members living in cities become unemployed or unable to find jobs they return 'home' to Newcastle. But Newcastle is not a rural area ... Most households interviewed derived some local income, and access to services and infrastructure is far greater than in rural areas. Further

> the availability of local employment and income has enabled households to live together to a far greater extent than in possible for rural based households [*Todes*, 1995b: 8].

There is, of course, another crucial sense in which greater Newcastle (defined to include Madadeni, Osizweni, and Blaaubosch) is not a rural area: other than house plots, some 95 percent of township households do not have access to land [*Data Research Africa*, 1993]. Yet a huge swathe of empty land, 15–20 km in length, separates the black townships from the formerly white town. Similar spatial configurations exist in Ladysmith and many other parts of South Africa.

These so-called buffer zones, designed to maintain racial separation, are one of the bizarre legacies of apartheid. They also represent major opportunities for agrarian reform – but of a very different character from the small farmer model promoted by the World Bank. Rather than conjuring up small farm households wherever land becomes available through the market, this alternative strategy would involve the allocation of resources to ensuring broadly-based access to small plots of land in buffer zones. These areas are richly supplied with infrastructure, so that the costs of supplying water, electricity, transport, waste disposal and so forth are likely to be far lower than in remote rural regions. Even a very small but well-watered piece of land which can support some intensive cultivation and which is close to other income opportunities, schools, and health facilities is likely to constitute a far more viable option to those who have borne the brunt of dispossession than taking up farming wherever land happens to become available through the market. In parts of Osizweni where house plots are large enough for gardens and water is available, a number of households cultivate vegetables for their own consumption and for sale. The potential for expanding and diversifying this type of very small-scale, part-time agriculture may in fact be quite considerable if well-watered land became available.[16]

Rather than relying on agricultural linkages to create non-farm jobs in hypothetical 'rural regions', agrarian reform to support multiple livelihoods is distinguished by proximity to existing non-agricultural resources, and by clustering of agricultural and non-agricultural activities. Spatial clustering is likely to be particularly important for women who, in addition to working for wages and other income, undertake vast amounts of unpaid reproductive labour – bearing and rearing children, housework, and care of the sick and elderly. Spatial proximity constitutes a sort of resource that cuts travel costs and makes possible the combination and sequencing of multiple activities.

Buffer zones and adjacent land are not simply physical spaces that happen to be strategically located, well-resourced, and unused: they also exemplify new political spaces. In the context of local government restructuring, newly-formed Local Councils have redrawn boundaries to unify former white towns and black townships. In the process, buffer zones have very recently become a part of new political entities.[17] Since large parts of these areas were owned by former white town councils, thousands of hectares will come under the jurisdiction of new local governments. If they are not so already, buffer zones and adjacent land will very quickly become intensely contested spaces, and the locus of multiple competing claims and aspirations. Whether or not these areas generate growth of livelihood opportunities based on democratic allocation of resources will depend first and foremost on mobilisation and the constitution of political forces around land access and land use.

Unlike the market-based small-farmer model, multiple-livelihood agrarian reform in the context of local government restructuring does at least hold out the possibility of broadly-based political mobilisation. Local political dynamics generated in intersecting institutional arenas constitute a key element of an explicitly spatial (as opposed to a sectoral and techno-cratic) strategy of agrarian reform. How these dynamics work out in practice, and who ends up getting access, is of course quite unpredictable; perhaps all one can say with certainty is that buffer zones are likely to become battlegrounds of one sort or another. The involvement of organised labour at all levels is likely to be crucial both in mobilising broadly-based political forces around the land question, and in negotiating the conditions of access to land. This would, of course, entail a significant shift away from the corporatist direction in which segments of organised labour seem to be moving, and a redefinition of debates cast in terms of low versus high roads of industrial competition [*Hart*, 1995c].

Questions of gender and women's property rights are also centrally important. Indeed, women's active and collective involvement in exercising pressure for access to land may well be the single most important determinant of the success of multiple-livelihood agrarian reform. This in turn could have repercussions in more remote rural areas of the former banstustans where tribal authorities are attempting to maintain control over land allocation in ways which, unless challenged, will almost certainly continue to exclude women [*Walker*, 1994].

While local dynamics are the primary crucible in which these and other possibilities for democratic resource allocation and equitable growth will be tested, they are not sufficient: supportive action at the regional and national levels is also vitally important. There is a pressing need for the Reconstruction and Development Programme to transcend conventional urban-rural and agriculture-industry dualisms, and to situate debates over resource allocation and redistribution within the context of the agrarian question in the late twentieth century.

NOTES

1. See Schreiner [1994] for a useful summary and analysis of corporatist debates in South Africa.
2. These debates have been brought together in Tomlinson and Addleson (eds.) [1987]. For a recent critique and reformulation, see Platzky [1995].
3. Lee demonstrated that Taiwan's agricultural sector had been heavily squeezed in the service of industrialisation, but that increasing agricultural productivity was essential to the continuous net outflow of resources from agriculture. He also showed that the per capita consumption of the rural population improved in the 1950s and 1960s due to increasing nonagricultural incomes, which offset all the taxes that the state extracted from the agricultural sector [Lee, 1971; also Karshenas, 1993]. Rising consumption in turn expanded the home market for industry in the economy as a whole, while low foodgrains prices provided the wages goods necessary to back expanded employment.
4. Consumption linkages in this sense are akin to the concept of social articulation in which wages make up the bulk of final demand in the economy as a whole [Kalecki, 1968; also Dobb, 1951].
5. As de Janvry points out, the assumption of an infinitely elastic supply of non-tradables becomes increasingly untenable as the catchment area increases: 'As the size of the NT [nontradable] sector incorporates more of the economy, its elasticity inevitably falls, for the same reasons that make an aggregate supply response inferior to that for a subset of commodities' [de Janvry, 1994: 1183]. He goes on to note that the analysis does not address the heart of the African development problem of low elasticity of supply response in the production of food and manufactures in a context where distortions in price incentives have been largely removed.
6. In fact, a central concern in the growth linkage modelling literature is to discern the optimal degree of inequality in order to maximise consumption linkages. The argument is that the consumption pattern of low income groups is limited in terms of consumption linkages, because poor people spend a relatively high proportion of their incremental income on foodgrains rather than on labour-intensive non-agricultural commodities. See Harriss [1987a] for a devastating critique.
7. Some proponents of flexible specialisation have recently tried to reinterpret Taiwanese forms of network production in these terms [e.g. Orru, 1991].
8. As I have argued more fully elsewhere [Hart, 1995b], classical debates on agrarian transitions together with recent feminist literature provide far greater analytical purchase on contemporary trajectories of capitalist development than does the flexibility debate; see also Goodman and Watts [1994].
9. In my forthcoming book, I shall provide a far more detailed exposition.
10. The proliferation of complex subcontracting networks, which are now being defined as a sort of Asian version of flexible specialization [e.g. Cheng and Gereffi, 1994; Orru, 1991; Hamilton, 1994; Chan and Clark, 1994], operate exclusively through male relationships.
11. Several village studies note that daughters' earnings were a key source of capital for rural enterprises [e.g. Niehoff, 1987]. Wolf [1992] contrasts parental control over daughters' earnings in Taiwan with the far greater autonomy of working daughters in Java.
12. As I discuss fully elsewhere [Hart, 1995a], Newcastle has become a node in a world-wide Taiwanese diaspora.
13. These data are discussed in greater detail in Hart and Todes [1995]. The data reported in the text refer only to Newcastle; in Madadeni, employment fell from 2,559 in 1989 to 1,210 in 1994. By mid-1995, however, a large Asian multinational clothing factory had established in Madadeni, and was employing in the vicinity of 600 women.
14. Transport between Madadeni-Osizweni and the industrial area of Newcastle consumes 25–30 per cent of wages.

15. Nominal wages are measured in market exchange rates, and real wages in terms of Purchasing Power Parity (PPP). Although measurements of PPP are obviously slippery and problematic, they do capture broad differences in living standards.
16. The ecological viability of intensive cultivation would, of course, have to be investigated and could well be quite controversial. It seems reasonable to suppose, however, that since towns are typically close to water sources, at least part of these buffer zones and adjacent areas may be relatively easy to irrigate.
17. Local government elections in KwaZulu-Natal are scheduled for March 1996; in the rest of South Africa they took place on 1 Nov., 1995.

REFERENCES

Amin, A. and K. Robins, 1990, 'Industrial Districts and Regional Development: Limits and Possibilities', in F. Pyke *et al.* (eds.), *Industrial Districts in Italy*, Geneva: International Institute for Labor Studies.

Amsden, A., 1985, 'The State and Taiwan's Economic Development', in P. Evans *et al., Bringing the State Back In,* Cambridge: Cambridge University Press.

Amsden, A., 1991, 'Big Business and Urban Congestion in Taiwan: The Origins of Small Enterprise and Regionally Decentralized Industry (Respectively)', *World Development,* Vol.19, No.9, pp.1121–35.

Anderson, D. and M. Leiserson, 1980, 'Rural Nonfarm Employment in Developing Countries', *Economic Development and Cultural Change* Vol.28, No.2, pp.227–49.

Bardhan, P. and J. Roemer, 1992, 'Market Socialism: A Case for Rejuvenation', *Journal of Economic Perspectives*, Vol.6, No.3, pp.101–16.

Bell, T. 1983. *The Growth and Structure of Manufacturing Employment in Natal.* University of Durban-Westville: Institute for Social and Economic Research Occasional Paper no. 7.

Bell, T., 1987, 'Is Industrial Decentralisation a Thing of the Past?', in R. Tomlinson and M. Addleson (eds.), *Regional Restructuring Under Apartheid: Urban and Regional Policies in Contemporary South Africa*, Johannesburg: Ravan Press.

Bell, C. *et al.,* 1981, *Project Evaluation in Regional Perspective,* Baltimore, MD: Johns Hopkins University Press.

Bernstein, H., 1994, 'Food Security in a Democratic South Africa', *Transformation* 24, pp.1–25.

Binswanger, H. and K. Deininger, 1993, 'South African Land Policy: The Legacy of History and Current Options', *World Development*, Vol.21, No.9, pp.1451–75.

Bowles, P. and X.Y. Dong, 1994, 'Current Successes and Future Challenges in China s Economic Reform', *New Left Review* 208, pp.49–76.

Buck, D., 1995, 'Geographical Industrialization: Factors Causing Overseas Dispersal of Taiwanese Industry', *Berkeley Journal of Asian Studies* VI, pp.19–33.

Byrd, W. and Lin Qingsong (eds.), 1990, *China's Rural Industry: Structure, Development, and Reform.* New York: Oxford University Press.

Castells, M. and J. Henderson, 1987, 'Techno-Economic Restructuring, Socio-Political Processes and Spatial Transformation: A Global Perspective', in J. Henderson and M. Castells (eds.) *Global Restructuring and Territorial Development*, New York: Sage Publications.

Castells, M. *et al.,* 1990, *The Shek Kip Mei Syndrome: Economic Development and Public Housing in Hong Kong and Singapore*, London: Pion.

Chan, S. and C. Clark, 1994, 'Economic Development in Taiwan: Escaping the State-Market Dichotomy', *Environment and Planning C: Government and Policy,* 12, pp.127–43.

Cheng, L. and G. Gereffi, 1994, 'The Informal Economy in East Asian Development', *International Journal of Urban and Regional Research,*Vol.18, No.2, pp.194–19.

Data Research Africa, 1993, *A Study of Income and Expenditure and Other Socio-Economic Patterns in the Urban and Rural Region of KwaZulu,* Vol.4, Durban: DRA for Kwazula Government.

Development Bank of Southern Africa, 1990, *Report of the Panel of Experts on the Evaluation of the Regional Industrial Development Policy as an Element of the Regional Development Policy in Southern Africa*, Midrand: External Relations Department.

de Janvry, A., 1981, *The Agrarian Question and Reformism in Latin America*, Baltimore, MD: Johns Hopkins University Press.

de Janvry, A., 1994,'Farm-Nonfarm Synergies in Africa – Discussion', *American Journal of Agricultural Economics*, Vol.76, No.5, pp.1183–5.

Delgado, C. *et al.*, 1994, 'Promoting Intersectoral Growth Linkages in Rural Africa Through Agricultural Technology and Policy Reform', *American Journal of Agricultural Economics*, Vol.76, No.5, pp.1166–71.

Dobb, M., 1951, *Some Aspects of Economic Development*, New Delhi: Delhi School of Economics.

Furuoka, F., 1995, *Japanese Indirect Investment in Kedah State*. Unpublished dissertation, University of Malaysia.

Gallin, B. and R. Gallin.,1982, 'Socioeconomic Life in Taiwan', *Modern China*, Vol.8, No.2, pp.205–46.

Gertler, M., 1992, 'Flexibility Revisited: Districts, Nation-States, and the Forces of Production', *Transactions: Institute of British Geographers* 17, pp.259–78.

Gold, T. 1986. *State and Society in the Taiwan Miracle*, Armonk, NY: M.E. Sharpe.

Goodman, D. and M. Redclift, 1982, *From Peasant to Proletarian: Capitalist Development and Agrarian Transition*, New York: St. Martin's Press.

Goodman, D. and M. Watts, 1994, 'Reconfiguring the Rural or Fording the Divide? Capitalist Restructuring and the Global Agro-Food System', *Journal of Peasant Studies*, Vol.22, No.1, pp.1–49.

Greenhalgh, S., 1994, 'De-Orientalizing the Chinese Family Firm' *American Ethnologist*, Vol.21, No.4, pp.746–75.

Haggblade, S. *et al.*, 1989, 'Farm-Nonfarm Linkages in Rural Sub-Saharan Africa', *World Development*, Vol.17, No.8, pp.1173–201.

Haggblade, S. *et al.*, 1991, 'Modelling Agricultural Growth Multipliers', *American Journal of Agricultural Economics* 73, pp.361–74.

Hamilton, G., 1994, 'Organization and Market Processes in Taiwan's Capitalist Economy', paper prepared for the SSRC conference on Market Cultures, Boston.

Harrison, B., 1994, *Lean and Mean: The Changing Landscape of Corporate Power in the Age of Flexibility*, New York: Basic Books.

Harrison, P., 1994, 'New Production Spaces: Changing Patterns of Uneven Development within the Province of KwaZuulu-Natal', paper prepared for the 34th European Conference of the Regional Science Association at the University of Groningen, The Netherlands.

Harriss, B., 1987a, 'Regional Growth Linkages from Agriculture', *Journal of Development Studies*, Vol.23, No.2, pp.266–89.

Harriss, B., 1987b, 'Regional Growth Linkages from Agriculture and Resource Flows in Non-Farm Economy', *Economic and Political Weekly*, 22, pp.31–46.

Hart, G., 1989, 'The Growth Linkages Controversy: Some Lessons from the Muda Case', *Journal of Development Studies*, Vol.25, No.1, pp.571–5.

Hart, G., 1993, *The New Agrarian Optimism: 'Regional Growth Linkages in the Era of Liberalization*, Geneva: International Labor Office. World Employment Programme Research, Working Paper 37.

Hart, G., 1995a, 'Industrial Restructuring Debates Through "Third World" Agrarian Lenses', Paper presented at the workshop on 'The Political Economy of the Agro-Food System in Advanced Industrial Countries: New Directions', University of California, Berkeley.

Hart, G., 1995b, '"Clothes for Next Nothing": Rethinking Global Competition', *South African Labor Bulletin*, Vol.19, No.6, pp.41–7.

Hart, G., 1996, 'Global Connections: The Rise and Fall of a Taiwanese Production Network on the South African Periphery', Working Paper No.6, Institute of International Studies, University of California, Berkeley, Feb.

Hart, G. and A. Todes, 1995, *Newcastle in the Changing Global Economy: Industrial Restructuring and Foreign Investment, 1989–95*. University of Natal: Center for Social and Development Studies (forthcoming).

Hazell, P. and C. Ramasamy, 1991, *The Green Revolution Reconsidered: The Impact of High-Yielding Rice Varieties in South India*, Baltimore, MD: Johns Hopkins University Press.

Hazell, P. and A. Roell, 1983, 'Rural Growth Linkages: Household Expenditure Patterns in Malaysia and Nigeria', *IFPRI Research Report 41*, Washington, DC: IFPRI.

Ho, S., 1982, 'Economic Development and Rural Industry in South Korea and Taiwan', *World Development*, Vol.10, No.11, pp.973–90.

Hsia, C.J., 1988, 'Dependency and Development in the Evolution of a Spatial Form: The Case of Chang-Hua, Taiwan', *Taiwan: A Radical Quarterly in Social Studies*, Vol.1, Nos.2/3, pp.263–38.

Hsing, Y., 1995a, 'Cheap Hands, Cheap Brains: Chinese Workers in Taiwanese Factories', Paper presented at the International Institute of International Studies, University of California, Berkeley.

Hsing, Y., 1995b, 'Blood Thicker than Water: Interpersonal Relations and Taiwanese Investment in Southern China', forthcoming in *Environment and Planning*.

Hsiung, P.C., 1991, 'Class, Gender, and the Satellite Factory System in Taiwan', unpublished Ph.D dissertation, University of California, Los Angeles.

Hu, T.L., 1983, 'The Emergence of Small-Scale Industry in a Taiwanese Rural Community', in J. Nash and M.P. Fernandez Kelly (eds.), *Women, Men and the International Division of Labor*. Albany, NY: State University of New York Press.

Hu, T.L., 1984, *My Mother-in-Law's Village: Rural Industrialization and Change in Taiwan*, Taipei, Taiwan: Institute of Ethnology, Academia Sinica.

Kalecki, M., 1968, 'The Marxian Equation of Reproduction and Modern Economics', *Social Science Information* 7, pp.73–9.

Karshenas, M., 1993, 'Intersectoral Resource Flows and Development: Lessons of Past Experience', in A. Singh and H. Tabatabai (eds.), *Economic Crisis and Third World Agriculture*. Cambridge: Cambridge University Press.

Lee, T.H., 1971, *Inter-Sector Capital Flows in the Development of Taiwan, 1895–1900*, Ithaca, NY: Cornell University Press.

Lipton, M. and M. Lipton, 1993, 'Creating Rural Livelihoods: Some Lessons for South Africa From Experience Elsewhere', *World Development*, 21, pp.1515–48.

Mabin, A., 1990, 'Limits of Urban Transition Models in Understanding South African Urbanisation', *Development Southern Africa*, Vol.7, No.3, pp.311–22.

Massey, D., 1993, 'Power Geometry and A Progressive Sense of Place', in J. Bird *et al.* (eds.), *Mapping the Futures: Local Cultures, Global Change*, London: Routledge.

McKinley, T. and K. Griffin.,1993, 'The Distribution of Land in Rural China', *Journal of Peasant Studies*, Vol.21, No.1, pp.71–84.

Mellor, J. and U. Lele, 1973,'Growth Linkages of the New Foodgrains Technologies', *Indian Journal of Agricultural Economics*, Vol.28, No.1, pp.35–55.

Mingione, E., 1994, 'Life Strategies and Social Economies in the Postfordist Age', *International Journal of Urban and Regional Research* 18, pp.24–45.

Murray, C., 1988, 'Displaced Urbanization', in J. Lonsdale (ed.), *South Africa in Question*, London: James Currey.

Murray, C. and G. Williams, 1994, 'Land and Freedom in South Africa', *Review of African Political Economy* 61, pp.315–24.

Nee, V,. 1992, 'Organizational Dynamics of Market Transition: Hybrid Forms, Property Rights, and Mixed Economy in China', *Adminstrative Science Quarterly* 37, pp.1–27.

Niehoff, J., 1987, 'The Villager as Industrialist: Ideologies of Household Manufacturing in Rural Taiwan' *Modern China*, Vol.13, No.3, pp.278–309.

Oi, J., 1992, 'Fiscal Reform and the Economic Foundations of Local State Corporatism in China', *World Politics*, Vol.45, No.1, pp.99–126.

Orru, M., 1991, 'The Institutional Logic of Small-Firm Economics in Italy and Taiwan', *Studies in Comparative International Development*, Vol.26, No.1, pp.3–28.

Platzky, L., 1995, 'The Development Impact of South Africa's Industrial Location Policies: An Unforeseen Legacy', Ph.D Thesis, Institute of Social Studies, The Hague.

Platzky, L. and C. Walker, 1985, *The Surplus People: Forced Removals in South Africa*. Johannesburg: Ravan Press.

Pred, A., 1989, 'The Locally Spoken Word and Local Struggles', *Environment and Planning D*, Vol.7, No.2, pp.211–33.

Ranis, G. and F. Stewart, 1987, 'Rural Linkages in the Philippines and Taiwan', in *Macroeconomic Policies for Appropriate Technology in Developing Countries*, Boulder, CO: Westview Press.

Roberts, B., 1994, 'Informal Economy and Family Strategies', *International Journal of Urban and Regional Research* 18, pp.6–24.

Rogerson, C. 1994, 'South Africa – from Regional Policy to Local Economic Development Initiatives', *Geography*, Vol.79, No.343, pp.180–3.

Sabel, C., 1989, 'Flexible Specializtion and the Re-Emergence of Regional Economies', in P. Hirst and J. Zeitlin (eds.), *Reversing Industrial Decline*, Oxford: Berg.

Sassen, S., 1988, *The Mobility of Labor and Capital: A Study in International Investment and Labor Flow*, Cambridge: Cambridge University Press.

Schmitz, H., 1990, 'Small Firms and Flexible Specialization in Developing Countries', *Labor and Society*, 15, pp.251–85.

Schreiner, G., 1994, 'Beyond Corporatism: Towards New Forms of Public Policy Formulation in South Africa', *Transformation* 23, pp.1–22.

Selden, M. (ed.), 1993, *The Political Economy of Chinese Development*, Armonk, NY: M.E. Sharpe.

Selden, M. and C. Ka., 1993, 'Original Accumulation, Equity, and Late Industrialization: The Cases of Socialist China and Capitalist Taiwan', in M. Selden (ed.), *The Political Economy of Chinese Development*, Armonk, NY: M.E. Sharpe.

Shih, J.T., 1983, 'Decentralized Industrialization and Rural Nonfarm Employment in Taiwan', *Industry of Free China*, Aug.

Standing, G., 1989, 'Global Feminization through Flexible Labor', *World Development* 17, pp.1077–95.

Stites, R., 1982, 'Small-Scale Industry in Yingge, Taiwan', *Modern China*, Vol.8, No.2, pp.247–79.

Storper, M., 1990, 'Industrialization and the Regional Question in the Third World: Lessons of Postimperialism; Prospects of Post-Fordism', *International Journal of Urban and Regional Research*, Vol.14, No.3, pp.423–44.

Surplus Peoples Project, 1983, *Forced Removals in South Africa: Natal*, Vol.4 of the Surplus People Project Report.

Todes, A., 1995a, 'From High Road to Low Road to No Road', Unpublished paper, University of Natal.

Todes, A., 1995b, 'Migration, Survival Strategies and the Gendered Impact of Regional Development Policies: The Case of Newcastle', Paper prepared for the GRUPHEL II Workshop, Durban.

Tomlinson, R, 1990, *Urbanisation in Post-Apartheid South Africa*, London: Unwin Hyman.

Tomlinson, R. and M. Addleson (eds.), 1987, *Regional Restructuring Under Apartheid: Urban and Regional Policies in Contemporary South Africa*, Johannesburg: Ravan Press.

Urban Foundation, 1990, *Policies for a New Urban Future: Urban Debate 2010*, Johannesburg: Urban Foundation.

Vaughan, A, 1992, 'Options for Rural Restructuring', in R. Schire (ed.), *Wealth or Poverty? Critical Choices for South Africa*, Cape Town: Oxford University Press.

Walder, A., 1995, 'Local Governments as Industrial Firms: An Organizational Analysis of China's Transitional Economy', *American Journal of Sociology*, Vol.101, No.2, pp.263–307.

Walker, C., 1994, 'Women, "Tradition" and Reconstruction', *Review of African Political Economy* 61, pp.347–58.

Weiner, D. and R. Levin, 1991, 'Land and Agrarian Transition in South Africa', *Antipode*, Vol.23, No.1, pp.92–121.

Williams, G., 1993, 'Setting the Agenda: A Critique of the World Bank's Rural Restructuring Programme for South Africa', unpublished paper.

Wilsenach A. and A.A. Lichthelm, 1993, 'A Preliminary Evaluation of the New RIDP and its Impact on Regional Development in South Africa', *Development Southern Africa*, Vol.10, No.3, pp.361–81.

Wolf, D., 1992, *Factory Daughters: Gender, Household Dynamics, and Rural Industrialization in Java*, Berkeley, CA: University of California Press.

Wolpe, H., 1972, 'Capitalism and Cheap Labor in South Africa: From Segregation to Apartheid', *Economy and Society,* Vol.1, No.4.

World Bank, 1993, *Options for Land Reforms and Rural Restructuring in South Africa.* Washington, DC: World Bank.

Peasants Speak:
The Land Question in Mpumalanga

RICHARD LEVIN and DANIEL WEINER

Research for this study was undertaken in the Mpumalanga Central Lowveld, which is located just east of the Drakensburg escarpment in an area of high ecological variability. The region has a long history of forced removals and now has intensive fruit plantation agriculture and forestry production in the relatively well-watered and irrigated areas to the west, with extensive game parks to the semi-arid east. Between these two zones lie the bantustans and the intersection of the Mapulaneng district of Lebowa, the Mhala district of Gazankulu and the Nsikazi district of Kangwane. The study area therefore has highly diverse social, political and environmental characteristics.

The research was conducted through the Community Perspectives on Land and Agrarian Reform (CPLAR) Project, a participatory and multi-disciplinary policy-oriented research programme. The major objectives of the project were:

(1) to enhance the participation of rural people in the processes of research design, implementation, analysis and dissemination;

(2) to generate detailed, site specific information which reflects the material realities and views of people living within varying agro-ecological regions and farming systems;

(3) to help formulate appropriate interdisciplinary methodologies for post-apartheid rural development policy-formulation;

(4) to contribute to the production of knowledge and understanding of

Richard Levin and Daniel Weiner, Department of Sociology, University of the Witwatersrand, Johannesburg, South Africa and Department of Geology and Geography, West Virginia University, Morgan Town, West Virginia, USA. The authors would like to express their sincere gratitude to the John D. and Catherine T. MacArthur Foundation for funding the *Community Perspectives on Land and Agrarian Reform in South Africa* Research Project on which this study is based. They would like to thank all villagers who participated in the process of generating the policy documents contained in this study, as well as the following research and field assistants: Lawrence Khoza, Sonnyboy Maphanga, Sam Mkhabela, Sello Ntai, Knox Nyathi, Ray Russon, Phorster Sambo, David Shabangu, Elkin Sigudla and Hilton Toolo.

South Africa's rural areas; and

(5) to better understand the politics of local natural resource utilisation.

The CPLAR employed participatory methods for both research and policy formulation involving people within four village clusters of the Central Lowveld in continuous discussion and dialogue around questions of land reform and research findings. Progress reports became central elements of this process, while workshops evolved as the ideal format through which land reform policies could be discussed and debated. This interactive approach was coupled with an attempt by researchers to immerse themselves in the villages concerned, and to establish a relationship with them based on a mutual commitment to progressive rural restructuring and land reform. The CPLAR team was thus able to facilitate involvement by village groups from Mpumalanga in the National Land Committee's Community Land Conference held in Bloemfontein on 12–13 February 1994.

The different elements of the research – a socio-economic survey, mapping, intensive interviewing and social histories – were discussed in five workshops held in each of the research sites over a one-year period. Initial workshop meetings were held with interested residents in each village in December 1992, where a report-back was given on the pilot survey conducted in July 1992. It was then proposed that a further workshop be held in January 1993, at which a report-back would be given to a wider audience on the objectives and progress of the research to date. This was done in each village, and at these meetings committees were elected to liaise with the research team. The hope was that these committees would become the focus of local land issues. At the January 1993 workshop, a variety of issues were discussed. One set of questions focused around issues of which land should be made available, how it should be obtained, and how and to whom it should be allocated. These questions generated discussion on issues of the historical geography of forced removals, compensation and the importance of land reform within the bantustans. Another set of questions focused on agriculture and agricultural production systems, while another centred on the problem of skills and resources. The final set of questions concentrated on development and local understandings of the issue.

A second series of workshops was held in June and July of 1993. Those in June were conducted with members of the village committees elected at the beginning of the year. The focus here was on a report-back of progress made in the research to date, and participatory mental mapping. These workshops were followed by broader village meetings in July, where the research team reported back on opinions expressed in the first workshops, and introduced local village maps as a mechanism for generating discussion around land reform in the bantustans. These workshops were invaluable in terms of unearthing knowledge of local historical geographies, and important information was generated in them on key CPLAR research themes, in particular, on forced removals and the chieftaincy. They also began to reveal the high expectations generated by the presence of the research team, and in cases, some impatience with the fact that little concrete progress or development had been experienced since the arrival of the CPLAR project in the area. It became increasingly important to stress that ours was essentially a research project, and that the aim of our participatory approach was to involve local people in policy-making, to engage them in drafting local policy documents which could be used as mobilising tools and the first step in development planning.

In order for the final workshop to lead to the production of practical policy documents, information gathered through the workshops and other relevant research data, was drawn together under five key questions or themes:

(1)   Where to get land;

(2)   How to get land;

(3)   How to allocate land;

(4)   What production systems to develop on the land;

(5)   Who should benefit from land reform.

This information was compiled into draft policy documents which were discussed and amended in the final village workshops held in January 1994. Two delegates were then elected in each village to attend the final CPLAR workshop in March 1994, where they presented the policy documents. Key project findings and the policy documents themselves are presented below:

TABLE 1

WHERE TO GET LAND

	Critical Issues	Key Research Findings	Policy Recommendations
1	Land Quality	Communities removed from more fertile and well-watered areas	Participatory rural land use planning which integrates local knowledge within a GIS
		People are identifying specific places for resettlement and are concerned about land quality	Move Kruger Park fence eastward and promote multiple land use strategies which include intensive irrigated smallholder production
		Local knowledge provides details on agro-ecological potential not available from land types data	
2	Politics of Water Access	Community concerns about accessing land without sufficient water	State must halt privatisation of dams, pending social impact analysis
		Privatisation of dams is reproducing apartheid water access/use inequalities	Democratisation of local water boards and associated water use
3	Under-utilised and Inappropriately Used White Farmland and Plantations	Local knowledge essential for identifying under-utilised and inappropriately used land	Restrict timber production on medium and high potentially arable land
		Communities more hostile to timber production than food (including fruit) production on arable land	Resettle under-utilised white farmland (example near Hazyview)
		'Expert' and 'Local' knowledge suggests reduced surface water supplies associated with exotic timber plantations	
4	Land Reform within the Bantustans	Chiefs allocate higher quality land to themselves and clients	Involve locally elected committees in identifying land for distribution
5	Conflicting Land Claims	Multiple and overlapping claims for the same white farmland will make operation of land claims court difficult	Avoid strict dichotomy between land restitution and redistribution to fairly accommodate the wide range of forced removal victims
		Willingness on the part of some community participants to share land with white farmers and farmworkers	Decision making and adjudication should be as inclusive as possible

TABLE 2

HOW TO GET AND ALLOCATE LAND

	Critical Issues	Key Research Findings	Policy Recommendations
1	How to make land available?	The new state is expected to play a leading role in land acquisition Great hostility towards chief allocating land	National Rural Land Reform programme that articulates regionally and locally Create democratic process to transform rural institutions
2	How should available land be allocated?	Many people reject land allocation functions associated with the chieftaincy	Democratic local land committees must be involved in land allocation Patriarchal structures of land allocation and control need to be transformed
3	Community reaction to 'market assisted' land reform	Widespread rejection of individual payment for land, but some acceptance if state provides compensation for victims of forced removals	Rural people with farming aspirations but with limited resources must be given land without co-payment requirement
4	Extension and infrastructural needs	Belief that in the short-term, land access is more important than extension	Transforming extension institutions must not delay land transfer process Address extension needs as defined within communities
5	Demand for agricultural land	Demand is high: 78% of households surveyed wish to participate in land reform, and 46 % are willing to move Land needs cannot be assessed through quick, 'felt-needs surveys' Petty capitalist farming class presently very small	Grassroots identification of agricultural land needs. This should inform provincial and national policy development about the spatial variability of agricultural land demand and local farming systems possibilities

TABLE 3

WHAT AGRICULTURAL PRODUCTION SYSTEMS SHOULD BE DEVELOPED?

	Critical Issues	Key Research Findings	Policy Recommendations
1	Defining a petty commodity producer	Bantustan households need and want multiple income generating options Demand for individual household and community or co-operative plots	'Smallholder Model' cannot be defined from the top-down: needs to be grounded locally Mistake of trying to separate 'workers' and 'peasants' in rural areas must not be made
2	Food security	Strong desire for increased production for domestic, household consumption Half of total household expenditure on food	Promote arable land access for household food security Women should be major recipients of land for domestic production for consumption
3	Appropriate farming systems	Unrestricted timber production is seen as an inappropriate land use There are people who express an interest in co-operative farming Only 11 per cent of survey population of 477 households have access to grazing land Livestock and grazing access associated with tribal authority structures	Restrict exotic timber plantations on land with medium and high agricultural potential Support mixed livestock and crop farming Petty commodity production will require greater access to draft animals and grazing land Promote democratic forms of common property
4	What happens to existing bantustan agricultural projects	Parastatal projects and associated bureaucratic structures very unpopular	Participatory land use planning must feed into popular project appraisal process
5	Land Tenure	There is a demand for security of tenure which must not be confused with private property	Need to democratise 'communal' forms of land tenure

TABLE 4

WHO SHOULD BENEFIT FROM RURAL LAND REFORM

	Critical Issues	Key Research Findings	Policy Recommendations
1	Black farming skills and World Bank assumption that poorer households and individuals have inferior farming skills to wealthier households	Farming skills found amongst all socio-economic strata of the rural bantustan population Access to land and capital a poor measure of black farming skills Lower strata have agricultural production potential CPLAR participants feel that the unemployed and landless who want to farm should get preferential treatment	Create democratic institutions in which all classes of the rural poor are adequately represented ANC's RDP must not deviate from its commitment to poorer segments of the community World Bank must not set agenda for project implementation
2	Support for production by women	Broad-based support for prioritising women's access to land Land, water and biomass access is crucial to women's reproductive activities Women are engaged in numerous forms of petty commodity production	Prioritise landless, female-headed households with farming aspirations Women prefer a range of farming systems, including small family plots and community gardens
3	Criteria for defining forced removal victims	The number of forced removal victims is likely to be far higher than generally assumed Strict legal definitions will exclude many victims Retrenched farmworkers have strong land claims and perceive themselves as forced removal victims	The definition of 'victims' needs to be broadened and determined through a participatory process Retrenched farmworkers with legitimate claims must be included in a land reform programme Victims of Betterment Planning must be included in a land reform programme
4	Land for farmworkers and labour tenants	Some willingness in bantustan communities to share land with farmworkers and labour tenants	Farmworkers need to be drawn into the participatory process De facto land rights must become de jure land rights Outlaw super-exploitation of farm labour including within former bantustans
5	Will petty capitalists and chiefs in the former bantustans become the major beneficiaries of 'market-assisted' land reform?	Market-assisted land reform will exclude poorer households including those with farming capacity Accumulation from below is constrained by the institutions of the chieftaincy Chiefs, headmen and clients will benefit from World Bank plan as will petty capitalists Households with access to wage income will benefit more	Pragmatic electoral alliances with chiefs will run the risk of alienating popular support on the ground Projects must be democratically run and extra-economic coercion must be outlawed Petty-capitalist beneficiaries must be rurally based and have genuine farming skills and aspirations

VILLAGE POLICY DOCUMENTS

Here we reproduce, in their English versions, the Village Policy Documents generated by the workshops described earlier. These documents are also available in Zulu (Cork, Marite) and Siswati (Malekutu, Manzini).

A. CORK

1. Where to Get Land?

1.1 Many people in Cork Village have been removed from land which presently falls within the boundaries of the Kruger Park and private game reserves including Malamala, Londolozi, Numbi Gate and Sabie Sand. Other areas, which are presently divided between the Kruger Park, private game reserves and white farms from which people were forcibly removed, include Toloni, Lisbon (part of which is now a Gazankulu Development Corporation citrus estate), Dumfries, Pretoriaskop, Newington and Ireagh. People were expropriated without compensation and settled in Cork. All this land needs to be considered for a future land reform programme. People were also forcibly removed through betterment planning from farms including Calcutta, Madras, Belfast, Justicia, Huntington, Lillydale and Somerset. These farms are now divided between white farmers and villages under the jurisdiction of the Mhala district of Gazankulu. Those sections of these farms presently under the control of white farmers also need to be considered for redistribution.

1.2 Land quality must be considered when identifying additional land to ensure that land acquired under a land reform programme has productive potential.

1.3 Unused land should be made available to people as additional land.

Resettlement:

1.4 People are prepared to leave Cork if they are offered good arable land, but they would prefer land near Cork.

2. How to Access Land?

2.1 Local people must play a decisive role in development planning and formulation of a land reform policy. A Land Claims Court is needed to facilitate the processing of land claims. Elders within the community can point out land from which people were expropriated. These lands must be returned and made available as part of a land reform programme. There is a concern that there will be practical problems if people target the areas from which they were removed. The following steps must be followed in getting back the land:

(a)   maps of all land from which people were removed must be obtained;

(b)   elders who know the area must be consulted;

(c)   the Land Affairs Office in Pretoria must be approached to obtain original maps of the area;

(d)   the claims must be submitted to a land claims court;

(e)   if the Land Claims Court is unable to return the land, mass action must be organised. Land occupations will take place and shacks will be erected until people are allowed to settle on the land.

2.2 In order to facilitate this process, a local land affairs committee should be established and should work very closely with the new government.

Compensation:

2.3 Black people were not paid any compensation when they were forcefully removed. By the same token, white farmers should not be paid for land taken from them under a land reform program. An exception may be made with regard to the development costs incurred by occupants, unless these costs have been recovered by the owners through profits.

2.4 White farmers who are prepared to live with black people and share the land, their skills and knowledge of farming, should not be forced to leave their farms.

3. How to Allocate Land?

3.1 The land where the community is located has deteriorated due to overgrazing. There is also a shortage of land as a result of it being fenced out (a fence protects and separates the chief's land, and also separates Lebowa and Gazankulu). Homeland borders will have to be removed for proper allocation and use of land.

3.2 A new government through local democratic government structures should allocate land to the people, but there should be effective participation of farmers' associations in the allocation of agricultural land and elected committees with which the government must liaise. A committee elected by the people should be empowered to give land to the people. It must also ensure that the given land is used productively.

3.3 Residential stands must be equal and each household will have some agricultural land. Farms must not necessarily be the same size because people with a greater capacity for farming (that is, full time, expertise, equipment, irrigation, and so on) will be allocated additional agricultural land.

3.4 People who fail to use their land should inform a committee elected by the people why they are failing to use their land. In a case where land is not used properly, the committee should consult with the owner of the land. This means that the local committee should not have the power to remove people from their land without their consent.

The Chieftaincy:

3.5 The chiefs have failed to meet the people's needs. On the contrary, the chieftaincy acts more in the interest of the government rather than the people. The chief should oversee civil disputes in the community and not be involved in the allocation of land and other responsibilities whereby corruption can arise.

4. How To Use Land?

4.1 Available land is far too small for the community's needs. Additional land of high quality with nearby water access is needed for residential sites, pasturage and agricultural production.

4.2 The bantustan government has proved itself unable to develop and/or allocate the land effectively and must be removed. Rural development cannot be facilitated by the bantustan system. Local people pay taxes and should be empowered to participate in land use and development planning and decision-making.

4.3 A mixed farming system of large-scale and small-scale units needs to be developed. Small-scale units need to be demarcated equally.

4.4 Fields should be adjacent to homesteads.

4.5 Communities must make the decision as to what crops to grow.

4.6 Within the household, women must be empowered to make decisions on what crops to grow. Emphasis should be given to growing food, that is, maize and vegetables. In the case of banana plantations made available for resettlement, half of the bananas should remain, with the remaining land being used for growing food.

4.7 If more land is secured, irrigation will be required due to low rainfall in the area. Government should create the necessary infrastructure for successful irrigation.

4.8 Within Cork, more land should be made available for pasturage.

Land Tenure:

4.9 Individual tenure should be a priority, and there should be areas under communal tenure as well.

4.10 All people can enter into agreements to use the land on a rotating basis. There should be communal grazing as well as camps for cattle.

Resources and Skills:

4.11 Without state assistance, people would not be able to use the land, because they have no money for farming inputs. The state must develop credit facilities as well as markets for small farmers.

4.12 There is a general shortage of basic needs and infrastructure in Cork, including: water supply for human consumption, agricultural and livestock production; firewood; roads; schools; electricity; telecommunications. There are no agricultural institutions or centres in the area.

4.13 While the state needs to play a central role in provision of these services, community-based initiatives also need to be developed through the establishment of farmers associations and agricultural co-operatives. Strategies must also be developed to raise loans from international develop-ment agencies. Committees must be formed to guide people on resource utilisation.

4.14 The civic association will be under the control of the community. Small sub-committees (for water, grazing, ploughing and so on) will be under community control. The civic association will co-ordinate local issues such as the usage of land for ploughing. The civic will liaise with the government to assist with transport and markets to black farmers.

4.15 The new government should provide agricultural inputs to encourage the landless to farm.

5. Who Should Benefit from Rural Land Reform?

5.1 Land should be given to all who want to farm. The selection criteria should include: those who are poor with no land and fields and who are most vulnerable regarding food security. This could end jealousy and food problems, and provide a rational measure for allocation. The giving of land should be as open as possible. There should be a differentiation between people wanting to farm for commercial purposes and those farming to feed their families.

5.2 The following additional criteria should be considered:

(a)   marginalised and landless should be the first group to be allocated land;

(b)   land should be given on the basis of 'land need'; gender biases should be discouraged – there should be no discrimination when allocating land;

(c)   the vulnerable groups of female headed households and those who are on pensions should also be prioritised;

(d)   there should be a feeding scheme for children at creches;

(e)   refugees from Mozambique should be provided enough land and reference books;

(f)   the giving of more land (for example, to the chiefs) should not be allowed;

(g)   preferences should be given to people without land rather than to those who currently have large plots, although there should be special consideration to those who are already providing food.

B. MALEKUTU

1. Where to Get Land?

1.1 There is a need for additional land. Land from the so-called white areas and from the white farms (in particular unused or unoccupied white farm land) must be given back to the people.

1.2 Many people in Malekutu have been forcibly removed from white farms and state land and resettled in Malekutu. Specific areas where people have been removed from include Ngodwana, the Kruger National Park, Eric's Place (Emgwenya), Plaston including Karino, Nelspruit including Mataffin, and White River.

1.3 The areas at Mataffin and Karino are largely under-utilised, and at Karino, tobacco is farmed instead of food crops. The Kruger National Park, while it should be protected, should have its size reduced in favour of a land reform programme that benefits the people.

1.4 The issue of land claims needs further research and investigation.

1.5 In the case of national parks, the state would have to identify some land within the national parks for redistribution. There is a feeling that the parks should remain even if some park land is given back to neighbouring communities.

Resettlement:

1.6 In the context of the current population explosion, resettlement options include:

(a)   building a house on the farm;

(b)   leaving some family members in the current household and building a house on the farm for other family members;

(c)   selling the old house to build a new one on the farm to avoid people having many houses.

2. How To Access Land?

2.1 Black people do not have the capacity to buy land. If land is to be subject to market prices, black people will be unable to afford buying back their land.

2.2 People should not have to take out loans to purchase white farm land. The legitimacy of white ownership is questionable and it would be like 'buying out the thief who stole your land'.

2.3 In the case of land being claimed from white farms, the state should arrange for the expropriation of farm land. This must concentrate on unused land, but more generally, the amount of land available to white farmers must be reduced.

2.4 In the case of forced removals, the appropriate mechanism for redistribution is a land claims court, but those without documents and/or oral historical evidence are unlikely to be catered for. Old people who are still alive should be consulted when processing land claims. A committee should be elected to present all land claims to the relevant structures.

2.5 It is essential that all land considered for redistribution be fertile and have high agricultural potential.

Compensation:

2.6 Compensation arrangements should only be implemented in the case of productive white farm land. There should be no compensation for unused land.

3. How to Allocate Land?

3.1 There are options regarding land allocation:

(a)   each family must have an individual farming plot. If a farmer is doing well, he/she can enter into a sharecropping agreement or other arrangement to use a neighbour's land. A person who fails to farm a given piece of land should give that land to somebody who needs the land;

(b)   land must be shared equally amongst members of the community.

3.2 The state should allocate land and manage a proper system of land ownership and registration in place of the chief.

3.3 The local state (including the Department of Agriculture) should work through locally elected committees and farmer's associations. The committee would oversee the allocation of land and ensure that the process is democratic and equitable.

3.4 Individuals should not get additional land on the basis of being a chief, a headman, or a member of the committee.

The Chieftaincy:

3.5 The chieftaincy must be democratised and made more accountable to the people.

4. How to Use Land?

4.1 Land use should be organised around crop production, livestock rearing, industry, or residential purposes. Agricultural land and plots allocated to individual household should be properly registered in their name to end arbitrary expropriation and land transfers. Land use and production should be decided upon either by

(a)   community representatives in liaison with government representatives;

(b)   individuals.

4.2 There are options regarding the placement of fields and homesteads:

(a)   people must get land for agricultural production away from residential areas;

(b) land must be within or near the residential site of families for reasons of security and manageability;

(c) all the fields should be in one place because it is impossible now to have fields next to homesteads because houses have already been built and people cannot be removed or resettled.

4.3 In terms of grazing land, present communal arrangements should be retained so that grazing land can be available for everyone to utilise.

4.4 Large-scale agriculture is more productive than small-scale; it benefits the whole country and creates job opportunities. Small-scale farms are necessary, however, for family subsistence. Both farming systems, therefore, are important for Malekutu.

4.5 Agricultural co-operatives should be formed.

Land Tenure:

4.6 There should be both individual and collective ownership of land. Collective ownership is essential for large-scale enterprises. People will be elected by the community to administer and run the farms. Individual ownership is necessary for small-scale family subsistence farms.

Resources and Skills:

4.7 The state is the major source of resources and skill provision. The state must develop a comprehensive development programme for agriculture. This would involve the development of infrastructure and mechanisms for supplying electricity, water, agricultural inputs, training (on the use of fertilisers and the examination of soil types), and equipment (including storages, tractors, and a machine for milling maize), as well as credit and financing facilities.

4.8 Specific resource needs include: a land bank for credit and finance, pools for tractors and other implements, fertilisers, electricity, water reservoirs, cattle dipping facilities, better road infrastructure, clinics, industrial sites, educational institutions (especially for agric training), creches, fencing.

4.9 Government subsidisation of black farmers must be introduced.

4.10 The resources for development should come from a variety of sources including: the KaNgwane government, VAT and PAYE taxes, the 'tibuse' fee collected through the chief, through the institution of farmers' co-operatives.

4.11 People are unhappy with Agriwane, banks, and similar institutions that have indebted their co-operatives. The Development Bank should allocate development funds directly to the co-operative with a clear credit agreement and terms of repayment.

4.12 The Community should establish a development committee with various sub-committees to decide on development programmes and the use of resources. These should include:

(a)   a sub-committee on health;

(b)   a sub-committee on agrarian issues;

(c)   a sub-committee on education.

4.13 In order to be effective, such committees must be structurally accountable to the community, and must be subject to periodic election. The development committee and its sub-committees should not be dominated by the tribal authority

5. Who Should Benefit from Rural Land Reform?

5.1 Land should be allocated on the basis of "land need" and not on the basis of gender. Priority should be given to the landless.

5.2 Every person can farm if given land, but there are people who are not willing to farm. People who want to farm should be the people to whom the land is given.

5.3 People who want to farm food crops (tomatoes, maize) should have priority over those who want to farm cash (non-edible) crops like tobacco. Tobacco farming does not address the problem of starvation.

5.4 People should be given the opportunity to say how much land they can plough. More land should be given to those who have the capacity to use the land productively. Households that want to make full use of their land should have access to tractors and implements to do so.

5.5 Those who are married but still living with their parents must be given priority.

5.6 Unemployed landless people including married couples and pensioners should also be at the top of the list for land allocation.

5.7 Female-headed households, either widowed or deserted and with children to feed, must be given enough ploughing land and agricultural implements in order to survive.

C. MANZINI

1. Where to Get Land?

1.1 The people of Manzini Village come from different areas from which they were removed. Much of these areas are white farms, including Della and Sallerson. Other areas include White River, Nelspruit, Graskop, Skukuza (in the Kruger National Park), Pretoriuskop, Plaston, Kiepersol, Mataffin, Karino, Malelane, Mayfair and Didimane.

1.2 The forest plantations do not help the people, and they hinder the growing of food crops.

Resettlement:

1.3 There are mixed feelings about moving in order to gain access to land as part of a land reform programme. Some people are prepared to move, while others are not, although they would still like to have more fields. Those who wish to farm may move as they choose, but people should not be forced to forfeit their residential plots as these plots should pass to their children.

1.4 Some people want to be resettled on an area about 1.5 km from Legogote Mountain. Also Hek's farm on the other side of Legogote.

2. How to Access Land?

2.1 The community should identify people who know the history of the area that people will claim, and these people should make up a local land committee.

2.2 The government should expropriate the land from the white farmers, but it must use peaceful means to avoid conflicts and violence.

Compensation:

2.3 Most people feel that compensation would be unjust in light of the forced expropriation of blacks and that the incoming government should not be burdened with the errors of the past one. In the interests of peace and preserving agricultural equipment, however, the issue of compensation can be negotiated.

3. How to Allocate Land?

3.1 There should be a local elected committee to handle land allocation. It is also important to talk to the new elected regional government. The size of residential sites must be increased, and all people should get equal plots.

3.2 If an individual or a household proves incapable of farming, the land can be lent to others who can work the land until the person to whom it was originally allocated can work it.

The Chieftaincy:

3.3 The institutions of the chief and the induna are problematic. There is support for the view that the chief and the induna should not have the power of land allocation, and that they should have the same amount of land as the residents.

4. How to Use Land?

4.1 People should have individual powers and rights to make decisions about what to crop, how, and when.

4.2 The community should farm for domestic consumption and also for commercial purposes.

4.3 Regarding the placement of fields and homesteads, the following options require further discussion:

(a) houses should be next to the fields for daily monitoring;

(b) there should be a residential village that is separate from the farming land;

(c) people should be given the option of relocating to live near or on farm land or remaining in the 'townships';

(d) people should obtain land for agriculture only. If people try to use all this farm land for housing as well, it will not be sufficient. Residential land should be kept separate from farm land;

(e) the land must be divided according to different purposes (that is, land for agriculture, land for grazing, land for residential purposes).

Land Tenure:

4.4 There are a variety of options regarding land tenure arrangements in Manzini:

(a) the possibilities of introducing co-operative farming must be explored. The co-operative should be entitled to request agricultural credit from the land bank. The money will be used to pay labourers and to purchase inputs, including a communal tractor;

(b) a mixed system of collective and individual farms would be the preferable arrangement;

(c) the farm as a whole should be collectively owned, but each family/ household should be allocated a morgen for its occupation and use for housing, agriculture, and grazing;

(d) each household should be allocated its own farm-land and should farm on the individual household basis. A 'commonage' is likely to produce conflict, and there will be free-riding;

(e) it is preferable that farms be broken down into small-scale family units, taking into account the different capacities of individual farmers;

(f) the extension officer should be responsible for checking how productive people are. If people are found to be unproductive, the extension officer should have the power to recommend reduction in land holdings to make way for those who can use the land productively.

4.5 Grazing land should be shared.

Resources and Skills:

4.6 Resources can be obtained, allocated, and used according to an elected committee from within the community. The civic associations should be responsible for carrying out and controlling development. There is disagreement about the role the chief should play in this regard, but most people feel the chief should play some role.

4.7 The people need agricultural inputs, tractors, fertilisers, seeds, dams/ irrigation, storage sheds, and credit for an effective development programme. The state should provide these to the community.

4.8 The community should have a farming-shed which shall be used to store all farming requirements such as tractors, fertilisers and seeds.

4.9 There is also a need for jobs, an end to gangsterism/crime, tertiary-level schools, and a spirit of co-operation, especially among mothers and fathers.

4.10 Agricultural education and training is important to empower those who will be farming with farming skills.

5. Who Should Benefit from Rural Land Reform?

5.1 The categories of beneficiaries include:

(1) landless; especially those without residential sites;

(2) those without agricultural land who need to work it;

(3) female-headed households;

(4) the unemployed who may gain employment or sustain themselves
     through agriculture.

D. MARITE

1. Where to Get Land?
1.1 Additional land is necessary for development.

1.2 The people of Marite Village have been forcibly removed from the
following areas: Diepdrift, Frankfurt, Richmond, Sabane, Erasmus, Inyaka,
Boschoek, Sandford, Ramanas, Kiepersol, Qwetha, Mac-Mac, Waterral
Boven. Also, the land owned by the HLH corporation and land that extends
towards Graskop and Bushbuckridge.

1.3 It is important to identify unused and under-utilised white farm land to
be made available for use by the community. State land and unused land
should be occupied before elections for a constituent assembly. Much of the
land at Sandford and Diepdrift is under-utilised.

1.4 Land to the northwest of Marite is the most suitable for farming. It is
currently being used by white farmers for a coffee plantation and not
benefiting the people.

Resettlement:
1.5 People should continue living in their current households, but some
people are willing to be resettled as long as the area is conducive to farming.

2. How to Access Land?
2.1 It is important to embark on a campaign to reclaim and gain access to
more land.

2.2 Acquiring adequate farming land necessitates the scrapping of the
bantustan system and the formulation of a participatory land claims procedure,
including a land dispute resolution committee and a land claims court.

2.3 A committee should be elected, excluding the chief, to facilitate the
process of land claims in Mathibela. Marite must develop an inventory of

land claims and a thorough historical case by identifying people who have a precise knowledge of the history of the area and the forced removals. This will facilitate the documentation of the forced removals and the resultant land claims. This process must begin before a land claims court has been set up, and the community must formulate demands and present them to all high level structures of government and other relevant authorities as soon as possible.

2.4 The Committee on Land Allocation (CLA) must be democratised.

Compensation:

2.5 If there is to be compensation, a controversial issue, the white farmers must claim their money from the government and not from the people.

3. How to Allocate Land?

3.1 Land should be allocated and distributed democratically and equitably.

3.2 If a person is under utilising his/her land, he/she should lend it out to others for their use.

3.3 A committee should be elected to deal with allocation and distribution, headed by an elected person who is not a chief or a king. The committee would be elected periodically, say for five years, to ensure accountability. An assessment should then be made as to whether the committee had succeeded in distributing land democratically. The committee should not be subject to the control of bantustan authorities or structures or the tribal authorities. It should be accountable to the democratic local government structures of a unitary national state.

3.4 Extension officers should be directly involved in land allocation

The Chieftaincy:

3.5 Chiefs should not maintain their present powers as they have become products of apartheid and have oppressed the people of Marite for too long. Land allocation should be handled by the people's elected representatives and committees, but ways can be sought to include the chief in this process.

Resources and Skills:

3.6 Farmers' associations, government, and private corporations are key structures for determining the use and allocation of resources. Local people have lost confidence in the traditional tribal authority and the chieftaincy in this regard.

4. How to Use Land?

4.1 Additional land must be made available for agricultural, residential, and grazing purposes, as well as for the establishment of industrial sites. Existing and newly allocated land should be used for a diversity of crop and livestock production. Crop farming should be a priority and there should be a farmer's support scheme.

4.2 The government must give the large farms to the community so that the community can divide the land for itself. There should be both small-scale and large-scale farming units. Everyone should have land for family farming on returned/reclaimed land.

4.3 People would like to have houses on their farms, but given financial constraints, houses should be separate from the farms. With time, people can build houses on their farms.

4.4 Organised farmers associations should be established to challenge the existing monopolies within agriculture.

Land Tenure:

4.5 There should be mixed forms of tenure: individual forms of ownership/possession for family farms, in conjunction with democratically controlled state farms for collective use.

Resources and Skills:

4.6 Under the present dispensation, the chief has to play a central role in securing resources which must come from the Lebowa and central government. In the future, community committees and democratic local bodies like civics need to be elected and mandated to seek assistance from development agencies, funding bodies, and the international community. In the meantime, existing resources must be shared through the establishment of agricultural co-operatives.

4.7 The community must play the major role in local development and a local development committee must be elected. The community must have the major powers of decision-making through an elected civic leadership.

4.8 Water is high on the list of priorities for purposes of irrigation and consumption. It is essential to investigate the possibility of building a dam in the area and to establish piping and pumping facilities.

4.9 Other resource needs which have been identified include more livestock, fertilisers and seeds, pesticides, insecticides, and implements such as tractors, ploughs, etc. The development of farmers' associations and the pooling of implements (such as tractors) will encourage a collective culture between farmers and further the joint utilisation of resources and skills.

4.10 Electrification, job opportunities, an efficient road network, comprehensive health services, education and day-care centres, proper recreational facilities (renovation of the Mathibela Stadium and a community library), and the improvement of public transport facilities are all crucial development issues.

4.11 Basic agricultural skills are available, but there is a lack of agricultural and non-agricultural training institutions in the area. The government and the community need to establish multi-disciplinary youth and adult education schemes. Skills centres should be established, controlled and administered by committees of parents, teachers, and students in consultation with the state.

Who Should Benefit from Rural Land Reform?

5.1 Meetings should be held where people who wish to farm can be listed. Those who want to farm should be given the land to do so. There should be a rule that establishes that a person failing to use land given to him or her is forced to relinquish the land or temporarily to give the land to somebody else. This necessitates committees which would ensure that all people benefit equally, and not a selected few as has been the case when land was controlled by the chieftaincy.

5.2 Families should be given first priority when allocating land. Married sons and daughters with children must get land.

5.3 Women must have adequate access to land (with protection for divorcees and widows). There must be no discrimination on the basis of sex.

5.4 For residential stands, those with no homes at all should be the first to benefit, and the richest and those with land should be last.

5.5 People who are dismissed from the farms (evicted labour tenants) must benefit from a land reform program.

5.6 Refugees who have become part of the community must also be helped. These refugees are normally expected to pay large monies (R500 in Khonza fees to the chief).

5.7 Marginalised/landless households, and especially their children, must get land.

5.8 The unemployed, especially those who lost their jobs during the struggle, should be helped by a land reform programme.

5.9 Children who finish their studies but do not get employment, as well as those who leave school, must also benefit.

5.10 Pensioners.

5.11 Those who can farm and make food available especially vegetables/foodcrops.

Abstracts

South Africa's Agrarian Question: Extreme and Exceptional?
HENRY BERNSTEIN

This introductory essay first sketches the context of the agrarian question in the trajectory of capitalist development in South Africa since the mining revolution of over a century ago. This provides a framework for a review of the contributions to this volume and the issues they illuminate. A third section addresses the question of the title. On one hand, the agrarian question in the sense of a transition to capitalist agriculture *and* industry has been completed, thereby resolved for agrarian and industrial/urban capital. On the other hand, it has not been resolved for those who long struggled against extreme national oppression. The legacy of massive dispossession is central to post-apartheid South Africa and democratic transition as 'unfinished business', as are widespread poverty and insecurity inherited from the structural crisis of the economy shaped by apartheid.

The Theory and Practice of the Agrarian Question in South African Socialism, 1928–60
ALLISON DREW

This contribution concerns the recovery of a lost history of the South African Left. For decades, South African socialists struggled with the problem of the relationship between rural proletarianisation and peasant aspirations, anticipating more recent scholarly debates on rural development and consciousness. None the less, using a discourse and concepts derived from European conditions, they initially treated the rural black population in polarized and gender-blind terms: either a rural proletariat or a land-hungry peasantry. These polarised conceptions were reflected in an oscillating practice between town and countryside. During the late 1920s and in the 1940s and 1950s, rural mobilisation was the cornerstone of much socialist practice; at other times socialists neglected the countryside. These sporadic efforts impeded the development of a network between those sections of the urban working class, migrant labour force and rural population which might potentially have had socialist aspirations. In the 1940s and 1950s, however, socialists began developing concepts and analyses based on South Africa's own specific conditions. Not coincidentally, this was also a period when, despite the intense sectarianism dividing the Left, the observations of rural activists often coincided and their analyses began to converge.

The Politics of Land Reform in South Africa after Apartheid: Perspectives, Problems, Prospects
RICHARD LEVIN and DANIEL WEINER

Democratic elections in April 1994 in South Africa signified a major advance in the national democratic struggle in South Africa. Nevertheless, the transition to democracy has seen the emergence of a new style of politics based on bourgeois elite bargaining, which threatens gains made through popular mass driven liberation struggle in which the role of the organised working class has been central. The limitations of these new politics are examined through an analysis of the prospects and problems of contemporary land reform. The study reflects on the limitations of rural organisation in the national democratic struggle, and its consequences for transforming historical racially-based land relations. It offers some democratic alternatives to the process of land reform pursued by the Government of National Unity, and concludes that if popular aspirations around land are to be realised, the democratic movement needs to take more seriously the contradictory social relations of the countryside.

The Political Economy of the Maize Filière
HENRY BERNSTEIN

This study first introduces the notion of *filières (vivrières)* – (food) commodity chains – as a useful approach to investigating the interconnected activities, agents and dynamics of the maize sector in South Africa. A political economy of maize is proposed in relation to the maize boom of the 1960s and 1970s, and the growing pressures on maize farming subsequently. This political economy links the analysis of class forces and forms of capital to that of specific institutional mechanisms of regulation (in its broad sense). It concludes that 'deregulation', in the narrow (and misconceived) sense of market liberalisation, is inadequate to restructure the maize industry to meet the needs of a democratic South Africa, including that of food security in conditions of widespread poverty, both rural and urban.

Labour Organisation in Western Cape Agriculture: An Ethnic Corporatism?
JOACHIM EWERT and JOHANN HAMMAN

This study examines labour organisation in South Africa's fruit and wine industries. It is argued that the economic and political pressures emanating from the sectors' insertion in export markets is the main reason behind the transformation of the labour regime from a low-wage paternalism to a variety of arrangements, including neo-paternalism, formal collective bargaining and corporatist equity-sharing and decision making. While the first cannot hold, it is not clear which of the latter two regimes is set to become the dominant future pattern. That, it would seem, depends mainly on the responses of white farmers to growing worker demand for the sharing of economic and political power.

Livestock Production and Common Property Struggles in South Africa's Agrarian Reform
BEN COUSINS

This study focuses on conflicts over livestock and rangeland resources in post-apartheid South Africa, and suggests that the roots of these struggles lie not only in the skewed distribution of land, but also in the important role of livestock in complex rural livelihood systems and in processes of social differentiation. Perspectives from the wider literature on livestock and rangelands in Africa and on common property regimes are brought to bear on the specifics of the South African case, and several axes of struggle over common property are identified. Complex interactions between the economic, ecological and political and institutional dimensions are explored in two case studies from the Eastern Cape and Kwazulu-Natal. These provide general lessons for the political economy of common property resources within South Africa's agrarian reform.

Land Reform in the Eastern Free State: Policy Dilemmas and Political Conflicts
COLIN MURRAY

Three complementary elements of South African land reform policy are examined through case studies drawn from the eastern Free State province: the restitution of land; the redistribution of land; and the achievement of security of tenure. Firstly, diverse restitution claims are shown to reflect diverse experiences of dispossession of land under apartheid. Secondly, policy dilemmas and political conflicts over the redistribution of state-owned land around the huge relocation town of Botshabelo are investigated. They pose the fundamentally important questions of who represents 'the community' and who are the legitimate beneficiaries of state-sponsored land redistribution schemes. Thirdly, two different land regimes in part of an erstwhile African 'homeland' – private landownership by individual Africans and 'communal' tenure administered by a tribal authority – are analysed in their historical context in order to illustrate dilemmas and conflicts of the mid-1990s over forms of land tenure that will prevail in the future.

The Agrarian Question and Industrial Dispersal in South Africa: Agro-Industrial Linkages Through Asian Lenses
GILLIAN HART

In South Africa today, debates over agrarian reform and industrial restructuring are taking place in separate domains. This study calls for a broader understanding of the agrarian question as South Africa opens to the increasingly competitive global economy. Possibilities for broadly-based land redistribution in South Africa will depend both on the constitution of political forces, and on the conditions of access to non-agricultural resources. The study draws on comparative Asian evidence (a) to contest the World Bank's claims that a market-based small farmer model of agrarian reform will generate non-agricultural jobs in rural regions, and (b) to analyse new impulses of industrial dispersal in South Africa. Ironically, it is in regions that have borne the brunt of apartheid spatial engineering that the political and economic conditions for land redistribution may be greatest.

Peasants Speak: The Land Question in Mpumalanga
RICHARD LEVIN and DANIEL WEINER

This study reports the results of participatory research undertaken in the Central Lowveld region of Mpumalanga (formerly the Eastern Transvaal). It outlines the methods employed during the course of the research, highlights key research findings, and ends with village policy documents generated by the inhabitants of four villages in the former bantustans.